Social History of Africa

A HISTORY OF PRISON AND CONFINEMENT IN AFRICA

Recent Titles in
Social History of Africa Series
Allen Isaacman and Jean Allman, series editors

Making the Town: Ga State and Society in Early Colonial Accra
John Parker

Chiefs Know Their Boundaries: Essays on Property, Power, and the Past in Asante,
1896–1996
Sara S. Berry

"Wicked" Women and the Reconfiguration of Gender in Africa
Dorothy L. Hodgson and Sheryl A. McCurdy, editors

Black Death, White Medicine: Bubonic Plague and the Politics of Public Health in
Colonial Senegal, 1914–1945
Myron Echenberg

Vilimani: Labor Migration and Rural Change in Early Colonial Tanzania
Thaddeus Sunseri

"God Alone Is King": Islam and Emancipation in Senegal: The Wolof Kingdoms of
Kajoor and Bawol, 1859–1914
James F. Searing

Negotiating Development: African Farmers and Colonial Experts at the Office du Niger,
1920–1960
Monica M. van Beusekom

The Bluest Hands: A Social and Economic History of Women Dyers in Abeokuta
(Nigeria), 1890–1940
Judith A. Byfield

Colonial Lessons: Africans' Education in Southern Rhodesia, 1918–1940
Carol Summers

Poison and Medicine: Ethnicity, Power, and Violence in a Nigerian City, 1966 to 1986
Douglas A. Anthony

To Dwell Secure: Generation, Christianity, and Colonialism in Ovamboland
Meredith McKittrick

Genders and Generations Apart: Labor Tenants and Customary Law in Segregation-Era
South Africa, 1920s to 1940s
Thomas V. McClendon

A HISTORY OF PRISON AND CONFINEMENT IN AFRICA

Edited by Florence Bernault

Translated by Janet Roitman

Social History of Africa
Allen Isaacman and Jean Allman, Series Editors

HEINEMANN
Portsmouth, NH

Heinemann
A division of Reed Elsevier Inc.
361 Hanover Street
Portsmouth, NH 03801-3912
www.heinemann.com

Offices and agents throughout the world

ISBN 0-325-07119-5 (cloth)
ISBN 0-325-07125-X (paper)
ISSN 1099-8098

Library of Congress Cataloging-in-Publication Data

A history of prison and confinement in Africa / edited by Florence Bernault ; translated
by Janet Roitman.
     p. cm.—(Social history of Africa, ISSN 1099-8098)
  Includes bibliographical references and index.
  ISBN 0-325-07119-5 (alk. paper)—ISBN 0-325-07125-X (pbk. : alk. paper)
    1. Prisons—Africa—History. 2. Imprisonment—Africa—History. 3. Detention
of persons—Africa—History. I. Bernault, Florence. II. Series.
  HV9837.H57   2003
  365'.96—dc21   2002027286

British Library Cataloguing in Publication Data is available.

Printed in the United States of America on acid-free paper.

07 06 05 04 03 SB 1 2 3 4 5 6 7 8 9

CONTENTS

Illustrations   vii

Acknowledgments   ix

1. The Politics of Enclosure in Colonial and Post-Colonial Africa   1
   Florence Bernault

2. Confinement in Angola's Past   55
   Jan Vansina

3. Captivity and Incarceration in Nineteenth-Century West Africa   69
   Thierno Bah

4. Juvenile Marginality and Incarceration During the Colonial Period:
   The First Penitentiary Schools in Senegal, 1888–1927   79
   Ibrahima Thioub

5. Punishment to Fit the Crime?: Penal Policy and Practice in British
   Colonial Africa   97
   David Killingray

6. Colonial Urbanism and Prisons in Africa: Reflections on Conakry
   and Freetown, 1903–1960   119
   Odile Goerg

7. Between Conservatism and Transgression: Everyday Life in the
   Prisons of Upper Volta, 1920–1960   135
   Laurent Fourchard

8. Ultimate Exclusion: Imprisoned Women in Senegal   155
   Dior Konaté

9. *L'Enfermement de l'Espace:* Territoriality and Colonial Enclosure in
    Southern Gabon   165
    Christopher Gray

10. Space and Conflict in the Elisabethville Mining Camps, 1923–1938   191
    Sean Hanretta

11. Administrative Confinements and Confinements of Exile: The
    Reclusion of Nomads in the Sahara   221
    Pierre Boilley

12. The War of the *Cachots:* A History of Conflict and Containment in
    Rwanda   239
    Michele D. Wagner

    Selected Bibliography   271

    Index   281

    About the Contributors   285

ILLUSTRATIONS

FIGURES

1.1	Dori Administrative Post (Niger, 1908)	17
1.2	Central Prison in Brazzaville (1943)	19
1.3	Map for a New Prison in Magaria (Niger, 1929)	20
4.1	Number of Juvenile Detainees at Bambey (1916–1926)	87
7.1	Monthly Variation of Disciplinary Sanctions (1925–1932)	139
10.1	UMHK Mining Camp with *Zone Boisée*	203
10.2	UMHK Mining Camp with Block of Houses	204
10.3	Plan of Lodgings for Two Families	208

PHOTOS

1.1	Courtyard and Cell Doors in the Prison at Daikana (Niger, 1992)	18
1.2	A Collective Cell in the Prison at Tillabéry (Niger, 1992)	21
1.3	Ceiling Opened by an Escaping Prisoner (Tillabéry, Niger, 1992)	31
1.4	Painting by Tshibumba Kanda Matulu, *Colonie Belge* (1971)	35
10.1	Building for Latrines in Mining Camp	209

MAPS

2.1	Ancient Angola	56
6.1	Prisons and Military Camps in Conakry	123
6.2	Jails in Freetown	124
7.1	Prisons in Upper Volta	136
9.1	Gabon (1948)	170

9.2   Concessionary Companies in the French Congo   174
10.1 Katanga Region   195
11.1 Tuareg Living Space in the Sahara   222
12.1 Rwanda Provinces (1996)   240
12.2 Active Prisons in Rwanda (1996)   243

TABLES

4.1   Schedule for Juvenile Inmates at Thiès   85
4.2   Annual Arrivals and Releases at Bambey (1921–1926)   88

ACKNOWLEDGMENTS

This book project originated from personal interest in the prisons in Africa, yet it could not have been completed without collective support from the Research Program on *"Pratiques répressives, violences politiques, prisons et enfermement"* at the University of Paris 7, in the Laboratory SEDET (Sociétés en Développement dans l'Espace et le Temps). In France, the Center for Urban History at the Ecole Normale Supérieure supported some of my field research. At the University of Wisconsin-Madison, the Graduate School granted a Vilas Fellowship for the completion of the book project. The Cartography Laboratory at the University of Wisconsin-Madison designed the maps and graphics.

I wish to thank individual colleagues who actively supported our four-year long research and debates: first, Christine Daure-Serfaty, the founder of the International Observatory of Prisons (OIP) who brought endless generosity and energy to our research group, and helped connecting our academic debates with the experiences of African prisoners. Christian Carlier and Denis Peschansky at the Institut d'Histoire du Temps Présent (Paris), Jean-Louis Triaud at the Institut d'Etudes Africaines (University of Aix-Marseille), Saliou Ndiaye and Ibrahima Thioub at the University Cheikh Anta Diop (Dakar), faculty members of the Centre d'études et de recherches en Géopolitique at the University Omar Bongo in Libreville (Gabon), the African Studies Program at the University of Wisconsin-Madison, and Frank Dikötter at SOAS invited me to present papers on prisons in Africa. Catherine Coquery-Vidrovitch (University of Paris 7), Jan Vansina (University of Wisconsin-Madison), and Marc Michel (University of Aix-Marseille) helped me with comments on the manuscript and invaluable friendship. Graduate students and my colleague Tom Spear at the African History Program in Madison provided me with relentless intellectual stimulation.

In Africa, I received support for visiting prisons in Niger and Congo-Brazzaville from Boureima Gado (University of Niamey), Bernard Mackiza (Brazzaville), the late Jean-Blaise Kololo (Brazzaville), and from the French embassy in Brazzaville. During a particularly intense field trip in war-ridden Congo-Brazzaville in 1995, Roger Djambou provided welcome companionship in Kinkala when our bizarre questions about the local prison led the police to detain both of us in the commissariat for a day.

1

THE POLITICS OF ENCLOSURE IN COLONIAL AND POST-COLONIAL AFRICA

Florence Bernault

By the seventeenth century, prisons were pictured in the western imagination as abhorrent microcosms of vice, shame, and misery. They offered a grotesque mirror of society—its radical Other. In 1618, Geffray Mynshull, an English author horrified by the excess and evil that reigned in King's Bench, compared his jail to the place that, to his mind, could best suggest disorder and moral darkness: Africa.[1] Three centuries later, in the aftermath of the 1994 genocide, the prisons of Rwanda have provided journalists and western commentators with another set of dramatic images. For a popular French magazine, the Gitarama penitentiary looked like "a Dantesque painting: four inmates for every square meter; a day of acrobatic feats just to get to the latrine; the floor oozing with cankerous toes; feet and hands eaten by gangrene, condemned at best to amputation. And more than 900 deaths in eight months."[2] Confronted by such extreme visions, western spectators can reflect on the recent events in the Great Lakes region. Most probably, however, the overmediatization of the Rwandan prisons calls for nothing more than a regressive voyage into an archaic penal epoch, inciting western audiences to recall the unsavory, anachronistic memory of the long-forgotten "hells full of vermin and cruelty" of the old jails of London and Paris, where a picturesque crowd of ladies of the night, indebted folks, and various criminals were amassed in morbid promiscuity.[3]

The degraded state of some contemporary African prisons might incite some commentators to think that African judicial systems have silently returned to pre-colonial, archaic forms of punishment. At best, some might explain away the lack of improvement in the prison system as an effect of "underdevelopment," imagined as an indefinite standstill in the penal phase prior to the prison reform. Return or retardation: the threatening horizon of western orientalism only obscures the long-term maturation of the African penitentiary. In fact, present-day Rwandan prisons, like most contemporary penitentiary systems in Africa, have nothing in common with the jails of the *ancien régime* in Europe, nor do they borrow from local practices associated with pre-colonial "traditions." To the contrary: Europeans imposed the prison system in Africa a century ago to serve a specific colonial objective; thus transforming a complex form of local repression. After independence, regimes carefully reworked the prison system to meet modern, if sometimes unfortunate, political purposes.[4]

This book seeks to historicize the emergence of the modern prison in Africa by shedding light on the articulation between ancient systems of physical captivity and the importation of foreign penitentiary systems. Penal incarceration was unknown to sub-Saharan societies prior to the European conquest, when colonial regimes built prisons on a massive scale for deterring political opposition and enforcing African labor. Since independence, African governments have unanimously maintained the prison at the heart of their legal systems, although penitentiary policies vary in considerable ways across the continent. Some governments, like Ghana, have been recently engaged in building several new, modern corrective facilities. By contrast, in a number of African countries, judicial systems have tended to neglect prison sentences as a major means of punishment and social control. In addition, even though urbanization, industrialization, and modern forms of criminality have increased at unprecedented rates since independence, popular perceptions of the prison remain ambivalent. Large components of African civil societies reject the idea of imprisonment as a legitimate form of punishment, thus shedding fresh light on the intricate ways in which Africans have reshaped colonial legacies. This paradox helps explain why today, from the shores of the Mediterranean to the tip of the Cape, prisons remain an inescapable element of African landscapes, while the ratio of imprisonment across the continent is one of the lowest worldwide.[5]

Of course, the prison cannot be explored without understanding broader problems: in particular, the emergence of modern criminality, law, and punishment in Africa. For the last decade or so, a fast-growing field has provided historians with greater knowledge about these questions, although few studies have examined the role of prisons.[6] This book seeks to fill this gap by focusing primarily on the penitentiary institution, although many chapters also reflect on the topics of punishment, criminality, and deviance in Africa.

Our investigation has benefited from the extensive literature on the birth of the western penitentiary that has accumulated since the early 1970s. Inspired by the pioneering studies of Michel Foucault and David Rothman,[7] historians have documented thoroughly how western legal and political cultures at the end of the eighteenth century progressively replaced the *ancien régime* economy of punishment based on *lex talionis* and the dramatic public display of chastisement with a centralized, homogenized, and secluded system of imprisonment based on a theory of amendment. As subsequent studies demonstrated, this movement was reinforced in Europe and in North America by the rise of centralized and bureaucratic states, the emergence of an industrial civilization, and the spread of a new culture of discipline. Other, more critical works, have questioned the failure of the western penitentiary, as well as the ideological and architectural inertia that has prevailed in the West since the nineteenth century.[8] Yet, very little is known about another extraordinary achievement of the penitentiary model: its worldwide dissemination in the nineteenth and twentieth centuries, a process largely supported by European imperial expansion.[9]

The birth of the penitentiary in Africa sheds considerable light on this invasion. Colonial conquest used the prison as an early instrument for the subjugation of Africans. Even before colonial powers were in full control of territories, early prisons were erected in all European garrisons and administrative outposts. Thus, the penitentiary did not emerge after European conquest had imposed full control over the colonies, but served as a crucial tool to carry on colonial wars against Africans. However, as it was imported in the colonies, the western prison model experienced substantial alterations. First, no overarching "carceral archipelago" ever emerged in the colonies, even though European colonizers tested a range of techniques of confinement and discipline, such as asylums, hospital wards, workers' camps, and corrective facilities for children.[10] Second, contrary to the ideal of prison reform in Europe, the colonial penitentiary did not prevent colonizers from using archaic forms of punishment, such as corporal sentences, flogging, and public exhibition.[11] In Africa, the prison did not replace but rather supplemented public violence. Third, colonial power put considerable emphasis on the economic ends of the prison, and its role in the organization of forced labor. Finally, the principle of amending the criminals was considerably altered in the colonies, and largely submerged by a coercive doctrine of domination over Africans, seen as a fundamentally delinquent race. Racial segregation served as an enduring—though tacit—basis for the architectural, moral, and bureaucratic management of colonial penitentiaries.

African prisons also speak to the transformation of models of social control imported from the West. Since Weber and Durkheim, this concept covers a wide array of state and social strategies destined not only to restrain forms of deviance defined by criminal law, but also to promote the reproduction of social order.[12] A significant theoretical gap remains between neo-Marxist perspectives (positing social control as the ideological instrument of the state, which represents the ruling classes, to impose and legitimate social coercion) and the functionalist/revisionist school. The latter maintains that social control, as imperfect as it is, does not serve particular interests; rather, it rests upon widespread consensus about threats to the collective order, as well as appropriate solutions.[13] Colonization provides both a more complex and a simpler case in point. In the racially divided colonies, order was imposed from above, since the idea of criminality rested on a racial understanding of deviance. No large social consensus, therefore, existed across the races about law, deviance, and the appropriate techniques for correcting delinquency. Moreover, colonial authorities hardly sought to alleviate tensions brought on by coercion: as a consequence, the aim of the colonial prison was not to ensure new forms of social harmony or conformity, but rather to guarantee European hegemonic control. Hence, by encouraging the consolidation of racial tensions and social inequality, colonial prisons participated in creating forms of social control that borrowed from, but deeply differed from western models.

Finally, prisons in Africa have been shaped from the outset by a larger project: For beyond the construction of penitentiaries, colonial authorities attempted to organize the physical space of the colonial territories.[14] Under colonial rule, Africans did not simply face a new repressive system; they also experienced broader mutations in the political construction of physical and spiritual space, the public and domestic spheres, the collective and the private, the invisible and the apparent. For this reason, the history of prisons must be located in the larger context of colonial and postcolonial tactics of confinement. Through the delimitation of borders, the sedentarization of villages, the classification of ethnic groups, and the stabilization of workers in model cities, colonizers and Africans inaugurated a series of new articulations between social identity and physical space.

PUNISHMENT AND CAPTIVITY AT THE END OF THE NINETEENTH CENTURY

At the end of the nineteenth century, the modern African prison system emerged through the massive importation of a foreign judicial order, and the eclipse of a large number of precolonial penal techniques. The construction of prisons represented a considerable break with local practices of social control, based essentially on the idea of reparation. But this historical rupture tends to obscure complex, hidden correspondences between European doctrines and African ideas about punishment and physical enclosure. Some aspects of the penitentiary resonated with ancient, local forms of spatial captivity and physical seclusion. Military captivity, legal techniques of body constraint, and spiritual retreats existed in Africa alongside a series of architectures of confinement generated by the slave trade. Imported as a by-product of foreign occupation at the end of the nineteenth century, the penitentiary in Africa was not the product of local initiatives by local societies. Yet, its rapid articulation with local forms of punishment and social control suggests that the birth of the penitentiary in Africa depended less on a moment of rupture than on a long period of exogenous mutations partially imposed from above and partially captured, adapted, and transformed from below.

For most African societies in the nineteenth century, power was exercised over people rather than over space; or, to borrow from the famous Foucaultian distinction, authority stemmed primarily from governing people *(gouverne-mentalité)*, rather than subordinating spatial territories. However, social groups were always located in well-defined territorial limits that demarcated community protection.[15] People experienced and played out notions of individual liberty and integrity within these boundaries. They perceived the outside—an open space devoid of social protection—as potentially threatening, marked by the risk of spiritual pollution, captivity, and sale into slavery—an ultimate form of degrading mobility.[16]

Within this particular configuration of relationships between men, power, and space, refined judicial procedures existed. In West Africa, the repression of crimes was founded on reparations, vengeance, and amendment, a philosophy similar to the justice system of the *ancien régime* in Europe. The right to punish belonged, for the most part, to heads of families, both in lineage-based societies and centralized state systems.[17] Yet, the entire society, including ancestors and the invisible world, worked to solve the disturbances brought about by the crime.[18] As the legal sphere connected to the invisible, some forms of punishment used physical confinement in order to submit the criminals to the sanctions of the other world, as the techniques of ostracism in Bandjoun society show (Bah). For the most serious crimes, besides the death sentence, radical exile from the community served as the main form of punishment, leading to the social or physical death of the convicted offender. In particular, sale into slavery subjected criminals not only to exclusion, but also to destructive geographical and social displacements.[19]

While small-scale and decentralized societies usually chained criminals out in the open, many centralized states in West Africa possessed permanent jails for holding convicts or suspects before trial, a form of physical constraint comparable to the function of *ancien régime* prisons of Europe. Instruments of aristocratic power, state goals mostly aimed to reduce political opponents. African states, however, did not use prisons as a penalty in itself. Captivity worked as an exceptional form of public and domestic power, both in daily life (domestic hostages, and pawns), or to meet unusual circumstances (prisoners of war, and, in some rare cases, dangerous criminals). The great warrior Samori, for example, imprisoned his own son who was accused of treason, and made him die of hunger. Yet, Samori's tragic decision was more a form of destructive captivity and extreme bodily torture, than the exercise of a standardized form of punishment based on reclusion (Bah). As in the case of European prisons before the reform, bodily constraint, or the restriction of physical and social mobility, existed everywhere, but seldom worked as a curative treatment for vice. Rather, in the centralized and militarized states, as in a number of so-called lineage-based societies, reclusion was a transitory moment that underscored the power of public authority. The detained was eventually integrated into a household as a dependent or a slave, or disappeared physically, the ultimate effacement of the crime. In this context, reclusion did not aim to correct, but rather to seize the body to inflict punishment and allow legal reparation.

The slave trade introduced a number of significant changes in this penal economy. First, judicial tactics fueled the new market by producing criminals condemned to be sold into slavery to the profit of those capable of accumulating wealth and power (usually expressed by the number of dependents). Second, new techniques for the physical restriction of slaves promoted a range of bodily techniques that reinforced the dread of capture and individual chaining. For example the *bois mayombe* in the Loango region, as it was named by French traders in the nineteenth century worked as a forked piece of wood that secured slaves who had tried to escape. The branches were opened precisely to the thickness of their neck, and the "collar" fitted so tightly that slaves were in danger of being choked.[20] Third, important architectures of confinement emerged along the trade routes. In Angola after the 1760s, the Portuguese authorities complained about the proliferation of private goals where slave traders jailed and retained porters, recalcitrant partners, and pawns, directly threatening the central government's monopoly over the restraint of criminals. Later on, after abolition, African and Portuguese-African traders built *barracons* (from the Portuguese *barracaõ*, a large cabin or hangar), where they hid slaves along the interior trade routes and the coast patrolled by French and English naval squadrons.[21] An original network of semi-enclosed communities also developed along the coasts of Africa: the "villages of liberty" set up by the missionaries to house and supervise recaptured slaves.[22] These architectures were to play a significant role as spatial and ideological models when Africans confronted the colonial prison.

By encouraging the commoditization of people, the slave trade considerably challenged the philosophy of the person. The value of the free person declined as it became easier to accumulate dependents through the slave trade market rather than by natural reproduction and the protection of families.[23] Dependency no longer meant being affiliated with a lineage in a more or less precarious status. Instead, it meant being passively inserted into the flow of degrading economic exchanges and a punitive mobility that led to social death. The slave trade, fueled by captivity (judiciary, war, and merchant) and radical exclusion, increased the negative perceptions attached to the experience of capture and confinement.[24] Hence, the later terrors associated with the arrival of the colonial prisons, which reconvened the physical memory of the slave trade, as well as the ideological memory of degrading reclusions.

During the same period, other penal edifices appeared on the margins of the continent. European trading forts, erected on the coast since 1500, possessed jails and military cells, mostly used for the incarceration of military personnel.[25] Outside the forts, Europeans had erected a few prisons in some coastal colonies in the nineteenth century. In Freetown (Sierra Leone), a prison opened in 1816. In Senegal, the *senatus-consulte* of July 22, 1867, allowed the construction of prisons at the trading and military stations of Saint-Louis and Gorée. In the mid-nineteenth century, colonial authorities started to use the prison of Saint-Louis to control African itinerant populations and petty urban criminals (Thioub; Konaté). Yet, in most cases, only a fraction of the inhabitants of the trading posts were liable to be detained in these prisons, and the experience of modern incarceration seldom touched the daily life of most Africans.

Away from the few European coastal jails, African societies relied on different penal principles: the productive recuperation of criminals in society, or their destructive exclusion. Even centralized states had not developed tighter forms of penal imprisonment, nor seemed ready to breed local forms of penal incarceration. Yet, long before the imposition of the colonial penitentiary, a considerable range of models of confinement, captivity, and seclusion existed. Ideas about the compensatory character of punishment, the commoditization of people in the slave trade, the link between physical reclusion and contact with the sacred world, and the association between public authority and punishment had all played a central role into local systems of knowledge, initiation, power, and punishment. When colonizers started to sever philosophies of punishment from the realm of local power relations, and, with the building of prisons and jails, to relocate legitimate violence into the sphere of foreign domination, Africans could borrow from local repertoires and experiences to confront the new judicial system.

SOUTHERN AFRICA

From the infamous political prison of Robben Island, to the narratives written by former victims of apartheid, literature on the late twentieth-century prison in Southern Africa abounds.[26] Yet, historians have conducted few systematic inquiries in the earlier development of the penitentiary and modern forms of confinement in this region.[27]

Southern Africa presents a fascinating exception to the development of the modern penitentiary South of the Sahara. First, instead of being imported by colonizers at the end of the nineteenth century, the penal prison emerged at the very beginning of the century, closely following the prison reform movements in Europe and the Americas. Yet, in the Cape colony, prisons did not target common criminals as much as offenders of the recently adopted pass laws, a system that diffused all over the territory of what would become South Africa.[28] Second, from the late 1880s onward, prisons provided early sites for testing racial segregation, thus offering crucial models for racial separation schemes in the larger society. Third, the needs of labor strongly prevailed in the shaping of the penitentiary system. The close association between criminal and economic incarceration remained as a key feature of the Southern penal apparatus until 1990. Finally, institutions for the incarceration of the insane and children existed at an early date alongside[29] confined architecture for the housing and control of African workers after 1870: the compounds for miners in Kimberley and Johannesburg, then urban hostels for migrant workers.[30] In Southern Africa, spatial confinement shaped the economic, medical, and political landscape in ways that far exceeded other policies of enclosure on the continent.[31]

Racial segregation, however, did not characterize the early penal system in Southern Africa. At the end of the Dutch occupation of the Cape, rudimentary jails and a policy of deportation,[32] torture and public punishment applied to all offenders with no distinction according to race. From 1807 to 1834, the abolition of slavery in the Cape colony, prompting new needs for cheap labor in the colony, inaugurated new penal policies. First, the British governor, following the European penal reform, replaced physical punishment in the colony with prison sentences.[33] But, in 1809, the imposition of pass laws to help white farmers compelling Africans to work on farms, encouraged the formation of a large population of Khoi Khoi and Bushmen offenders. Most ended up in local jails ("lockups"), whereas criminals sentenced to long-term sentences were detained in newly created "convict stations." The classification of prisoners rested on the basis of offense committed, not on racial lines.

In 1828, Ordinance 50 abolished the system of passes for Khoi Khoi inhabitants of the colony. Yet, the number of prisoners in lockups and convict stations continued to grow, and threatened to overwhelm the poorly organized prison system. In 1843, prisons in the Cape underwent a major reform under John Montagu, the new colonial secretary. Montagu improved the detainees' diet, supervision, and access to education. Most importantly, inspired by reformers' ideals in Europe and the United States, Montagu emphasized the reformatory role of the prison, and the importance of penal labor in the construction of roads and harbors for the colony.[34] The emerging state of the Cape colony built large, portable wooden convict stations that could be transported to the vicinity of public works. All prisoners in the stations were forced to labor outdoors in chain gangs. No racial distinction existed; rather, a reformative classification was based on each prisoner's behavior. Yet, this period consolidated a key feature in the Southern African penal system: the prominent role of the state in combining penal policy and the handling of labor.

Detainees of the Breakwater Prison, many of them Bushmen and Khoi Khoi, provided the main labor for the construction of the breakwater around the Cape Town harbor from 1852 to 1870. Public work in Cape Town, particularly on the dock, never ceased to be supported by large gangs of convict laborers. In the 1870, the Harbour Board employed, on average, over 300 workers on maintenance and construction, of which 200 were convicts. In the mid-1880s, the Board relied increasingly on cheap penal labor: the proportion of convicts to free workers rose from two-fifths in 1882 to three-quarters by 1887.[35]

By the late 1880s, the state started to implement racial discrimination in the prisons and convict stations of the colony. Concerns for the lack of civilized amenities for white prisoners arose in the Cape as more white convicts were sentenced to hard labor for illegal diamond buying.[36] In contrast to earlier white offenders, these convicts appeared as refined, intelligent, and rich, thus promoting a new divide between the rich and poor, the good and bad criminal. In 1884, a Cape Town magazine complained that, in prison, "The coarser criminal, the black, the brute, has a more comfortable life than probably he had before his 'punishment' commenced, while . . . the white man has every decent susceptibility [to be] everlasting shocked and outraged."[37] The penal administration introduced a policy of differential treatment among white and nonwhite prisoners: the physical separation of inmates inside all penal facilities in Cape Town (1892),[38] a different diet (1898), and physical punishment for black prisoners. By 1901, authorities had erected a new building at the Breakwater Prison to house white prisoners. While blacks were forced to perform hard labor, white detainees had access to greater opportunities for skilled and industrial training in workshops.[39] John Montagu's rehabilitation ideals had degenerated into a racialized, differential treatment that split amendment procedures into hard labor for blacks, and reformative treatment for whites.

By the late 1890s, therefore, blacks provided most of the prison labor in Southern Africa.[40] At that time, pass laws were generating an increasing flux of pass offenders, or people accused of idleness and vagrancy.[41] Yet, their work was not confined anymore to urban public works, docks, and harbors. Confronted by incessant demands for cheap labor from private farmers, the state had begun hiring out convicts to wine farms in 1889. In 1934, the practice expanded dramatically with the sixpence scheme: Short-term prisoners could be compelled to spend their sentence working for white farmers who paid six pence to the department of prisons for each laborer.[42] By 1947, the number of black convict workers on white farms had increased massively, prompting, in 1948, the establishment of farm-jails housing nonwhite prisoners sentenced to long-term sentences (over two years). White farmers financed the construction of these facilities by buying shares of the farm-jails, and drawing convict labor in proportion to their contribution.[43] According to some historians, "The fact that large prison outstations were built in response to the pressure of farmers suffering from a shortage of labor showed the extent to which South African agriculture had become dependent upon crime."[44] Moreover, farmers frequently imposed corporal punishment on laborers, thus undermining the state's monopoly of violence and the theoretical purposes of the penal legislation.[45]

The creation of closed compounds for black workers in the mining area of Kimberley sheds further light on the role of private initiatives in creating original models of confinement.[46] Historians are still debating the nature and function of the compounds. For C. Van Onselen and R. Turrell, the mining companies sought to discipline black workers, first by controlling alcohol consumption and preventing diamond theft, then by attempting to model all aspects of the miners' life.[47] According to Van Onselen's compelling comparison between prisons and compounds in the Witwatersrand, mining compounds belonged to a "web" of coercive legislation (pass laws) and confining institutions (camps, prisons, workers housing) established by whites to secure cheap labor and the superior position of Europeans in the labor process.[48]

In addition, De Beers was the first company—and the first corporate, non-state entity—to use massive convict labor. The number of prisoners employed by the company increased from 200 per day in 1885 to 600 in 1889 (of a total number of 11,000 native laborers). By that time, De Beers had gone so far as to build a private prison branch (the De Beers convict station), with staffing and regular supplies, in order to secure a steady supply of penal labor.[49] Although the existence of a connection between the model of the prison and the compound system is left open to debate,[50] the history of native and penal labor in Kimberley suggests that the physical settings of the closed compound belonged to the striking architectural repertoires of confinement that emerged in South Africa.

Arguably, the second major distinctive feature of penal and spatial confinement in South Africa has been the spectacular rise of political detention in the twentieth century, particularly after World War II, and the parallel, extraordinary prisoners' resistance to the regime. Robben Island, that had served in the nineteenth century as an asylum for the insane, the leper, and the chronically sick, transformed into a prison after the closure of the hospital in 1931, and the use of the Island as a military headquarters during World War II. In 1961, after the Sharpeville massacre and the subsequent ban of the ANC and the PAC, the apartheid regime decided to open a maximum security prison on the Island to deport political prisoners.[51] From 1964 to 1990, Robben Island achieved world visibility through the fate of its most famous prisoner, Nelson Mandela. In prison, Mandela and his fellow detainees organized systematic resistance against the wardens and the apartheid regime.[52] By

1976–1977, the resistance took the form of an extraordinary program of political education among prisoners, who organized writings, readings, and collective training through courses offered by the University of South Africa.[53] Since the liberation of Mandela in 1990, and the closing of the prison, Robben Island has remained the symbol of political resistance for South Africans.[54]

PRISONS AND THE COLONIAL CONQUEST

At the end of the nineteenth century, the penal system in South Africa was an exception. But within a few years, colonial prisons had invaded the rest of sub-Saharan Africa.

During the first decades of the colonial partition of Africa (1885 to 1910), the conquest was brutal but remained incomplete. The Europeans' military and administrative presence was superficial, concentrated only in a few strategic points that kept fluctuating according to revolts to be quelled or routes to be secured. Soon, however, colonial rule increased its impact by creating permanent administrative posts, and enforcing taxes, censuses, portage, and forced labor. By 1910–1920, even in the territories that had been given over as concessions to private companies, Europeans and their auxiliaries controlled a large part of local economic activities and migrations.[55] The prison played a central role in this transition.

In all colonies south of the Sahara, the abrupt and intrusive spread of the prison proved massive and systematic. In British territories, the authorities issued a comprehensive series of prison ordinances and built jails in all new administrative posts early in the twentieth century. Moreover, in regions under indirect rule, such as Buganda and northern Nigeria, paramount chiefs were authorized to open their own prisons (Killingray). In French West Africa, the penal dispositions of the *indigénat* (a special system of administration that applied to African subjects), promulgated in 1887, allowed white administrators to sentence Africans to fifteen days in prison without trial. The massive use of administrative sanctions encouraged functionaries to build prisons as soon as they settled in the new districts, oftentimes using a spare room or a cellar in the administrative buildings as temporary jails. In the circumscriptions under military control, where resistance remained considerable, fortified garrisons provided ample space for incarceration. Captured African leaders could be sentenced to immediate "administrative internment," a form of prolongation of the war against the political opponents of French colonization.[56]

The impact and nature of the colonial prison system did not seem to vary significantly from one colonial regime to another. In the French, Belgian, and Portuguese colonies, the administration exercised direct control over Africans, and monopolized—at least in theory—civil authority and criminal justice. The colonial state appointed African administrative "chiefs," who, like their counterparts, the so-called customary judges, were merely subaltern administrators. This profoundly destabilized existing legal systems, public order, and the resolution of private conflicts. In British and German colonies, indirect rule proved as disruptive for African penal orders. First, local chiefs had to conform to the new fiscal system, and to distribute a portion of the collected resources to the colonial state, thus upsetting existing power relationships. Second, even though some native judicial institutions (courts, police) remained in place, chiefs had to abandon penal practices that were deemed unacceptable by European law such as physical mutilation, torture, and stoning (Killingray). Finally, the ossification of chiefdoms within the confines of precise limits, and their integration into a protonational territory, deeply changed the historical nature of local power.[57] Political entities that were once fairly decentralized, putting few constraints on people and things, transformed into coercive microstates that triggered new judicial processes and new power relations.

After 1910, administrative detentions had increased everywhere, while African detainees were forced to labor on public works and the building of new detention facilities. Prior to World War 1, official inspectors in French West Africa denounced the chronic overcrowding of prisons. For instance, the prison at Kindia (Guinea) consisted of two rooms each measuring 5-by-6 meters, and contained twenty-nine prisoners in December 1907.[58] In the Upper Volta in 1932, during the peak of the farming season, the administrators pronounced at least 1,900 monthly disciplinary sentences of imprisonment—an average of one imprisonment for every 140 persons annually (Fourchard).[59] In Tanganyika, one decade later, the state enforced regulations on soil erosion by imprisoning recalcitrant peasants on a large scale.[60] In Kenya, the colony's thirty prisons (twenty-three of which were district prisons) received approximately 28,000 detainees in 1931—36,000 in 1941 and 55,000 in 1951, or one detainee for 146,136 and 109 Africans, respectively.[61] The highest figures come from the Belgian Congo, where, in the late 1930s, the administration evaluated the number of annual detainees at 10 percent of the male population. In 1954, in the province of Kivu, almost 7 percent of the adult males spent some time in prison.[62]

Although the available data does not always distinguish between long criminal detentions and short administrative sentences, most Africans during the first half of the twentieth century probably experienced the colonial prison through administrative sentences, a system of short and arbitrary detention affecting a wide spectrum of adult males.[63] Colonizers used administrative imprisonment as an economic incentive to enforce tax collection, forced labor, or cultivation, and to provide colonial companies with a constant influx of cheap labor. This form of incarceration is perhaps not best captured by the term "mass imprisonment," but it imposed high levels of short, widely distributed detentions on Africans. Administrative imprisonment proved remarkably enduring: in the French colonies for example, they were still in use in the early 1950s, long after the abolition of forced labor and of the *indigénat* regime.

Most prison systems remained under the tight control of the central state. In most cases, the penitentiary administrations worked as an autonomous service in the colonial government, and were in charge of defining program and budget lines. Although local administrators disposed of the everyday tasks of maintenance, central inspection services paid regular visits to the prisons, even before the First World War.[64] Only the prisons directed by paramount chiefdoms under indirect rule benefited from a relative autonomy.

Colonial states sought to build a coherent penitentiary apparatus. In French West Africa and Equatorial French Africa, every level of territorial authority had to open penal facilities. At the level of small administrative posts (circumscriptions and districts), smaller prisons *(maisons d'arrêt)* and houses of correction held persons waiting for trial, and detainees condemned to short-term sentences. Moreover, each police precinct provided "security rooms" *(cachots)* to hold the accused.[65] In the capital of each colony, central facilities *(maisons centrales)* sheltered prisoners sentenced to six months to five years of detention. Finally, at the federal level, a few larger, fortified penitentiaries *(pénitentiers)* held prisoners serving more than five years, as well as political prisoners (e.g., the *pénitentiers* at Fotoba, Guinea; Kidal, Mali; and Ati, Chad).[66]

In East Africa, British Kenya offered the most extraordinary attempt to organize a full hierarchy of penal institutions. In 1911, when an autonomous Prison Board was appointed to manage the administration of penal facilities, the colony already possessed thirty penitentiaries. These establishments were classified according to the duration of the detainees' sentences: two prisons held long-term prisoners (condemned to more than three years of detention), five accommodated medium-term sentences (six months to three years), and twenty-three, labeled "district prisons," received short-term prisoners. But starting in 1925, prisoners were relocated according to productive tasks: In 1927, twenty-two "detention camps" supervised hard labor in the territory. By 1933, forced labor had become such a frequent sentence that the government began building "prison camps" entirely devoted to agricultural and public works. This system of detention, perhaps one of the few in Africa to resemble a "carceral archipelago,"[67] included two "approved schools" for delinquent juveniles in 1934. During the Mau-Mau crisis, in the mid-1950s, the government organized fifty additional "emergency camps" in which entire villages and thousands of Gikuyu prisoners were forced to resettle. At that time, the entire colony—whites excepted—was subject to incarceration on a massive scale.[68]

At the time prisons were invading the African continent, colonial rule initiated a series of different reclusive tactics, with mitigated success. In South Africa, a solid and varied arsenal of asylums for the insane had existed since the middle of the nineteenth century, but the confinement of the insane proved unsustainable in other colonies. In Nyasaland, asylums remained attached to prisons and never became autonomous institutions.[69] In Senegal, the government and physicians initiated ambitious projects at the beginning of the twentieth century, but abandoned them soon after.[70] In Southern Africa, reformatories for children and minors had opened in the early 1880s, followed by penitentiary schools in Senegal (1888) and Guinea (*Jardin de Camayenne* in the suburbs of Conakry). In Central and East Africa, state initiatives proved slower. In Kenya, "approved schools" opened in 1934, in Equatorial French Africa, the governor-general set up agricultural "colonies" for delinquent and unemployed juveniles only after the Second World War.[71] Most of these projects met with resounding failure (Thioub).

Subtler forms of temporary confinement emerged through medical initiatives and private entrepreneurship. In the Belgian Congo and Cameroon, scientific advice prompted the government to organize sanitary camps to protect Africans against sleeping sickness epidemics. The colonial state put entire regions in quarantine, and hundreds of people imprisoned behind *cordons sanitaires*, cordoned off by mobile medical teams.[72] In West Africa, leper houses worked on the principle of the isolation and confinement of ill persons.[73] After the Second World War, the detention camps of the Mau-Mau war—where British officers hoped to extinguish the revolt by isolating and "disinfecting" warriors from evil beliefs—can be analyzed not only as an extreme form of political imprisonment, but also as hybrid products of sanitary incarceration.[74] Finally, the Church and private companies participated in this general economy of confinement. In the Catholic missions in Cameroon, the *sixa*—made famous by Mongo Beti's novel, *The Poor Christ of Bomba*—set up as temporary retreats for young girls before their marriage, were transformed into reservoirs of cheap domestic labor for the missionaries. They closed after the Second World War.[75] But in the working compounds of Rhodesia, South Africa, and the Belgian Congo (Hanretta), paternalistic policies succeeded in using physical enclosure to promote the formation of a stabilized African working class.

Derived from penal purposes, ideological principles, and economic paternalism, physical confinement whether permanent or transitory, provided one of the core models for European hegemony, and the emergence of colonial states in Africa.

PUNISHMENT AS PERMANENT CONQUEST

Unlike the broader judicial system to which they belonged, prisons remained firmly controlled by the colonial order. Most Africans experienced the prison in terms of submission, rejection, or resistance. The enduring violence of colonial incarceration suggests that not every colonial encounter can be fully explained by the "negotiation" paradigm.[76] By imposing a repressive system that was exogenous to the society subjected to it, the prison did not aim at solving social tensions. On the contrary, it sought to consolidate the profound upheaval of the conquest. A tool of disorder more than order, the prison arose as a strategic outpost, a front-line bastion of colonial power, inaugurating a frontier form (in Turner's geopolitical sense) of carceral strategy. Indeed, colonial conquest did not stop after the "pacification" of Africa, but rather endured as a style of governance, a relentless effort to subjugate both the colonized and the physical space in which they lived.[77]

The constant drive to combine the domination of men and territories explains some of the specific features of colonial penology. Numerous punishments that had practically disappeared in Europe a century earlier flourished again as legal sentences in the colonies. In the Belgian Congo, the law allowed capital punishment and public executions in 1898, thirty years after such sentences had been abandoned in Belgium. For Jean-Luc Vellut, "According to the almost unanimous opinion of the colonizers, death sentence and major punishments should strike hard at the Africans' imagination." In Elisabethville, the spectacle of the torture of François Musafiri, a man who had stabbed a European who had seduced his wife, took place in front of a crowd of a thousand Europeans and three thousand Africans. He was hung on the public square on September 20, 1922.[78] After 1940, as the colonial government became increasingly reluctant to enforce capital punishment in public,[79] some high-ranking administrators privately criticized the fact that executions were taking place "in private quarters, inside the prison courtyard, a thousand miles away from the site of the crime."[80]

In most African colonies, both administrative and "customary" legislation put into place by Europeans enforced physical punishments. The *Code de l'indigénat* allowed French administrators to arbitrarily inflict forced labor and corporal punishment. Native courts, both in British and French colonies, could impose corporal punishments as long as they did not contradict European "principles of civilization." As a result, many of the so-called customary sentences worsened. In French Guinea, for instance, colonial executioners started to carry out whipping sentences using their whole arm, failing to observe the age-old rule of hitting with the forearm only.[81] In the Belgian Congo, the famous *chicotte*—whipping administered by agents of the Force Publique—became so widespread that it later remained as an icon of colonial punishment in the memories of contemporary Zairians.[82] Under increasing criticism from the international community, Belgian law limited the number of blows, originally set at fifty in 1906, to a dozen in 1903, eight in 1933, and four in 1951.[83] Yet the legislation testified to the endurance of the *chicotte* as a legal sentence up to the end of colonial rule. Similarly, English colonies abolished the whip in the 1930s, but replaced it with cane beatings.[84] Physical torture was routinely administered inside the prison as an additional punishment. In 1906, the governor of Dahomey reported that detainees who did not comply with the internal regulations of the prisons in Cotonou and Porto Novo were routinely submitted to "palm beating" *(correction palmatoire)*, as guards violently beat the detainees' hands with a flat wooden cane twenty or thirty times.[85] In 1947, in Brazzaville (French Congo), an inspector discovered that several detainees were chained in the prison, a practice that violated the law. Nevertheless, the governor of French Equatorial Africa later justified chaining dangerous criminals or detainees prone to escape.[86] The frequency of physical violence in the prison suggests that administrators failed to believe that detention and the loss of liberty was a sufficient sentence for Africans.[87]

Public sentences of physical punishment did not exhaust corporal violence between colonizers and Africans. Private European settlers enjoyed a large measure of impunity when physically mistreating and abusing Africans, or even practicing expeditious executions. Their misdeeds remain invisible in the archives, but linger in the memory of the colonized.[88] Hence, the corporal punishments instituted by the state resonated with the private vengeance of white civilians, and relegated imprisonment to a relatively marginal position in the penal economy.[89]

At the outset, the historical function of colonial prisons differed dramatically from the western penitentiary. In western societies, penal reform emerged at the heart of a large social consensus—in response to the convulsive passage of European economies to industrial capitalism—seeking to resolve the most dangerous social aspects of this economic disruption to the benefit of the dominant classes. In the colonies, by contrast, economic profit depended upon political despotism and the enduring antagonism between different segments of colonial society. The tropical prison did not seek to separate lawful citizens from marginals and delinquents; it aimed to reinforce the social and political separation of the races to the sole benefit of white authority by assigning the mark of illegality to the whole of the dominated population. As such, the colonial prison did not supplant, but rather encouraged penal archaism. This is why the colonial prison did not *replace* physical torture in the colonies; it only *supplemented* it—recycling, far from the European metropoles, the long-forgotten practice of state violence and private vengeance.

SEGREGATED ARCHITECTURES

The colonial prison reproduced this economy of violence, as the separation of black and white prisoners remained the major element of the penitentiaries' internal geography until the end of the colonial period.

The transitory period of makeshift jails and cells, hastily set up in the first administrative garrisons, ended before the period of military conquest was over. Interestingly, nowhere in Africa did colonial authorities try to establish permanent prisons based on a prereform model, when jails and dungeons could not be distinguished from civil and private buildings. Even though most of the first colonial jails had followed this scheme for circumstantial reasons, and even when lack of resources later prevented the construction of carefully planned projects, local authorities started to build prisons as separate and specialized buildings during the first decade of the twentieth century.

Different architectural periods can be distinguished in the colonies. The oldest model was the block-prison, which simply consists of a single strip of collective cells built around a vast open space (e.g., Dori prison, Niger, Figure 1.1). The prison at Daïkana (Niger), dating from the early colonial period, juxtaposed two large courtyards surrounded by a rectangular ring of cells that

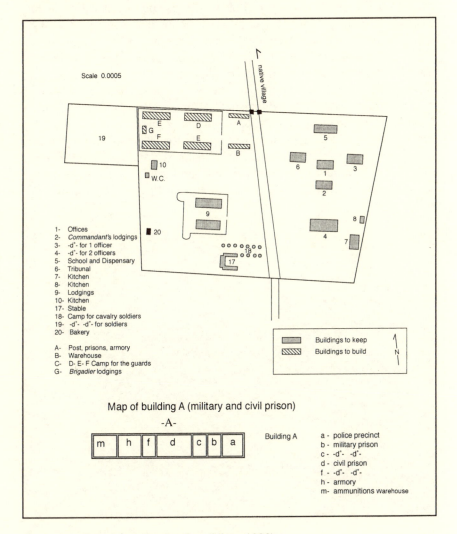

Figure 1.1. Dori Administrative Post (Niger, 1908).

served as the fortified walls of the building (Photo 1.1) Around 1920–1930, prison architecture became more sophisticated, and started to follow panoptic models more closely. Behind a monolithic facade, the prison at Conakry (Guinea, 1903) for example, deployed the famous diagram of separate wings spanning out from a central hall (schema dating from Pentonville, England, 1842). Elsewhere, compact and walled-off sections aligned along a symmetrical axis consisting of a covered or open corridor, as in the *maison centrale* in Brazzaville (Congo, 1943, Figure 1.2).[90] The presence of miradors, or some kind of watchtowers for a panoptical, constant surveillance of the courtyards (Conakry, Brazzaville), seemed to have been quite common. No chronological succession always existed between block-prisons and panoptical penitentiaries: simple block-prisons in rural posts of the interior coexisted with more elaborate, panoptical prisons in the large urban centers.

The internal architecture of colonial prisons almost always provided for separate cells and courtyards for whites and blacks.[91] When the buildings did not allow for separation, Europeans were incarcerated in a separate room in the police precinct or in the administration's residential housing. Even when detained in the regular jails, the rare white prisoners enjoyed preferential treatment. In the prisons of the Haute-Volta, for example, white prisoners enjoyed privileges related to food, sanitation, and clothing (Fourchard). Everywhere, they were exempt from forced labor. Penal segregation lasted well into the 1950s. Even when interracial marriages increased, urban segregation

Photo 1.1. Courtyard and Cell Doors in the Prison at Daikana (Niger, 1992).

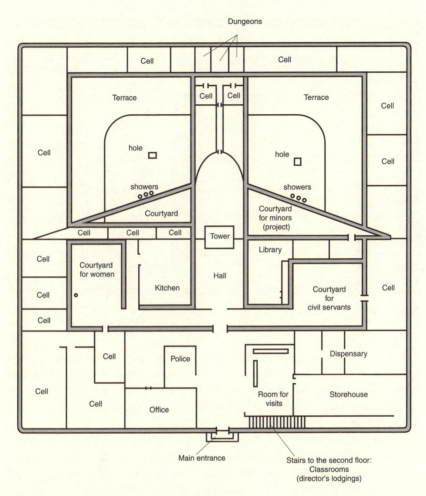

Figure 1.2. Central Prison in Brazzaville (1943).

declined, and political privileges multiplied, the collective detention of Europeans and Africans was never practiced nor even envisioned by colonial authorities. In fact, most European detainees were rapidly transferred to the European metropole to be judged and sentenced, as the symbolic impact of whites' detention appeared detrimental to the preservation of racial "prestige" in the colonies.[92]

The penal system enforced racial compartmentalization at other levels. Europeans perceived Africans as a collective entity, and as gregarious people. In 1929, the plan for the new prison and guard camps at Magaria (Niger, Figure 1.3) inscribed this principle in space. The building was set along a longitudinal wall separating "common law detainees" from "administrative detainees," which corresponded to the legal separation of prisoners arbitrarily

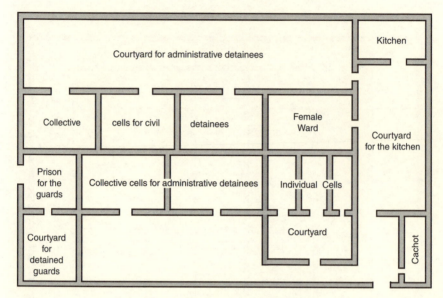

Figure 1.3. Map for a New Prison in Magaria (Niger, 1929).

sentenced by administrators according to the *Code de l'indigénat* (refusal to work, refusal to pay the headtax, etc.), and common law criminals sentenced to imprisonment by the legal courts. In Magaria, cells were divided into six collective quarters, with only three individual cells set aside for the isolation of recalcitrant prisoners.[93]

The Magaria architectural diagram takes up a fundamental dimension of the colonial prison. No individual jails existed for Africans—only large chambers for collective detention that often remained open onto the courtyard during the day (Photo 1.2). Colonial reports insisted upon the impossibility of isolating Africans, seen as gregarious and incapable of enduring solitude. This vision was only one of the many elements of colonial discourse depicting Africans as an undifferentiated mass, "a steady sea."[94] The Magaria prison provides a spectacular example of such racist visions. A specific site of detention existed for the guards, who were almost all Africans.[95] This prison within a prison demonstrated that the African population as a whole, not delinquents only, was under surveillance; including the native "collaborators" of colonial rule.

In the collective jails of the colonial prisons, women experienced the worst conditions of detention. Their triple exclusion as women, prisoners, and Africans subjected them to specific abuses. Only very late in the history of the colonial prison did female prisoners benefit from distinct jails and specialized female wardens. Before then, imprisoned women were forced to endure promiscuity and sexual abuses from both prisoners and guards. They were forced

Photo 1.2. A Collective Cell in the Prison at Tillabéry (Niger, 1992).

to work as cooks in the prison kitchens and as maids for the maintenance of the prison buildings: But the law did not recognize women's labor, and thus did not compensate for it (Konaté).

Since the separation of normality from marginality derived a priori from the racial division of society, not from individual, specific acts of delinquency, the internal geography of the prisons physically promoted the subaltern position of Africans. Penal architectures in the colonies were not envisioned as a therapeutic device. Colonial penitentiaries did not aim at organizing standardized punishment in a neutral space, since no such equality of status and right existed outside the walls of the prison. To the contrary, prison architectures sought to reproduce colonial hierarchies, erected not only upon the race distinction, but also upon a subtler contrast between individual citizens (whites) and the collective, untitled mass of African subjects. Although other forms of racial hierarchy existed in the colonies, the spatial segregation that Africans experienced in the penitentiary was particularly crude and graphic.

PENAL LABOR

The violence of the colonial prison derived also from its central role in the colonial economy. This role was twofold, as penitentiaries imprisoned Africans who resisted forced labor and colonial extractions, and implemented the systematic use of detainees as cheap labor. The prison, therefore, participated in the "artificial" economic system of the colonies, where surplus value derive from wages maintained at a low level.[96]

African prisoners worked primarily in areas where the shortage of labor was most acute, both in the public and private sector. From the colonial perspective, prisoners provided a docile, cheap, and constantly available labor force for underpaid tasks of handling and packing, urban maintenance, and unskilled domestic work. In a confusion typical of the colonial situation, the recourse to penal labor obliterated the barriers between the private and public sectors, and erased the difference between free labor and forced labor. As a hidden form of forced labor, penal labor endured up to the end of colonial rule, well after the abolition of mandatory labor.[97]

Whether detainees belonged to the central prison of an urban capital or a rural prison in the interior, they mostly worked for the agricultural sector. This included working in the fruit and vegetable gardens of penitentiary administrators, as well as in the yards of district administrators. Prisoners also labored on private plantations, such as the large, barely mechanized banana farms in Kindia (Guinea) that needed large amounts of cheap labor.[98] Finally, convict labor also supplemented forced labor for tasks that demanded hard physical activities: public and private work on quarries, roads, construction sites (wharves, bridges), trash hauling, ship loading, or warehousing in the colonial towns.

The use of penal labor rested upon three principles. First, all African prisoners had to work, including women. Only the infirm were exempt.[99] No geographical exceptions existed: both urban and rural prisons made systematic use of penal labor. Second, the penal administration routinely assigned detainees to work for private entrepreneurs, especially after the abolition of forced labor. Third, colonial rulers perceived penal labor as a necessary, even vital, part of the colonial economy.

At times, the high demand for penal labor resulted in competition between different detention centers. In French Guinea, in the early 1920s, the governor tried repeatedly to convince rural district chiefs to send part of their prison population to Conakry, in order to meet the need for labor in the capital. Most administrators of the interior resisted vigorously, arguing that their prisoners hardly met local demands, and were occupied in wood-gathering, water hauling, and the maintenance of administrative buildings and European gardens. In Dinguiraye, the circumscription commander pleaded that the prisoners were indispensable for the survival of the colonists: "In a colonial station . . . where the climate is particularly difficult, it seems to me that the sustenance and general hygiene of the Europeans must be assured in the best possible conditions."[100]

Colonizers perceived penal labor not as a marginal supplement to the ranks of African "free" wage earners, but, rather, as a crucial tool for the ongoing creation of colonial labor. The importance of African detainees' economic role explains why prisons were generally built near administrative and residential buildings in rural outposts (see Dori, Niger). Everywhere, penal labor and forced labor constantly overlapped: Africans who resisted forced labor were sentenced to prison; prisoners, in turn, were compelled to work for colonizers. To a large extent, the prison functioned as a site for observing and selecting the productive population.[101]

Penal labor informed the internal geography of the colonial prisons. Contrary to the western penitentiary, the colonial prison did not provide a therapeutic space of virtuous domesticity, nor a utopian cellular architecture.[102] To the contrary, public violence saturated their architectures, seeking to assemble African prisoners as a compact mass, separate them from Europeans, and herd them into forced labor. Not surprisingly, treadmills remained rare in the colonial prisons, as Africans were not supposed to partake in any personal reformation, but in the economic construction of European hegemony.[103]

THE IDEOLOGICAL LIMITS OF COLONIAL INCARCERATION

The violent consolidation of European hegemony in Africa should not mask its enduring fragility. John Lonsdale and Bruce Berman's work on Kenya, and Sara Berry's on Ghana have demonstrated how colonial domination was constrained by lack of resources, lack of will, and the divergent interests of the colonial community.[104] From a penal perspective, the colonial project was bound by a fundamental tension between different aims. Should the penitentiary only punish the criminals? Should prison administrators, discipline the natives as a controlled, subaltern labor force? Or should colonial prisons participate in the education and moral upbringing of Africans?

All evidence demonstrates that colonial regimes focused on the second option in Africa, until at least the Second World War. The rehabilitation of prisoners, but also the repression of civil crimes, remained marginal; colonial prisons served primarily as a tool for economic oppression. The lack of resources explains to some extent the limitations of penal objectives. Most importantly, however, limited objectives derived from ideological deficiency. In the colonies where research has been conducted, the theoretical debates about the role of the colonial prison seemed to have been remarkably sparse.[105] In Upper Volta, for example, the paucity of local European discourse on the reformatory functions of the prison (Fourchard) is stunning.[106]

In fact, at the time of the conquest, European ideas about penal incarceration had already considerably atrophied. The prison model that colonizers were importing in Africa was no longer the ideal penitentiary of the reformers, but, rather, a failing institution that had survived the decline of the great reform movement.[107] In Europe, ideas about rehabilitation no longer played a prominent role in the penitentiaries; in the colonies, the concern for repression easily prevailed. The long history of the western penitentiary ended up in Africa in a high-ranking officer's prosaic opinion: "Punishment is an expiation."[108] The failure to put forth a specifically colonial vision of the prison pointed up the relative intellectual void that shaped the transfer of the European prison to Africa, and the deficiencies of the colonial intelligentsia. Only administrative milieus and some missionaries initiated a few reforms after World War II. But neither dared to challenge the punitive and coercive essence of the colonial prison.

Colonizers often argued that incarceration was mild compared to existing African punishments, a notion debunked in this collection by Jan Vansina. Many Europeans shared the opinion of the commission for the supervision of prisons in Guinea in 1909: "[The elimination of meat and fish from the prisoners' rations] has produced an excellent effect: the condemned will no doubt eventually understand that imprisonment is a punishment, not a compensation for their misdeeds."[109] The concern that Africans could misunderstand the penal functions of the prison, and take the prisoners' living conditions as proof of the colonial state's generosity, indicated that most colonizers realized that the prison would remain utterly foreign to the very people it was supposed to correct.

Two intellectual traditions helped inform colonizers' views. The first, arising from the ashes of the prison reform, was the notion of "criminality" invented by Cesare Lombroso in his *Uomo Delinquente* (1876). Lombroso thought that criminality was an inner quality of evildoers that stemmed not from their contacts with the delinquent world, but rather from hereditary factors and a marred nature that separated criminals from the rest of humanity. For Lombroso, criminality was an innate flaw, a defect revealed by certain physical and psychic characteristics.[110] At the end of the nineteenth century, phrenologists studied and classified such characteristics, supporting the idea that criminals belonged to a degenerate, unredeemable race.[111] This school of thought was challenged by a second intellectual tradition—that of criminal sociology, which studied crime as the result of social conditions and the delinquent's social environment.

Both Lombroso's ideas and the school of criminal sociology provided a scientific armature for a vision of Africans as belonging to a class of outcasts either by virtue of their physiological nature or their social environment. For many colonizers, Africans were potential criminals. Only a minority of Europeans believed that some among them—the amenable, the *évolués*[112]—could eventually extricate themselves from this plight thanks to the contact with European education, moral standards, or Christianity. Almost none thought about the prison as a likely place for promoting such transformation, since they saw detainees as belonging to the most unredeemable class of African society. For most Europeans, therefore, penal discipline was to be limited to the body, and should not attempt to reach the native's soul.[113] Containing crime, intimidating wrongdoers, disciplining the masses into an amenable workforce—those were the only realistic prerogatives of a colonial prison.

The intellectual movement that had given birth to the reform of the western penitentiary, based on faith in the good nature of humanity, never played a major role in the colonies. Paradoxically, its echo resonated only in the idea that vice, like a disease, could contaminate the body and the soul.[114] The colonial distaste for physical contact with Africans, the fear of epidemics, intermarriage, the possibility of degenerating contagion, the political desire for physical separation from the inferior race all played out in the prison discriminating architectures that separated blacks from whites.[115]

The racial distance that helped create political hegemony in the colonies put the prison beyond the reach of any reform debate. In the colonial imagination, the colonial prison was an immobile rampart against barbarous punishments.[116] Even indirect rule, by authorizing paramount chiefs to open their own jails, aimed to redress the morals of the guards as much as the detained. Such penal fantasies entirely obscured the concrete abandonment, within the walls of the colonial prison, of any projects of rehabilitation and education. From a distance, the colonial prison could be perceived as a monument to a higher, benevolent civilization. Within its walls, however, it never stopped promoting hopeless forms of corporal and psychological coercion.

Only after 1945 did authorities start to devote more attention to the moral rehabilitation and the professional reformation of adult prisoners. The increasing globalization of criminology and penology worldwide partly fueled these new concerns. Scientific exchanges circulated widely throughout the world between different penal systems, and new theories reached the African colonies. Investment in penal rehabilitation also derived from the colonial regimes' need for legitimization in the face of internal and external anticolonial movements. Yet, concrete results seem to have been few, although some rehabilitation schemes provided the blueprint for penal reforms later undertaken by post-colonial governments.[117]

Political and penal inertia, plus the deficiency of material and intellectual resources among colonizers, prevented colonial regimes from implementing any project of *grand refermement* in Africa—with, arguably, the exception of

South Africa.[118] No colony ever tried to organize the whole panoply of penal architectures, carceral institutions, and disciplinary institutions that had spread in Europe and in the Americas from the eighteenth century on. On the contrary, prisons in colonial Africa were based on an implicit principle: to keep the impact of incarceration within strict ideological limits. By maintaining legal and physical distance between colonizers and Africans, the colonial prison was not supposed to transform Africans, but simply to promote the reproduction of the dominant power. This project also resulted form a conscious strategy to constrain bodies rather than disciplining minds, to control crime and labor rather than initiating social engineering. In this perspective, colonial prisons never served as true penitentiaries, but as practical fortresses where the conquest of Africa could be safely pursued.

In Europe, the passage from the old penal order to the prison reform at the end of the eighteenth century had become possible through the extension of civil and political rights, popular consent to the law, increasing popular intolerance toward delinquency, and the tightening of the legal grip over disobedient individuals. A century later, colonization imported the modern prison in Africa as a material device severed from the very principles that had presided over its birth. Instead of seeking to rehabilitate criminals and promote social stability through popular consent over legal punishment, Europeans used the prison for to secure control over a subaltern, racially defined social category that comprised the majority of the population. The juxtaposition of archaic and modern elements in the colonial prison did not derive, as in the West, from a long penal history. It grew out of colonizers' systematic reliance on confinement as a device that could allow, behind the façade of rational, disciplinary architectures, the use of pre-penitentiary punitive practices.

APPROPRIATIONS AND ESCAPES

Is the meaning of the modern prison in Africa to be found only at the heart of the imperial project? Even if popular perceptions of the modern prison have remained ambivalent, penal incarceration seems to have triumphed as an instrument of state power.[119] Today, African governments have unanimously preserved the penitentiary apparatus at the center of their judicial systems.

During the colonial period, however, and contrary to other colonial institutions that could be more easily assailed or appropriated, the prison left little room for African initiatives. The penal system could be diverted from the reproduction and consolidation of colonial inequalities only with great difficulty. For ordinary Africans, the prison remained at the core of political repression and economic extraction. Yet, as the penitentiary did not aim at resolving the social and political crisis initiated by the European conquest but participated in the permanent confrontation between Africans and Europeans, it engendered considerable resistance.[120]

Prisoners' life stories are difficult to document. For moral and social reasons, few ex-detainees wish to speak about their imprisonment. Moreover, the prison was often experienced as a space of annihilation and silence. Although a large body of literature exists as former prisoners wrote autobiographies, political denunciation, and fiction about life in prison, such narratives cannot entirely express what lies behind the silent experience of those who did not testify.[121] Historians can turn, of course, to statistical or anecdotal data, such as the records of acts of transgression and political organization among prisoners (Fourchard).

By all accounts, African resistance to the prison appears not only to have been ubiquitous, but also to have persisted well beyond the first years of the twentieth century.[122] Different phases existed in this confrontation. Early on, the frequency of suicide and morbid forms of prostration among African prisoners suggested that the detainees, especially free men, experienced imprisonment as an extremely traumatic situation.[123] Reclusion could lead to irreversible annihilation, as it often meant the immediate destruction of the individual's social status and spiritual protection. The historical experience of captivity played a determining role in this, but the prison seems to have exacerbated the association between capture and personal degradation. Those who crossed the prison threshold expected to get stripped of their social, physical, and spiritual integrity. The inhabitants of Guinea compared the prison to a grave, a vision fueled by detainees' testimonies about the obscurity of the stockades, the darkness of the jails and chambers. Many believed in the otherworldly nature of the prison. They described how all those who had the misfortune of being imprisoned for more than three months would lose their vision progressively, becoming totally blind after a year in prison.[124] These images of decay also resonated with the ancient and incessant fear of the vampirization of souls and black bodies by Europeans and their henchmen.[125]

After the 1910s and 1920s, escapes became the major form of revolt against the prison. Throughout the colonial period, the ratio of escapes remained considerably high. They often denoted the collective character of mobilization against incarceration, as escapees benefited from many forms of complicity: the help of African guards, protection from relatives, and public consensus that strongly rejected the prison as a tool of foreign oppression. Spiritual initiatives emerged to defeat the prison. In Senegal, for example, charms such as the "Ndémène horn" *(lokki Ndémène),* or the *Koular* charm, could protect prisoners from getting involved with the administration and could render one invisible.[126] Other charms could help to escape, or to restore detainees' spiritual protection after incarceration.

Yet, by its massive presence in the legal landscape, the prison introduced new repertoires of judicial practice. First, the prison transformed collective sentences into standardized, individual punishments applied to all. This radically challenged older practices of proportional sentence based on the social status of the conflicting parties. The prison also individualized punishments by truncating social responsibilities, severing the criminal from collective protection and the possibility—for the victim—of mobilizing powerful patrons for reparation and vengeance. Second, imprisonment circumvented public vengeance directed at delinquents, leaving the victim in the shadows—a crucial shift from past inquisitorial procedures. In other ways, the influence of the prison model could derive from its very proximity with local understanding. For example, forced penal labor could be apprehended in terms of compensatory reparation, or as a form of pawnship to the benefit of the new (white) masters. In this case, however, the overarching meaning of punishment changed radically. Forced labor as "compensation" no longer contributed to the resolution of local conflicts, but only signaled the foreign, arbitrary power of the whites. Racial inequality, physical punishment performed by colonizers, and the whites' impunity probably weakened the normative force of the principle of standardized, fair imprisonment.

But evidence exists that suggests how the colonial prison contaminated local taxonomy and the popular imagination. European missionaries and African catechists served as zealous intermediaries in this rhetorical diffusion: in 1936, for example, a ten-year-old plaintiff accused a catechist in the village of Zouma (Gabon), of having accused her of singing badly during the night prayers, ordering her "to stay in prison" in his own house, and raping her.[127] In 1943, a typical conflict involved a white catholic missionary, Father Le Clanche, and several African plaintiffs. The father had threatened to ask the commandant to put all Protestant converts in prison. Plaintiffs also accused missionaries of kidnapping and forcibly detaining children in the Catholic Mission.[128]

To what extent did some Africans accept the colonial prison? Chérif Diallo suggests that, in Guinea, a certain popular consent can be detected as of the 1930s.[129] Even earlier, a significant number of Africans had entered the prison as indigenous guards and wardens—although little is known about their origins and motivations. For the ruling class, and for some ambitious individuals, the new penal system presented obvious opportunities. Aside from the few paramount chiefs who owned their own prisons, some chiefs did not hesitate to take advantage of the possibility of incarcerating undesirable people. A detailed history of the sentences pronounced by the customary courts would show the extent to which imprisonment was incorporated in local judiciary practice, and to whose benefit. Individual anecdotes give an idea of these initiatives. We know, for example, the story of an administrative agent of the circumscription of Dori (Niger), who managed to devise a whole series of clandestine operations around the local prison. Denouncing criminals and petty offenders to the French administrator in residence, he ransomed and threatened families, or extorted money from the detainees' relatives, in order to help the prisoner to survive or to escape. In 1915, the district authorities arrested the zealous agent after three plaintiffs protested the confiscation of twenty of their cattle.[130] This episode speaks to a relative absence of compromise between the colonial and indigenous elites around the penitentiary. Apart from the few paramount chiefs who were allowed to manage their own jails, ordinary Africans could find ways to make use of the colonial prison. But they had to do so through illegal enterprises of diversion, not as recognized partners of colonial authorities.[131]

Therefore, resistance to the colonial prison further cast Africans as subaltern agents of the colonial system. Most colonial prisons survived until the period of decolonization in a context of undisturbed inequality.[132] Their walls delimited a space of domination that, while surely not infallible or total, was unyielding to any significant sharing of power between colonizers and colonized. In a different context, but with the same concern for keeping the penitentiaries under the control of the state, post-colonial penitentiaries inherited this coercive agenda.

THE CONTEMPORARY PRISON IN AFRICA: A NEW MODEL OF INCARCERATION?

The main hypothesis of this book is twofold: It argues that the prison system was successfully "grafted" onto Africa,[133] but that this transplant gave birth to specific, highly original models of penal incarceration.

The repressive functions of the colonial prison—submission to the laws of production and assent to the dominant order—have been adopted by many contemporary regimes. Across the continent, the most likely candidates for imprisonment today are the real or imaginary political opponents of established regimes. But contemporary prisons also help tame classes deemed as dangerous. In Senegal in the 1990s, the police raids and the mass incarceration of unemployed youth in the cities can be analyzed as a state attempt to subordinate the middle classes that fueled opposition to the regime.[134] Oftentimes, however, the function of political detention has changed since the colonial era. Imprisonment is now less a question of pure repression than one of forced capture, as governments use arbitrary sentences to intimidate, weaken, and subjugate opponents before ultimately integrating the most compliant into the ruling class. Rwanda is the most spectacular exception to this rule, where the massive incarceration of entire political and social groups, perceived as enemies of the regime, appears as extremely equivocal.[135] Do the judicial authorities believe in the suspected *génocidaires'* reintegration in society after trial, and their submission to the state? Or do they purposefully transform the

overpopulated prisons of Rwanda into silent machines for the physical reduction of the opposition? The filth and material degradation of the jails, and
the judicial disorganization of the country, have already worked as "anonymous tribunals" carrying death sentences on a massive scale (Wagner).[136] An
extreme case, no doubt, but one that illuminates how the most repressive
carceral apparatuses in contemporary Africa, far from being connected to any
form of ante-penitentiary penal customs, have been shaped by the legacy of
colonial penitentiaries and the tragic modernity of contemporary political
strife.

Many penitentiary regimes have failed to remodel the colonial prison by
lessening its violence and renewing the penal link between the state and civil
society. On the contrary, some penal regimes have encouraged other forms
of violence inherited from the colonizers; in particular, corporal punishment
and forced labor. Anglophone countries have not only retained physical torture, but many have reinstated whipping and beating for minor offenses.[137]
All over Africa, the obligation of prisoners to work remains widespread, as
penal labor contributes significantly to national production, especially in the
agricultural and public works sectors.[138] In some countries, however, governments have made a conscious effort to break away from this colonial legacy
and transform penal labor from a productive to a reformatory technique.[139]

In some cases, post-colonial regimes have also tried to renovate penal facilities. Yet, they have mostly done so by opening highly modern facilities
that worsen, rather than improve the convicts' conditions of detention. In
Pretoria (South Africa), the maximum security prison (also known as "Super-
Max") is equipped with all modern penal innovations relating to incarceration,
and holds serial killers and white political prisoners.[140] In Ghana and the Ivory
Coast, public rumor describes the ultramodern, maximum security prisons as
horrific places, where wardens can exert unchecked, sometimes lethal, violence on detainees.

Despite the lack of reliable studies and statistics, highly divergent visions
of the prison system seem to exist among the public. On the one hand, indi-
cators show that society accepts and even desires the incarceration of criminals and delinquents—at least in the cities. On the other hand, a fierce
rejection of carceral institutions seems to linger in popular mentalities continentwide. Escapes, for example, have multiplied in many present-day prisons. As before, prisoners typically attempt to escape during outdoor work,
promenades, and excursions for forced labor. Some rely on charms, or supernatural tools that defy the most solid chains and the highest walls (see
Photo 1.3).[141] Official figures evaluate successful escapes from the Congolese
prisons (Congo-Kinshasa) at three times what they represented at the end of
the colonial period. Reported in terms of the average number of prisoners per
day, they involve a third of the detained population.[142] This indicates not only
the persistent and predictable rejection of the prison among detainees, but

Photo 1.3. Ceiling Opened by an Escaping Prisoner (Tillabéry, Niger, 1992).

also civilians' enduring support of escapees, as well as a remarkably negligent attitude among the penal administration.

Modern juridical practices reflect this ambivalence. Penitentiaries often operate as marginal appendices of the judiciary system. In many countries, only specific categories of people belonging to categories deprived of strong connections in the social fabric, and lacking protection and even minimal social relations, such as labor migrants and foreigners, end up in prison and live out their sentences there.[143] Social vulnerability can result from the nature of the crime itself. Witchcraft, a crime legally recognized in several countries, generally lands the perpetrator in prison, as incarceration proves an effective means of protecting the alleged criminal from popular vengeance.[144] Spontaneous sentences—stoning, beating, murder by fire—might also occur in cases of both high banditry and petty theft. In Cameroon, plagued by violent bandit gangs attacking people on the roads *(coupeurs de route),* exasperated crowds try to get rid of petty thieves to prevent them from developing into underworld bosses *(katchika).*[145] For common delinquents, a broad array of informal strategies exist outside the carceral system, sometimes initiated by the state itself. As large-scale financial fraud, or crimes perpetrated by high-placed persons usually escape judicial sanctions entirely; at the other extreme of the social ladder, many petty crimes are managed within families and neighborhoods, or are solved at the level of local police precincts.[146] This "second legal economy" does not derive from the decline or the judicial failure of the African state; rather, it points to the perpetuation of the rich layers of informal, hidden judicial tactics initiated during the colonial period. At that time, European law only touched upon a superficial stratum of crimes; local communities kept handling illegalities underground.

Across the African continent, the physical management of most prisons has been largely abandoned, with the spectacular exception of the few maximum-security facilities in South Africa and Ghana. The maintenance, let alone modernization, of penal facilities is often relegated to the last lines of national budgets. Outsiders have tended to analyze the material degradation of African penitentiaries as a pathological decline of African penal philosophies, and as the failure of the reformatory purposes of the prison. Yet, it would be best explained as an intensification of colonial penal practices, paralleling the historical failure of most western reformative projects.

Interestingly, in Africa, in contrast to the West, state negligence has resulted in original initiatives to preserve the living conditions of detainees. In two countries as different as Niger and Congo-Brazzaville, the general abdication that reigns both inside and outside the prison is striking. The buildings date from the colonial period and are no longer maintained. Financial resources are nonexistent or unpredictable, a situation that forces prison directors to rely upon charity organizations and the detainees' families in order to ensure the prisoners' subsistence (food, clothing, bedding, health care). Such outside support is facilitated by the considerable permeability of the prison buildings. Families and donors can enter the prison yard on a daily basis, while prisoners can leave the buildings for work, visits, walks or errands, or casual conversation with visitors.[147] As a result, many older facilities end up offering much milder experiences of incarceration to the detainees, and preserve social connections between the prisoners and their relatives. The "open prisons" of Africa are not simply depleted avatars of the western penitentiary; they propose original solutions for prisoners' sanction, physical control, and preserved socialization.

More dramatic realities exist. In Uganda, the Central African Republic, and Guinea, to cite but a few cases, post-colonial dictators have built sites of detention and torture that speak to no other logic than that of megalomaniacal and murderous power. Spectacular and mediatized descriptions of Sékou Touré's Camp Boiro in Conakry (Guinea), Bokassa's prison at Ngaragba (Central African Republic), and Idi Amin Dada's jails in Kampala (Uganda) have repeatedly evoked the sinister images of Nazi camps or Soviet gulags to western audiences.

However, as Didier Bigo has shown in his provocative study of Ngaragba, these references obscure, rather than elucidate, the logic of these prisons. Ngaragba did not operate according to the panoptical laws of the modern and bureaucratic penitentiary; instead, it responded to the imperatives of a local political culture shaped by arbitrariness, physical torture, and the personalization of violence.[148] By contrast with Nazi concentration camps, driven by industrial and impersonal technique, Ngaragba's wardens did not seek to punish detainees by isolating them in a confined, invisible world. To the contrary, Ngaragba functioned like an open-air theater, where torturers and prisoners enacted tragic scenes of power and submission that celebrated Bokassa's personal will and grandeur. A monstrous excrescence of arbitrary power, Ngaragba and its involuntary actors dramatized the cruel confrontation between the weak and the strong, in an institution where inconstancy, contingency, and impredictability—not bureaucratic routine—provided the organizing principle.

This principle stemmed less from pre-colonial punishments than from the later archaism of the colonial penitentiary. Colonial jails, whose carcass mimicked the reformed penitentiary, submerged African prisoners in corporal punishment, the personalization of sentences and authority, and the confusion between political and economic imperatives. Colonial legacy, moreover, has encouraged radical forms of political detention, later practiced extravagantly by post-colonial regimes.[149] African prisons today reflect the exasperation of colonial modes of governance and social control, as well as their articulation with earlier, pre-colonial forms of despotism. These legacies are reinvented today in the context of a new political order (clientelism, personalization of power, prebendal culture). Through the lens of its penitentiary regime, the African state does not resemble the Weberian or even the Foucaultian state based on techniques of power, general surveillance, and the citizens' interiorization of omnipresent discipline. Its prisons shed light on the personalization of relations of power, and the prevalence of social coercion over social protection.[150]

What post-colonial prisons suggest, too, is that the state no longer exercises the monopoly of (il)legitimate violence. In the many places where governmental authority is dissolving or has never consolidated, private forms of incarceration proliferate along the multiple fractures of the social fabric. In times of peace, the agents of the small precincts and police stations capture and sanction a significant number of delinquents who escape the central justice system entirely. In times of political crisis, situations of civil war have encouraged the creation of clandestine jails set up by paramilitary gangs and militias. These transient, localized tactics of incarceration strengthen local networks of power. Their ubiquity speaks to the existence of many zones where the state does not penetrate, and where unregulated juridical and social innovation proliferates. On a different scale, the extraordinary proliferation of refugee camps testifies to the state's loss of control over national territories. Yet, the case of the Sahrawi and Tuareg camps in Algeria, Mali, and Libya (Boilley),[151] suggest how sites of massive fixation and physical constraint forged out of contemporary disasters can foster considerable social renewal.[152]

Here lies perhaps the characteristic mark of African models of incarceration today. Inherited in part from colonial incarceration, the physical capture of criminal bodies in the open, permeable prisons of contemporary Africa is shaped primarily by local power relations,[153] much more than by a regulated policy of punishment and discipline, or by the omnipotence of official justice. Modern African prisons attest, above all, to the unstable deployment of coercive powers—whether by the state or by political and social groups. In this perspective, the increasing diffusion of reclusive models over the continent continues to follow an archaic model of conquest.

BEYOND THE PRISON: SPACE, POWER, AND CONFINEMENT

During the colonial period, the prison belonged to a larger doctrine of spatial confinement. western tactics of enclosure aimed at controlling not only criminals and delinquents, but multiple aspects of African life and physical space. As the conquest rested on a specific mode of governing that combined the subjugation of physical territories with the control of human groups, colonial rulers sought to impose power relations that could be inscribed on the mastering of physical and social spaces. This effort applied to the "natural" and human landscapes, as perceived by the colonizer (ethnic groups, districts, and villages), as well as the social (control and stabilization of workers, urbanites, peasantries), and the cultural landscape (mapping of languages and customs).[154] Such perceptions were not dictated only by circumstances, but belonged, more fundamentally, to a widespread style of government that firmly associated social and political decisions with the implementation of geographical and social rigidity.[155]

The most famous painting of the Congolese artist Tshibumba Kanda Matulu, *Colonie belge, 1885–1959*, provides a striking illustration of colonial strategies (Photo 1.4). *Colonie belge* portrays an agent of the Force publique whipping a prisoner in a striped uniform while a white officer supervises the spectacle. In the background, prisoners in uniform are busy fetching wood and water. Another African character, pants down, is bending over in front of a guard who is ready to beat him. In the rear portion of the scene, a prisoner escapes under the threat of a large Belgian flag flying at the top of the painting.[156] Three women, sitting on a bench, watch and lament the scene.

Neither walls nor fences close this pictorial enumeration of colonial coercions. Yet, Tshibumba's composition plunges the viewer into a strong feeling of physical enclosure and inescapability, as the punctilious ordering of the various scenes forces the eye to wander and rest on colonial buildings and scenes of terror. In the upper portion of the canvas, the symmetrical axe of the police station and a row of dwellings forming a line of flight to the background block the horizon. At the center and foreground, the Belgian officer and his whipping agent form a strong vertical axe, resting upon the horizontal

Photo 1.4. Painting by Tshibumba Kanda Matulu, *Colonie Belge* (1971). Reproduced with permission from J. Fabian, *Remembering the Present* (Berkeley: University of California Press, 1996)

lines of both the beaten prisoner and the threatening whip, in an excruciating cross of torture and malignant power. The other groups satiate the material space of the painted scene with a relentless, proliferating inventory of colonial punishments, cadenced by the ubiquity of the three colors of the Belgian flag—yellow, red, and black. As actors, buildings, and objects bear the colors of colonial power, the viewer's perspective is masterfully captured in the visual field of colonial power, and saturated with the mobile reflections of Belgian authority.[157] This mental enclosure, well beyond the walls of the colonial prison, constitutes the hidden horizon of the history of modern confinement in Africa.

At the end of the nineteenth century, the enclosure of Africa began with the drawing of colonial frontiers, a blunt and banal technique for the construction of the nation-state. Today, colonial borders have survived, and sometimes worsened.[158] The Western Sahara, where an entire society has been imprisoned behind a wall of military fortifications since the mid-1980s, presents an extreme case of the rigidification of national borders.[159] In addition, the colonial enterprise extended the model of the border to the organization of the colony's interior space. First, colonial rule took on the mobility of men. To simplify administrative tasks (taxes, census, sanitary measures), colonizers attempted to restrain liberty of movement on either the individual level (defined as "vagabondage" in court registers) or the collective level, such as Tuareg nomadism in Mali (Boilley).[160]

Europeans tended to describe mobility as aberrant, apprehending local "crises" and disorders as provoked by pathological fluidity. In Gabon, for instance, starting in the early 1930s, administrators and sociologists explained away the Fang social crises (induced, in fact, by colonial disruptions) as stemming from Fang's enduring migrations, the dispersion of their communities, and the intensification of rural exodus. Colonial officers prescribed and finally imposed the regrouping of Fang villages along major roadways, and the settling of young men in "equipped," modernized, and enlarged villages. Other colonial campaigns were driven by the same principles, such as the rampant ideas that the uncontrollable movements of people and the spreading of urban areas were leading to the moral and physical degeneration of Africans, and to the breeding of parasite classes of delinquents, free and uncontrollable women, or jobless migrants.[161]

Therefore, outside the prison, colonial rule privileged spatial confinement as a transformational and eugenic technique. At the end of the nineteenth century, Senegalese correctional houses wished to inculcate children who "run the streets . . . free [and] unoccupied" with new habits of work and obedience (Thioub). A few decades later, the mining companies in Katanga devised a series of working camps to transform African peasants, seen as unstable, undisciplined, and physically vulnerable, into docile and prolific industrial workers (Hanretta). Later still, at the end of the Second World War, colonial authorities in Central and West Africa established agricultural colonies for minors. In these isolated, disciplinary communities, young people extirpated from the vices of the modern city were supposed to become model farmers, and replenish the declining peasantry.[162] Hundreds of administrative reports, briefings, and memoranda invoked the modernizing virtues and civilizing spirit of such spatial enterprises. Colonial territories themselves were oftentimes portrayed as wild archipelagos progressively encircled and penetrated by roads, trails, administrative posts, schools, medical dispensaries, and mission stations. The ideal colony developed as a fortified, rationally structured space, upheld by islands of civilization, energized by a productive, well-controlled circulation of men and resources.

In rare instances colonial camps and prisons could themselves be envisioned as spaces of limited redemption. In these islands, protected from their barbaric surroundings, the quest for the moral improvement of Africans could be engaged in by encouraging the mimicry of whites (Hanretta). In extreme circumstances, the radical transformation of Africans involved physical and mental isolation (e.g., the Mau Mau camps). Such projects shed light on a colonial imagination that linked social and moral changes to a strategy of *place*.

But in the mining camps of Katanga, Africans observed and sabotaged the principles of the colonial spatial order. National borders formed passageways toward better economic or political opportunities. Prisoners escaped from the prisons, and those who remained behind transformed them into sites of transgression and defiance. In shelter camps, refugees sustained their specific social dynamics through incessant innovation (Boilley).[163] And more generally, ancient relations to the land, unnoticed by colonial authorities, kept forging innovative connections with the sacred and invisible world.

The spatial techniques of the colonial conquest probably induced profound mutations in the way Africans articulated social relations with physical space. These transformations are difficult to trace, but a series of symptoms suggest the existence of far-reaching alterations.[164] In contemporary Gabon, for example, relations to the land have become increasingly governed by exogenous authority (Gray). The decline of farming migrations, the regrouping of villages along major roads, the crystallization of populations into inventoried and mapped ethnic groups—have transformed ancient, more largely "open" approaches to physical space in Africa. The most significant changes probably took place in the political realm, as the repertoire of colonial confinements revived the bonds between authority and the management of space. During the nineteenth century, the religious and political direction of territories was ensured by local ruling classes.[165] Colonization confirmed this situation by delimiting new sites of power and proposing new modes of action with respect to land.

Even when colonial rule relocated the ultimate source of authority in the creases of the central, distant, white state, it did not necessarily destroy existing repertoires of power. Hidden in their capitals and palaces, covetous of their political privileges, white rulers organized the symbolic basis of their authority according to the register of imprisonment, secrecy, and enclosure. The enactment of colonial power partly recalled local techniques of the secret, the inaccessible, and the dramatization of confinement. In pre-colonial Africa, ritual specialists protected social harmony through techniques that oftentimes involved episodes of reclusion. During the night, the enclosure of sacred woods or shrines, or the ritual confinement for initiation, was considered necessary in the quest for contact with ancestors and deities. The prison itself was viewed as a space open to the invisible world, and infused with magical threats. The prisoner who disappeared from the living world into the vault of the prison penetrated a world that involved two complementary and opposing principles: the risk of pollution and the opportunity to capture extraordinary power unleashed by supernatural forces.

The imagination of confined power has been repeatedly re-enacted since independence. In Africa today, the tenants of public authority cordon themselves off from ordinary citizens. The fortress-palaces of reigning presidents, popular gossip about rulers performing supernatural acts, the agile apparitions and disappearances of high-profile politicians—all resonate not only with pre-colonial repertoires of leadership, but also with the memory of colonial rituals of power.

CONCLUSION

Unlike western penitentiaries, the colonial prison system did not incarcerate delinquents according to a single judicial register; nor did it subject criminals to a standard regime of punishment. On the contrary, it sought to maintain the racial and juridical hierarchies upon which colonial rule was founded, thus reproducing a violent, personalized, and circumscribed power. After the conquest, European rulers never stopped privileging physical reclusion and fixation as a method of control over Africans. As the vanguard of these confining tactics, colonial prisons illuminate how European regimes in Africa survived as enterprises of unending conquest.

The various phases in the installation of the colonial penitentiary start with the period from 1890 to 1910–1920. This was the time of the triumphant prison in Africa, accompanied by several aborted attempts at erecting penitentiaries for children and asylums for the insane in Southern and Western Africa (1880–1900). Between 1900 and 1930, the campaigns for the medical prevention of epidemics represented the only totalitarian attempt at enclosing entire populations and quarantining territories. Yet, because the African continent was invaded by multiple, fragmentary, and archaic forms of imprisonment, complete carceral archipelagos fail to emerge. Colonial governments' lack of material resources, but, more importantly, their lack of ambition for using confinement as a transformative tactic for the natives, explains some of the original features of modern confinement in Africa.

Colonial punishments not only reflected, but helped create colonial societies. The law constructed the colonial subject as a free, responsible, and rational individual, but at the same time criminalized African life through the codification of taxes, labor, and spatial behavior (in particular, sedentarization). Colonizers read deviance both as an individual act (qualified crime), and as a collective quality (general African resistance to colonial order). Therefore, the colonial prison held people apart according to major colonial divides: Detainees guilty of "administrative" crimes kept away from detainees convicted of common crimes; white prisoners from African inmates. Simultaneously, most prisons failed to separate prisoners according to age, gender, or criminal status (accused or convicted), because the colonial order considered such qualities as less important than inmates' race and submission to administrative regulations.

Colonizers never envisioned experimenting with penal models in the tropics that could later be transported back to Europe. The diffusion of the western prison in Africa remained a one-way operation. Even between different colonies, neither real exchange nor mutual influence developed during the colonial period; no model prison—such as Pentonville in nineteenth-century Europe—ever inspired the building of colonial facilities. In other words, an autonomous penology did not emerge in colonial Africa. The remarkable ideological and material isolation of the penitentiary echoed another symbolic separation. As white colonizers found themselves surrounded by a formidable majority of Africans, prisons separated, isolated, and confined African convicts under colonial gaze. With the penitentiary, Europeans could reverse the racial and spatial confrontation they faced every day in the colony, and organize, in the small enclosure of the prison, a new spatial order. As a result, the prison remained a tool of foreign coercion, and never achieved significant popular favor.

Today, only highly bureaucratic states, endowed with a solid industrial and urban economy, such as South Africa, have managed to maintain the penitentiary systems at the heart of their judicial systems. Elsewhere, and despite considerable regional variations, African prisons are increasingly alienated from judicial institutions, especially when reigning regimes manipulate penal incarceration as a tool of political oppression. In many countries, the social pact between civil society and the state, and the state's duty to protect citizens, have receded under the drive for unilateral domination. The deadly prisons of authoritarian regimes, from Camp Boiro to Ngaragba, where the basic task of maintaining the health of detainees is entirely ignored, provide an extreme illustration of this defeat. Meanwhile, the proliferation of illegal cells and clandestine jails, and the increasing spread of temporary confinements linked to conflict and war, constitute a growing portion of African incarcerations. By using private, unregulated forms of imprisonment to subjugate communities and physical territories, modern warlords and leaders of political rebellions perpetuate some of the coercive spatial tactics of colonial domination.

From the outset of the colonial penal invasion, strategies of punishment and physical restraint never stopped borrowing from ancient repertoires. Because the imposition of the western penitentiary in Africa did not dissolve, but stimulated local representations and methods of confinement, the colonial prison opened a critical site where the direct, physical contact between colonial rulers and African subjects gave birth to a new language about power, escape, and submission. Today, around and against the model of the tropical prison, the crystallization of social and physical space continues to transform the African continent.

NOTES

1. Geffray Mynshull, *Certain Characters and Essayes of Prison and Prisoners*, London, 1618, cited in R. Evans, *The Fabrication of Virtue: English Prison Architecture, 1750–1840* (New York: Cambridge University Press, 1982).

2. V. Hugueux, "Les démons du Rwanda," *L'Express* (December 7, 1995), 96.

3. Evans, *The Fabrication of Virtue*, chap. 1.

4. The names in parentheses refer to the authors of the various chapters of this book. Where necessary, footnotes refer the reader to the original French edition of this book: F. Bernault, ed., *Enfermement, prison et châtiments en Afrique du 19ᵉ siècle à nos jours* (Paris: Karthala, 1999).

5. See the statistics published in the annual report of the *Observatoire des prisons* (Paris: Ulysse/Dystique, 1995).

6. As the collection does not cover the entire continent, the reader should take the book's provisional conclusions as working hypotheses. For classic studies on law in Africa, see S. Falk Moore, *Social Facts and Fabrications: Customary Law on Kilimandjaro, 1880–1980* (Cambridge: Cambridge University Press, 1986); K. Mann and R. Roberts, eds., *Law in Colonial Africa* (Portsmouth, NJ: Heinemann, 1991); and M. Chanock, *Law, Custom and Social Order: The Colonial Experience in Malawi and Zambia* (Portsmouth, NJ: Heinemann, 1998), in particular his theoretical discussion: v–xxii, 3–47, and 219–39.

7. D. Rothman, *The Discovery of the Asylum: Social Order and Disorder in the New Republic* (Boston: Little Brown and Co., 1971); M. Foucault, *Surveiller et punir: Naissance de la prison* (Paris: Gallimard, 1975); M. Ignatieff, *A Just Measure of Pain: The Penitentiary in the Industrial Revolution* (New York: Pantheon Books, 1978). See also R. Evans, *The Fabrication of Virtue*, one of the rare attempts at a complete spatial analysis of the western penitentiary. For a class analysis, see D. Melossi and M. Pavarini, *The Prison and the Factory: Origins of the Penitentiary System* (1ˢᵗ ed., *Carcere et fabbrica*, Bologna, 1977; English translation, London: MacMillan, 1981). And on the intellectual and literary birth of the prison, see J. Bender, *Imagining the Penitentiary: Fiction and the Architecture of the Mind in Eighteenth-Century England* (Chicago: University of Chicago Press, 1987).

8. Soon after the publication of *Discipline and Punish*, many scholars questioned Foucault's argument about the birth of the prison as a complete break with earlier practices. See discussion in M. Perrot, ed., *L'impossible prison: Recherches sur le système pénitentiaire au XIXe siècle* (Paris: Seuil, 1980). In France, this first critique was followed by a collection of essays edited by J.-G. Petit, *La prison, le bagne et l'histoire* (Paris: Librairie des Méridiens, 1984). P. Spierenburg's authoritative study of torture in modern Europe, *The Spectacle of Suffering. Executions and the Evolution of Repression: From a Preindustrial Metropolis to the European Experience* (Cambridge: Cambridge University Press, 1984) argues that no abrupt transition in western modes of repression happened at the end of the eighteenth century; instead, sensibilities changed over several centuries. See also his *Prison Experience: Disciplinary Institutions and Their Inmates in Early Modern Europe* (New Brunswick and London: Rutgers University Press, 1991). R.D. Salvatore and C. Aguirre, eds., *The Birth of the Penitentiary in Latin America: Essays on Criminology, Prison Reform and Social Control, 1830–1940* (Austin: University of Texas Press, 1996), one of the rare studies of colonial prisons, is essentially devoted to the nineteenth century in spite of its title.

9. M. Ignatieff correctly notes that historians have largely failed to explore the twentieth-century prison: "State, Civil Society and Total Institutions: A Critique of Recent Social Histories of Punishment," in S. Cohen and A. Scull, eds., *Social Control and The State* (Oxford, Basil Blackwell, 1985), 78. N. Morris and D. Rothman, eds., *The Oxford History of the Prison: The Practice of Punishment in Western Society* (New York and Oxford: Oxford University Press, 1998) partly fills this gap but does not investigate the non-western prison.

10. Foucault coined the concept of "carceral archipelago" in the last chapter of *Discipline and Punish*, 297–308. He described how penal incarceration gave birth to a continuum of disciplining institutions (asylums, reformatory schools, military garrisons) that used extrapenal incarceration to mold the mind and the body according to the norms of the bureaucratic society.

11. On colonial prisons, see David Arnold's pioneering work, "The Colonial Prison: Power, Knowledge and Penology in Nineteenth Century India," in D. Arnold and D. Hardiman, eds., *Subaltern Studies VII: Essays in Honor of Ranajit Guha* (Oxford: Oxford University Press), 148–87, and F. Dikötter, *Crime, Punishment and the Prison in Modern China* (New York: Columbia University Press, 2002). Peter Zinomann's work on prisons in colonial Vietnam presents striking parallels with the present collection. He shows in particular how the use of premodern forms of punishment in the colonial penitentiary fueled Vietnamese resistance to the colonial state. P. Zinoman, *The Colonial Bastille: A History of Imprisonment in Vietnam, 1862–1940* (Berkeley: University of California Press, 2001).

12. On social control, read the classic study of "total institutions" by E. Goffman, *Asylums: Essays on the Social Situation of Mental Patients and Other Inmates* (Chicago: Aldine Publishing Company, 1962), and further discussions in S. Cohen and A. Scull, eds., *Social Control and the State* (Oxford: Basil Blackwell, 1985).

13. Cohen and Scull, eds., *Social Control and the State*, 1–14.

14. Recent works have analyzed the normative "gaze" that accompanied the conquest of the continent. T. Mitchell, *Colonising Egypt* (Cambridge: Cambridge University Press, 1988); Marie-Louise Pratt, *Imperial Eyes: Travel Writing and Transculturation* (London and New York: Routledge, 1992).

15. Public and private authority also applied to what we call "things." However, objects were part of interpersonal relations and did not have any autonomy—or exchange value—in themselves. The slave trade intensified the commodification of persons, yet it did not consolidate specific categories of inanimate items as means of exchange. For a good review of contemporary debates on this question, see J. Guyer, "Wealth in People as Wealth in Knowledge: Accumulation and Composition in Equatorial Africa," *Journal of African History* 36 (1995), 91–120; and J. Miller, *Way of Death: Merchant Capitalism and the Angolan Slave Trade, 1730–1830* (Madison: University of Wisconsin Press, 1988). On exchange value/use value, see J. Vansina, *Paths in the Rainforest: Toward a History of Political Tradition in Equatorial Africa* (Madison: University of Wisconsin Press, 1990), 251.

16. It is important to avoid applying western romantic notions of a boundless and inviting "landscape" on African notions of environment. In addition, territories protected by communities hardly corresponded to our modern experience of a univocal and largely inactive space. Intrusions from beyond, the transmigration of persons, and many other contacts between the visible and the invisible world contributed to complicate the cognitive texture of space. Finally, settlements were rarely closed and anchored onto permanent locations. In Central Africa, for example, most agrarian societies subsisted through an elaborate system of itinerant crops that linked villages to a complex and changing framework of spaces of production. Mobility took place either by the slow drifting of whole villages, or by fragmentation and dispersion of the households. See Vansina, *Paths in the Rainforest*.

17. In modern Europe, inquisitions and sentences remained largely in private hands before the penal reform in the eighteenth century. In France, the state only intervened in

the event of "extraordinary affairs." During the prison reform, the state did not achieve definitive control of penitentiaries before the late nineteenth century. Cf. J.-G. Petit, *Ces peines obscures. La prison pénale en France, 1780–1875* (Paris: Fayard, 1990); and N. Castan, "Le régime des prisons au XVIIIe siècle," in Petit, ed., *La prison*, 31–42.

18. Spierenburg, *The Spectacle of Suffering*, has shown how in Europe during the sixteenth and seventeenth centuries, the state executioner had to share the power to punish with the crowd.

19. For narratives of spatial and social wanderings, see M. Wright, *Strategies of Slaves and Women in East Africa. Life Stories from East/Central Africa* (New York and London: Lilian Barber Press and James Currey, 1993).

20. P. Martin, *The External Trade of the Loango Coast, 1576–1870* (Oxford: Clarendon Press, 1972), 119.

21. Paul du Chaillu visited the Sangatanga barracons in 1856, as quoted by K. David Patterson, *The Northern Gabon Coast to 1875* (Oxford, Clarendon Press, 1975), 83–86: "Men were chained in collars in groups of six, but women and children were allowed to wander at will within the well-guarded compound. The slaves subsisted on rice and beans while awaiting shipment. Most of the slaves in West Central Africa believed that the whites needed such a great number of slaves for food, not for labor: they fatten and eat them."

22. D. Bouche, *Les villages de liberté en Afrique noire française, 1887–1910* (Paris and La Haye: Mouton, 1968).

23. This pattern is well described along the Congo River by R. Harms, *River of Wealth, River of Sorrow: The Central Zaire Basin in the Era of the Slave and Ivory Trade, 1500–1891* (New Haven: Yale University Press, 1981).

24. Historians have not paid attention to the ideas of exclusion and infamy that probably stigmatized prisoners in Europe as well.

25. A. W. Lawrence, *Trade Castles and Forts in West Africa* (London: J. Cape, 1963). Slaves usually stayed in open quarters outside the fort.

26. For an excellent review and analytical articles on prisoners' political writings, see C.J. Driver, "The View From Makana Island: Some Recent Prison Books From South Africa," *Journal of Southern African Studies* 2, no. 1 (1975), 102–19; D. Schakwyck, "Writing From Prison," in S. Nuttall and C.A. Michael, eds., *Senses of Culture* (New York: Oxford University Press, 2000), 279–97; and P. Gready, "Autobiography and the 'Power of Writing': Political Prison Writing in the Apartheid Era," *Journal of Southern African Studies* 19, no. 3, (1993), 489–523. I would like to thank Patrick Harries for providing me with invaluable insights for this section.

27. Exceptions to this rule can be found in the pioneering article by D. Van Zyl Smit, "Public Policy and the Punishment of Crime in a Divided Society: A Historical Perspective on the South African Penal System," *Crime and Social Justice* 21–22 (1984), 146–62; and among an extensive literature on Robben Island, the recent collection edited by H. Deacon, *The Island: A History of Robben Island, 1488–1990* (Cape Town: Mayibuye Books, 1996). For a broader study of the South African legal context, see M. Chanock, *The Making of South Africa Legal Culture, 1902–1936* (New York: Cambridge University Press, 2001).

28. At the end of the nineteenth century, the settlers' communities in South Africa developed pass laws to control the movement of the black population and to reduce the cost of labor. Under apartheid, the various passes were strenghened and consolidated, extending to women. Over 17 million blacks were imprisoned for breaking these laws between 1916 and 1986, when the pass sytem was finally dismantled. R. Davenport and C. Saunders, *South Africa: A Modern History* (London: 2000), 511.

29. When the first asylum in West Africa was built in Accra in 1888, four psychiatric hospitals were already operating in the Cape colony. Mostly destined for white patients, and then duly organized according to race during the 1890s, these asylums received European patients from all over Southern and Eastern Africa up until the 1920s and 1930s, at which time the English and Portuguese colonies created local establishments. South Africa had several penitentiaries for children as early as the beginning of the 1880s; these were mostly colonies for the training of young delinquents. These institutions had no significant impact on large portions of the African population, with the exception of urbanites. See S. Schwartz, "The Black Insane in the Cape, 1891–1920," *Journal of Southern African Studies* 21, no. 3 (1995), 399–415; M. Vaughan, "Idioms of Madness: Zomba Lunatic Asylum, Nyasaland in the Colonial Period," *Journal of Southern African Studies* 9, no. 2 (1983), 218–38; and L. Chisholm, "The Pedagogy of Porter: The Origins of the Reformatory in the Cape Colony, 1882–1910," *Journal of African History* 27 (1986), 481–95, and "Education, Punishment and the Contradictions of Penal Reform: Alan Paton and Diepkloof Reformatory, 1934–1948," *Journal of Southern African Studies* 17, no. 1 (1991), 23–42.

30. The cloistering of female domestic labor in the cities has been analyzed by D. Gaitskell, "Christian Compounds for Girls: Church Hostels for African Women in Johannesburg, 1907–1970," *Journal of Southern African Studies* 6, no. 1 (1979), 44–69.

31. On the issue of scientific argument for racial segregation, see H. Deacon, "Racial Segregation and Medical Discourse in Nineteenth Century Cape Town," *Journal of Southern African Studies* 22, no. 2 (1996), 287–308.

32. Robben Island served as the outlet for deported convicts under Dutch (1652–1806) and early British occupation. Convicts, both white and black, came from the Cape along with a few political prisonners from the East Indies. After British occupation (1806), African political prisoners from the frontiers of the growing colony joined common criminals on the Island. See H. Deacon, "Introduction," and N. Penn, "Robben Island 1488–1805," in Deacon, ed., *The Island*, 1–32.

33. Van Zyl Smit, "Public Policy," 148–49.

34. Ibid., 150–52, and Deacon, "Racial Segregation and Medical Discourse," 305.

35. V. Bickford-Smith, *Ethnic Pride and Racial Prejudice in Victorian Cape Town* (New York: Cambridge University Press, 1995), 17 and 96.

36. According to Van Zyl Smit, the first segregated prison outside the Cape colony was the one in Kimberley. Bickford-Smith, *Ethnic Pride*, 102–4, shows how the smallpox epidemic in 1882 encouraged white prisoners in the Breakwater Prison to obtain sanitary privileges.

37. Quoted in Deacon, "Racial Segregation and Medical Discourse," 305.

38. Bickford-Smith, *Ethnic Pride*, 139.

39. Deacon, "Racial Segregation and Medical Discourse," 306–7.

40. For a useful comparative perspective on the relationship between forced labor (*shibalo*) and prison labor in Mozambique, see J.M. Penvenne, *African Workers and Colonial Racism: Mozambican Strategies and Struggles in Lourenço Marques, 1877–1962* (Portsmouth, NJ: Heinemann, 1995), particularly 39, 42, 63–77, 103–30, and 146 (for minors' participation in *shibalo*).

41. This pattern was hardly confined to South Africa, as the large literature on the criminalization of idleness and vagrancy in nineteenth-century Europe demonstrates. For a good overview, see R.A. Nye, *Crime, Madness, and Politics in Modern France: The Medical Concept of National Decline* (Princeton: Princeton University, 1984), 175–80.

42. M. Wilson and L. Thompson, eds., *The Oxford History of South Africa* (New York: Oxford University Press, 1969), 145–50. Later, the sixpence scheme was replaced by the "Volunteers Scheme" that allowed petty offenders to choose to work as farm laborers on parole.

43. The state financed all other needs, such as a staffing, maintenance of prisoners, etc.

44. M. Wilson and L. Thompson, eds., *The Oxford History of South Africa*, 148–49.

45. Ibid., 162–63.

46. Compounds for black miners in Kimberley were literally closed, unlike the ones in Johannesburg.

47. Van Onselen, *Studies in the Social and Economic History of the Witwatersrand, 1886–1914*, vol. 2: "New Nineveh" (New York: Longman, 1982); R.V. Turrell, *Capital and Labour on the Kimberley Diamond Fields, 1871–1890* (New York: Cambridge University Press, 1987), 146–73.

48. Van Onselen, *Studies*, 178–79. In 1889, a total of seventeen compounds existed in Kimberley. Patrick Harries, in *Work, Culture and Identity: Migrant Laborers in Mozambique and South Africa, c. 1860–1910* (Portsmouth, NJ: Heinemann, 1994) challenges the totality of the prisonlike compounds as an institution. He notes that De Beers created the first closed compound in 1885, at the height of the Depression, not only to prevent diamond theft and drinking, but also to propose engaging living conditions to African workers. The company never forcibly recruited workers, but instead crafted a system of "racial paternalism" that provided workers in the compounds with comparatively high wages, eight-hour shifts, short contracts, and significant social benefits.

49. Van Zyl Smit, "Public Policy and the Punishment of Crime," 155–56; and Turrell, *Capital and Labour*, 155.

50. Drawing heavily on Erving Goffman's work, both Van Zyl Smit and Turrell argued that De Beers' convict station provided the model for the "total institution" of the closed compound.

51. The first political prisoners arrived on Robben Island in 1962, after the South African Prison Service officially took control of the Island on April 1, 1961. F. Buntman, "Resistance on Robben Island, 1963–1976," in Deacon, ed., *The Island*, 97.

52. N. Mandela, *Long Walk to Freedom* (Boston: Little Brown, 1994).

53. On Robben Island as a "university" for political education, see P. Gready, "Autobiography," 500, 515–21, and F. Buntman, "Resistance on Robben Island," in Deacon, ed., *The Island*, 93–136.

54. This celebration has tended to romanticize the violence of everyday life in the prison, as well as the sharp conflicts that divided prisoners. For a critical analysis of romanticized Robben Island, see D. Schalkwyk, "Writing from Prison," in Nuthall and Michael, *Senses of Culture*, 278–97. A century earlier, resistance to the prison in Southern Africa took the spectacular form of prison gangs. In the nineteenth century, Jan Note, alias "Nongoloza" Mathebula, a charismatic road bandit who was detained in the prison of Johannesburg, managed to organize a network of several thousand gang members largely from his jail. Nongoloza later joined the prison administration as a warden, but his conversion did not stop the development of prison gangs, a characteristic of South African prison life. From 1974 to 1977, at least forty gang murders happened within the prisons of the Western Cape alone. C. Van Onselen, "Crime and Total Institutions in the Making of South Africa: The Life of 'Nongoloza Mathebula, 1867–1948," *History Workshop Journal* (1979), 62–81. For recent studies of gangs in South Africa, see D. Pinnock, *The Brotherhoods: Street Gangs and State Control in Cape Town* (Cape Town: David Philip, 1984), and C. Glaser, *Bo-Tsotsi: The Youth Gangs of Soweto, 1935–76* (Portsmouth, NJ: Heinemann, 2000).

55. C. Coquery-Vidrovitch, *Le Congo au temps des grandes compagnies concession-naires, 1898–1930* (Paris and the Hague: Mouton, 1972); and B. Jewsiewicki, "Rural Society and the Belgian Colonial Economy," in D. Birmingham and P. Martin, eds., *History of Central Africa*, vol. 2 (London and New York: Longman, 1983), 95–125.

56. I. Thioub, "Sénégal: la prison à l'époque coloniale," in Bernault, *Enfermement*, 287.

57. Many of these supposed traditional chiefdoms were, in fact, invented according to the general model put forth by Frederick Lugard. F.D. Lugard, *The Dual Mandate in British Tropical Africa* (London: Franck Cass, 1965). M. Crowder and O. Okime, eds., *West African Chiefs: Their Changing Status under Colonial Rule and Independence* (New York: Africana Pub. Corp.: 1970). On German Tanganyika (and then British as of 1918), see J. Iliffe, *A Modern History of Tanganyika* (Cambridge: Cambridge University Press, 1979).

58. C.M.D. Diallo, "Histoire de la répression pénitentiaire en Guinée française (1900–1958)" *(Thèse de l'université, Université de Paris 7*, 1998), 56–57.

59. The total population of Upper Volta numbered 3.2 million at that time.

60. In a single province (the Lac), 14,408 imprisonments relative to this legislation were pronounced in 1944. D. Williams, "The Role of Prisons in Tanzania: A Historical Per-spective," *Crime and Social Justice* (1980), 28.

61. L.C. Kercher, *The Kenya Penal System: Past, Present and Prospect* (Washington, DC: University Press of America, 1981), 138. For these three years, the African population of Kenya was estimated at about 4.1 million (1931), 4.8 million (1941), and 5.9 million (1951). Figures come from J.D. Fage and R. Oliver, eds., *The Cambridge History of Africa*, vol. 3 (Cambridge: Cambridge University Press, 1975), 576.

62. Figures cited by M.-B. Dembour, "La chicotte comme symbole du colonialisme belge?," *Canadian Journal of African Studies* 26, no. 2 (1992), 207–8. See also her article, "La peine durant la colonisation belge," *Recueils de la société Jean Bodin, LVIII, La Peine/ Punishment* (Brussels: De Boeck, 1991), 67–95.

63. In 1956, the distribution in the Belgian Congo numbered 27,209 sentences for crimes and common offenses, and 21,192 disciplinary sentences. A. Rubbens, "Congo Democratic Republic," in A. Milner, ed., *African Penal Systems* (London: Routledge & K. Paul, 1969) 27.

64. Diallo, "Histoire de la répression pénitentiaire," 145.

65. In Rwanda, under German and Belgian rule, these *cachots* played a crucial role in the penal system (Wagner).

66. In Equatorial French Africa, the *Arrêté du 18 août 1955* regulated penitentiary es-tablishments and convict labor. *Journal officiel de l'AEF* (September 15, 1955), 1158–1201. For French West Africa, two decrees in 1887 and 1891 provided for bodily constraint. Articles 603 to 618 of the Colonial Code for Criminal Instruction *(Code co-lonial d'instruction criminelle)* distinguished between three types of prisons: houses of arrest and houses of justice for the accused, prisons *(maisons de force)* for individuals condemned to more than five years, houses of correction for those detained for eleven days to five years, and police prisons for sentences derived from the *Code de l'indigénat*. Diallo, "Histoire de la répression pénitentiaire," 57.

67. South Africa would be the second exception.

68. Statistics from Kercher, *The Kenya Penal System* 14–15. In less than twenty years the number of penal institutions more than doubled in the colony, rising from 85 to 177.

69. Vaughan, "Idioms of Madness," 218–38.

70. R. Collignon, "Le traitement de la question de la folie au Sénégal à l'époque colon-iale," in Bernault, ed., *Enfermement*, 227–57.

71. P. Morel, *Enfance délinquante et rééducation en AEF et au Congo belge (Mémoire de l'Ecole nationale de la France d'outre-mer*, no. 43, 1955–56; housed in the *Centre des Archives nationales, Section outre-mer, Aix-en-Provence.* Hereafter CAOM).

72. M. Lyons, *The Colonial Disease: A Social History of Sleeping Sickness in Northern Zaire, 1900–1940* (Cambridge: Cambridge University Press, 1992).

73. Eric Silla has shed fresh light on the authoritative aspect of leper houses in *Mali, People Are Not the Same: Leprosy and Identity in Twentieth Century Mali* (Portsmouth, NJ: Heineman, 1998), 120–21.

74. Among the rare historical studies of the detention camps, see L. White, "Separating the Men from the Boys: Construction of Gender, Sexuality, and Terrorism in Central Kenya, 1939–1959," *International Journal of African Historical Studies* 23, no. 1 (1990), 1–25.

75. M. Beti, *Le pauvre Christ de Bomba* (Paris: R. Laffont, 1956).

76. For a different argument, see K. Mann and R. Roberts, eds., *Law in Colonial Africa* (Portsmouth, NJ: Heinemann, 199), 3–58.

77. Historians have documented this enduring violence—especially in Central Africa where it took on particularly visible forms and lasted until the 1930s. On the Belgian Congo, see J. L. Vellut, "La violence armée dans l'Etat Indépendant du Congo. Ténèbres et clartés dans l'histoire d'un Etat conquérant," *Cultures et Développement* 16, nos. 3–4 (1984), 671–707.

78. In France, the last public execution in time of peace took place in 1939. In Belgium, the death penalty was not applied between 1863 and 1944, and disappeared definitively in 1950. J.-L. Vellut, "Une exécution publique à Elisabethville (20 septembre 1922). Notes sur la pratique de la peine capitale dans l'histoire coloniale du Congo," article ms., Louvain-la-Neuve, April 21, 1989.

79. As in French Guinea, where public executions had been performed on the square adjoining the Conakry prison until the 1920s, then abandonned, the colonial government probably feared the risk of urban riots. See chapter by Goerg in this volume.

80. Vellut, "Une exécution," 3–4. According to this historian, indulgence in the realm of crime marked the last ten years of Belgian colonization; colonial authorities did not prescribe or prescribe capital punishment.

81. Diallo, Histoire de la répression pénitentiaire, 124–25.

82. See the painting series of *Colonie belge* by artist Tshibumba, analyzed in J. Fabian, *Remembering the Present: Painting and Popular History in Zaire* (Berkeley: University of California Press, 1996). In German East Africa before World War I, colonial agents used the *kiboko* whip.

83. See Dembour, "La chicotte," 207–8. This sentence was abolished in 1959.

84. Milner, ed., *African Penal Systems*; and A. Milner, *The Nigerian Penal System* (London: Sweet and Maxwell, 1972), 297ff. See also Kercher, *The Kenya Penal System*; 72–75.

85. *Archives nationales du Sénégal, Rapport du governeur du Dahomey au gouverneur général de l'AOF*, no. 378, March 31, 1906.

86. *Archives nationales du Gabon, Fonds Ndjole, 6, Prison. Lettre du gouverneur général de l'AEF aux gouverneurs chefs de territoire*, July 23, 1947.

87. For a superb discussion of the decline of the role of pain in western ideas of punishment, see K. Shoemaker, "The Problem of Pain in Punishment: Historical Perspectives," in A. Sarat, ed., *Pain, Death, and the Law* (Ann Harbor: University of Michigan Press, 2001), 15–41. Colonial punishment represents a striking exception to this historical trend.

88. Hence the ordeal related by Mundo Swalu near Kikwit (Belgian Congo) around 1947: "A few months after returning to school, I learned that one of my father's cousins, Uncle Mbala, a palm nut cutter, was in prison. He had forgot to make the ring [circle] around the palm tree. The local agronomist flagellated him, and had him arrested. Uncle Mbala spent two weeks in prison, and lost a lot of weight. My father's younger brother, Mulaba, a nervous, strong, and quarrelsome man . . . decided to avenge this injustice. . . . He dug a big hole in the ground and covered it with leaves. When the agronomist came by for inspecting the trees, he fell in the hole and broke a leg, besides other wounds. Arrested, my uncle swore that he wanted to avenge his cousin. He was going to die. The whites drove a nail in his head with a hammer. This is how he was killed." Narrative reported in Bogumil Jewsiewicki, *Naître et mourir au Zaïre. Un demi-siècle d'histoire au quotidien* (Paris: Karthala, 1993), 111.

89. Michelle Perrot explains that corporal punishment also disappeared very late in the French reformed prisons in France. Perrot, ed., *L'impossible prison*, 59.

90. On Pentonville, see Evans, *The Fabrication of Virtue*. I drew the plan of the central prison of Brazzaville during a visit to the prison in the summer of 1995.

91. In South Africa, however, modern imprisonment appeared earlier but racial segregation did not occur before the late 1880s.

92. For a spectacular example of the way Europeans evaded sentences in the colonies, see M. Crowder's study of the scandal that followed a native chief's decision to inflict punishment on a white man in Botswana, *The Flogging of Phineas McIntosh: A Tale of Colonial Folly and Injustice, Bechuanaland 1933* (New Haven: Yale University Press, 1988).

93. Single cells could also isolate potential European detainees.

94. Vellut, "Une exécution"

95. Numerous affairs referring to the condemnation of guards for complicity with detainees exist in the archives of Niger. Guards were particularly susceptible to being imprisoned. Thus, in 1951, the 580 guards of Niger spent a total of 620 days in prison. *Rapport d'inspection 341/2/ICGC, 2 november 1951. Archives nationales du Niger 4N-43.*

96. See similar view in D. Williams, "The Role of Prisons in Tanzania," 27–38.

97. The transfer of prison labor gangs to private entrepreneurs had been definitively forbidden in metropolitan France at the end of the nineteenth century. Petit, *Ces peines obscures*. Forced labor was abolished in the French colonies in 1946.

98. This case is detailed in Diallo, "Histoire de la répression pénitentiaire," 77–79.

99. The law usually mentioned the obligation of penal labor. It was sometimes simply part of prison regulations, such as the 1895 decree in French Guinea stating that work was obligatory for all prisoners except on Sundays, holidays, or for a medical reason. In French Equatorial Africa, a first decree instituted forced labor for prisoners in 1894 and called for the transfer of labor to private enterprises. The *Arrêté* of August 18, 1955, reiterated obligatory labor for all detainees, and the construction of penal camps for those condemned to more than one year of prison. Prisoners in penal camps were forced to labor in public works. A medical visit classified each prisoner in one of the following categories: (1) apt for all works, (2) apt for light labor, (3) inapt for work. This last category of prisoners, usually reserved for women, minors, or accused persons awaiting trial, had to do maintenance and cleanup of the penitentiary. All others inmates had to work for sixty hours a week, including travel time. The prison administration received a fee calculated according to the minimum wage practiced in the territories, and the prisoner only received a portion

of this money—fixed by the order of the territorial chiefs—which constituted his prison earnings (*pécule*). Article 6, *arrêté du 18 août 1955, Journal officiel de l'AEF* (September 15, 1955), 1189.

100. Ibid., 425; and *Télégramme*, May 15, 1922. *Archives nationales du Niger, 3N 35.*

101. An exemplary case is preserved in the archives of Niger. In 1926, in the circumscription of Maradi, the population resisted against forced labor and military conscription. Many men fled to neighboring Nigeria. The circumscription commander ordered sixty young men to report to the district headquarters and "labor on the prison construction work-sites." The ten days of service were a means to select the fifteen "most solid and best constituted" workers, who would be presented to the commission for army recruitment. Four "volunteered," and the others were sequestered in the prison that they had just erected. After forty-seven days of detention, they were turned over to the commission for recruitment as conscripts. *Enquête et plaintes concernant le maintien des recrues à Maradi, 1927. Archives nationales du Niger, 3N 35.*

102. On the private and domestic space of the "good life" as the model penitentiary, see Evans, *The Fabrication of Virtue*, 404–7.

103. The administration introduced a treadmill in the Cape Town prison in the 1820s, but abandoned it after it broke.

104. B. Berman and J. Lonsdale, "Coping with Contradictions: The Colonial State in Kenya, 1895–1914," *Journal of African History* 20, no. 4 (1979), 487–506, and *Unhappy Valley: Conflict in Kenya and Africa* (London: James Currey, 1992). See also S. Berry, "Hegemony on a Shoestring," in *No Condition is Permanent: The Social Dynamics of Agrarian Changes in Sub-Saharan Africa* (Madison: University of Wisconsin Press, 1993), 22–42.

105. This hypothesis levels regional variations. A flurry of discourse on penal programs in the British East African colonies emerged during the 1930s, when official commissions for study and reflection were created (1923: *Kenyan Commission on Native Punishment*; 1931: *Tanganyika Legislative Council Committee on Penal Policy*; and, especially, in 1933: *Bushed Committee of Inquiry into the Administration of Justice in Kenya, Uganda and Tanganyika Territory in Criminal Matters*). The last of these concluded that corporal punishment should be restrained, imprisonment should be seen as the most efficient of civilized solutions, and compensation for victims in the payment of fines should be applied. Description and analysis in Read, "Kenya, Tanzania and Uganda," in Milner, ed., *African Penal Systems*, 110–18.

106. Debates among lower-ranked administrators, especially district officers and *chefs de circonscription* have not yet been examined. Administrators who worked in the interior and had direct contact with Africans were probably more apt to question the function of imprisonment and repression.

107. All scholars document the early failure of the penitentiary almost instantly after the first modern prisons were built in Europe and in North America.

108. Report of the vice president of the French West Africa court of appeals, 1907, cited by Diallo, "Histoire de la répression pénitentiaire," 136.

109. *Rapport de 1909*; ibid., 206.

110. Delinquent children were the only exception. In 1870 sixty-five farms were created in England for the reform of children. In 1879, fifty-two agricultural colonies were founded in France. Evans, *The Fabrication of Virtue*. On the French case, see the study by C. Carlier, *La prison aux champs. Les colonies d'enfants délinquants du Nord de la France au XIXe* (Paris: Editions de l'Atelier, 1994).

111. The degeneration school occupied a middle ground between the atavistic criminal described by the Lombrosians, and the abstract free man imagined by Enlightenment jurists and philosophers. One of its leaders, the psychiatrist Charles Féré, argued in his book *Dégénerescence et criminalité* (1888) that criminal degenerates were produced by an unhealthy milieu that weakened the individual's ability to resist the "impulses" of criminal temptations. For a lengthy discussion of degeneration, see R.A. Nye, *Crime, Madness, and Politics in Modern France* (Princeton: Princeton University Press, 1984), especially chap. 4.

112. *Evolués* is a colonial term that appeared in the Francophone colonies at the end of the 1930s. It designated western-educated Africans. In the French Congo and the Belgian Congo, it gave rise to a specific juridical status.

113. David Arnold argues that this principle was fairly generalized among English colonizers in India; cf. "The Colonial Prison," in Arnold and Hardiman, eds., *Subaltern Studies VII*, 175.

114. The architecture of the reformed prison was supposed to cure criminals by severing them from the contamination of evil, and by infusing discipline into them from the ordered, rational architecture of the penitentiary.

115. Ann Stoler explored these anxieties in "Sexual Affronts and Racial Frontiers: European Identities and the Cultural Politics of Exclusion in Colonial Southeast Asia," *Comparative Studies in Society and History* 34, no. 2 (1992), 514–51. Panics were particularly virulent in colonial cities, and justified the first programs for spatial separation. P. Curtin, "Medical Knowledge and Urban Planning in Colonial Tropical Africa," *American Historical Review* 90, no. 3 (1985), 594–613. For Equatorial Africa, see P. Martin, *Leisure and Society in Colonial Brazzaville* (Cambridge: Cambridge University Press, 1995).

116. In the French colonies, these visions crystallized around the supposed contrast between the benevolent prison and the barbarous *sharia* law: "*Notre répression (emprisonnement) reste bénigne à côté du châtiment corporel prévu par la loi coranique (ablation du poignet),*" *Rapport du colonel Venel, commissaire du gouvernement général au territoire militaire du Niger, 2 mai 1915, 76/AE. Archives Nationales du Niger, 23-6-16.*

117. On contemporary reform programs in Senegal, see S. Nédélec, "Etat et délinquance juvénile au Sénégal contemporain," in Bernault, ed., *Enfermement*, 411–35. On present-day Kenya, see Kercher, *The Kenya Penal System*.

118. Underscored by M. Vaughan, *Curing their Ills: Colonial Power and African Illness* (Stanford: Stanford University Press, 1991).

119. On the paradigm of the transplant *(greffe)*, a notion developed with respect to the state and the nation, see the luminous introduction by J.-F. Bayart in his edited volume, *La greffe de l'Etat* (Paris: Karthala, 1996).

120. Only a few prisoners collaborated with colonial penitentiary rulers. Some provided "good-willed" Europeans with "trustworthy" detainees converted into gardeners, cooks, or guards. Despite European rhetoric, their motivations stemmed probably more from urgent needs for survival and the lack of possible alternatives, rather than the will to cooperate. See, for example, R. Gauthereau, *Journal d'un colonialiste* (Paris: Seuil, 1986), 113–15.

121. Among many outstanding works, see J.M. Kariuki, *Mau Mau Detainee* (1963), Wole Soyinka, *The Man Died: Prison Notes* (1972), Ngugi Wa Thiong'o, *Detainee: A Writer's Prison Diary* (1981), Ken Saro Wiwa, *A Month and a Day: A Detention Diary* (1995), and the fiction novel by Ibrahima Ly, *Toiles d'araignées* (1982). Ch.D Gondola

proposes an interesting analysis of prison novels in his chapter "Le cercle de craie: l'enfermement dans le roman africain," in Bernault, ed., *Enfermement*, 337–61.

122. For another reconstituted vision of prison experience, see C. Van Onselen on the itinerary of Nongoloza Mathebula, "Crime and Total Institutions in the Making of Modern South Africa: The Life of "Nongoloza Mathebula, 1867–1948," *History Workshop Journal* 19 (1985), 62–81. Bandits and rebels have generated an extensive literature in the 1980s. See D. Crummey, ed., *Banditry, Rebellion and Social Protest in Africa* (London: Heinemann, 1985); and a good discussion by S. Cohen, "Bandits, Rebels or Criminals: African History and Western Criminology (Review Article)," *Africa* 56, no. 4 (1986), 468–83.

123. Thioub, "Sénégal: la prison à l'époque coloniale. Significations, évitement et évasions," in Bernault, ed., *Enfermement*, 292, explains how free men *(gor)* and nobles *(garmi)* experienced the prison as an unbearable social degradation. Many committed suicide, such as the ruler *(damel)* of Kayor, Samba Yaya Fall, after he was confined to the Island of Gorée in 1891.

124. Diallo, "Histoire de la répression pénitentiaire en Guinée," 125.

125. On idioms of extraction during the time of the slave trade, see Miller, *Way of Death*, 157–58. And on their endurance throughout the colonial and contemporary periods, see the works of L. White, especially *Speaking with Vampires* (Berkeley: University of California Press, 2000).

126. Thioub, "*Sénégal*," in Bernault, *Enfermement*, 294.

127. *Archives nationales du Gabon, Fonds présidence 629. Procès verbal de plainte 1032, à G. Thomas, chef de poste à Mékambo*, April 1, 1936

128. *Archives nationales du Gabon. Fonds présidence 8-308. Procès verbaux d'enregistrement de plainte, Tribunal indigène du 1er degré de l'Ogooué-Ivindo*, August 1, 1943.

129. Diallo, "Histoire de la répression pénitentiaire en Guinée," 122.

130. *Minutes du tribunal de subdivision de Djibo, cercle de Dori. Audience du 18 mai 1915. Archives nationales du Niger, 7-8-2.*

131. Victims of the system could ally themselves with African civil servants against the threat of the prison. In early colonial Sierra Leone, for example, the courts realized that a number of supects had evaded the law through bribery, as the court messengers on their way to arrest a suspect were sometimes "begged" with "presents" to let the suspect go. C. Magbaily Fyle, *History and Socio-Economic Development in Sierra Leone* (Freetown: SLADEA, 1988), 91–92. I thank Odile Goerg for this reference.

132. To my knowledge, no research has been done on rebellions in colonial prisons in Africa.

133. Gondola, "Le cercle de craie," in Bernault, ed., *Enfermement*, 358.

134. Nédélec, "Etat et délinquance juvénile," in Bernault, ed., *Enfermement*, 411–35.

135. Mass incarceration in Rwanda does not date back to 1994: before then, the Rwandan government imprisoned opponents (Wagner).

136. See also C. Deslaurier, "Un système carcéral dans un Etat en crise: Prison, politique et génocide (1990–1996)," in Bernault, ed., *Enfermement*, 437–71; and for a recent analysis of contemporary Rwanda, R. Brauman, S. Smith, and C. Vidal, "Rwanda: politique de terreur et privilège d'impunité au Rwanda," *Esprit* (August–September 2000).

137. This is the case for the criminal codes of Nigeria, Kenya (1973), and Uganda. See Milner, ed., *African Penal Systems*, 111; and *The Nigerian Penal System*, 305. See also Kercher, *The Kenya Penal System*, 250. In Tanzania, the government introduced a "Minimum Sentences Act" in 1963, that required caning for scheduled offenses such as robbery,

cattle theft, and theft by public servants and state officials. The Act sparked vigorous criticism in Tanzania, until a new law canceled all physical punishment in 1972. See discussion of the 1963 Act in J.S. Read, "Minimum Sentences in Tanzania," *Journal of African Law* 9, no. 1 (1965), 20–39. For a good analysis of the 1972 Act, and discussion of earlier debates, see D. Williams, "The Minimum Sentences Act, 1972, of Tanzania," *Journal of African Law* 18, no. 1 (1974), 79–91. In Ghana, the British colonial government never legalized corporal punishment, and after independence independent regimes never introduced it. R.B. Seidman, "The Ghana Prison System: A Historical Perspective," in Milner, ed., *African Penal Systems*, 68 and 85.

138. The modern airport of Embakasi in Nairobi was constructed by 3,000 recidivist prisoners. James S. Read, "Kenya, Tanzania, and Uganda," in Milner, ed., *African Penal Systems*, 137.

139. Williams, "The Role of Prisons in Tanzania," 32, and 36–37. In 1961, the establishment of revolutionary tribunals in Ghana reflected Nkrumah's longstanding suspicion that the existing legal system has been made "for application to an imperialist and colonial purpose." In the 1970s and 1980s, a continentwide trend tried to restructure legal systems inherited from the colonial past. The creation of special courts in Nigeria, the adoption of Customary Law in Zimbabwe along with the creation of Village and Community Courts, and in Mozambique, the sweeping replacement of Portuguese courts by people's tribunals, marked this period of renovation. See an excellent overview by R. Gocking, "Ghana's Public Tribunals: An Experiment in Revolutionary Justice," *African Affairs* (1996), 197–223.

140. Among these are the heads of the worst death squads that operated in the 1980s and 1990s. I thank Patrick Harries for this information.

141. The night before I visited the Tillabéri prison (Niger, 1992), a handcuffed prisoner had managed to free himself and escape through a hole in the log roof of his cell, more than three meters off the ground.

142. The figures are as follows: in 1956, 1,425 escapes for 22,680 (6.3%) prisoners [average per day]; in 1963, 4,743 escapes for 12,285 detainees (38.6%); in 1973, 3,126 for 15,322 (20.4%). *Administration pénitentiaire, Imprimerie de Ndolo, Archives nationales du Congo.* It is extremely difficult to gain access to an even imperfect series of figures on this point. The detailed data of Milner, ed., *African Penal Systems; The Nigerian Penal System*; and Kercher, *The Kenya Penal System*, are all silent on this point. In addition, available date is hardly reliable; figures can be manipulated so as to put pressure on governments to increase budgets for maintenance and security.

143. In the Brazzaville prison, detainees are said to be foreigners, particularly Zairians.

144. On the Cameroonian case, see C. Fisiy and M. Rowlands, "Sorcery and Law in Modern Cameroon," *Culture and History* (Copenhagen) 6 (1990), 63–84; and C. Fisiy and P. Geschiere, "Judges and Witches, or How is the State to Deal with Witchcraft? Examples from Southeastern Cameroon," *Cahiers d'études africaines* 118 (1990), 135–56.

145. S. Issa, "La répression du grand banditisme au Cameroun," *Crime, histoire, et sociétés* (forthcoming).

146. Nédélec, "Etat et délinquance juvénile," in Bernault, ed., *Enfermement*, 411–35.

147. Author's visits to the prisons at Tillabéry, Niamey, Daikana, and Kollo (Niger, 1992); and to the Brazzaville prison (Congo, 1995).

148. D. Bigo, "Ngaragba, 'l'impossible prison," *Revue française de science politique* 39, no. 6 (1989), 867–85.

149. See reports by human rights organizations (Amnesty International, Human Rights Watch/Africa); and the memoirs of political opponents.

150. What Achille Mbembe calls the *caporalisation* of colonial and African governments. See his article, "Traditions de l'autoritarisme et problèmes de gouvernement en Afrique sub-saharienne," *Africa Development* 17, no. 1 (1992), 37–64.

151. R. Villemont, "Le cas du Sahara occidental," in Bernault, ed., *Enfermement*, 387–410.

152. L. Malkki, *Purity and Exile: Violence, Memory and Cosmology among Hutu Refugees in Tanzania* (Chicago: University of Chicago Press, 1995) shows how a complex network of social, ethnic, and national identities is constructed among Hutu refugees from Burundi in the camps of Tanzania.

153. A good theoretical overview can be found in R. Marchal, "Surveillance et répression en postcolonie," *Politique africaine* 42 (1991), 41–50.

154. Apart from Pratt's pioneering study; see also, J.K. Noyes, *Colonial Space: Spatiality in the Discourse of German South West Africa, 1884–1915* (Philadelphia: Harwood Academic Publishers, 1992); and M.-A de Suremain, "Cartographie coloniale et encadrement des populations en Afrique française dans la première moitié du XXe siècle," *Revue française d'histoire d'outre-mer* 324–325 (1999), 29–64.

155. For elaboration on this idea, see C. Gray, *Colonial Rule and Crisis in Equatorial Africa* (Rochester: The University of Rochester Press, 2002).

156. A reproduction of this painting is provided by J. Fabian in *Remembering the Present: Painting and Popular History in Zaire* (Berkeley: University of California Press, 1996), 68–69. I thank Jan Vansina for noting an interesting anachronism in the painting. The colonial flag of the Belgian Congo was blue with a yellow star, but it was later appropriated by independent Congo. The painting uses the contemporary Belgian flag (three bands of yellow, red, and black) in order to mark the difference between the colonizers and the colonized.

157. This formal analysis is inspired by Ilona Szombati-Fabian and Johannes Fabian, "Art, History and Society: Popular Painting in Shaba, Zaire," *Studies in the Anthropology of Visual Communication* 3 (1976), 1–21.

158. P. Nugent and A.I. Asiwaju, eds., *African Boundaries: Barriers, Conduits and Opportunities* (London: Pinter, 1996) offers a subtle study of modern frontiers, and points out that the artificiality of African borders is similar to the artificiality of most modern borders worldwide.

159. R. Villemont, "Le cas du Sahara occidental," in Bernault, ed., *Enfermement*, 387–410.

160. See also the case of transborder labor migrations in A. Duperray, "*Une frontière fantôme: le 11e parallèle entre Gold Coast et Haute Volta*," in Bernault, ed., *Enfermement*, 133–62.

161. Of a fast-growing literature, studies of colonial policies aiming to control urban women include N.R. Hunt, "Domesticity and Colonialism in Belgian Africa: Usumbura's *Foyer Social*, 1946–1960," *Signs: Journal of Women in Culture and Society* 15 (1990), 447–74; and L. White, *The Comforts of Home: Prostitution in Colonial Nairobi* (Chicago: University of Chicago Press, 1990). For South Africa, J. Wells, *We Have Done with Pleading: The Women's 1913 Anti-pass Campaign* (Johannesburg: Ravan Press, 1991). A continental overview is available in C. Coquery-Vidrovitch, *African Women: A Modern History* (Boulder: Westview Press, 1997).

162. On Equatorial Africa, see Morel, *Enfance délinquante*.

163. See also the vitality of social formations in the closed space of Honde Valley, in H. Schmidt, "Love and Healing in Forced Communities: Borderlands in Zimbabwe's War of Liberation," in Nugent and Asiwaju, eds., *African Boundaries*, 183–204.

164. The history of environment in Africa is now a mature field, but does not necessarily cover the history of space. On cultural notions of space and their transformations in colonial Africa, see, for example, Achille Mbembe's work on the notion of regional spaces *(terroirs)* and the invisible world in *La naissance du maquis dans le Sud-Cameroun 1920–1960* (Paris: Karthala, 1996). On the formation of sacred and political territories, see F. Bernault, "The Political Shaping of Sacred Locality in Brazzaville: 1959–1997," in D. Anderson and R. Rathbone, eds., *Africa's Urban Past* (London: James Currey, 1999), 283–302. Michele D. Wagner looks at precolonial and postcolonial perceptions of space in Tanzania in her article "Environment, Community and History: Nature in the Mind," in G. Maddox, J. Giblin, and I. Kimambo, eds., *Custodians of the Land* (London: James Currey, 1996), 175–99.

165. On Central Africa, see Georges Dupré's study of "lords of the earth," among the Beembe, *Les naissances d'une société. Espace et historicité chez les Beembé du Congo* (Paris: ORSTOM, 1985); and among the Teke, P. Bonnafé, *Histoire sociale d'un peuple congolais* (Paris: ORSTOM, 1987). See also the chapters on Africa in J.-F. Vincent, D. Dory, and R. Verdier, eds., *La construction religieuse du territoire* (Paris: L'Harmattan, 1995).

2

CONFINEMENT IN ANGOLA'S PAST

Jan Vansina

Given the importance of prisons and penal servitude in the founding of the contemporary system of coercion in Central Africa, historical studies are compelled to demonstrate the elaboration of this order. No doubt, the present system emerged at the start of the modern colonial period.[1] But one wonders: Did antecedents exist either in African societies themselves or in the old Portuguese colonies? Since we find no traces of prisons or penal incarceration (or even places where slaves were confined) in the ethnography of the region, and since terms designating "the prison" in African languages are either borrowed or recent innovations, we can presume that pre-colonial African societies did not practice penal servitude as a judiciary institution or institute prisons as a specific place for incarceration. Institutionalized incarceration appeared in Central Africa only around 1485, with the founding of the Portuguese colonies. The latter, then, are central to our inquiry. How did they contribute to more recent colonial regimes? And did neighboring African societies ever adopt the institutions and the penal techniques of the old Angolan colony?

We should note at the outset that the history of incarceration in the former Portuguese colonies involved two distinct practices: (1) incarceration for criminal cause and (2) the incarceration of slaves. Moreover, we must constantly remind ourselves that these colonies were always under military government, being thus well adapted to receive those condemned to banishment (*degredados*). As of September 1493, the first colony at São Tomé (established in 1486) was peopled with the children of Jews expelled from Castille. They were baptized and condemned to banishment because of their parents' religion.[2] This practice was also introduced to Angola shortly after its founding (1575) and continued throughout the history of the colony. However, in this

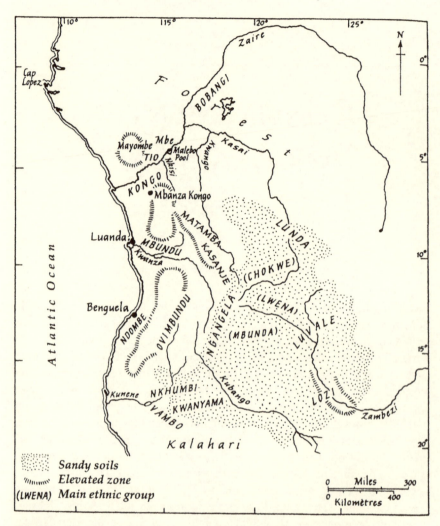

Map 2.1. Ancient Angola. Map drawn from Joseph C. Miller, "The Paradoxes of Impoverishment in the Atlantic Zone," in D. Birmingham & P. Martin, eds., *History of Central Africa*, vol. 1 (London and New York: Longman, 1983), p. 142.

instance, the great majority of those banished were not Jews or Gypsies, but rather prisoners of common law who had been condemned for crimes such as murder, rape, assault and battery, or theft.[3] As of 1600 or earlier, they constituted the majority of European immigrants. They contributed to the climate of violence and extreme disorder that had already been established by the slave trade. The practice of banishing criminals to Angola was never abandoned. To the contrary, after the abolition of the death penalty in Portugal in 1869, this method was reaffirmed and continued until 1932.[4] These two major facts—military control and the presence of numerous banished persons—a third was added: slavery and the slave trade. Together, these elements characterized all aspects of the social history of the Portuguese colonies, and especially the application of criminal law and the practice of incarceration.

THE PORTUGUESE PRISON OF THE PAST

Upon installation in Africa, the Portuguese constructed fortresses that contained prisons. The latter were erected mostly for Europeans, but Africans were also locked up behind their walls. At São Tomé, the first significant edifice was a tower[5] where the military and local governors were housed. This tower also contained a prison for defendants, who were chained and shackled until judgment and eventual condemnation.[6] Contrary to other European and contemporary African practice, condemnation to penal servitude—that is, condemnation to punitive incarceration for a determined period of time—did not exist. At the time, the prison had no place in the repertory of punishments meted out. Thus the first known reference to its use in 1499 recounts how a prisoner's associates tried, in vain, to free him. With regard to the same affair, the text mentions sentences pronounced: execution by quartering, execution by impalement, and exile outside of the only inhabited space at the time.[7]

Evidently, the law in use was still wholly medieval. This impression is confirmed by the use of a collection of Manuelian decrees (printed in 1514, and used as a penal code). For example, the punishments mentioned in only one chapter of these decrees include fines, suspension of wages, confiscation of goods, whipping "for those who are not exempt" (by status), banishment, "natural" death (probably by hanging, which was a frequent decision), and death by torture. Mutilation (severing of a member) is not cited in this particular chapter even though it was an equally common punishment.[8] Interrogation by torture was practiced, but only at the stage of judicial discovery. And this range of punishments was completed with condemnation to the galleys.[9] These decrees remained in force until the middle of the nineteenth century. In 1841, and still in 1875, cases of banished persons having been whipped to death are noted.[10] In Luanda by the mid-nineteenth century, a square in the neighborhood called Bungo was still a site of public executions.[11] And, as we will see, these same decrees were sent to the king of the Kongo around 1514 as models of civilized justice!

During the Middle Ages, the Portuguese Catholic Church possessed a well-developed and systematized judicial code that was distinct from royal justice. Under the authority of the bishop, each diocese constituted a distinct jurisdiction with its own prison. The criminal law practiced by the church had its own panoply of punishments, from fines to reclusion; these included excommunication, banishment, and the death penalty. The organization and exercise of ecclesiastical criminal law developed in Africa with the foundation of dioceses in Central Africa (first in São Tomé in 1535; then in Kongo/Angola in 1578, with headquarters at Mbanza Kongo until 1614, and then in Luanda). But despite vigorous judicial activity, which often led to fierce conflict between the bishops and political authorities, there were never any episcopal prisons in Central Africa. An agreement between the king and the bishops foresaw the incarceration of those held by the church in ordinary prisons, where they could only be freed by order of the diocese.[12] In Angola, the history of ecclesiastical imprisonment is thus not much different from that practiced by secular authorities. In fact, the latter sometimes made abusive use of criminal law associated with the church. For instance, this ecclesiastical code provided for punishment by reclusion in cases where a defendant could not manage to pay a fine. Certain parsons exploited this precept, arresting African chiefs and using them "as slaves" while waiting for the payment of an arbitrary fine supposedly imposed for evasion of religious obligations.[13]

As we can see, the prison held a relatively modest place in the panoply of punishments meted out by the state. And the history of the sites established for these activities confirms this point. The first major construction project in Luanda (founded in 1576) was the fortress of São Miguel, which of course contained a prison. Two other fortresses, Penedo and São Pedro, were built in Luanda shortly thereafter.[14] However, São Miguel continued to serve as the main place of internment up until the nineteenth century, at which time the dungeons of Penedo partly took over.[15] Military guards served as jailers and the occupants were mostly banished persons and other military personnel. Andrew Battell, an English seaman who was banished from Rio de Janeiro around 1592, refers to jail in his memoirs: "Here I was presently taken out of the ship and put into prison, and sent up the River Quansa, to a town of garrison . . ." He then tried to escape on a Dutch ship: "But I was betrayed by Portugals which sailed in the ship, and was fetched on shore by sergeants of the city and put in prison, and lay with great bolts of iron two months, thinking that the governor would put me to death. But at last I was banished forever to the Fort of Massangano, to serve in the conquest of those parts." Six years later, he escaped with three Gypsies and seven Portuguese. They fled to the border of the Kongo kingdom, where they were informed on and then attacked by a Portuguese patrol. In the face of this, Battell declared: "rather than I will be hanged, I will die amongst you. Then the captain came near unto me and said 'Deliver thy musket to one of the soldiers;' and I protest, as I am a gentleman and a soldier, to save thy life for thy resolute mind." Thus he returned to prison in Luanda for three months, "with collars of iron, and great bolts upon our legs." Afterward, his banishment for life "to the wars" was pronounced and he was sent to the hinterland.[16]

While originally prisons were destined for white inmates, over time they also held black prisoners. This was especially true after the construction of the so-called "public" or "civic" prison (at an unknown date, but certainly before 1750) that was connected to the town hall.[17] Only renowned Africans were jailed in the fortresses. The best-known case is that of Alexis, a prince of Kongo, a political prisoner who was incarcerated at Penedo in 1836 for having asserted the independence of the kingdom of the Kongo. He was held in chains like the other prisoners, without ever having been condemned; the authorities hoped that he would die in prison.[18]

Before 1624, there was neither a separate administration nor a specific budget for prisons. At this time, the *Santa Casa de Misericordia* was founded, attached to the hospital, and operated by the ecclesiastical establishment. These two institutions were largely financed by donations from the wealthy classes of Luanda. At the *Santa Casa*, there was a supervisor, and a salaried lawyer was in charge of the release of prisoners. Meals seem to have been provided by the hospital's kitchen.[19]

There is much evidence of the subsidiary role of the prison in the system of incarceration at this time. There is no map or description of Luanda that mentions a building or site referred to as a "prison," and for the entire period under consideration there is no single building consecrated entirely to incarceration. The prison was a simple dungeon in a fortress, a room in the barracks at a garrison post or in the official warehouse of other provincial administrative centers, or even a room in the Luanda city hall. The latter was the city's "public" or "civil" prison, designated no doubt for the seclusion of defendants from the city who were not banished persons. However, despite this "civil" title, the military were also in charge of this house of detention. This was facilitated by the fact that it was located just across from the main guardroom of the governor general's palace. But even this prison was so rarely used that, in about 1816, it was falling into ruins. Having been restored in 1817, it is referred to in 1819, along with the city hall, as one of the most distinguished structures in the city. At this time, it was also used to imprison those arrested during nightly patrols.[20] Aside from banished persons, and persons awaiting confirmation of their death sentences from Lisbon, the Luandan prisons were "almost empty [of Portuguese]."[21]

On the other hand, many sources refer to the common practice in the provinces of detaining African chiefs as hostages, especially to force their subjects to pay up tithes or to recruit porters.[22] Other Africans were also imprisoned: men for indebtedness or as collateral, and women as hostages or as lures for their husbands.[23] Decisions on incarceration in the provinces were left to the judgment of those heading administrative centers (*capitães mor*). These decisions are particularly arbitrary, especially concerning local Africans. Thus, still in 1875, a provincial administrator had a local African man chained and whipped for having danced in public. But only four weeks later, the same administrator organized a show of this same dance in order to please his new mistress.[24] These kinds of practices turned official jails into private prisons.

It is not surprising, then, that simple Portuguese residents, or even merchants who were just passing through, had private prisons where they held Africans. Private individuals, who were mostly slave traders, certainly had the means to do so. As of 1765, certain governors tried to eliminate this practice, but to no avail.[25] One hundred years later, merchants were still arresting and judging thieves on their own initiative.[26] This was still the case in the neighboring colony of Congo, where such methods were used in trading posts before the advent of the Congo independent state. One of the future founders of that state, A. Delcommune, an employee in a trading house in Boma, explains how, in 1876, a moot *(lit de justice)* condemned a group of Africans to death, chaining them and throwing them into the river. An English patrol found their bodies at sea.[27]

In Angola, the role of the prison in the penitentiary system was slow to lose its character—that is, to prevent accused parties from fleeing. The first sign of a *condemnation* to a prison term for a determined period as a *punishment* appears only in 1742. Even then, this sentence was applied only to wealthy people, having been decreed for those who contravened the laws on sumptuary displays.[28] Even then, and for the duration of the nineteenth century, condemnation to prison sentences was extremely rare.[29]

Even minor changes in this system only came much later. In the Angolan interior, the sole—yet enigmatic—innovation, reported in 1846–1848, involved two separate prisons in each garrison, one at either side of a guard-house.[30] The question is: Why two? They were surely not intended to separate Blacks from Whites, or men from women. More likely, one prison was for the military and the other for civilians, as was the case in Luanda.

While the old system endured in Luanda, it seems that in around 1840 the civil prison was finally established in a separate building from the town hall.[31] But by 1861, it was in ruins once again. At this time, it is described as "disgusting," and both "black and white criminals" were imprisoned pell-mell within, to the disgust of the commander of an American squadron.[32] The governor promised to build a new town hall, but he forgot to include the prison in the plans. One of the town councilors had to remind him that the construction of a prison was an urgent matter. On this advice, the decision was taken to rebuild one, albeit it in the interior of the town hall.[33] But things hardly changed; at the end of 1874, the governor referred to Luandan prisons as "dens," or "lairs."[34] Evidently, we are still far from the concept of a central prison as a site for the internment and reformation of criminals condemned through penal servitude. Undoubtedly, this is because such punishment remained exceptional. The first indications of a transformation in mentalities appear only with the Decrees of 1869 and 1876, through which Lisbon ordered the creation of special housing (repositories) and penal farms for the condemned. These establishments were finally installed in 1883, but not without setbacks.[35] And central prisons were not constructed until the twentieth century.

In modern colonial Angola, then, there was no violent rupture with the old system. Banishment as punishment was only abolished in 1932, as were bodily harms. In 1961, forced labor still represented the main form of punishment, whether in the context of penal farms or not. As far as penal reforms were concerned, Angola was then about two centuries behind Europe. The penal practices of old Angola were thus not the origin of the system of incarceration practiced in more recent European colonies.

AFRICAN ATTITUDES TOWARD INCARCERATION

In 1514, the Court at Lisbon sent a copy of the Manuelian decrees to the Kongo as an example of civilized criminal law. King Afonso read them and, "after having examined the decrees and particularities of each law, article, and mode of execution, remarked that it was impossible to impose such rules of life upon his subjects." He was said to be most impressed by the massive interference in people's lives reflected in the decrees. He once told Balthasar de Castro, in amusement, "Castro, what punishment does Portugal mete out for those who place their foot on the ground?"[36] The king rejected the code, and we can suppose that the extreme physical violence imposed as punishment for criminality was a primary motivation for this refusal.

In the sixteenth and seventeenth centuries, the main difference between criminal law in the Kongo and the Ambunda of Angola, on the one hand, and Portugal, on the other, was that African law never had recourse to corporal punishment or mutilation. Capital punishment was reserved for high treason and witchcraft, as in the case of the death of a person accused of witchcraft following the forensic test of poison.[37] This may come as a surprise since European observers of the seventeenth century—notably, Battell (Jaga), Cavazzi, and Cadornega (Queen Njinga)—place so much emphasis on cannibalism and infanticide (Jaga), the occasional decapitation of well-known prisoners of war,[38] and human sacrifices (Jaga, Ambundu). However, these acts were not executed in the context of criminal law or penal practice. The only exception was mutilation (the ablation of genital organs), practiced by Queen Njinga in the 1640s as punishment for the infidelity of her consorts.[39] But this is a unique case, and the queen subsequently abandoned this practice. Moreover, it is not impossible that her approach to the question was inspired by Portuguese methods of judiciary mutilation. Despite their great efforts to underscore the savagery of Africans, none of the European authors—even in the seventeenth century—refers to punishment by thrashing or the whip.

A less significant difference resides in the fact that, contrary to the Portuguese system of justice, these countries had no prisons. And this is so even for the incarceration of defendants whose parents were the guarantors of their appearance before the tribunal. Otherwise, their respective legal codes were rather similar with regard to procedures and punishments. African laws imposed fines and restitution for injured parties, which even entailed the enslavement of the guilty party (or a substitute) to the injured party. Since tribunals treated almost all crimes—including blows and wounds, rape, homicide and murder—as violations of public property, whose value could be determined, condemnation to restitution with punitive damages was the "rational" solution. But sentencing to exile was also customary. At the time, this essentially meant condemnation to sale as a slave. This was the fate of incorrigible repeat offenders, who overstepped the boundaries of their kinfolk's patience. Later, after the establishment of the slave trade, this sentence was imposed more and more often, even for minor offenses.[40]

The kingdom of the Kongo copied neither the Portuguese penal code nor its prisons. True, in 1554, the king imprisoned a group of people one evening in the confines of his palace and had them executed the next day at noon.[41] But this is not proof of the existence of a veritable prison. Around 1650, the prison as a site of specialized confinement did not exist. Indeed, the concept of the prison is translated by the word *esamba*, which also signifies, "praetor, chief, commander." Evidently, there was no Roman praetor at Mbanza Kongo . . . nor was there a prison.[42] Nor is there any subsequent evidence of prisons. Thus, in 1704, when Beatriz Kimpa Vita, the prophet who led the "Antonian" religious and political movement, was incarcerated before her execution, there is no mention of a prison.[43] In the nineteenth century, the term *boloko*, which signifies the warehouse of a commercial trading post, is added to the Kongo language with the new meaning "prison."[44] There is also no mention of a prison in the African domains surrounding Portuguese Angola, with the exception of a single (probably fictive) account recounting how, in Kisama, two "mulattos" were shut up in a hollowed baobab tree, from which they escaped.[45]

In these regions, African law never made use of bodily constraint, even for prevention. And this attitude has not changed much over the centuries, in spite of the fact that bodily constraint was an integral part of the slave trade. These bodies of law never allowed for corporal punishment for crimes even though there was frequent recourse to political violence and terror by certain African courts, and despite the regularity of *razzias* and brutal wars inspired by colonial aggression and the quest for slaves.

SLAVERY AND BODILY CONSTRAINT

From the outset, the Angolan colony was a Mecca of the slave trade and the incarceration of slaves. Therefore, an understanding of incarceration in this country cannot be limited to bodily constraint for criminality; it must also consider the much more prevalent confinement of slaves. Domestic slavery seems to have existed in Central Africa before the arrival of the Portuguese;

however, the sale of slaves did not precede them.[46] Slaves were then either criminals condemned to servitude or prisoners of war. Thus, in the Kongo, the term *mwai* signifies "slave, domestic prisoner"[47] and in Bushoong, the word *ntwiingy* designates both booty and prisoners of war. It is possible that bodily constraint was practiced on prisoners at least during the first days of their incarceration. This probably involved tying their hands, putting them in a wooden shackle, or even, in certain communities, putting a net over them. It is only the advent of the slave trade that gives rise to the need to systematically constrain the body. Among the instruments used to do so were metal chains, shackles for the feet or the neck, and yokes, which were all used in Portuguese prisons well before the slave trade. Indeed, the Portuguese were the first to use these methods in the transport of slaves.

Therefore, these instruments came to Central Africa with the Portuguese. In a chapter on "the phases of the trade," dated 1793, Oliveira Mendes says that, after their sale at a market in the interior, slaves were freed from yoke or shackles so that their right hands could be tied to a ring attached to a chain long enough to link together from thirty to one hundred people. This was the *libambo*, which the coastal traders had brought with them. The *libambo* for women was slightly different. Sometimes the ring was fixed around the neck and sometimes two rings were used, one around the neck and one around the hand. Thus this ambulatory prison, a caravan, could walk. The chains stayed in place day and night and no shelter was offered until arrival at the port, sometimes after six months of travel.[48] Once sold at the ports of Luanda or Benguella, the slaves were freed and put in an enclosure called a *quintal* ("cattle pen") until their boarding—unless they were lucky enough to be taken as a domestic slave by a local inhabitant. These enclosures, which were rebuilt every two years, were surrounded by very high walls and sometimes equipped with small peepholes. They were not paved, but contained a hangar or a roofed straw hut where the slaves could spend the night or wait out the rain. These enclosures were distributed throughout the entire lower part of the city of Luanda, each shipper having his own.[49] After the official abolition of slavery, the enclosures were replaced with *barracons*, which were large structures built near the coast in out-of-the-way places, imperceptible from any vantage point of the sea. Slaves were crammed into these buildings where they awaited departure, and were kept chained up in "large groups."[50]

Contrary to this scenario, domestic slaves in Luanda were not subject to shackles. They lived in cabins erected in courtyards behind the "big house."[51] All descriptions of Luanda underscore the liberty of movement of slaves, at least in the city. The fear of being sold to cross the Atlantic was sufficient to prevent most of them from attempting to escape to the interior in spite of the harsh treatment they endured from their masters.

To what extent did neighboring African populations take up these techniques of constraint? As far as we know,[52] they did not make use of enclosures or *barracons*. But they did utilize diverse forms of shackles, especially in markets in the interior where slaves were sold to Portuguese agents. Those who specialized as escorts of slave caravans to markets or to the coast— especially Vili traders—adopted and copied constraining techniques employed by the Portuguese. No case of such use is reported outside of the large commercial roads. It seems that these techniques did not spread outside the context of the slave trade, through which they were introduced into the region. And even in this context, incarceration in closed quarters was refused. Moreover, and most remarkably, even Africans who used these techniques, like the Vili, seemed never to apply them to common criminals.

CONCLUSION

This rapid review[53] of incarceration in old Angola shows that, in the framework of the Portuguese penal code, judiciary imprisonment was largely a preventive measure that preceded judgment. These practices, which are medieval in origin, grant a large place to institutionalized physical violence as punishment. Chaining, or the use of iron chains and the *golilha* to limit the movements of the detained—a practice that also gave rise to techniques of constraining the bodies of slaves in the context of the slave trade—was current. Despite the significant penal reforms that took place at the end of the eighteenth century and the beginning of the nineteenth century, this old code was still in use in Angola (at least for Africans) up until 1961.[54] The modern legacy of this quite distinctive penal practice was the predominance of whipping as a sentence and the restriction of the liberty of movement of the detained. These practices were transmitted to the first French and Belgian colonial establishments via methods for treating slaves and detainees employed in coastal trading posts—a treatment that was subsequently institutionalized in colonial legal texts.

African societies that lived in the area surrounding the Angolan colony did not put the institution of the prison to their own use, nor did they reproduce sentences of corporal punishment. But some did adopt techniques for constraining the body, as applied to slaves. The view of René Pélissier, who repeats the widespread belief that, "there is nothing extraordinary to corporal punishment in one form or another in Black Africa, be it in traditional or in colonial society"[55] is absolutely erroneous, at least in the case of Central Africa. The present-day use of these methods stems only from the Portuguese model. In the past, the rejection of physical violence and of the prison is a reflection of an African vision of human, individual, and social dignity which has remained intact over the centuries for free persons—in spite of the slave trade—and constituted an integral and fundamental part of these societies and cultures.

NOTES

1. The Congo independent state published a penal code in 1888. Penal servitude was referred to as an applicable punishment, prisons were erected at each station, and the condemned were put to work. Cf. A. Chapeaux, *Le Congo* (Brussels: Charles Rozez, 1894), 647, and 649–50. The founding of French legislation goes back to the *senatus-consulte* of May 3, 1854. Prisons and penal servitude were introduced to the colonies as soon as Gabon and Congo were organized as colonial states.

2. R. Garfield, "A History of São Tomé Island, 1470–1655" (Ph.D. thesis, University of Michigan, Ann Arbor, 1971), 7–9.

3. For a sample in 1714–1748, see R. Boxer, *Portuguese Society in the Tropics: The Municipal Councils of Goa, Macao, and Luanda: 1500–1800* (Madison: University of Wisconsin Press, 1965), 197–209.

4. G. Bender, *Angola Under the Portuguese* (London: Heinemann Educational, 1978), 57–94, who gives details about this political program and its social consequences.

5. Cf. A. Brásio, *Monumenta Missionaria Africana: Africa ocidental* (Lisbon: 1952–1988), 15 vols. Vol. 1: 168 (July 30, 1499). Subsequent references are noted MMA, followed by the number of the volume, and the date of the document. Brásio, António, ed., *Monumenta missionaria africana. Africa occidental* (Lisbon: Agência Geral do Ultramar, Divisão de Publicações e Biblioteca, 1952–988).

6. The main term in Portuguese for prison was (and still is) *cadeia*: "chain," "shackle."

7. MMA, I: 172 (July 30, 1499). MMA, I: 384 (March 15, 1517), 383–384 for an example of the use of the prison as prevention.

8. See the chapter of these decrees in MMA, 4: 70–83 (June 28, 1514).

9. On the galleys, cf. Maria T. Amado Neves, *D Francisco Inocêncio de Sousa Coutinho* (Lisbon: 1958), 62 (1771 for Africans only); João Carlos Feo Cardoso de Castello Blanco e Torres, *Mémorias* (Paris: 1825), 315 (1816–1819 for Europeans and Africans). I found no cases of judiciary mutilation in either Angola or São Tomé (Lisbon: Sociedad national de Tipografia, 1958).

10. G. Tams, *Visit to the Portuguese Possessions in South-Western Africa* (London: 1845, reprinted New York: 1969), vol. 2, 12–13. At this time, banished persons were still condemned to up to 2,000 lashes. H. Soyaux, *Aus West-Afrika (1873–1876)* (Leipzig: 1879), vol. 2, 111 (London: Newbury, 1845).

11. J. Lopes de Lima, *Ensaios sobre a statistica das possessões portuguezas* (Lisbon: 1846), vol. 3, part II, 5 (Lisbon: Imprensa national, 1846).

12. In 1578 in São Tomé (MMA, X: 558), and in 1703 in Angola (*Arquivos de Angola*, series 1, II, document 9 of May 20, 1703, 145–46).

13. Tito Omboni, *Viaggi nell' Africa occidentale* (Milan: 1845), 95 (Milan: Cirelli, 1845).

14. Francisco Xavier Lopes, *Três fortalezas de Luanda em 1846* (Luanda: 1954) (Luanda: Museu de Angola, 1954).

15. Tams, *Visit to the Portuguese*, vol. 2, 13, 17–19; and Omboni, *Viaggi nell' Africa*, 108.

16. E. Ravenstein, ed., *The Strange Adventures of Andrew Battell of Leigh* (London: 1901), 7 and 9–13. One notes the (officially recompensed) role of the informer, the fact that prisoners were always in chains, the waiting period before hanging, and the exceptional use of the garrote. But Battell was not put in a garrote since he was tied to a wooden post in a standing position with the garrote around his neck and the stake. This is a punishment called *golilha*, which was still in use around 1830. See *Annaes do conselho ultramarino*.

Parte não official (Lisbon: 1958), series I, p. 458; and Jean-Baptiste Douville, *Voyage au Congo* (Paris: 1832), vol. 1, 200–2.

17. The date of construction remains unknown. Ilídio do Amaral, *Luanda* (Lisbon: 1968), 40, places its construction before 1680, but his source (Cadornega) does not mention it. It is reasonable to think that it was built around or before 1750. On the subject of black and white prisoners in the same prison, see, for example, Torres, *Mémorias*, 279–88 (for 1788) and S. Lopes de Calheiros e Menezes, *Relatório do Governador Geral da Provincia de Angola* (Lisbon: 1867), 213.

18. Tams, *Visit to the Portuguese*, vol. 2, 19–24, visited him in 1841.

19. A. de Oliveira de Cadornega, *História de Angola* (Lisbon: 1942), vol. 3, 19–21.

20. Torres, *Mémorias*, 91, 318, 349. On the night rounds, see 56, 62–64, 79–80.

21. Omboni, *Viaggi nell' Africa*, 108 (for the situation in 1835); Tams, *Visit to the Portuguese*, vol. 2, 19 (on those condemned to death).

22. See, for example, Douville, *Voyage au Congo*, vol. 1, 200–2, 314–15. And see the numerous references in *Annaes do conselho ultramarino. Parte não official*, for instance, 1858, series 1, 458. H. Soyaux, *Aus West-Afrika*, vol. 2, 11–12, 84, mentions the execution of chiefs who did not furnish the required number of roadworkers (71) and fines imposed upon them for not providing laborers (84, 110).

23. On indebtedness for adultery, cf. *Annaes do conselho ultramarino. Parte não official*, series 2, 1860, 124.

24. Soyaux, *Aus West-Afrika*, vol. 2, 124. This case was recounted to Soyaux by a incensed "civilized" African. On the excesses of the captains, more generally, see Carlos Couto, *Os capitães-mores em Angola no século XVIII* (Lisbon: 1972).

25. Decrees of 1764 and 1765 prohibit this practice: M. Neves, *D Francisco Inocêncio de Sousa Coutinho*, 44–45, 47, 53. These prisons made use of collar shackles (45). The banished persons who traded in the countryside (but captains as well) are accused of "seizing women and children; whipping them; deposing chiefs; despoiling them; and sometimes exposing them to the sun, tied up in the shape of the cross of Saint André with a heavy load of iron shackles; and leaving them tied to trees" (39). "Moreover, they run their own courts, commit murder and inflict wounds (53)." For criticism of these abuses expressed in a text dated 1763, cf. Couto, *Os capitães-mores*, 134, n. 78.

26. Soyaux, *Aus West-Afrika*, vol. 2, 87 (arresting thieves, imprisonment, private judgment, and punishment).

27. C. Jeannest, *Quatre années au Congo* (Paris: 1886), 190–92, referring to a robbery in his trading post in 1871, speaks of "tying up," "shackling," and "chaining together" various suspects. See also 15, 27, 28, 35, 53, 75, 86–87. A. Delcommune, *Vingt années de Vie africaine* (Brussels: 1922), vol. 1, 56, first says, "Naturally, no prisons existed and every European was free to punish criminals as they saw fit." He then reminisces about the use of the *palmatoria*, the whip, and the chain. The narrative about the *lit de justice*, consisting of "all the Portuguese living in the Congo," follows (58–59).

28. *Arquivos de Angola*, series 1, II, 7, 1936 (October 5, 1742), 28. The prison term was five months; ten for repeat offenders.

29. The only case I found was in 1765 and involved condemnation to five years of forced labor with shackles. This punishment was reserved for White offenders, who were not subject to the five hundred whip lashes and two years in the galley. Cf. Neves, *D Francisco*, 62 (1765).

30. For the different presidios, see *Annaes do conselho ultramarino. Parte não official*, series I (Lisbon, 1854), 7, 57; 1858: 457, 475, 476, 478; series II, 1859: 57; 1860: 136,

144 (the prisons on either side of the guardhouse were built by order of the governor Alexandrino da Cunha (1845–1848).

31. Joao Vieira Carneiro, *"Observações feitas em 1848,"* Annaes do conselho ultramarino. *Parte nao official,* series 2 (Lisbon: 1876), 178.

32. Menezes, *Relatório do Governador Geral da Provincia de Angola* (Lisbon: 1867), 213, 214, 217, 224. For the dossier on Mr. Birnie, an imprisoned American agent, see 49–50; 202–229. Far from protesting against this description, the governor promised to attend to Mr. Birnie's plight.

33. Ibid., 179, 181, 185.

34. I. Amaral, *Luanda* (Lisbon: 1968), 58.

35. Bender, *Angola,* 76–86.

36. L. Jadin and M. Dicorato, *Correspondance de Dom Afonso, roi du Congo: 1506–1543* (Brussels: 1974), 115–116, translated from the *Crónica* of Damião de Góis (1516). The chronicler adds that one should praise this king since "he is from such a barbaric country."

37. For a fairly systematic exposition of African justice at the time, cf. G. Cavazzi de Montecúccolo, *Descrição histórica dos três reinos: Congo, Matamba e Angola,* translated by G.M. de Leguzzano (Lisbon: 1965), Book 1, paragraphs 15, and 25, 102–113 and 155–158 (original written in 1667).

38. Also practiced by the Portuguese at the same time.

39. In Cavazzi's "Araldi" manuscript (A, 2)—but dropped from the published text—there is a gruesome description of trees where such organs were hung as a public warning. Cf. C. Skidmore-Hess, "Queen Njinga, 1582–1663" (Ph.D. thesis, University of Wisconsin, Madison, 1995), 319–320.

40. Sale into slavery had become a very common punishment by the seventeenth century. It was even imposed in the case of petty theft, which was denounced by many authors, who forgot that the analogous punishment of exile was imposed for equally trivial reasons in Portugal. Banishment for life or slaves; what is the difference?

41. MMA, XV: 190.

42. J. Van Wing, *Le plus ancien dictionnaire Bantu* (Louvain: 1928), 23. *Kisamba* means "dignity of the lender." The notion of *samba* designates the "delegate of an authority" in Kongo and Kimbundu. The dictionary referred to follows a Latin model; since both "lender" and "prison" appear within that exemplar, the author was, of course, obliged to translate! This is not an unusual situation; cf. F. Bontinck, *"Remarques marginales à Vansina:* The Dictionary and the Historian," *History in Africa* 3 (1976), 155–56 for others.

43. J.K. Thornton, *The Kongolese Saint Anthony* (Cambridge: 1998), 169–176. However, Beatriz was chained up (174). She was imprisoned for less than two months. Evidently, the crime of heresy was thought to be the equivalent of witchcraft since she was condemned to the stake—the usual punishment in the latter case.

44. K.E. Laman, *Dictionnaire Kikongo-Français* (Brussels: 1936), vol. 1, 51. This was the place where Africans who were arrested by the agents of European trading houses were imprisoned.

45. Douville, *Voyage au Congo,* vol. 2, 261–62. The Portuguese were surprised to find that hollowed out baobab trees served as water tanks, but there is no other allusion to oubliettes in numerous other references.

46. This is suggested by the analysis of the terminology relative to the subject. In the African world, the slave was someone who had lost his or her legal parentage and was under the sole jurisdiction of his or her master.

47. Van Wing, *Le plus ancien dictionnaire*, 240.

48. Luís A. de Oliveira Mendes, "Discurso academico ao programa," republished in António Carreira, "As Companhias Pombalinas," *Boletim cultural da Guiné Portuguesa*, XXIV, 94 (1969), 423–25. Mendes lived in Brazil and obtained his information from Portuguese coming from Angola around 1770.

49. Ibid., 426–27; J. Miller, *Way of Death* (Madison: 1988), 390–91; and Silva Correa, *História de Angola* (Lisbon: 1942), vol. 1, 79–80.

50. Jeannest, *Quatre années au Congo*, 125–126, for description of a visit to an old *barracon* at Kinzau.

51. This was the case even before 1640. Cf. J. von Augspurger, *See-Reisen von Amsterdam in Holland nach Brasilien in America, und Angola in Africa . . . 1642* (Schleusingen: 1644), 6. I thank B. Heintze for this reference. And for 1841, cf. Tams, *Visit to the Portuguese Possessions*, vol. 1, 237.

52. Written and oral sources on this subject are extremely rare, including the ethnographic observations of "explorers" or the first ethnographers.

53. This paper is but a first review of a question that has been ignored in the historiography. As it is only based on published information, and is narrowly limited to "the prison," we are still far away of what will be one day a well-grounded social history of penal confinement in Angola.

54. R. Pélissier, *La colonie du Minotaure* (Paris: 1978), 131.

55. Ibid.

3

CAPTIVITY AND INCARCERATION IN NINETEENTH-CENTURY WEST AFRICA

Thierno Bah

Historians of Africa have seldom made captivity and incarceration objects of study. Yet the issues appear to be of great significance in Africa today, where human rights are trampled upon and extreme violence has become a means of managing political and social relations. Many reasons explain the relative lack of observation and information on this theme. First, the modern prison, conceived as a space of internment and privation, occupied a negligible place in the regulation of traditional African societies. Second, in most West African societies, places of captivity were hidden universes or worlds of silence. Most chroniclers—from Ibn Battutah in the fourteenth century to Heinrich Barth in the nineteenth century—described at length the pomp and sumptuousness of imperial courts and military campaigns, but seldom alluded to the conditions of captives. Third, a polarized field of African studies has long prevented the emergence of law as a significant field of inquiry. This explains why two important and lengthy studies by Yves Person on Samory, and Claude Tardits on the Bamoun kingdom,[1] conducted a detailed analysis of military campaigns but had almost nothing to say about the conditions of war prisoners.

The following reflections represent an effort to correct this perspective. To do so, I use an array of resources, including chronicles, travel narratives, and oral histories taken in West Africa and in Cameroon. Unfortunately, the information gathered is limited and fragmented, and thus precludes a coherent synthesis. Nonetheless, this material provides the basis for further reflection on local forms of sanction exercised upon slaves, captives, and criminals, and on the original forms of incarceration that were practiced in diverse societies of pre-colonial West Africa.

THE EMPIRES OF THE WESTERN SUDAN

In his study of the Sokoto Caliphate, J.P. Smaldone argues that well-defined systems of incarceration first appeared as instruments of aristocratic power in centralized, militarist, and bureaucratic states.[2] It is tempting, therefore, to turn to the great empires of the Bilad-es-Sudan in order to locate some of the oldest forms of state imprisonment. Unfortunately, Arab chroniclers and the authors of the *Tarikhs* are silent on this issue. In reference to the capital of Ghana, Al Bekri mentions only that "the king's city is surrounded by huts, hills, and small fields and hedges, which harbor the magicians of this nation, those who are responsible for this cult. . . . This is where the king's prisons are located: as soon as a man is shut away there, you do not hear about him anymore."[3]

Mahmoud Kati's *Tarikh El Fettach* contains some information on incarceration in the Songhay Empire during the sixteenth century. The Songhay ruler Chi Ali (Sonni Ali), known for his cruelty, "had live people buried in walls and let them die that way."[4] During Chi Ali's reign, political prisoners and all those who contested the king's authority were sent to a prison located on an island on the Niger River, shackles bound their feet, as in the case of two dignitaries, Môri Es-Sâdiq and Môri Djeiba. Later, Askia Mohammed Bounkan exiled one of his paternal uncles to Gao, where the prisoner was forced to live in reclusion on the island of Kangâga.[5] Mahmoud Kati also mentioned how the Kabara-Farma threw an offending slave in prison after caning him one hundred times.

The *Tarikh El Fettach* explains how members of the intelligentsia and Sudanese dignitaries went into exile to Morocco just after the famous battle of Tondibi (1591) that sounded the death knell of the Songhay empire: "Pacha Mahmoud sent prisoners to Marrakech along with some of their children and close relatives, men and women. They were a little more than seventy people. None of them ever came back, with the exception of Sîdi Ahmed Baba."[6] Taking place at a time of strained relations between the Bilad es-Sudan and North Africa, this famous deportation episode merits detailed study. What were the conditions of detention at the point of departure in Timbuktu? What happened to the prisoners during the travel across the desert? And what fate awaited them upon arrival in Morocco? The scholar Ahmed Baba, for instance, seemed to have experienced relatively humane conditions of incarceration: he was assigned to residence in a house at Marrakech, received visitors, and made legal consultations. Nonetheless, loss of liberty and exile from his homeland made Ahmed Baba inconsolable.

These few observations provide evidence of the existence of a prison system in the empires of the western Sudan. But our understanding of this system remains extremely vague. Spaces of banishment probably received prisoners condemned for their political attitudes and for crimes of *lèse-majesté*, since competition for political power was ruthless in the Songhay empire. But we lack precise indications of the conditions of incarceration. We will never know, for example, whether the Ghanaian forest and the island of Kangâga on the Niger river had specific buildings or structures to receive the prisoners.

In many regions of West Africa, the transition period from the end of the eighteenth to the beginning of the nineteenth century was characterized by intimate interconnections between war, slavery, and commerce. This was a determining factor in the restructuring of political space, or the emergence of centralizing states whose economic activity was largely based on slave trading and/or the exploitation of slave labor. Slave raids and captivity were highly lucrative activities: as Jean Bazin has shown for the case of Segou, the production system was based on the *jon* (captive).[7]

Most societies in West Africa celebrated the end of a military campaign by the distribution of war booty, including prisoners who were executed, ransomed, exchanged or enslaved. I have elected to inquire into the fate of these prisoners with reference to the cases of two eminently militarist states that enacted powerful coercive structures: the kingdom of Dahomey and the empire of Samori Touré.

In Dahomey, royal power sacrificed large numbers of prisoners of war during the great Celebration of Customs *(Fête des Coutumes)*. Often more than 3,000 prisoners came under the executioner's hatchet. Others, who were destined for the slave trade were crammed into barracks where they were fed only cassava flour. They traveled to the coast shackled with thick iron chains in groups of eight.[8] In Dahomey itself, slavery involved a form of forced labor based on spatial confinement. The condemned were sent to the valley of Couffo and Zou, about 20 kilometers away from Abomey, in a swampy zone called Afomayi ("the foot cannot go there"). No prisoner could escape and they were forced to cultivate the earth in perpetuity for the king.

In Abomey, the capital of the kingdom, the palace of Simboji played an important role in the history and practice of captivity and servitude. Around 15 percent of the capital's population was of slave origin. Some 5,000 to 8,000 slaves and dependents of the king lived behind the high walls of the palace, including prisoners of war and women. The latter were given the title of *Ahori* (king's wives). Strictly speaking, no state prison existed either inside or adjacent to the palace; only a distinction in residence allowed one to distinguish between slaves and former war captives born outside the borders of Dahomey, and "citizens." Furthermore, many palace slaves—especially women—experienced high social mobility, often ceding to important political and military positions thanks to their prowess in the army of the Amazons. Maurice Glélé demonstrates that the king authorized certain ministers and dignitaries belonging to his inner circle to establish prisons in their respective domains. Delinquent or offending princes were imprisoned in the domain of the *Mehu*. Common criminals were detained in the domain of the *Kpakpa*; hence *kpakpahue* (the house of *Kpakpa*) became a synonym for "prison."[9]

Did a penitentiary system exist beyond the royal capital, at the regional and local levels? The evidence on this subject remains tenuous. Glélé argues that village and regional chiefs had small cabins or huts to confine petty criminals. It seems that this form of detention could not exceed the duration of four days and that corporal punishment was forbidden unless administered with bare hands (thus excluding the use of clubs and whips). Le Hérissé, on the other hand, affirms that the *Tôhosou*, the provincial rulers who represented the kings of conquered tribes, had no prison and no remand center.[10] Ultimately, justice in Dahomey appears to have been the personal responsibility of the king, who convened court meetings *(lits de justice)* at his residence *(akaba),* which was specially designed for this purpose. There, he judged serious criminal affairs and pronounced sentences: the death penalty, imprisonment, flagellation, fines, and so on. This system of sanctions, privations, and internment emanating from a centralized jurisdiction allowed Dahomey's military aristocracy to consolidate its authority and to serve as an integrative force on both political and cultural levels.

Samori Touré created another great military state in nineteenth-century West Africa. Unfortunately, Yves Person's remarkable study on this subject offers only minor details on the topic of captivity in war, in a section on central government, justice, and police.[11] In Samori's empire, warfare and slavery were fundamentally linked, as constant *razzias* created a continuous influx of captives. According to Person, practices relating to war captivity were generally uniform in the Upper Niger. Those captured in combat lost their liberty, and were confined as quickly as possible to prevent their escape. If their relatives recognized the sovereignty of Samori's empire, they could purchase their kin back, and restore their free status. Otherwise, captors shared prisoners at the end of the war. Those who were attributed to *Kélitigui* (war chiefs) or to Samori often served as domestic servants and porters, or worked the land for their masters in special villages.

Samori sought to organize a repressive judiciary system in order to enforce commercial security in the empire, and respect for his authority. This system was stabilized by 1886, the date of Samori's first great military expedition. In keeping with Manding views about the exercise of justice as the privilege of sovereignty, Samori reserved the right to punish certain infractions. At a lower level, preoccupied with public order and state stability, he delegated some powers to provincial governors, the *Dugu Kunnangi*, who were in charge of repression in every *kafu*. In the empire, summary executions were common and performed by decapitation with a saber.

But Samori did not create a systematically organized penitentiary system. His moving empire changed capitals in accordance with conquests, and proved too mobile to sustain a permanent penitentiary system. Nonetheless, tradition notes that Samori once detained a famous prisoner: his own son, Dyaulé Karamogho. On the basis of European observations and oral tradition, Yves Person traced the tragic destiny of Samori's third and favorite son. To demonstrate his good faith vis-à-vis France, Samori sent Karamogho on a diplomatic visit. Karamogho fully appreciated the military grandeur of this European nation that had received him with ceremony. However, several years after returning to his country, Karamogho was accused of spying for colonial troops. To make him confess his crime:

> Samori had him walled up in a hut under the guard of Fila Sana, who passed food to him every day by way of a narrow orifice. Soon, he ordered him on half-ration. Each time, he asked if he had confessed, but Karamogho remained silent. After a month, Samori came to see him, without success. And so he went away without saying anything. Did Fila Sana take the initiative to do away with all food in the hope of making the prisoner talk? Did Samori give him the order to do so? In any event, Karamogho died three days later. His father sent notables to confirm the death and declared: "He was a bad son, bury him."[12]

If the favorite son of Samori could meet with such tragic fate, many anonymous people must have faced similar repression. The Great Revolt *(Ban nue)*, which involved vehement popular uprisings against the political and religious order (theocracy) imposed by Samori, probably initiated a period of purges, banishments, and internments. State repression did not disappear in post-colonial West Africa. During Sékou Touré's regime in Guinée, hundreds of prisoners died of hunger in the sadly renowned *Camp Boiro* in Conakry.[13] Evidently, certain continuities exist between the pre-colonial and the post-colonial periods.

CAMEROON: CENTRALIZED STATES AND ACEPHELOUS SOCIETIES

In Cameroon, a number of historical case studies complement the observations made above, allowing us to expand and refine our understandings of imprisonment. Historians have noted Cameroon for the great diversity of its ethnic and sociopolitical organizations. In the northern part of the country, conversion to Islam meant incorporation into centralized and hierarchical states. In the western Grasslands, political formations (chiefdoms) also exhibited marked social hierarchy. Acephelous societies regulated by diverse criminal sanctions, inhabited the central, southern, and eastern regions of Cameroon. Punishments ranged from simple fines to ostracism, and included beatings and imprisonment.

Standardized state imprisonment seems to have been practiced by centralized states, such as the Mandara kingdom, which reached its pinnacle during the nineteenth century. The Mandara system of official titles proves that the kingdom used a classical penitentiary system, complete with torture and squads of guards. Castration led to the founding of the official role of the eunuch. The *Tlavungé* managed the palace prison *(gulfunye)*, which held condemned prisoners. The *Tlavungo Ndunda* (children's guard: *gardien des petits*) was responsible for children taken captive in war. The *Tliksé* (the sovereign) decided upon their placement. The *Tloho* dignitary assessed cases of adultery, imposing fines and terms of imprisonment. The *Zaka Ukdle* (or guard of the testicles) was charged with punishing rape and murder through whipping and incarcerating. And the *Ndoko Hudgo*, chief of royal eunuchs, supervised the division of labor among palace slaves. This rigorous system is indicative of the elaborate penitentiary system that had developed in Mandara, where repressive practices included isolation, starvation, threats, and beatings.

The Fulani emirate of northern Cameroon, founded in the wake of Usman dan Fodio's *jihad* (1804), also established a judiciary system with punishments that varied from fines to long prison sentences, and included forced labor. Each political unit of command *(lamidat)* had a prison, perceived by local populations as a place of terror. The prison cells, which apparently were ordinary huts, were equipped with materiel used to "trap" the prisoner: ropes, locally produced handcuffs, iron chains, and stakes or tree trunks planted in the floor.

In the *lamidat* of Mindif, the *Bongo*, a Muslim convert who did not belong to the Fulani ethnic group, acted as the chief of police and prison guard. He supervised the guards who accompanied the condemned to labor the sovereign's fields. Prisoners worked the entire day before returning to their cells. Physical cruelty and starvation were frequent. Recalcitrant prisoners were tortured by being shut up in a stifling hut, and exposed to the smoke of hot peppers thrown onto fire. The suffocating prisoner soon confessed. Jailers, however, often proved compassionate if the prisoner and his family provided generous bribes.[14]

Curiously enough, German and French rule did not put an end to this institution. Indeed, both the French and the Germans instituted a system of indirect rule based on alliances with traditional chiefs. Thus, the prison of the *lamidat* of Ngaoundéré, which was created in 1831, closed down only in 1961, just after independence. Today, the powerful *Lamido* Rey Bouba, a close ally of President Paul Biya, has sovereign power over his own prison. Opponents daring to contest the *Lamido*'s authority are shut away in jail. Modern regimes in Cameroon, therefore, have protected the traditional penitentiary system for reasons of political clientelism.

In the case of the Bamoun kingdom, Claude Tardits refers to *Mitngu*, a secret society that was both a police and judiciary institution. Its chief, *Tangu*, was the true master of the land, along with the king. The *Tangu* examined criminal cases, arrested guilty parties, and punished infractions. The center of the village consisted of twelve houses set in a square, the left side of which was lined with a blind wall that was part of the "house of the prisoners' shackles."[15] This is where the condemned served their sentences and suffered numerous punishments. The prisoners' conditions could improve with time, however, if they proved obedient and loyal.

In acephalous societies, a different range of repressive techniques emerged. In the Bamileke chiefdoms of western Cameroon, war was as rampant as in the centralized states.[16] But the fate of war captives proved quite different. Here, prisoners were kept in a specific place in the court of the *Fo* (chief). They were free to conduct business so as to provide for themselves. At the end of the conflict they could return home. In traditional Bamileke society, there was no real prison per se, though the chief had a secret place where he incarcerated suspects for indeterminate periods of time. He left the prisoners alone, and surrounded them with fetishes in order to to provoke terror and confession.

In the Banjoun chiefdom, a fairly original type of imprisonment was practiced: prison-in-residence. This form of ostracism prohibited criminals from performing any economic or social activity in the public domain (e.g., participation in meetings of secret societies, funerals, markets, etc.). Convicted criminals were not allowed to leave their compound, and could not receive visitors. In order to materialize their isolation, executioners erected wooden stakes laced with *toun* (a plant with evil and daunting powers—no one dared to cross a fence adorned with it) around the condemned's domicile. The psychological and ideological aspects of this form of incarceration were critical. Banished from all social relations, the incriminated party suffered moral depression, and oftentimes committed suicide.

The Nso, an ethnic group of Tikar origin living in the region of Bamenda, established relatively elaborate sociopolitical structures. But these did not give rise to a penitentiary system. As in the Bamileke case, the Nso punished crimes by isolating the condemned. The *Nwerong* secret society carried out sentences: after having completed certain rites, the affiliates excluded the criminal from relations with kin, or banished him from the community. The Nso had specific territories to deport social delinquents: Kutupit in Bamoum country and Mbinkar in the Ndop plain.

The case of the Bassa people provides further evidence that acephelous societies lacked prisons, even if bodily constraint and privations were practiced. In the decentralized but strongly hierarchical Bassa societies, patriarchs *(Mbombock)* and holders of authority and sacred power were in charge of judging criminal cases. To immobilize a prisoner, they fixed solid wooden shackles to the tibia, a technique known as *ndi-keng*. And, here too, ostracism predominated. The sentence of *ngwaga* involved loss of customary rights, the exclusion from family meetings and exchange networks, and from speaking in public.

RITUAL INCARCERATION

In most traditional societies of Cameroon, confinement was also part of a system of values promoting individual accomplishment and group cohesion. Sacred reclusion was linked to a whole ensemble of rituals and a symbolic repertoire that conveyed meanings to those involved. This system should be distinguished from repressive imprisonment. Rituals of confinement had a sacred dimension and forced an individual or group to end all contact with others for a certain amount of time.

In the Beti society (central and southern Cameroon), *So* was an initiation ritual for all young adolescents who aspired to become accomplished men. The youth were deported by age groups to an encampment in the deep forest where indiscreet eyes could not peer. There, they underwent terrible ordeals and learned the fundamental principles of social life. *Akus*, a ritual for widowers, necessitated reclusion in a delimited space and environment, beyond which it was forbidden to venture.

Among the Bamileke in western Cameroon, initiatic reclusion played an important role in the production of public authority. Upon the death of the chief *(Fon)* and during the nine-month mourning period, initiates captured the successor to the throne and enclosed him in the *laakam*, a sanctuary made of bamboo and mats that housed the skulls of the ancestors. Nine initiates took charge of the successor's surveillance and initiation. For a neophyte chief *(Moken)*, reclusion in the *laakam* involved a period of study and contemplation, during which he was introduced to the esoteric realm and instructed in customary law. In addition, the future chief ate and drank to satiety, and was supposed to prove his virility with the young women who accompanied him. Children borne of this moment of retreat received the name *Toukam*. After seclusion in the *laakam*, the new chief was enthroned.[17]

This brief overview reveals that systems of incarceration in traditional West African societies were numerous, highly variable, and in close connection with diverse historical and cultural contexts. I have argued that the existence of a penitentiary system was related to the degree of political centralization and social hierarchy. Centralized states that developed in these regions used a significant set of coercive and repressive techniques, and invented strict regulations for imprisonment. One important question remains: to what degree did endogenous factors versus exogenous influences (for example, Muslim practices of punishment) shape the penitentiary system of centralized states in West Africa? In contrast to centralized states, acephelous societies relied on social reprobation and exclusion to punish crimes. Yet, their use of sacred reclusion and ritual confinement expand and enrich the notion of incarceration in Africa.

NOTES

1. Y. Person, *Samori Turé, une révolution Dyula* (Dakar: IFAN, 1968); C. Tardits, *Le royaume Bamoum* (Paris: Colin, 1980).

2. J.P. Smaldone, *Warfare in Sokoto Caliphates: Historical and Sociological Perspectives* (Cambridge: Cambridge University Press, 1977).

3. Al Bekri and Abou Obeid, *Description de l'Afrique septentrionale*, MacGuckin de Slane, trans. (Paris: Maisonneuve, 1965), 328–329.

4. Mahmoud Kati, *Tarikh El Fettach,* O. Houdas and M. Delafosse, trans. (Paris: Maisonneuve, 1971), 83.

5. Ibid., 110 and 156.

6. Ibid., 232 and 307.

7. J. Bazin and E. Terray, eds., *Guerres de lignage et guerres d'états en Afrique* (Paris: Archives contemporaines, 1982).

8. Le Hérissé, *L'ancien royaume du Dahomey* (Paris: Larose, 1911), 113–14.

9. M. Glélé, *Le Danxome: du pouvoir Aja à la nation Fon* (Paris: Nubia, 1974), 148.

10. Le Hérissé, *L'ancien royaume*, 78.

11. Person, *Samori Turé*, vol. 3, 883–88.

12. Ibid., 1533, footnote 233.

13. Diallo Telli, former secretary general of the AOU, was among the victims.

14. S. Issa, *Le système carcéral dans le nord-Cameroun traditionnel*, ms.

15. Tardits, *Le royaume Bamoum*, 944.

16. Data from diverse monographs written in my doctoral seminar on carceral systems in Cameroon, *University of Yaoundé-1*, 1996.

17. For instance, *Nguri*, a secret society of the Bamoum people, imposes the reclusion of young, circumcised boys in the "house of lions." *Jengu*, an initiation society of the coastal Douala people, requires adolescents to be shut up in a sacred house *(pamba).*

4

JUVENILE MARGINALITY AND INCARCERATION DURING THE COLONIAL PERIOD

The First Penitentiary Schools in Senegal, 1888–1927

Ibrahima Thioub

During the second half of the nineteenth century, the abolition of slavery (April 27, 1848),[1] the spread of colonial wars of conquest, and the specialization of local economies in peanut production considerably disrupted the territory that was to become the colony of Senegal. Intense urbanization also made its mark on the period following the economic boom of the trading posts at Saint-Louis and Gorée during the 1850s, the expansion of the peanut sector, and the installation of railways and seaports in Dakar, Rufisque, and Thiès.[2]

Many excellent publications have thoroughly studied these changes, allowing us to examine an aspect of colonial history that Senegalese historians have mostly neglected: social marginality in booming colonial cities.[3] The rich documentation preserved in the Senegalese national archives establishes the existence of groups in urban centers whose material privation, social status (e.g., recently freed slaves), and/or supposedly deviant behavior disturbed the logics of reproduction of the colonial system. Colonial authorities devoted constant attention to the control of these groups of people at a fairly early stage. In a remarkable mimesis, administrators transposed in the colonies solutions that had generally failed in the metropole. In a context of less favorable conditions, and with inadequate means, the French imported techniques such as the tutelage and patronage of delinquent individuals, and their incarceration in first private, then public, reformatories.

Different methods of social control, punishment for deviant behavior, and corporal discipline emerged in the metropole and in Senegal. While in France techniques of social control at the end of the nineteenth century were based on a long history of incarceration,[4] Senegalese communities only encountered this mode of punishment in the context of colonial domination. Contrary to the expectations of colonial authorities, the transplant did not succeed completely. Colonizers established age criteria to determine the imprisonment of various delinquents.[5] For children recently freed from slavery, colonists had recourse to private persons who agreed to educate the children. Subsequently, the colony established public institutions and formal welfare for minors, both freed slaves and youth who had been in trouble with the law.

This chapter examines the management of marginalized youth in Senegal through the establishment of penitentiary schools as private institutions (1888–1903), and public ones (1916–1927). The history of these institutions highlights the difficulties encountered by colonial power in controlling marginal groups in Senegal.

BEFORE THE PENITENTIARY SCHOOLS: PATRONAGE POLICY

After many hesitations and arduous negotiations with slave owners, the colonial authorities decided to apply the decree of August 27, 1848, and abolish slavery in Senegal. Slave masters, led by the *signares*, vigourously resisted the abolition. In the end, however, they accepted state indemnities for the loss of their property. But the hundreds of young freed slaves who had benefited from abolition found themselves in a state of dire poverty.

Colonial authorities were not prepared to take responsibility for the material needs of the freed slaves. They tried to find a solution by promoting a patronage system among affluent residents in the coastal towns: those were, of course, the masters who had just been dispossessed of their slaves. In Saint-Louis and Gorée, the *signares* boycotted the sponsorship of minor freed females, thus dashing the colonial governor's hopes that former slave masters would be the pillars of a new welfare system. The disillusioned governor of Senegal deplored how "indigenous ladies" thought it inadmissible that "after having emancipated their captives and removed them from their authority, [the authorities] wanted them to bear the responsibility of their education."[6] Minors represented a large part of the freed population, between 34 percent and 49 percent of the total number in 1881.[7] In addition, the Senegalese colony attracted captives from neighboring countries despite the hesitations and ambiguities of a French policy trapped between philanthropic principles, the need for labor, and the desire to maintain good diplomatic relations with neighboring states that still practiced slavery.[8] The number of liberated slaves, and the risk of deviant behavior concerned the colonial administration, as this statement attributed to the governor of Senegal suggests: "The captives that we have declared free, as soon as they touch our territory, [they] overcrowd our cities, especially Saint-Louis. They refuse to work, and live off pillage and begging."[9]

Colonial power soon took initiatives to control the urban fringes: The decree of April 13, 1849, instituted two Counsels for Tutelage *(Conseils de tutelle)* in Dakar and Saint-Louis.[10] Each *Conseil* was presided over by the deputy mayor, assisted by two notables and two work managers. They appointed guardians for freed minors, who were in charge of instructing the children in a profession until they came of age. The Counsels also supervised the conditions of the apprenticeship, the work schedules, and the disciplinary practices.

In both Saint-Louis and Gorée, the Counsels had no difficulty placing their pupils with former owners who, having overcome their initial negative reaction to abolition, seized the opportunity to obtain cheap labor, a commodity always in short supply in the colony.[11] Soon the *Conseils* faced insurmountable obstacles in trying to end the overexploitation of freed slaves, who began deserting the workshops and houses of their new masters, their living conditions having hardly evolved from those experienced in captivity. On October 11, 1862, a decree terminated this experience and gave tutelage power to the head of the colonial judicial system, who became the legal guardian of freed slaves.[12] In 1880, the Bureau of Political Affairs took over from the Counsel for Guardianship.[13]

The many changes in the tutelage policy for minors suggested the difficulties encountered by colonial authorities in defining and applying a program to control marginalized youth. Alongside freed slaves "thrown into a chaotic life of idleness and vagabondage,"[14] delinquent minors crouched in colonial prisons, "mixed up with malefactors of all ages and all kinds . . . their only masters being their jail companions; their only training being in evil . . . They come out of prison without resources, without professional instruction . . . having, in general, a great aversion to work, which has only been presented in forms the least likely to give them such an inclination. Thus ready for crime, they can only become a burden or a danger for the society that opens before them." Moreover, the administration also took care of "the children of Europeans, mulattos, and even Blacks, who had been abandoned or practically abandoned by their parents. . . . Most often, they run the streets or the bush, lacking in instruction and education. Completely free, with nothing to do and nowhere to lay their heads, they form a generation of vagabonds."[15]

During the entire half-century following the abolition of slavery in the Senegalese colony, the fate of young freed slaves preoccupied the administration, as their number, difficult material conditions, and deviant behavior threatened the norms promoted by colonial power. The expansion of urban areas widened the social field that harbored groups considered marginal by the public authorities. At the turn of the century, private judiciary or administrative tutelage appeared to be an insufficient strategy. The head of the colonial Judicial Service exhumed Article 66 of the 1810 Penal Code in order to provide a judicial basis for a new solution: entrust marginal youths to a private institution supervised by public authorities.[16] In 1901, with great enthusiasm, the head of the Judicial Service proposed the founding of the first colonial penitentiary school at the Catholic mission *(Mission des Pères)* of the Congregation of the *Saint-Esprit* in Thiès. The penitentiary school would teach children to "obey and work, two qualities which are often lacking in the indigenous people."[17]

THE PENITENTIARY SCHOOL OF THE *PÈRES DU SAINT-ESPRIT* (1888–1903): "TAMING REBELLIOUS CHARACTERS" THROUGH WORK, EVANGELISM, AND SHACKLES

The decree of August 13, 1888 instituting the penitentiary school at Thiès, was largely inspired by the metropolitan law of 1850 opening reformatories in France.[18] The law determined which minors would benefit from the penitentiary school: "detained youths who have been acquitted in virtue of Article 66 of the Penal Code as having acted without discernment but not given back to their parents (art. 2)," "detained youths condemned to more than six months and less than two years of imprisonment (art. 3)," and, finally, "young freed slaves who were insubordinate (art. 6)."[19] Annual reports published by the Supervision Council for the school described the pupils' living conditions. A magistrate representing the Judicial Service, assisted by a delegate from the Director of the Interior Affairs and a member of the Legislative Council (art. 4), presided over the Supervision Council. The reports, kept in the Senegalese national archives, were accompanied by correspondence between the colonial authorities and the Mission's *préfet apostolique* who directed the school.

Budgetary conditions weighed heavily on the colonial authorities' decision to charge the missionaries with the detention of delinquent minors. "Missionaries, being already established in the area, would be compensated by the product of the children's labor . . . [the authorities], therefore, would only assume the expenses required for the building of the school." The authorities also sought to decongest colonial prisons, hoping that the reformatory would incite the tribunals to pronounce more acquittals for minor delinquents.[20] The fact that youth detained in the reformatory either for correction or condemnation would be handled in a way that was consistent with norms established for Senegalese prisons attenuated the judges' doubts about acquitting delinquent minors and sending them to the penitentiary at Thiès. Children "would be raised together under severe discipline, and consigned to agricultural work as well as related industries," "their elementary education will be provided for" (art. 2). The Mission paid in advance for medical, travel, and educational costs, and was later reimbursed by the colony. The colonial governement also paid for the school directors' salaries.

Considerable enthusiasm and optimism infused the preliminary report published at the opening of the school. But the actual operations of the school soon encountered unexpected difficulties.

LIVING CONDITIONS AT THE PENITENTIARY IN THIÈS

Contrary to the authorities' expectations, the number of pupils at the school in Thiès increased very slowly after it had opened as a penitentiary for minors. The figures for 1892—twenty-nine detainees under Article 66 of the Penal Code, one freed slave, and twenty "orphans"—dropped quickly and then stabilized from 1895 to its close in 1903, at an average of twenty acquitted minors and two freed slaves interned for insubordination. Statistics in the 1892 *Comité de surveillance*'s report revealed that economic delinquency was the primary cause of incarceration.[21] Studies of criminality and prison populations in Senegal for the same period indicated a similar pattern.[22]

In the beginning, detainees lived in a wooden cabin. The structure could shelter eight children; the others had to spend the night on the veranda, all sleeping on beds made of straps.[23] Later, the Mission built a concrete structure with subsidies from the colony. Annual reports from the Supervision Committee described the penitentiary as "a very healthy place where crops were abundant, and the water plentiful . . . Three superb structures served the needs of the evangelical, agricultural, and penitentiary personnel, as well as the dispensary." Nonetheless, nothing indicated that incarcerated children ever benefited from the installations built with colonial subsidies. According to the Catholic Fathers (the sole source of information for the Supervision Committee that only visited the penitentiary once a year), children were relatively well nourished in comparison with other prisons, a "privilege" due to the fact that the government spent 1 franc per day per minor, while the ordinary prisons laid out only 0.35 francs per prisoner. The main meal generally consisted of couscous with meat; other meals offered mostly rice with "pistachio oil." A doctor working for the Indigenous Medical Assistance Service *(Assistance Médicale indigène)* tended to the minors' health.[24] Available reports refer to two deaths between 1888 and 1903.[25]

Discipline in the penitentiary preoccupied the Supervision Committee. Annual reports often mentioned the missionaries' laxity, or their tendency for

paternal familiarity with the detainees. These views must be revised to account for the Fathers' correspondence with administrative authorities, referring to the use of iron shackles to punish "rebellious spirits" among the
detained. Thus, "Touti Ndiaye broke his irons and went to get drunk." For
lack of a surrounding wall that would dissuade the prisoners from escaping,
"we attached the feet of this incorrigible runaway with an iron cord that was
not tight enough to prevent him from walking, but only allowed him to walk
with tiny steps."[26] The Fathers did not hesitate to use iron shackles, which
colonial prisons seldom employed at that time, and only for prisoners deemed
dangerous.

According to the missionaries, deviant behavior was inscribed in the inmate's character and individual nature. Alongside positive remarks—"excellent boy, good gardener," "tough worker"—we find numerous pejorative and
even contemptuous comments—"barren head," rebellious nature," "suffering
from primitivism," "incorrigible thief," not "enough brain" to learn to read.[27]

Ironically, the Fathers also viewed deviance as a contagious pathology, with
physical contact being the main vector of transmission. Consequently, isolation of the "carriers of evil germs" could only prevent the "propagation of
the illness" and the contamination of healthy individuals. The Fathers offered
the following explanation for the detainees' desire to escape incarceration:
"The idea of finding themselves in security in English territory troubles these
young turbulent minds and pushes them to escape, especially since several
of their former comrades flew there at the time of my predecessor—among
others, the infamous François Kane, an accomplice to the assassination of the
late Mr. Jeandet. The horror of work and the love of liberty is so very strong
among them . . . only the fear of being arrested again by the police can force
some lazy, mean, and hypocritical characters to remain here and work."

Administrative authorities largely shared the Fathers' point of view. The
1892 annual report recommended that charity and kindness were not enough
to "avert perverse inclinations, and correct the vicious instinct of children."
In a "Lombrosian" fashion, Europeans thought that the origins of juvenile
delinquency resulted from a natural predisposition to crime, a behavior that
emerged as soon as the minimal conditions for its expression were in place.
In order to prevent contagion and the degeneration of society, strict discipline
and incarceration must eradicate evil in predisposed criminals at a very young
age.[28]

To confront the children's "naturalized" deviance, the missionaries developed two remedies that reflected the material and ideological interests of the
Mission: redemption through work and the Gospel. The detainees labored for
the Mission's agricultural enterprise: by developing a "laborious therapy" for
deviance, the Fathers secured cheap labor. The Fathers did not train the children in schooling and apprenticeships in manual trades,[29] which represented
the major part of the children's official programs. Rather, they enforced "se-

vere discipline in agricultural work" (in the custom of the Physiocratic spirit). Thanks to subsidies from the colonial budget, abundant equipment helped the prisoners accomplish their chores: annual reports repeatedly underscored the healthy state of the Mission's agricultural enterprise.[30]

The children's contribution to the economic prosperity of the Mission was far from negligible. They were subject to long days of work, although the program of daily activities, according to the Fathers, remained quite low (see Table 4.1).[31] Nevertheless, the author of the report indicated that the information was "dictated by the director of the penitentiary."

The use of young detainees for the maintenance of roads (paid for by the colonial administration to the benefit of the Mission), and the predominance of rural activities were not the best means for reinserting young prisoners into society, since most of them came from urban backgrounds. Nonetheless, the issue of the delinquent youths' social reintegration preoccupied the colonial and ecclesiastical authorities.[32] At the end of their term in detention, some minors returned to their parents or former guardians.[33] The Mission informed the authorities of upcoming releases, indicating the future destination of the freed person, since the colonial administration took care of the costs of transportation. After 1892, the authorities became less and less interested in compensating the Mission for its services. In 1903, the collaboration between the Mission and the administration stopped.

THE MISSION AND THE GOVERNMENT OF SENEGAL: DETERIORATING RELATIONS

The relations between the colonial powers and the Mission began to deteriorate in 1892. That year the Supervision Committee's report was particularly critical of the missionaries' use of public subsidies. The report accused

Table 4.1.
Schedule for Juvenile Inmates at Thiès.

Time	Activity	Time	Activity
5:30 A.M.	Wake Up	12:00–1:30 P.M.	Recess
7:15 A.M.	Breakfast	1:30 P.M.	Singing Class
7:30 A.M.	Manual Labor	2:00 P.M.	Class
9:30 A.M.	Recess	3:00 P.M.	Recess
9:45 A.M.	Classroom	Until 6:45 P.M.	After School
Noon	*Dawal* (Main Meal)	6:45 P.M.	Dinner and Recess
		7:30 P.M.	Bedtime

the fathers of not having used sums received from the public treasury (35,000 francs) for initial setup costs and designated materiel. The report also blamed the Mission's duplicity, for having waited until the minors were settled to ask for maintenance costs (in October 1888) of 1 franc per child per day. The total sum amounted to 700 francs for clothing, 300 francs for medicine, and 582 francs for the doctor.

The report concluded: "Everything, apart from the house of correction, has been well conceived," and praised the Mission's prosperity and the "energetic will, the tenacious persistence of the Father Superior, who benefited from a most favorable situation, using local materials, the labor of young detainees, subsidies from the administration and the Mission itself, asking for and obtaining aid and assistance from all parties to assure the success of the enterprise." But, contrary to the initial project, there was "neither refectory, nor gymnasium, nor bathroom . . . , nor laundry room, nor infirmary."

The conclusion was particularly severe for the reformatory: "More a model farm than a house of correction. The colonial subsidies intended for the penitentiary have been used to the benefit of the Mission." The report recommended a new contract to regulate the relations between the mission and the administrative authorities. The contract was signed in 1894, and stipulated a substantial compensation for the missionary personnel who worked for the penitentiary.

After 1903, the contract between the Mission and the government ended. The decision derived, in part, from the exorbitant costs of the penitentiary. The administration also wondered about the location of the penitentiary, now close to a railway crossroads, and deemed inappropriate as a site for education. But the most important factor in the administration's decision was probably the rise of the anticlerical movement in France advocating for the separation of the State and the Church.[34] Thirteen years later, the first public colonial penitentiary opened its doors in Senegal.

THE AGRICULTURAL PENITENTIARY IN BAMBEY (1916–1927) AND THE PUBLIC MANAGEMENT OF JUVENILE MARGINALITY: NEGLIGENCE AND IRRESPONSIBILITY

The termination of the contract between the missionaries of Saint-Esprit and the administration left the colony without a penitentiary for minors. Young delinquents acquitted by virtue of Article 66, those who were under eighteen years of age and condemned to less than two years imprisonment, were interned in a public orphanage in the town of Richard Toll (on the Senegalese River). The administration had created the orphanage on March 12, 1912, and eventually transferred it to the village of Makhana, in the same region, on July 20, 1917. In order to end the "dangerous" situation that prevailed in the orphanage, where "the condemned and innocent orphans" were in "direct and constant contact," an official decree opened an agricultural penitentiary for the minor delinquents on March 12, 1916 in the town of Bambey.[35]

The choice of Bambey, a town situated in the heart of the peanut basin, far from the temptations of the large urban agglomerations, suggests that the colonial administration still believed that agricultural work could cure juvenile delinquency. Moreover, this locale offered good conditions for the construction of a penitentiary, since it was the site of the experimental agricultural station specializing in the peanut crop; the station's premises and personnel were at the disposal of the penitentiary.

Bambey agricultural station allowed detainees to labor in agricultural work associated with the peanut economy, the core of Senegalese colonial production. The administration's primary concern in this initiative was budgetary savings.

From the time of its creation—decree of February 5, 1916, signed by the lieutenant-governor of Senegal—to its closure in 1927, the agricultural colony at Bambey received 108 minors "acquitted in virtue of Article 66 of the Penal Code as having acted without discernment." (See Figure 4.1.) Customary tribunals sent forty children; the remainder came from the French colonial court system.[36] Among the detainees were numerous subjects of the colony of the Sudan.[37] The relatively important number of detainees sent to Bambey

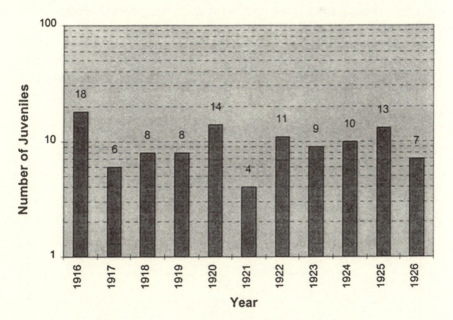

Figure 4.1. Number of Juvenile Detainees at Bambey (1916–1926).

by French colonial first-degree courts (tribunals in Dakar and Saint-Louis responsible for incidents involving citizens, Europeans, and subjects living under their jurisdiction) suggests the colonial administration's preoccupation with urban juvenile delinquency.

In 1916, the penitentiary registered the greatest number of new detainees (eighteen) during its eleven years of operations. At this time, the flow of entries had somewhat stabilized, although sources do not allow for the determination of the number of annual releases due to the termination of sentences, or reaching majority age. The number of detainees present at the penitentiary from one year to the next greatly fluctuated mostly because of the frequent numbers of escapes, rather than releases. Table 4.2 shows that exits—escapes were not included in the documentation consulted—remained more numerous than entries.[38]

The director of the agricultural station was in charge of administering of the penitentiary. The station buildings housed the penitentiary, and the station personnel ensured the primary training of the detained minors. The police commissioner of Bambey managed all penal operations at the agricultural colony (keeping the registers, monitoring the detainees). But the delegation of responsibilities undermined the good management of the penitentiary. In spite of numerous rules of conduct for detainees as well as for guards, one problem haunted the penitentiary: the station employees, not responsible for supervision of the minors, were hardly interested in the correctional aspects of the detention center. In turn, police guards who were in charge of disciplinary matters paid little attention to the minors' agricultural work.

Interior regulations obliged the minors to complete ten hours of work per day.[39] More than Thiès, the colony at Bambey attempted to use physical labor for "the correction of delinquent minors." In a Physiocratic and calculating spirit, the colonial administrators decided that "the detained will be employed

Table 4.2.
Annual Arrivals and Releases at Bambey (1921–1926).

Year	Arrival	Number of Detainees	Release
1921	4	26	
1922	11	15	21
1923	9	19	15
1924	10	16	13
1926	7	23	0

for diverse tasks at the agricultural station." On average, the administration reimbursed the work completed by the detainees at a daily rate of 0.75 francs. For the children, penal labor took precedence over educational and correctional objectives. The pupils split into two groups every week, sent to different areas of work, that they joined "in tight rows."

Administrative regulations also stipulated that each minor should own a pair of pants (renewed every six months), a working blouse (one year), a beret (two years), a pair of sandals (six months), and a blanket (one year). The director of the agricultural station performed initial medical examinations and, if need be, sent patients to the dispensary in Diourbel. A decree of December 16, 1907, "[fixed] the daily ration delivered to indigenous prisoners and *horses* in the confines of the colony."[40]

A strict discipline aimed at training the body for work. The administration enforced complete isolation for two, four, and eight hours for the following faults: "disputes followed by blows, inappropriate responses, uncleanness, bad maintenance of materiel, tools left at a work site." Isolation with a half-ration was ordered for "repeat offenders, lack of will for work, and theft of fruits and vegetables." Children guilty of "fights leading to wounds, loss or sale of materiel, attempted escape" were confined to a cell "with or without shackles" for at least three months. By contrast, good subjects could get more satisfying positions, and work as stable boys, herders, drivers, gardeners, or warehouse keepers. They could also benefit from conditional liberation, which involved transfer to the orphanage at Makhana. The regulations specified equally harsh punishment for guards: detention, prison, and dismissal in cases of negligence with respect to the obligations of surveillance.

However, the increasing gap between the rigors of written regulations and the decay in discipline suggests that the administration was more interested in producing a model text, than in creating an efficient tool for helping the minors interned at the agricultural station. The dissociation of responsibilities between the police commissioner of Bambey, entrusted with enforcing discipline, and the station personnel, responsible for the minors' education, lacked coherence.

Early on, the situation at the penitentiary deteriorated to the point where all authorities who visited the establishment recommended either its closure, or the complete reform of its structures and orientation. In general, the authorities overlooked the administration's negligence, and blamed the children's behavior or the guards' laxity. The director of the agricultural station alerted his hierarchical superior to the poor mentality of the children, which manifested itself in frequent thefts, the unwillingness to work, mass protests, and "even rebellions against the guards." The Bambey police commissioner, who was responsible for surveillance, also pulled the alarm and informed the commander of the Diourbel circumscription that "Escapes followed one after the other as quickly or even more quickly than the arrival of new detainees.

The penitentiary in no way served the purpose of purification, to which it was destined." He admitted his powerlessness in applying the rules: "Punishments inflicted upon guards did nothing to change the situation, nor did the replacement of agents," and proposed the transfer of the penitentiary to Diourbel in order to bring the establishment closer to the surveillance services. The head of the agricultural services explained the demise of the colony in terms of the imposition upon the station's director and its personnel of the tasks of a warden, for which they were not prepared.

The following year, the commander of the Diourbel circumscription took charge of the case. While deploring the duality of attributions between the station's director and the commissioner of Bambey, the commander blamed negligent guards and the "bad and often dangerous little rascals."[41] The heads of the penitentiary, lacking experience and unprepared for the task at hand, consistently reported their inability to handle the situation. The breach between the principles set forth by the regulations and the reality revealed by an inspection report[42] prompted the authorities at Saint-Louis to reorganize the agricultural colony that very same year. The report described the penitentiary as consisting of four small, unfenced buildings. The first building had two rooms measuring 3.5 by 3 meters and, since the tin roof on one of the rooms had caved in, "the minors squeezed into the other to sleep during rest hours." Two buildings served as a stockroom and lodging for the guard, respectively; and the last, "whose roof had fallen in ruins, housed the second guard." The detainees were dressed in rags at the time of the inspection team's visit; they had never received the clothing allotted by the public service. They also had insufficient food rations.

In spite of deplorable living conditions, the minors performed a work schedule in flagrant violation of established rules. Of the twenty-three minors detained, five were cleaning the port of Bambey alongside "common law prisoners," with whom they had their meals and shared dormitories. The seventeen other detainees served as apprentices (1), metalworkers (3), masons (2), carpenters (1), assistant gardeners (1), peanut sorters (2), domestics of the European functionaries working at the station (3), and cooks (1). Three were inactive. Minors' forced labor shows that the local administration totally ignored the principles of work as a means of correction. The central administration, preoccupied with juvenile delinquency in the major urban centers, had delegated the management of the penitentiary to local administrators who were unprepared to deal with youth delinquency. Their disinterest resulted in the pathetic living conditions of the minors detained at the Bambey station.

Was it surprising that the penitentiary deviated from its original goal: "the moral rectification of delinquent children"? The 1927 report underscored the lack of respect for the decree of August 13, 1888, and the law of 1850, that had provided the models for moral education through professional instruction.[43] At Bambey, the situation had become too degraded for effective reform:

Twenty-one of the forty-four detainees had escaped. The commander of the Baol circumscription visited the penitentiary and left with a negative impression: "The disciplinary quarters were partly demolished; half of the roof was torn off. The children were in rags and complained that they were underfed. The buildings were dirty and poorly maintained; no rule of hygiene was observed."

These deficiencies proved fatal to the first public agricultural penitentiary of Senegal. And so did one of its main administrators—the police commissioner of Bambey—who suggested that: "Labor at a low price rendered great service to the experimental station in agricultural production. Several ex-detainees have been arrested again after their liberation, I think any idea of amending these young wrongdoers is useless. However, their incarceration is socially beneficial: During their internment, they cannot harm society." The commissioner proposed the militarization of the station, with the obligation to wear uniforms and the institution of individual records, gratuities, and elementary instruction.[44]

But the governor of Senegal issued a decree declaring that the establishment "no longer served its purpose" and created "in Carabane (Casamance) a "reformatory home," which later became the *École professionnelle spéciale* (EPS) of Carabane.[45] The management of urban juvenile marginality entered a new period. After thirty-nine years of fruitless experience, the colony finally decided to open a establishment specializing in the detention of minors, and appoint personnel who were in the exclusive service of the penitentiary.

CONCLUSION

Being private or public, the penitentiary schools of the Senegalese colony only received a relatively small proportion of youth who had been sentenced to detention. The majority remained detained in the regular prisons during the entire colonial period. In 1931, the civil prison in Dakar alone held forty-seven prisoners aged from twelve to seventeen years of age, originating from the different territories of French West Africa.[46] Some archival material refers to some very sad cases, such as Léonie Guèye, sentenced to eight years in the prison of Saint-Louis for petty theft, after her father's death. Acquitted by virtue of Article 66 of the penal code, and not returned to her mother, Léonie Guèye shared the adult female cell for three years; it was impossible to send her to Bambey where she would have had to live in close promiscuity with the detained boys.[47] Ironically, Léonie Guèye would have served a shorter term if common law had been applied to her case. Children detained in correction houses had the advantage of being subject to lesser surveillance. They could express a radical critique of incarceration by staging escapes. Two key factors contributed to the failure of carceral institutions for children—escapes and the administration's financial greediness.

Paradoxically, the colonial state in Senegal entrusted a private religious institution with the first reformatory at the very moment when the metropole, having learned lessons from more than a half-century of experience, condemned, by an "official notice . . . the very principle of the delegation of the powers of correction to private establishments."[48] In Senegal, difficult circumstances reinforced the errors that had led to the abolishment of the private management for the incarceration of youth:[49] the heterogenous statuses of the detained, the lack of financial resources for the management of marginalized youth, and the lax control over the use of public funds. The political situation in the metropole, with the rise of the anticlerical movement, prompted the government's decision to end the private administration of the penitentiary colony.

When the colonial authorities switched to a public institution, they introduced the seeds of failure into their project by making use of an institution that was devoted to aims other than the incarceration of minors. The favorable technical conditions offered by the peanut station for minors' labor were not the deciding factor in the placement of the penitentiary at Bambey. The authorities' main concern was to save money on the costs of installation and personnel. The agricultural station was thus incapable of fulfilling the functions of a penitentiary for lack of personnel, appropriate quarters, and funding.

Private and public attempts to reproduce metropolitan agricultural reformatories satisfied the demand for cheap labor, rather than the rehabilitation of juvenile delinquents according to the norms defined by the colonial order.[50] Moreover, the failures of the European model were exacerbated by the colonial situation. In the colonies, as in the metropole, the early effort to take into account the specificity of childhood in the definition of prison policy failed to create special jurisdictions for minors.[51] Only in 1928 did a decree institute special jurisdictions and probation[52] for minors in the colonial territories. But the decree was not promulgated in French West Africa before June 28, 1958.[53] Despite this late date, and the earlier failures examined in this chapter, the extension of educative modes of detention to minors in the French colonies of West Africa remains a remarkable fact.

NOTES

1. Abolition affected the trading posts of Saint-Louis, Gorée, and Sedhiou in Casamance and, indirectly, all neighboring territories in the French domain. M. Guèye, "La fin de l'esclavage à Saint Louis et à Gorée en 1848," *Bulletin de l'IFAN*, 28, B, 3–4 (1966); R. Pasquier, "A propos de l'émancipation des esclaves au Sénégal en 1848," *Revue française d'histoire d'outre-mer*, 54, 194–97 (1960), 189–208.

2. R. Pasquier, "Villes du Sénégal," *Revue française d'histoire d'outre-mer* (1960), 387–426.

3. On the colonial conquest, see M. Crowder, *West Africa Under Colonial Rule* (Evanston, Ill: Northwestern University Press 1982); and on urban processes, see C. Coquery-

Vidrovitch, *Histoire des villes d'Afrique noire des origines à la colonisation* (Paris: Albin Michel, 1993).

4. M. Foucault, *Discipline and Punish* (Paris: Gallimard, 1975); J.-G. Petit, ed., *Histoire des galères, bagnes et prisons XIIIe-XXe siècles* (Paris: Privat, 1991); M. Mollat, *Les pauvres au Moyen-âge* (Paris: Complexe Editions, 1978).

5. The administration later took into account other criteria for discriminating between the various groups of prisoners—penal category (accused/condemned, delinquent/criminal), status (civil/military), and gender.

6. *Archives nationales du Sénégal* (ANS), 2 B 26, *Correspondance du Gouverneur au ministre des Colonies*, May 10, 1849.

7. *Moniteur du Sénégal et Dépendances* (1881).

8. The *Moniteur du Sénégal et Dépendances* notes that, between 1894 and 1895, 1,916 slaves were liberated in Saint-Louis.

9. ANS, Dossier K 15, *Captivité et esclavage*, 1900–1903.

10. ANS, Dossier K 17, *Rapport Poulet*, 1905.

11. I. Kâ, "L'évolution sociale à Saint Louis du Sénégal du XIXe au début du XXe siècle," (*Mémoire de maîtrise, Université Cheikh Anta Diop*, 1981), 81.

12. In 1823, colonial authorities adopted a new system *(le régime des engagés à temps):* purchased slaves could be liberated after fourteen years of service to those who acquired them. The Senegalese government appointed the presidents of tribunals as the guardians of the *engagés* slaves. The presidents liberated *engagés* at the end of their "term," or in the case of proven mistreatment. F. Zucarrelli, "Le régime des engagés à temps au Sénégal," *Cahiers d'études africaines* 7, no. 2 (1962), 420–61.

13. One can trace the rate of emancipations by using the Bureau lists published in the *Moniteur du Sénégal et Dépendances*.

14. ANS, 3, F, 28, *Procureur de la République au gouverneur général*, December 20, 1900.

15. Ibid., *Directeur du pénitencier de Thiès au gouverneur général*, March 10, 1901.

16. Article 66 of the Penal Code stipulated: "If the accused is under sixteen years of age, and has acted undiscerningly, he will be acquitted. According to the circumstances, he will be given back to his parents or assigned to a house of correction, where he will be held for a number of years, to be determined by the judge and that cannot exceed the delinquent's twentieth birthday."

17. The head of the Judicial Service had already given over young freed slaves deemed rebellious or perverted to the Catholic priests. They labored for the Mission "according to their particular abilities in agricultural or domestic work."

18. C. Carlier, *La prison aux champs. Les colonies d'enfants délinquents du nord de la France au XIXe siècle* (Paris: Editions de l'Atelier, 1994), 299.

19. The reports noted the presence of a girl among the detainees once. In order to separate her from the boys, she moved to the quarters of the Mission's Sisters.

20. Tribunals acquitted an average of twelve minors every year.

21. In 1892, the infractions for the detention of the twenty-eight minors in the penitentiary were described as follow: 68 percent for theft, 10 percent for bodily harm, 7 percent for vagabondage, and the rest for abuse of confidence, attempted homicide, indecent assault, and attempt to derail a train. ANS, 3 F 28, *Rapport du Comité de surveillance*.

22. C.D. Bâ, "La criminalité à Diourbel, 1925–1960" (*Mémoire de maîtrise, Université Cheikh Anta Diop*, 1994); N.C. Diédhiou, "L'évolution de la criminalité au Sénégal de 1930 aux années 1960" (*Mémoire de maîtrise, Université Cheikh Anta Diop*, 1991); O.

Faye, "L'urbanisation et les processus sociaux au Sénégal: typologie descriptive et analytique des déviances à Dakar d'après les sources d'archives, de 1885 à 1940" (*Thèse de
3e cycle en histoire, Université Cheikh Anta Diop*, 1989).

23. ANS, 3 F 28, *Rapport sur l'installation d'une école pénitentiaire*, 1888.

24. A conflict with the Mission's personnel—for unknown reasons—interrupted the doctor's activities. From then on, the Mission's sisters provided health care at their dispensary.

25. Alassane Guèye (December 9, 1894), *"victime,"* and Omar Mbaye (January 23,
1896), "arrived with pneumonia; he became worse here due to several careless acts."

26. ANS, 3 F 28, *Rapport sur l'installation d'une école pénitentiaire à Thiès, arrêté du
13 août 1888.*

27. ANS, 3, F, 28, *Rapport Comité de surveillance, 1892.*

28. A.-C. Ambroise-Rendu, "Les enfants criminels de la Belle époque," *L'Histoire* 198
(1996), 62–66.

29. Missionary brothers taught manual trades: A tailor, a cartwright, a carpenter, and a
blacksmith were joined by a teacher and a head gardener, the gardener serving as general
superintendent. ANS, 3, F, 28, *Rapport annuel du Comité de surveillance, 1892.*

30. The benefits of the detainees' labor for the mission were considerable. For example,
the Fathers asked a prisoner to maintain the penitentiary, offering him separate lodgings,
remuneration for his services, and outings.

31. ANS, 3 F 8, *Rapport annuel du Comité de Surveillance, 1892.*

32. The *Journal Officiel* informed future employers of the termination of the minors'
detention and their technical competences.

33. Madame Farrereau, a merchant in Saint-Louis, asked for the liberation of Amadou,
her former employee who had been condemned to five years in the penitentiary of Thiès
for stealing from her store. "I have learned that the young Amadou has become a good
subject, and considering that I am absolutely alone in my work, this child, punished and
corrected, can help me enormously." ANS, 3 F 26, *École pénitentiaire de Thiès, 1888–
1900, Correspondance départ et arrivée, directeur de l'intérieur, Lettre du 18 juillet 1892.*

34. J.-R. De Benoist, *Eglise et pouvoir colonial au Soudan français. Administrateurs et
missionnaires dans la boucle du Niger, 1885–1945* (Paris: Karthala, 1987), 111.

35. ANS, 3 F 28, *Lettre du chef des services agricoles au Secrétaire général du gouvernement*, August 10, 1923.

36. ANS, 3 F 28, *Extrait d'un rapport du chef du Bureau politique, 1927.*

37. We found no evidence, in the documentation consulted, of minors being sent by the
other territories of French West Africa.

38. ANS, 3 F 28, Diverse correspondence.

39. This length of work time was equivalent to an adult's workday. Unions judged it
excessive and hotly contested it. They obtained a reduction to eight hours when the law
of April 23, 1919, was promulgated in French West Africa. See I.D. Thiam, *Histoire du
mouvement syndical africain, 1790–1929* (Paris: L'Harmattan Editions, 1993), 142.

40. *Journal Officiel Sénégal* (1907), 689, author's emphasis. The ration was composed
of the following elements: 0.5 kg of rice (replaced by 1 kg of millet when the price of rice
surpassed 40 francs/100 kg), 0.015 kg of oil or locally produced butter, 0.015 kg of salt,
and 0.125 francs allotted to each detainee per day in place of meat or fish.

41. ANS, 3 F28, *Lettre au gouverneur du Sénégal*, April 30, 1924.

42. An extract of this report, addressed to the Secretary General of the government by
the head of the Political Bureau, exists in the archives, and probably dates to 1927. ANS,
3 F 28.

43. This despite the passage, "Professional education that is to be given to the children of the penitentiary of Senegal must include agricultural instruction . . . for those coming from the bush, and industrial instruction that will prepare the others to be urban workers."

44. ANS, 3 F 25, *Lettre au commandement de cercle du Baol*, January 27, 1926.

45. The EPS of Carabane was situated in an isolated spot at the mouth of Casamance and functioned until 1953. The *Centre de rééducation*, created after Carabane at Nianing, 100 kilometers south of Dakar, still functions today along with numerous other institutions for delinquent children. see O. Thioune, "L'éducation surveillée au Sénégal" (*Mémoire de maîtrise de philosophie, Université Cheikh Anta Diop*, 1980). Since the closing of the penitentiary of the Mission at Thiès in 1903, public institutions have monopolized the detention of minors.

46. F. Cazanove, "L'enfance criminelle indigène," *Bulletin de la Société de Pathologie Exotique* 25, no. 7 (1932), 826–828.

47. ANS, 3 F 73, *Dossier d'une détenue mineure Léonie Guèye*, 1925.

48. Carlier, *La prison aux champs*, 586.

49. Ibid., 527.

50. O. Faye, "Les métis de la seconde génération, les enfants mal-aimés de la colonisation française en Afrique occidentale, 1895–1960," *Colleque L'AOF: esquisse d'une intégration africoune* (Dakar: Direction des archives du Sénégal, 1997), has studied how colonial authority encountered many difficulties with marginal persons who had been created by its very policies, such as "second generation mulattos."

51. In France, jurisdictions for children, which had taken hesitant first steps at the end of the first decade of the twentieth century, were clearly affirmed with the declaration of the law on children's courts of July 22, 1912. This law provided social investigations in favor of minors who had been in trouble with the law. See M.A-Perret, "L'enquête sociale (loi 1912). Les services sociaux près le tribunal pour enfants de la Seine à Paris dans l'entre-deux-guerres" *(Mémoire de maitrise, Université de Paris 7, 1989)*, 22 and 27.

52. Thioune, "L'éducation surveillée."

53. *Journal Officiel de l'AOF (1958)*, 934–47.

5

PUNISHMENT TO FIT THE CRIME?

Penal Policy and Practice in British Colonial Africa

David Killingray

In 1911 C.E. Ward told the boys of his former preparatory school about his duties as an administrative officer in the East African Protectorate. "We are responsible," he wrote, "for the administration of justice, for the collection of the revenue (which is in the form of a native poll tax), the control of the Police, regulation of the Prisons, and for preserving the lines of communication through the territory."[1] It is doubtful whether Ward gave much thought to what he meant when he used the word *justice*. Most colonial officials of that period unequivocally saw their role as bringing peace and order and the benefits of modern law to darkest Africa. To enforce alien rule, as Ward rightly observed, required a paramilitary police force and prisons that were among the earliest institutions created and built by colonial rulers in Africa. The first was needed to establish authority and to ensure that vital revenue was collected, the second to punish those who committed offenses against the new system of order. The civilizing mission, as Mahmood Mamdani says, soon shifted in perspective and practice to being primarily concerned with the administration of law and order.[2]

Although prisons and punishment were central to the workings of the colonial state in Africa relatively few historians have looked at the principles and practices of this often unpleasant aspect of colonial governance. Scholarly interest has focused much more on the important questions relating to the framing and working of colonial legal codes and processes;[3] it has been left largely to a few lawyers to comment on African colonial penal policies.[4] This is in marked contrast to the very large and continuing interest shown by scholars in the history of imprisonment and punishment in Europe and North America.[5] So this chapter is a rather brief attempt to fill that gap. It looks at official penal policies introduced and applied in British colonial Africa, at the various forms of punishment inflicted upon colonial subjects by government and native administrative courts, and the arguments for and against certain measures of reform. Penal policy and practice in each colony always concerned the Colonial Office in London, which sought to ensure that what was done in the Imperial name appeared to be both consistent and humane. English law, as exported to the British colonies, was based on ideas of equity and impartiality, but because colonial rule—most specially in white settler colonies such as Kenya and Southern Rhodesia—was largely about racial dominance and economic hegemony, these principles were often absent from local legal codes or at best ambiguous.

British colonial rule introduced into Africa new ideas of law and "crime" and also new forms of punishment. Most colonial administrators regarded customary law as "primitive" and African means of retribution generally as "barbaric"; English law was seen as both superior and necessary as an agent of gradual modernization. There were occasional dissenting voices to this widely held view, but they were rare.[6] What constituted appropriate punishments for Africans was also debated at some length, although with little understanding or knowledge to inform judgments. In the period when colonial rule was being established, the measures adopted to coerce and punish were largely dictated by military and political expediency. Thus in "unsettled" districts, punitive expeditions, often referred to as "extreme measures," inflicted collective punishments by destroying houses and crops and removing cattle. As colonial rule was placed on a firmer basis, notions of good government and social control dictated the need for a regular system of courts and codified penal policies and punishments. But what was appropriate? Whipping was instant and cheap; fines required a money economy, while prisons locked up potential labor and burdened treasuries. Invariably, it was argued that flogging was a more effective punishment than imprisonment, but a lack of solid information other than subjective comment makes it difficult to determine what if anything actually served as a deterrent. Any detailed study of penal policy and practice also needs to take into account the perceptions of those who suffered from the rigors of the law; such information is rare.

There has been little systematic study of sentencing policies in British colonial Africa. It would appear that sentencing practices varied considerably from court to court, colony to colony, often determined by the ideology of an individual magistrate or judge. Sentences tended to be harsher in white settler colonies for a whole range of offenses. Cultural settings also influenced sentencing. For example, in Nigeria more fines were levied in the Western Province where money more readily circulated than in Northern Nigeria, which had a smaller modern monetary base.[7] Certain European administrators and judges were sympathetic to African intellectual ideas and institutions and this was reflected in their understanding of and leniency in interpreting colonial law and making judgments.[8] From an early twenty-first–century perspective, many aspects of British colonial policy relating to sentencing and penal practice seem mild when compared with the draconian measures employed by certain successor governments—minimum sentences mainly for offenses against property; mandatory death sentences for armed robbery, drug offenses, and stock theft; the increased use of corporal punishment, public executions, and a range of harsh sanctions for economic crimes.[9]

The penal system established in British Africa mirrored, in part, the experience and practices pertaining in the United Kingdom, modified by the experience of colonial rule in India and the Caribbean. In most African colonies there was created a system of indirect rule, of native authorities subject to colonial government and possessing parallel institutions such as treasuries, courts, police, and prisons. This system, adopted for Buganda and Northern Nigeria in the early part of the century, was gradually extended over a large part of British Africa in the 1920s–1930s as indirect rule was applied as a practical, pragmatic, economic, and gradualist means of ruling large areas. The penal laws and methods of native authority courts and prisons were subject to the principle of repugnancy. In the words of Lugard, they were "bound solely by native law and custom, provided that the punishment is (a) not in excess of the powers conferred upon it and (b) does not involve mutilation or torture, and is not repugnant to natural justice and humanity."[10] Only in Northern Nigeria and in Buganda did native courts have complete jurisdiction, including powers to impose capital sentences. The dual system inevitably caused some confusion. In certain cases punishments under customary law exceeded in severity those permitted by the colonial criminal code.[11] Plural legal systems also raised jurisdictional questions and problems with African nonsubjects being illegally sentenced and punished by native administration courts. Native authority penal practices were supposed to be regulated by colonial officials but were often overlooked. In the early years of indirect rule in Northern Nigeria, it appears that certain repugnant policies continued and only slowly became subject to European scrutiny.

Officials in the Colonial Office in London closely watched penal policies and practices in each colony to ensure that humanity prevailed and that the various systems were standardized. Before the Second World War this was usually done by monitoring annual colonial reports of prison departments, receiving the papers of local committees of inquiry, or by commissioning reports by penal specialists charged to inquire into specific aspects of penal policy. For example, the question of "native punishment" in Kenya was examined in some detail in the early 1920s, while Alexander Paterson, chief commissioner of prisons in England and Wales, inquired into the prison system of East Africa in a report issued in 1939.[12] In the late 1930s, and especially after 1945, the prison services in the African colonies became much more professional. This is reflected in the creation by the Colonial Office in the late 1940s of the Advisory Committee on the Treatment of Offenders in Colonies, which met regularly to discuss penal matters. Throughout the years of colonial rule, various humanitarian and interested bodies acted as watchdogs of colonial penal practice. These included the Aborigines Rights' Protection Society, the Anti-Slavery Society, the Howard League for Penal Reform, the Fabian Colonial Bureau, various political parties and individual parliamentarians, and representatives of Christian missionary societies.[13]

IMPRISONMENT

Imprisonment was comparatively rare in sub-Saharan African societies before the advent of colonial rule. Punishments for crimes and misdemeanors varied and included beating, ordeal by poison (which was often a sentence of death), mutilation, reparations and compensatory payments, various forms of torture, enslavement, and banishment. The history of indigenous African penal practice has been clouded by ideology. Most colonial rulers emphasized the innate savagery of African societies and the brutal punishments meted out to offenders. This was countered by scholars in the decolonization years who toned down the idea of savagery and in its place emphasized that indigenous law was concerned with reconciliation rather than harsh retribution. More recently this "Merrie Africa" view of the pre-colonial past has been abandoned by scholars for a more exacting analysis of the complexities of power, status, class, and gender within African societies.[14]

Prisons were comparatively rare throughout most of pre-colonial sub-Saharan Africa. They existed in certain parts of the sudanic region; for example, in Kano, their main purpose was to house the emir's political enemies rather than common criminals.[15] A more common form of detention was to restrain prisoners by attaching them to a log or a tree. More commonly, as indeed in early modern Europe, convicted criminals were dealt with in ways other than by incarceration. Thus the prison system introduced into colonial Africa represented a new, different, and largely unknown form of punishment. Prisons were among the earliest examples of colonial architecture. The first were converted forts; for example, Fort Jesus at Mombasa or some of the old trading castles on the West African coast. As colonial rule was established, new prisons were built. When Port Harcourt, in Southern Nigeria, was created as a new town and railway port in 1911–1912, among its public buildings was a prison capable of holding 1,100 prisoners.

Although prisons existed throughout British colonial Africa, officials constantly questioned whether prison was an appropriate method of punishment for Africans. There was no doubt that prisons were necessary to detain a certain number of violent criminals, recidivists, and also the criminally insane.[16] In certain territories—for example, the South African colonies and Kenya—relatively large numbers of Africans were sent to prison convicted of petty offenses. In the 1950s, prison sentences in Tanganyika averaged three times the length of those given for comparable crimes in the United Kingdom.[17] It is debatable whether Africans attached any social stigma to imprisonment. Ekechi argues that this was so in southern Nigeria, although in East Africa people mockingly referred to government prisons as "Kingi Georgi Hotel."[18] Prisons were not comfortable and were not intended to be so. Convicts generally had a drab existence. For the colonial authorities, imprisonment raised a number of major questions: Did prison serve as a deterrent to crime? Were there more economical and effective ways of punishing offenders? Was prison the best place to remand prisoners, many of whom would not be convicted? There was also the more exacting problem of how to run a humane prison system with adequate food and care for inmates in societies where social and economic conditions might often be harsh and food periodically in short supply.[19] Imprisonment may not have carried a stigma but the deprivation of liberty was certainly a severe form of punishment for many Africans because, as more than one report suggested, they were accustomed to living a close, communal life.[20] One perceptive colonial official in London commented in 1920:

> A man is taken from his village, from his family and kindred, from the only life which he knows, and confined to a prison cell. . . . The cell where he sleeps is provided with ventilation based on British ideas of fresh air. The result is often such that it would be more merciful to hang him at once. He pines at the loss of freedom; the unaccustomed food and sleeping arrangements cause disease—and he *dies*. To all intents and purposes he had been sentenced to death as surely as if he had been sentenced to hanging.[21]

In addition to being deprived of their liberty, convicts were sometimes in chains and employed as forced labor. Describing Owerri prison in southeastern Nigeria in the first decade of this century, Ekechi says that many of the prisoners were young men who had resisted compulsory labor, captives brought in by military expeditions and hostages. By 1919 there were over 900 prisoners in a building that had been built to accommodate just over 100. Conditions were unsanitary and food was in short supply; predictably, many prisoners fell sick and died.[22] The poor physical conditions and the relatively high mortality among those incarcerated in early colonial prisons, can be seen in the reports of prison medical officers.

The debates about appropriate deterrents ranged from harsher prison regimes to flogging in place of imprisonment, and various forms of restitution and compensation, which, it was often argued was more in accord with customary legal processes, and also other forms of punishment, including those involving public humiliation which would "cause a native to be laughed at by his own people especially his women folk."[23] For much of the colonial period imprisonment was widely regarded as a less than satisfactory method of punishment, while the alternatives such as fines and flogging were frequently viewed as inappropriate or out of step with modern penal practice and humanitarian ideas. This was increasingly the view from London on corporal punishment, although the dilemma was to find an alternative form of retribution that was economical to apply, practical in operation, and did not incur the opposition of the liberal and humanitarian bodies that kept a close watch on colonial rule. One of the problems in managing the colonial penal system was that, with the extension of indirect rule, increasingly there were two different systems requiring administrative control: There were government courts, police, and prisons, which were subject to direct colonial administration, and those under native authority jurisdiction.[24]

CENTRAL GOVERNMENT PRISONS

Government prisons varied in size, strength, and purpose. The pattern that emerged in most colonies by the 1930s was for a number of central prisons, usually in provincial capitals, with a lower tier of local prisons and also numerous lock-ups attached to police stations and district offices. In most cases colonial legal codes and the government prison system closely mimicked aspects of British penal policy and practice although reforms, if they came, invariably lagged well behind reforms in Britain. Thus, imprisonment for debt ended in most colonies long after it had ceased to be treated in this way in Britain; similarly Master and Servants laws continued in colonial legal codes for many years after they had been withdrawn from the English statute book. The gap between British penal reforms and the impulse for change in the colonial territories began to narrow by the 1950s, a good example being the moves to end corporal punishment following its abolition in England and Wales in 1948.

The earliest prisons in colonial Africa were those in the West African possessions. The colony of Freetown regularized its prisons system with the completion of a three-story stone building in 1816 that remained largely unaltered for a century.[25] The Gold Coast prison system of the late nineteenth century, following a Colonial Office circular of 1860, had adopted the three pillars of British punitive practice: the separate system, penal labor and a minimal diet.[26] Although the separate system was never imposed—inadequate and overcrowded prisons prevented that—crank and shot drill and the treadmill continued until 1907. Broad Street Prison in Lagos, opened in 1872 with accommodations for 300 prisoners, was modeled on the British prisons of the time, although, unlike those of Gambia and the Gold Coast, the regimen contained neither crank nor shot drill.[27] But the idea of "reform rather than punishment," enunciated by the Gladstone Committee in Britain in 1895 that swept penal labor into the dustbin, was only effectively introduced into the Gold Coast by the new regulations of 1922 initiated by Governor Frederick Gordon Guggisberg; in other colonies these reforms followed later. The "mark" system, whereby prisoners could earn up to a 25 percent remission of sentence, also followed British practice; it had been used on the antipodean penal colony of Norfolk Island and then introduced to Cape Colony in 1840 by John Montagu.[28] The practice continued in most colonies long after it was abandoned in Britain.[29]

In the first years of this century, Northern Rhodesia had no prisons and convicts served their sentences in the jails of Southern Rhodesia. By the Prison Ordinance of 1911, eleven central prisons were set up (reduced to six by 1938) and by 1921 there were also twenty-one local prisons. Although regarded as a necessary institution, the prison system in Northern Rhodesia, as indeed in many other colonies, was the Cinderella of the colonial order. It was characterized by a shortage of funds and administrative neglect. In the pecking order of colonial administration, the post of jailer was near the bottom. Expenditure on the prisons of Northern Rhodesia amounted to only £14,666 in 1928 and this declined by nearly 12 percent along with all colonial budgets during the Depression years of the 1930s. Control of prisons often was the responsibility of the police. This was the case in Southern Nigeria until 1920 and in Northern Rhodesia until the late 1940s. Alexander Paterson, the commissioner of prisons for England and Wales, in a memorandum to the Colonial Office as early as 1930, urged that separate prison departments be created.

Certain reforms to penal policy and practice did take place before the 1940s but they were slow and slight. For example, in Northern Rhodesia in the 1920s, a lack of adequate accommodations for juvenile offenders meant that they were sent to South African reformatories, habitual criminals were separated from first-time offenders, and some move was made toward training and rehabilitation following the passage of the Prisons (Amendment) Ordinance and Rules of 1927. A riot in Livingstone Prison in the 1930s, which, some commentators suggested, mirrored the disturbances in the notorious English prison on Dartmoor, focused official attention on the system. The Fynn Report of 1938 found the prison service "greatly neglected." The Livingstone Central Prison, the report continued was "antiquated and thoroughly unsatisfactory from every point of view," while Kasama prison was in "a dangerous state of repair" with the only water half a mile away. Prison clothing consisted of "inadequate" canvas garments and most prisoners slept on the floor without mats. Fynn, the prison commissioner for Southern Rhodesia, recommended a centralized prison at Lusaka, further European staff and a "single cell system," which he regarded as a "very important deterrent factor in prison administration . . . [and] essential for the proper treatment and reform of habitual criminals." He further commented on the policy of using "mechanical restraints" to control violent and dangerous convicts in Livingstone prison.[30] This was reported on by visiting justices in 1940: "One of the greatest disgraces and condemnations of the present prison in Livingstone lies in the fact that it appears to be necessary to chain large pieces of railway ties to the legs of prisoners to prevent them from escaping." One commissioner commented that "the practice of using chains and railway ties may be medieval but it is certainly effective."[31] The penal reforms recommended by Fynn and also by the Dowbiggin *Report on the Northern Rhodesia Police* of 1937 were held up by the outbreak of war and only implemented after 1945.

Harsh regimes existed in certain government prisons but the general picture of the interwar years is of a service ill-funded and accorded low consideration by many colonial governments and with reform only grudgingly and slowly accepted. The control of prisons often depended upon ex-soldiers and former policemen employed as wardens. Abuses were common although Paterson commented on great improvements in prison discipline in East Africa during the 1930s.[32] By 1939 graduates of Makarere College were joining the prison service as assistant jailers. Paterson approvingly reported that they were "humane and good at sport" and he went on to suggest that there might be in Africa "wander races," that is "tribes more suited to the discipline of restraining Africans." Study courses run by the Home Office for European prison officers employed in the colonies were begun in 1926.

A restricted "penal diet" was used as a form of punishment, often for cases of disciplinary infractions, in British and in colonial prisons. The classic example is the regime of bread and water. Generally, colonial prison diets were purposely restricted as part of the deterrent element of imprisonment. But constant care and some specialist knowledge of nutrition was needed to tread the narrow margin between restriction as policy and dietary neglect. The latter often prevailed. Most colonial prisons had ration scales graded by race and sociocultual status; the one in Northern Rhodesia differentiated between "Europeans, Cape Boys, Asiatics and colonial kaffirs, and uncivilized natives."[33] Poor diet as a result of either restriction, ignorance, or low budgets led to disease and malnutrition for many prisoners. In the Freetown Prison in 1928 – 1929 there was a high incidence of beriberi; 166 out of 252 prisoners had the deficiency disease, which, said an official report, was because "the statutory diet . . . fell below that regarded by dietetic authorities as a famine ration."[34]

One change to the prison system designed to deal with tax defaulters and those serving short sentences was the introduction of detention camps. Established first in Kenya in 1925, followed by Northern Rhodesia in 1928 and Tanganyika in 1933, the camps aimed to be self-sufficient in food supplies. Prisons frequently served as sources of extra-mural labor. The old idea of work as punishment was replaced with the idea of prison labor as a financial asset to the colonial state. Prison workshops turned out boots and clothing, convict gangs carried out public works and were used in anti-malarial and anti-tsetse schemes. Prison labor was also hired out "as a convenience to the more privileged members of the community to work on white-owned farms and gardens," a practice condemned by Paterson in his report on Kenyan prisons in 1939.[35] In the same report Paterson urged that prisoners be provided with hard work and also education that would be useful to them on their release. Prison farms, often producing model farmers, were established in certain colonies mainly after 1945.[36]

In the years after the Second World War, the prison population in the African colonies increased. This was due to a number of factors: There was an increase in crime, especially in the urban centers, that had began to grow rapidly during the war years; police forces were expanded and more effective policing may have led to a higher detection rate;[37] and growing opposition to colonial rule led to an increase in the number of people detained for political reasons.[38] The greatest increase in the prison population, and in prison staff, occurred in Kenya during the Mau Mau emergency of 1952–1960. At the height of the emergency in the mid-1950s, a daily average of 86,634 prisoners were being held in 176 prisons and detention camps guarded by 457 European and 14,000 African prison staff. This compared with a prison population of roughly 9,000 in 1952 when the Emergency was declared.[39]

NATIVE AUTHORITY PRISONS

From the outset of formal colonial rule, a dual system of prisons was established in Northern Nigeria and Uganda. With the extension of the system of indirect rule, native authority prisons were created in other colonies. The retreat from indirect rule in the years after 1945 led to a decline in native administration so that by 1949 prisons subject to native jurisdiction remained in only four colonies—Northern Nigeria, Uganda, the Gold Coast and a lone prison in Northern Rhodesia. Lugard, who had served in Uganda before moving to Nigeria, urged that "it was essential that every Native prison should be under the eye of a European Administrative Officer, who will see that the place is kept in a sanitary state, that the sick are properly cared for and prisoners properly fed."[40] There was often considerable difference between official instructions posted in colonial capitals and how policy was implemented on the ground, especially in the provinces. European supervision of native authority prisons was often slack, as Hailey pointed out in his *Survey* of 1938 and the conditions of some prisons in Northern Nigeria were little different from what they had been in pre-colonial times.[41] Even as late as 1952, a Colonial Office committee reported that "information about them [native authority prisons] was so scanty that it was not possible to judge what conditions in the prisons were like."[42] Three years earlier, the members of the same committee had commented that "they had an uneasy feeling that there were many possibilities of grave abuse" in native authority prisons and that they should be brought more speedily under the control of central government in each colony. By 1952 most of these prisons were little more than temporary lock-ups, although the system of indirect rule continued to give powers to autocratic African rulers to act in an arbitrary way toward the people that they ruled.

Dual control of native authority prisons was exercised in all colonies with the exception of Buganda. There the commissioner of prisons was not empowered to visit native authority prisons, although many did so at the invitation of district commissioners.[43] Native courts, police, and prisons undoubtedly allowed African indigenous rulers to abuse their positions of authority; references are numerous in the standard literature to instances of native authority police being used to extort payments and labor on behalf of chiefly rulers and of peasants being punished and imprisoned for refusing to comply. In Uganda in the mid-1930s, it was reported that 60 percent of those in native authority prisons were convicted of either tax default or adultery.[44] The native authority prisons helped underpin indigenous rulers' powers; they "serve as a mild but none the less effective penal sanction towards the maintenance of tribal discipline," said the Uganda Prison Report of 1946.[45] The reality may have been more severe than the "mild" of the official report.

CORPORAL PUNISHMENT

Various alternative punishments to imprisonment existed in most colonies. The pillory and stocks, favored by Lugard, were introduced into Nigeria in 1904 and only abolished in 1932.[46] Levying fines on individual offenders presented difficulties. In communities where the majority of people were poor or on the fringes of a money economy, a monetary fine was either impossible or represented severe punishment. Extreme disparities between rich and poor also made fines palpably unjust. The principle of fines also had to be understood and appreciated by the offender for the punishment to have meaning. Compensation to a victim, commonly applied in customary legal processes, was understood but fines paid to a government were not. And if people could not or would not pay, then court and police services were stretched and prisons filled with defaulters.[47] The large number of people who were brought before the colonial and native courts for failure to pay taxes, and the many who were subsequently imprisoned for this offense, indicated all too clearly the difficulties of levying fines as a penal measure.

Collective punishments continued to be used throughout the colonial period, often taking the form of removing cattle but also levying a fine on a community. Such actions under collective punishment or stock theft ordinances were widely used against pastoralists in the early years of colonial rule.[48] Later, collective punishment was reserved as an emergency measure applied, for example, during the Mau Mau emergency.[49] Various methods to effect restitution or compensation for crimes were also introduced into colonial legal codes, especially in the 1950s. The alternative punishment to prison favored by many Europeans, and which they often argued was endorsed by African customary practice, was whipping or flogging. The use of the whip or cane, it was frequently advanced, had the advantage of "expeditiousness and cheapness."[50] As one proponent of corporal punishment told the Commission on Native Punishment in Kenya in 1923, flogging was "inexpensive, summary, that the native is a child and should therefore be punished as a child and that it is effective."[51]

Corporal punishment was widely used in nineteenth-century Britain. Flogging was employed as a punishment in the penal system and also in the army. In both institutions, its use was reduced between 1861 and 1881, although retained as an appropriate punishment for certain offenses within prison. Corporal punishment for juvenile offenders remained on the statute book for the first half of the twentieth century. In most schools, children were caned for breaking rules or for poor work and this was a practice familiar to most colonial administrators and Christian missionaries working in Africa. Thus it is hardly surprising that corporal punishment should be advocated for colonial penal systems. As in Britain, so in colonial Africa, "this institutionalized punishment was carefully measured, shaped and gradually controlled by law and regulation: . . . in prison . . . there was the careful ordering of the body and the regulated number of lashes, with a medical practitioner in attendance. Physical pain was regarded as a salutary means of dealing with offence, the short sharp shock that would punish, discourage and, pre-eminently, provide a warning to other offenders."[52]

The instruments of corporal punishment were the "cat" (the cat-of-nine-tails, a nine-thonged leather whip with each thong weighted with a knot or small piece of concealed lead), which in Africa was mainly confined to prisons; the hide whip; and the rod or cane. The "cat" was a brutal instrument that cut the body of the victim unless he (women were very rarely beaten with it) were protected in some way. Its use was banned by the early part of the twentieth century and the hide whip or cane became the most common instrument for flogging. A hide whip could also cut the body of the victim; it ceased to be used in Uganda in 1925, Tanganyika in 1930, and Nigeria in 1933. Caning as an official punishment was usually applied on shoulders, back, or buttocks. The length, diameter, and weight of the stick, and its prescribed use, varied from one colonial territory to another. Alexander Paterson described as a "barbarous weapon" the "instrument prescribed by law for the beating of small boys" in Kenyan prisons, although he added that jailers were generally humane and refused to use a stick of more than 10 millimeters in diameter.[53] Flogging could be inflicted by order of both government and native authority courts and also for offenses committed by convicted prisoners. Officially, native courts only had jurisdiction over the African subjects of an indigenous ruler; when this was breached there might be an outcry, and in the rare occurrence of a European being beaten, as in the case of Phinehas McIntosh in Bechuanaland in 1933, this could result in a minor political crisis and armed intervention.[54] Under *shari'a* law in the Northern Nigerian emirates, lashings in public were supposed to be "humanely" inflicted.[55]

In the late nineteenth century and the first decades of the twentieth century, colonial officials and Europeans in nonofficial positions arbitrarily used corporal punishment; control was slight. Flogging was applied as a means of punishment but also to enforce and regulate African labor for road and railway building and carrying. Colonial officials used their powers to order African rulers to compel and punish recalcitrant laborers by fines and floggings.[56] Even women were beaten on the order of Northern Nigerian native courts, a punishment that was strongly opposed in Britain. One notorious case occurred in Bauchi in late 1918 when two African women were stripped naked, publicly beaten, and then exposed in the stocks. This incident, and an earlier case in 1914 when two African clerks, not subjects of the emir, were flogged in Zaria, led to strong denunciations in the West African press and fueled the growing opposition in Britain to the unregulated use of corporal punishment in the colonies.[57] Chanock, in his study of Central Africa quotes from legal records to show the liberal use made of the whip in attempts to instill in Africans new notions of social order: "Charges," he wrote, "were not framed in terms of law; some taken from the Fort Jameson Court Book were wasting time instead of buying food—four lashes; sitting around fire instead of working—five to ten lashes."[58]

Colonial officials differed in their attitudes to the extent of use and the severity of corporal punishment. Lugard was a "flogger" while Walter Egerton, High Commissioner and Governor of Southern Nigeria from 1904 to 1912, regarded flogging as degrading for both those who inflicted it and those who suffered the punishment.[59] Hugh Clifford, Governor of Nigeria after Lugard from 1919 to 1925, denounced sentences of flogging given by Northern Nigerian native courts as "excessive" and "shocking," although he was told in no uncertain terms by the Colonial Office that he had not been sent there to undermine the indirect rule policies introduced by his predecessor.[60] This did not mean that the Colonial Office in London was not interested in regulating corporal punishment in the African colonies. It clearly was, and each abuse that became public, such as the "flogged to death" case in Kenya in 1923, stressed the need for reform and a much tighter hand to be exercised over judicial proceedings and penal practice.[61] A Commission on Native Punishments, appointed to Kenya in 1921, heard many European witnesses who demanded an extension of corporal punishment. Despite this, the Commission recommended that flogging had a brutalizing effect and should be restricted only to those who committed particularly brutal crimes. A majority of the Commissioners believed that caning was a useful alternative to imprisonment for juveniles and minor offenders. Ten years later, the Bushe Committee of Inquiry opposed any extension of corporal punishment and rejected caning and flogging of adults except in cases of the most serious crimes.[62]

In 1932 the Governor of Nigeria voiced official opinion in the colony on the restriction of corporal punishment. At a Residents' conference later in December the generally held view was that native administration courts should retain the power to impose sentences of corporal punishment. All but one of the Northern emirs and chiefs supported retention while the Resident of Plateau Province declared that "flogging has not among primitive people the same brutalizing effect that it has among more civilized peoples."[63] Nevertheless, an amendment to the Criminal Code in 1933 abolished flogging with a leather whip while retaining beating with the rod, cane, or birch. The new regulations prescribed the instrument and the number of strokes that could be administered.[64] Tighter control over sentences involving corporal punishment imposed by native courts in Nigeria reduced the number of such punishments from 7,000 in 1933 to 900 in 1935.

Penal policy and practice in the colonies were influenced by policy and practice in the United Kingdom. Following the Cadogan Committee's recommendation in 1938 for the abolition of judicial corporal punishment in England and Wales, the Secretary of State for the Colonies asked the Governor of Nigeria to consider whether such a recommendation could be applied to that West African colony. The favorable replies, says Milner, indicated "that even at that early date, the administration throughout the country was moving rapidly towards the limitation and abolition of the penalty."[65] The Second World War effectively shelved any plans for immediate reform although it did lead the Colonial Office, against the judgment of the War Office and most military commanders, to bring to an end corporal punishment in the African Colonial Forces.[66] When judicial corporal punishment was abolished in England and Wales in 1948, it set a precedent for the colonies. Two years later, James Griffiths, the new Secretary of State for the Colonies, said that the colonies must follow suit.[67] The Governor of Tanganyika proposed an end to corporal punishment but the Legislative Council opposed such a move, as did various African local councils, for example, that of the Chagga. In its report in 1953, the Tanganyika Committee on Corporal Punishment argued for retention as "a punishment and a deterrent." A similar committee in Kenya similarly endorsed the continued use of corporal punishment and the infliction of a maximum of twenty-four strokes for an adult offender and twelve for those under the age of sixteen years, while the Northern Rhodesia committee recommended "abolition as an aim" but not until "adequate alternative sanctions have been provided."[68] In the 1950s, sentences of corporal punishment increased in both Kenya and Tanganyika, despite the reforming noises from London.[69]

CAPITAL PUNISHMENT

Under British rule, the death penalty in most territories was under normal circumstances restricted to a single crime, murder.[70] This was in line with judicial practice in Britain for the whole of the modern colonial period. In Britain, capital punishment was a contentious issue and was only abolished in 1965 after a long political struggle. The death penalty for offenses other than murder was introduced as an exception into one or two colonies, usually those with a sizable minority of white settlers and in response to a local panic, for assault and attempted rape of white women by Africans, the so-called "Black Peril" offenses. These crimes carried a capital sentence in Kenya from 1927 to 1955 and at various times in Basutoland and in colonial Natal.[71] Another exception was the use of the death sentence in times of emergency. Treason remained a capital offense in Britain and the colonies but was rarely invoked, even in wartime. In Kenya during the Mau Mau emergency, mandatory capital sentences were extended to offenses such as carrying firearms; as many as 1,083 people suffered the death penalty with a further 500 pardoned.[72] The Colonial Governor, as representative of the Crown, had absolute powers as to whether a death sentence should be carried out, although an appeal to a higher court, which might lead to the Privy Council itself in London, could place the power of reprieve in the hands of the Secretary of State.[73]

The most common form of capital punishment was hanging, although early in the twentieth century shooting was occasionally used in remoter areas.[74] Few colonial officials advocated the abolition of capital punishment although there was pressure to ensure that executions should not be held in public but behind prison walls, as had been the case in Britain since 1868. Nevertheless, in many parts of rural Africa well into the 1930s executions were carried out in public, sometimes at the scene of the crime in order to provide a stark deterrent message. An outbreak of what the Uganda government thought of as murderous crime in parts of the country in the early 1930s led to the reintroduction of public hanging.[75] In these circumstances a district officer might find himself with the responsibility of executing a convicted criminal, an unpleasant task that was frequently bungled and brutally performed.[76] But generally by the 1930s most capital sentences took place in government central prisons. Some colonies employed a regular hangman. For many years Northern Rhodesia did not, using either a jailer or a volunteer from the police who was paid ten pounds. The Fynn report in 1938 condemned "in the strongest possible terms the conditions under which this grave responsibility is carried out" and recommended the employment of a professional hangman.[77]

Alone among the native authority courts of British colonial Africa, those of Buganda and Northern Nigeria had powers to impose capital sentences until 1917 and 1936, respectively. The *Kabaka's* courts in Buganda had the power to impose death sentences according to customary law but the sentence was subject to confirmation by the protectorate government. In Northern Nigeria the Governor and the Chief Justice read through the proceedings but, since the accused did not have the benefit of counsel in the trial, this led some critics to argue that the government was failing to give "natives less than the British justice they had the right to expect."[78] Lugard laid down that executions by native authorities in Northern Nigeria "may be carried out in accordance with the local custom, by beheading or drowning, provided it is not contrary to humanity," an elastic interpretation of the principle of repugnancy that was not shared by all of his officials.[79] Dark practices by the emirs in disposing of enemies are hinted at in one or two of the memoirs of men who served as officials in Northern Nigeria during the Lugardian period.[80] Under the Northern Nigerian native authority system, persons convicted of capital crimes were invariably executed in public by beheading with a sword, a method only abolished in 1936.[81] According to one account from Sokoto, the convicted man entered a public area followed by the executioner who suddenly tripped him and as he fell expertly severed his head from his body.[82]

By the Second World War, all capital sentences were confined to within government central prisons. Following the war and with the evidence available from the British Royal Commission on Capital Punishment in 1948, there was added clamor for abolition of the death penalty not only in Britain but also in the colonies. Coming at a time when there was an increasing challenge to colonial rule, any demand for abolition was drowned out by officials who argued that it was an appropriate punishment for people in developing societies and needed to be retained for emergency situations. Kwame Nkrumah, while he was in prison for political activities in 1950–1951, recalled the somber day in most months when a prisoner was hanged:

These unfortunate men were brought in chains and were kept in solitary confinement away from the ordinary prisoners. We all knew when the day of execution arrived for we were made to get up earlier than usual and taken from our cell to an upstairs room where we were locked in before six o'clock. Some people used to try and peep through the window to see if they could catch a glimpse of what was going on, but it was quite impossible. By about ten o'clock we were let out and the only sign of the grim event was that there was sometimes an occasional bloodstain on the ground near where we went to have our ablutions, for the gallows was situated in the vicinity of the washroom. . . . There must have been on an average one execution a month during the time I was imprisoned and most of these men were hanged for killing their wives or for killing men who they had believed were having illicit relations with their wives.[83]

At the transfer of power, all of Britain's African colonies retained the death sentence on their statute books. In many of those former colonies since independence, the number of offenses carrying the death penalty have increased, as have the number of people put to judicial death.

REFORM

In the colonial period before the late 1940s, officials were concerned about reform of the penal system. Early policies and practices were introduced in a rule-of-thumb sort of way, pragmatic adaptations of what was done in Britain but in different circumstances and with different people who were perceived in a markedly different way. Reforms did occur because the system was so often *ad hoc*; abuses surfaced, reform-minded officials were alarmed, inquiries reported and improvements were implemented but usually very slowly and as limited resources allowed. Reform focused on regularizing as far as was practical the penal policies and practices of each colony and ensuring that they were not out of step with one another.

There were various questions that figured prominently in official thinking: how best to deter law breakers; how to limit the growth of a criminal class; how recidivists and also first offenders should be treated; what policies should be adopted to deal with women prisoners; what facilities should be provided for the criminally insane; and what measures should be introduced to deal with juvenile offenders? In a brief essay not all of these can be dealt with. Reform and rehabilitation of convicted men and women became an aim of the colonial prison services from early on, although the resources to implement adequate programs and to employ suitable staff were lacking. The professionalization of the colonial prison service was slow. In some colonies, prisons remained under the control of police well beyond 1930. Only in the interwar years were men and some women with experience in the British prison service increasingly advertised for and recruited to work in the colonies. Reformist ideas came from Britain but also from South Africa where the prison service was more developed and had been professionalized much earlier than in the territories to the north of the Limpopo. Certain ideas on rehabilitation emanated from South Africa, albeit ideas framed within the context of the needs of a white-dominated agrarian and manufacturing society, which helped influence thinking on prison policy and administration in British colonial Africa, most notably in Southern Rhodesia and Kenya.[84] Gradually, rehabilitation became a central part of prison activity with selected prisoners being taught craft and artisan skills by prison staff specifically employed for that role.

The question of juvenile offenders was important because young men—and the vast majority of offenders were males—posed special problems if placed in prisons with older and often practiced criminals. Current practice in Britain was to separate juveniles and attempt to rehabilitate them in order to prevent them from developing into persistent offenders. In the African colonies, this was also the concern of the authorities and various Christian missions, which played a prominent role in education and welfare services. A reformatory school was established in Kenya in 1909 and a modified "Borstal" system opened in 1924.[85] In the Gold Coast, the Salvation Army ran a home for delinquent boys at Ada, which was formally taken over by the Department of Social Welfare in 1946. A single, Borstal-type establishment, set up in Accra in 1940 for young men aged 17–21, provided some vocational training and formal education. The need for separate juvenile institutions was generally recognized, although the resources and the provision of proper facilities invariably lagged well behind intention. For example, in Uganda a reformatory was proposed in 1915, an ordinance to that effect passed in 1930, but the first school was not actually opened until 1951.

The other concerns of penal reformers—probation services, schemes for after-care of prisoners—only began to be implemented in the African colonies after 1945. Tanganyika introduced a small probation system only in 1951. As Hailey wrote in the mid-1950s: "European penal methods are now being gradually applied to African prisons. The conception of punishment is giving way to the ideas of rehabilitating the offender and training him to useful employment."[86] Such ideas cost money and, although this was in short supply, the principles of good government, humanity, and welfare economics demanded that the late colonial state should have a modern system for dealing with those who broke the law. But, as with much of colonial rule, changes came but slowly and then were too little and too late.

NOTES

1. C.E. Ward, *Roydon Hall Magazine* (Norfolk), Easter Term 1912, 91.

2. M. Mamdani, *Citizen and Subject: Contemporary Africa and the Legacy of Late Colonialism* (Princeton: Princeton University Press, 1996), 109. A gallows and a pillory were among the first constructions erected by the Spanish conquistadors in the Americas; see V.S. Naipaul, *The Loss of Eldorado* (New York: A.A. Knopf 1969; 2d ed. 1973), 35.

3. A recent volume of essays is by K. Mann and R. Roberts, eds., *Law in Colonial Africa* (Portsmouth, NH: Heinemann 1991). See also M.J. Hay and M. Wright, eds., *African Women & the Law: Historical Perspectives* (Boston: Boston University, African Studies Center, 1982).

4. A. Milner, *African Penal Systems* (London: Routledge & K. Paul, 1969); A. Milner, *Nigerian Penal System* (London: Sweet and Maxwell 1972); L.C. Kirchner, *The Kenya Penal System: Past, Present and Prospect* (Washington, DC: University Press of America, 1981).

5. The studies are numerous, of which these are but a sample: L. Radinowicz and R. Hood, *A History of English Criminal Law and its Administration from 1750, vol. 5. The Emergence of Penal Policy* (London: Stevens 1986). M. Ignatieff, *A Just Measure of Pain: The Penitentiary in the Industrial Revolution 1750–1850* (New York: Pantheon Book, 1978), M. Foucault, *Surveiller et Punir. Naissance de la prison* (Paris: Gallimard, 1975). Douglas Hay et al., *Albion's Fatal Tree. Crime and Society in Eighteenth-century England* (New York: Pantheon Books, 1975). P. Linebaugh, *The London Hanged. Crime and Civil Society in the Eighteenth Century* (Cambridge: Cambridge University Press, 1991). V.A.C. Gatrell, *The Hanging Tree. Execution and the English people 1770–1868* (Oxford: Oxford University Press, 1994). P. Spierenburg, *The Spectacle of Suffering: Executions and the Evolution of Repression* (Cambridge: Cambridge University Press, 1985).

6. See, for example, C. Clifton Roberts, *Tangled Justice. Some Reasons for a Change of Policy in Africa* (London: MacMillan and Co., 1937).

7. Milner, *Nigerian Penal System*, chap. 4.

8. See for example, F. Lugard, *Political Memoranda. Revision of instructions to political officers on subjects chiefly political and administrative 1913–18* (First edition 1906; 2d. edition 1919; reprinted London: F. Cass, 1970), part III, para. 30, 97–98: "Sentencing for crimes which are not offences under Native Law."

9. R.F.S. Tanner, "Penal practices in Africa: Some restrictions on the possibility of reform," *Journal of Modern African Studies* 10 (1972).

10. Lugard, *Political Memoranda*, Part VIII, para. 51, 289, "Punishments." The Native Courts Proclamation 1901, in Nigeria, stated that punishments should be "not repugnant to the natural justice or to the principles of the Law of England." Quoted by Milner, *Nigerian Penal System*, 22.

11. Milner, *Nigerian Penal System*, 23–27, 300–2.

12. *Commission on Native Punishment in Kenya (1923). Report on a Visit to the Prisons of Kenya, Uganda, Tanganyika, Zanzibar, Aden and Somaliland by Alexander Paterson, M.C.* (1939).

13. For example, Rhodes House Library, Oxford (hereafter RHL). Mss. Brit. Emp. 22 s. G136. Fry or Howard League to Harris, August 13, 1925, asking if someone were available to observe penal matters in the Gold Coast and Nigeria.

14. See the discussion by M. Chanock, *Law, Custom and Social Order. The Colonial Experience in Malawi and Zambia.* (Cambridge: Cambridge University Press, 1985), 5–6, 125ff.

15. *Northern Nigeria Annual Report 1902*, 29.

16. On colonial asylums for those deemed mentally ill, see M. Vaughan, "Idioms of Madness: Zomba Lunatic Asylum, Nyasaland, in the Colonial Period," *Journal of Southern African Studies* ix (1983), 218–38.

17. Tanner, "Penal practices," 451 n. 1.

18. F.K. Ekechi, *Tradition and Transformation in Eastern Nigeria. A Sociopolitical History of Owerri and its Hinterland, 1902–1947* (Kent, OH: Kent State University Press, 1989), 148.

19. Lord Hailey, *An African Survey Revised 1956* (London: Oxford University Press, 1957), 625. PRO. CO 859/379, "Problems of the relation between prison conditions and normal standards of living [1953–54]."

20. See Tanner, "The East African Experience of Imprisonment," in Milner, *African Penal Systems*, 293–315. There are few firsthand accounts by Africans of prison experience, other than those of political prisoners, but see G.S. Mwase, "Outward and Inward

of the Prison and Prisoners," in *Strike a Blow and Die* (Cambridge, Mass: Harvard University Press, 1967), 101–14.

21. Public Record Office, Kew (PRO). CO 583/87/29835, Minutes by A.J. Harding on Clifford to Milner, May 19, 1920, quoted by Ekechi, *Tradition and Transformation*, 148–49.

22. Ekechi, *Tradition and Transformation*, 149–50.

23. P.A. Igbafe, *Benin Under British Administration. The Impact of Colonial Rule on an African Kingdom 1897–1938* (Atlantic Highlands, NJ: Humanities Press, 1979), 214.

24. The great variety of penal structures, policies, and practices in native authorities can be seen in the 5 volumes of Lord Hailey, *Native Administration in the British African Territories* (London and New York: Oxford University Press, 1957).

25. C. Fyfe, *A History of Sierra Leone* (Oxford: Oxford University Press, 1962), 134.

26. R. Seidman, "The Ghana Prison System: Historical Perspectives," in Milner, *African Penal Systems*, 429–72.

27. On Nigeria, see Milner, *Nigerian Penal System*; and B. Awe, "History of the Prison System in Nigeria," in T.O. Elias, ed., *The Prison System of Nigeria* (Lagos: University of Lagos, 1965).

28. For example, by the Gold Coast Penal Ordinance 1876, all convicts serving sentences of two years or more were given marks that "he shall by hard and steady labour earn."

29. See *Rules and Standing Orders for the Government of Prisons, Sierra Leone* (Freetown: 1941), 8.

30. *Report on the Prison System in Northern Rhodesia and Recommendations for Reorganization* (Lusaka: 1938).

31. Quoted in I. Graham, "A History of the Northern Rhodesia Prison Services," *Northern Rhodesia Journal* V (1964), 558.

32. *Report on a Visit to the Prisons of Kenya, Uganda* (1939), which is a humane and well-written document.

33. European prisoners usually had separate accommodations in colonial prisons. This was a more urgent problem in white-settler colonies, although judges sometimes said that they would not give a white person a sentence of imprisonment if there were not suitable accommodations. In non-settler colonies, Europeans sentenced to prison might serve their sentences in the prison of a neighboring white-settler colony or in the United Kingdom.

34. J. Niel Leitch and M. Watson, *Beriberi and the Freetown Prison. A Report of an Investigation* (Freetown: 1930).

35. *Report on a Visit to the Prisons of Kenya, Uganda* (1939), 17–19. Hailey, *An African Survey* (London: 1938), 310–11.

36. C. Harwich, *Red Dust. Memories of the Uganda Police, 1935–55* (London: V. Stuart, 1961), 42; Hailey, *An African Survey Revised 1956*, 626.

37. On policing in British colonial Africa, see D. Killingray, "The Maintenance of Law and Order in British Colonial Africa," *African Affairs* 85 (1986), 411–37. D.M. Anderson and D. Killingray, eds., *Policing the Empire. Governments, Authority and Control, 1830–1940* (Manchester: Manchester University Press, 1991); D.M. Anderson and D. Killingray, eds., *Policing and Decolonisation. Nationalism, Politics and the Police, 1917–65* (Manchester: Manchester University Press, 1992).

38. Kwame Nkrumah, *The Autobiography of Kwame Nkrumah* (London: 1957), chap. 11, "Trial and imprisonment," provides an account of the inside of the prison at Cape Coast in 1950–1951.

39. G.H. Heaton, *Report on General Administration of Prisons and Detention Camps in Kenya*, July 1956. J. Mwangi Kariuki, *"Mau Mau" Detainee* (Oxford: Oxford University Press, 1963), offers a searing account of these camps.

40. Lord Lugard, *Political Memoranda*, Part VIII, para. 55, 290.

41. For a brief description of the large native authority prison in Kano, Northern Nigeria, which seems to have been well-regulated, see M. Perham, *Native Administration in Nigeria* (London 1937), pp. 97–98, and also her *West African Passage* (London and Boston: Peter Owen, 1983), 120. Hailey, An *African Survey*, 311.

42. PRO. CO 859/377. "Notes of Committee Chairman," February 25, 1952, attached to "Colonial Office Treatment of Offenders Sub-Committee," November 14, 1949.

43. PRO. CO 858/377. "Colonial Office Treatment of Offenders Sub-Committee," 14 November 1949.

44. PRO. CO536/190/40173, *Report of Prison Committee*, Entebbe, 1936.

45. *Uganda. Annual Report of the Prison Department for the Year ending 31 December 1946*, 18.

46. Lugard to Flora Shaw, April 7, 1906, in Margery Perham, *Lugard. II. The Years of Authority 1898–1945* (London: Collins, 1960), 199. Also Lugard, *Political Memoranda*, part VIII, para. 55, 290.

47. See the arguments of the Committee of the Legislative Council of Tanganyika, 1931, examined by J.S. Read, "Kenya, Tanzania and Uganda," in Milner, *African Penal Systems*, 112–13.

48. See W.R. Crocker, *Nigeria. A Critique of British Colonial Administration* (London: Allen & Unwin, 1935), 78–80 and 93, for examples of distraining goods. See R.L. Tignor, *The Colonial Transformation of Kenya. The Kamba, Kikuyu and Maasai from 1900 to 1939* (Princeton, NJ: Princeton University Press, 1976), 75–7, for examples of the use of the Stock Theft Ordinance of 1913 in Kenya.

49. Hailey, *An African Survey*, 628.

50. Crocker, *Nigeria*, 59.

51. Quoted by Read, "Kenya, Uganda and Tanganyika," in Milner, *African Penal Systems*, 111. See also the comments by Lt. Col. J.G. Kirkwood, a member of the Kenya Legislative Council in 1941, quoted in B. Berman and J. Lonsdale, *Unhappy Valley: Conflict in Kenya and Africa. Book One: State and Class* (London: James Currey, 1992), 107.

52. D. Killingray, "The 'Rod of Empire': The Debate over Corporal Punishment in the British African Colonial Forces, 1888–1946," *Journal of African History* 35 (1994), 203. Given that corporal punishment in various forms was so widely used in colonial Africa, it is surprising that so little scholarly attention has been directed to it. See D.M. Anderson, "Corporal Punishment and the 'Raw Native': Social Attitudes and Legal Action in Colonial Kenya, 1895–1932," paper given to the African History seminar, School of Oriental & African Studies, University of London, February 20, 1991. David Anderson is preparing a book on law, crime, and punishment in colonial Kenya. S. Peté, "Punishment and Race: The Emergence of Racially Defined Punishment in Colonial Natal," *Law and Society Review* (Natal), 1 (1986), 102–6. M.-B. Dembour, "La chicotte comme symbol du colonialisme belge?," *Canadian Journal of African Studies*, XXVI (1992), 205–23.

53. *Report on a Visit to the Prisons of Kenya, Uganda* (1939), 15.

54. This relatively minor incident is splendidly treated by M. Crowder, *The Flogging of Phinehas McIntosh. A Tale of Colonial Folly and Injustice, Bechuanaland 1933* (New Haven: Yale University Press, 1988). In the case of floggings of Southern Nigerians on the orders of native courts in Northern Nigeria, the Colonial Office predictably acted with far less alacrity.

55. Lugard, *Political Memoranda*, part VIII, para. 52, 289. Lugard, *The Dual Mandate in British Tropical Africa* (London 1922), 561–63; also p. 563, note 1, for speech by Governor Hugh Clifford, December 1920.

56. There are numerous instances of this, especially in the period before 1914; see Ekechi, *Tradition and Transformation*, chap. 3.

57. I. Duffield, "John Eldred Taylor and West African Opposition to Indirect Rule in Nigeria," *African Affairs* 70 (1971), 252–68. On the Bauchi case, I am grateful to Steven Pierce for his unpublished paper, "Punishment and the Political Body: Flogging and Colonialism in Northern Nigeria," presented to the Annual Meeting of the American Anthropological Association, Philadelphia, PA, December 5, 1998. As Pierce comments, in Northern Nigeria "the most frequent reasons women were flogged was for adultery (that is, married women's infidelity) and slander."

58. Chanock, *Law, Custom and Social Order*, 108.

59. I.F. Nicolson, *The Administration of Nigeria 1900–1960* (Oxford: Clarendon Press, 1969), 112.

60. Ekechi, *Tradition and Transformation*, 150–51.

61. On the 'flogged to death' case, see RHL. Mss. Brit. Emp. 22 s. G136. Also *House of Commons Debates*, February 26, 1924.

62. *Committee of Inquiry into the Administration of Justice in Kenya, Uganda and Tanganyika into Criminal Matters*, chaired by Sir Henry Grattan Bushe (1933), for which see Read, "Kenya, Tanzania and Uganda," in Milner, *African Penal Systems*, 110ff. Also H.F. Morris and J.S. Read, *Indirect Rule and the Search for Justice. Essays in East African Legal History* (Oxford: Clarendon Press, 1972), 95–96.

63. See Milner, *Nigerian Penal System*, chap. 11.

64. Milner, *Nigerian Penal System*, 297–302; Milner, *African Penal Systems*, 264–65.

65. Milner, *Nigerian Penal System*, 300.

66. Killingray, "The 'Rod of Empire,'" 214–16.

67. PRO. CO 859/387. 'Corporal Punishment Policy 1950–53." CO circular dispatch to colonial governors, August 1950.

68. PRO. CO 859/387 contains the three reports. See also CO 859/389, "Corporal Punishment Tanganyika," which contains a letter from Sir L. Fletcher to Lord Aberdare with the immortal postscript: "The African is only scared of one thing, a thrashing."

69. Hailey, *An African Survey*, 627.

70. For one colony, see R. Gocking, "Murder and Capital Punishment in the Gold Coast," unpublished paper presented at the 42nd Annual Meeting of the African Studies Association, Philadelphia, PA, November 11–14, 1999.

71. On the "Black Peril" in Southern Rhodesia, see P. Mason, *The Birth of a Dilemma* (Oxford: Oxford University Press, 1958), 246–53. The South African *Report on the Commission Appointed to Enquire into Assaults on White Women* (1913), was followed by similar legislation by the Australian administration in Papua, for which see A. Inglis, *The White Women's Protection Ordinance. Sexual Anxiety and Politics in Papua* (1974; published in Britain as *Not a White Woman Safe* [London: 1975]).

72. D.M. Anderson, "Capital Crimes, Colonial Law, and Human Rights: The Mau Mau Trials, Kenya 1952–58," unpublished paper given at the Sixth Stanford-Berkeley Symposium on Law and Colonialism in Africa, May 1999.

73. See A. Burns, *Colonial Civil Servant* (London: 1949), 168, 219ff. Burns was Governor of the Gold Coast, 1941–1947; in 1944 his administration was disturbed by a local murder that became an explosive political issue with reverberations in Britain. This case

is superbly discussed by R. Rathbone, *Murder and Politics in Colonial Ghana* (New Haven: Yale University Press, 1993).

74. W.R. Foran, *The Kenya Police 1887–1960* (London: R. Hale, 1962), 29–30.

75. Roberts, *Tangled Justice*, chap. XI "Public Executions—Capital Punishment."

76. For example, see H.A.L. Ward Price, *Dark Subjects* (London: Jarrolds, 1938), 90–91; D. Rooney, *Sir Charles Arden-Clarke* (London: R. Collins, 1982), 33–34; James Barber, *Imperial Frontier* (Nairobi: East African Pub. House, 1967), 207.

77. *Report on the Prison System in Northern Rhodesia*, 19.

78. W.N.M. Geary, *Nigeria Under British Rule* (London: Barnes and Noble, 1927), 280.

79. Lugard, *Political Memoranda*, Part VIII, para. 34, 280.

80. RHL. Mss. Afr. s. 1734 (111), Cromartie, 2, where he suggests that an emir's opponents may have been fed to the crocodiles.

81. Perham, *West African Passage*, 79 and 162.

82. "The Last Public Execution in Sokoto," in H.A.S. Johnston, ed., *A Selection of Hausa Stories* (Oxford: Clarendon Press, 1966), 167–69. It is worth remembering that public execution by the guillotine, albeit discreetly and very early in the morning, continued in France until 1939. A motion to abolish this "public spectacle of suffering" was defeated in the Chamber in 1908 by 334 votes to 210.

83. Nkrumah, *Autobiography*, 131.

84. See the two articles by L. Chisholm, "The Pedagogy of Porter: The Origins of the Reformatory in the Cape Colony, 1882–1910," *Journal of African History* 27 (1986), 481–95, and "Crime, Class and Nationalism: The Criminology of Jacob de Villiers Roos, 1869–1913," *Social Dynamics* 13 (1987), 46–59.

85. Borstals were prisons for young offenders, named after the first such institution opened at the village of Borstal, in Kent, in October 1902.

86. Hailey, *An African Survey*, 625.

6

COLONIAL URBANISM AND PRISONS IN AFRICA

Reflections on Conakry and Freetown,
1903–1960

Odile Goerg

In Africa, as elsewhere, colonial domination engendered new urban centers where administrative operations were headquartered. These towns were linked through a hierarchical network capped by the colony's administrative center *(chef-lieu)*. They were the sites of both organizational and repressive activities that were concretized in increasingly elaborate edifices. Various buildings symbolized colonial power: the main government hall; customs offices; schools; churches; hospitals; sometimes post offices; and always the military barracks and the prison, which were generally adjoining. What were the statuses and functions of these last two buildings with respect to urban colonial space, architectural models, and the repressive dimension of colonial domination? Did the reinforcement of colonial rule have an impact on their architectural evolution?

While the fortress represented the power of European trading posts on the African coast—combining military, commercial, and residential functions[1]— the military post gave birth to colonial towns or, if other forms of contact preceded colonization, served as points of spatial anchorage for the colonial enterprise.

The military post was the first symbol of new authority and lost sovereignty. From the outset, it included a jail. Two functions—military and repressive— were directly linked from the beginning of colonization. Initially, it was hard to distinguish between opposition to colonial domination, resistance to the new political order, and certain attitudes defined as transgressions of law. The new political masters put forth definitions of punishable misdemeanors and sanctions. Subsequently, various factors led to the separation of functions; the division of labor and the nomenclature of offenses became more precise, even though the garrison and the prison remained tightly bound. However, with the general decline of military power, the two places and their respective functions were increasingly disassociated.

These factors, derived from the organization of the penal system, were complemented by others associated with the process of urbanization. In the history of colonial towns, the military post and its annexes often preceded all effective domination and any concerted plans for the development of urban space. Therefore, the military post was not situated according to a general plan; it was located according to immediate needs and property rights issues or political dealings. Likewise, since the building itself was often constructed hastily and on an ad hoc basis, plans for a permanent structure were occluded. Because of this, the logic behind both the placement and the conceptualization of structures designated for repression was later challenged.

As in other domains, the tenets that guided the organization and construction of prisons in the colonial empire were inherited from the European metropole. These principles included notions about the scale of crimes and incarceration, definitions of misdemeanors and, more concretely, ideas about the very structure of the penitentiary building. The ideological and intellectual movement that renewed approaches to these questions in Europe, being motivated at first by the Enlightenment and, later, by the urban and industrial developments of the nineteenth century, influenced ideas and practices. It led to the institutionalization of new norms and mentalities among colonial administrators.[2] These were characterized by a decline in physical punishment, the application of prison sentences for the most serious misdemeanors, incarceration as a means of dissuasion and correction, a clear distinction between the prison and the outside world, and the institutionalization of rules and regulations inside prisons (clothing, schedules, food, hierarchies of authority). To what extent were these practices transposed directly from the metropolitan schema onto colonial situations? And to what extent were they adapted to the specific cases of diverse colonial societies?

Conakry (French Guinea) and Freetown (Sierra Leone) provide responses to these questions in the remarks that follow. These two case studies are interesting because they offer two discrete examples. The first city, founded in the 1880s, is a direct artifact of the late nineteenth century. The second is a century-old town that reflects the long-term evolution of penal practices that crossed the Atlantic at a rather late date due to lack of financial means. This chronological gap also refers to differing origins and modes of populating towns. While Freetown resulted from a philanthropic gesture linked to the struggle for abolition of the slave trade, Conakry was created during the imperialist phase of the partition of Africa. Freetown was populated in a more complex manner than Conakry, with diverse identities—from the first settlers (Black poor, Nova Scotians, and Maroons) to the liberated Africans or "re-captives"—being progressively integrated into a common culture. This latter category, called Sierra Leoneans, Creole, or Krio, was contrasted with those officially categorized as "Aborigines" (Mende, Temne). Krio discourse on delinquency, colonial justice, and repression—most notably, imprisonment—is worth analyzing. The Krio had high regard for the judicial profession and willingly appealed to colonial justice.[3] Furthermore, they often looked upon migrants from the interior, or the Aborigines, with incomprehension or even disdain, which stemmed from their ignorance about these people and their lifestyle. The Aborigines were subjected to the justice exercised by their "tribal headman," except in the case of very serious transgressions. We will not dwell on this last point, however, since this study is concerned with space relations and strategies for localizing penitentiary structures in the history of colonial urbanism.

Far from being exceptions, both Conakry and Freetown, having being con-firmed *mutatis mutandis* by other cases, are representative of the entire co-lonial empire.

THE PRISON: AN APPENDIX TO THE MILITARY POST

In the beginning was the military post. Over time, it accrued new forms of authority associated with colonization.[4] As colonial domination was affirmed, the post evolved from its situation as an entrenched fort in a hostile environment.

In Conakry, the French post was erected in a context where the European presence was sparse. In the 1880s, only two French commercial houses op-erated on the peninsula of Tumbo: the future *Compagnie française de l'Afrique occidentale*[5] and the Maillat establishments (as well as the German concern, Colin F. and Cie). Tumbo was not a significant commercial center—Freetown dominated just 150 kilometers away—rather, it was an area of po-tential development. Tumbo was populated by three villages, with approxi-mately 300 inhabitants. These were loosely connected to the confederation of Dubreka, which led a resistance movement against the French.[6]

In this turbulent context, which was aggravated by problems related to succession in the chiefdom of Dubreka, the French representative obtained land for the construction of a post. However, matters relating to land tenure proved more complicated than anticipated because African leaders were now conscious of the real stakes in European claims. While the administrators expected the cessation of the whole western part of Tumbo[7] in return for a "nice gift" *(un beau cadeau),*[8] its demarcation was not without difficulties. Agreement on a parcel measuring fifteen acres (slightly enlarged sometime later) was finally made in 1886.[9] For reasons of defense, the post was situated inland, halfway between the towns of Conakry and Boulbinet. Shortly thereafter, in 1887, the French bombed villages and announced the outright annexation of the peninsula, thus making use of the land as they saw fit.

The post was initially maintained on the original site. On the schematic but in other ways detailed map of its emplacement (indicating, for example, the positioning of wells and certain trees), the administrator Péreton does not mention the building that was used as a prison in 1889. He only makes note of the post since this structure combined military, repressive, and political functions.[10] Administrative sources give little precise information on the installation of the post, but effective prison operations are indirectly revealed by reference to the use of prisoners as laborers. At a time when France was questioning the penal colonies and forced labor, the interned were used for works contributing to the general good. Forced laborers were in no short supply, since the French had just arrived and there were no public works enterprises in the new town of Conakry. Although the French authorities were barely installed at the end of the 1880s, the administrator of Conakry made reference to the clearing of the peninsula of Tumbo, which was undertaken by penal laborers.[11] This practice continued. The road that ran along the periphery of the peninsula was built in 1901 using prisoners who were supervised by professional construction workers. Completed in 1906, this *corniche*, with coconut and palm trees along its borders, was the preferred spot for promenades in Conakry.[12] When infrastructure installations were terminated, the prisoners were used principally for cleanup work, such as garbage collection.[13]

At the time when the French sought to establish their definitive presence, a new site was selected in 1889 for the governor's residence. This was to be situated on the seaside (for reasons of ventilation) on land that extended from the parcel obtained in 1886. Encapsulated in a building plan titled "Cadastral Plan and Project for the Alignment of the Town of Conakry," which was put into effect in the spring of 1890,[14] the old [military] post found itself not far from the governor's residence in the heart of the newly built city (lot 25). This initial locale was reserved for repressive functions: surveillance (militia, police) and punishment (prison). The administrative organization of these different services went hand in hand with the specialization of space, which now entailed the juxtaposition of militia and police forces. The buildings housing the militia and prison (lot 25) adjoined those occupied by the *tirailleurs* (lot 9), not far from the parade grounds (lot 20bis [see Map 6.1]).[15]

Conakry's first prison, as an entity differentiated in space and by function, was built in several phases from 1892 to 1896.[16] A police precinct was constructed in 1898. No special materials or construction techniques were utilized in creating these first buildings due to time constraints and their ultimate uses. Although indispensable to colonial power, they were not considered to be prestigious structures. The use of wood for reasons of cost was not, in the

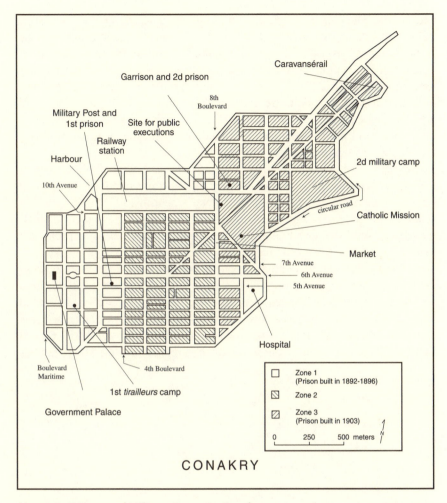

Map 6.1. Prisons and Military Camps in Conakry.

end, a wise decision; it was often prey to fires and termites. Built rapidly, the precinct was attacked by insects in spite of its rock foundation 1.4 meters high. All the wood had to be replaced by iron, which was an ideal but more expensive material; and the ceiling and roof also had to be redone.[17] The lack of originality in the construction of this building is not specific to Conakry. A. Sinou notes the same phenomenon in Saint-Louis of Senegal: the prison was part of the civil infrastructures that did not need "architectural marking."[18] Their function sufficed to specify them.

During this first phase, methods for surveillance, policing, and repression were increasingly systematized and fine-tuned. In 1899, the militia consisted of twenty-four people (twenty of whom were basic militiamen, paid 40 francs per month). The police included a commissioner, a deputy sergeant, and nine indigenous agents who were ex-militiamen known for their irreproachable behavior (compensated 55 francs per month). The ex-militiamen were to report incidents committed in public places (slaughterhouse, dog pound, market) on a daily basis. They were given uniforms that would heighten their authority: a dolman, blue duffel pants with braids and red piping, a fez, and a belt equipped with a sword-bayonet.[19] These thirty people, who were potentially aided by the *tirailleurs* stationed on the peninsula, were to supervise the 10,000–15,000 inhabitants of Conakry.

The repressive arsenal included prison sentences, which, in this same year (1899), totaled over 50 percent of correctional sanctions imposed.[20] This trend became even more marked a few years later when, in 1902, there were 178 prison sentences for 233 incidents involving 250 accused persons.[21] In 1901, the prison could shelter a hundred of detainees, and its judicial capacity extended beyond the town of Conakry.

As in Conakry, the first detention site in Freetown was located in the very confines of the old fort (Fort Thornton), which, situated on a hillside, had served as the residence of the director of the Sierra Leone Company. (See Map 6.2.) This coupling of the power to command and the power of repression was thus normalized. After the subjugation of the colony by the British Crown in 1808, Freetown became a base for the struggle against the slave trade as

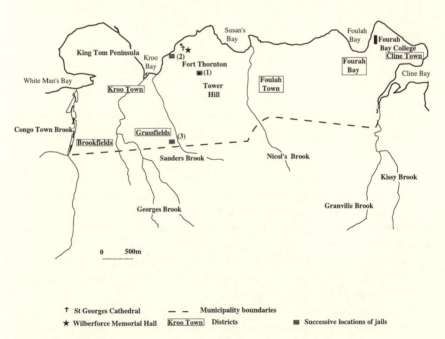

Map 6.2. Jails in Freetown.

well as a maritime tribunal. At this time, a separate building was erected in response to the new functions of the city. This building housed a court of justice and the prison. It was situated, along with the colonial hospital, in the enclosure where freed slaves landed. This ensemble was set on the waterfront, near the administrative zone and King Jimmy's wharf. This building, constructed of stone and finalized in 1816 under Governor Charles MacCarthy, was to endure until 1914, a testament to the technical mastery of the local artisans and builders. However, it proved ill-adapted to what colonizers expected of a detention center. Despite repeated complaints of filth and promiscuity, the prison was not improved for lack of funds. The only significant alteration was the relocation of the tribunal in 1862, which made room for the prison and physically separated judiciary and repressive functions. The barracks, which for sanitary and defensive reasons was relocated to the hills overlooking the city, remained disassociated from the prison, which sat virtually in the heart of Freetown.

FROM THE CENTER TO THE PERIPHERY: THE IMPERATIVES OF NEW URBAN PLANNING AT THE TURN OF THE TWENTIETH CENTURY

Situated just a few hundred meters from the seat of government (*Hôtel du gouvernement*), Conakry's prison, being set in an administrative and residential zone, confronted the great expansion of the city. It was eventually transferred out of the European zone, in accordance with the principles of colonial urbanism formulated at the end of the nineteenth century. These set forth the idea of the division of colonial towns into zones defined by different categories of people. This new urban policy was based on notions of order, hygiene, and the functionality of neighborhoods.

Evidently, this plan for segregation required resettlement, which was typically justified by arguments relating to sanitation and culture.

> The question of knowing whether or not, in colonial cities, it is best to seek to separate the indigenous element from the European gives rise to long discussions. Our judgment on this point is affirmative; the health of the European requires a lifestyle, infrastructures, and hygienic measures that the indigenous people, to their advantage, forgo. . . . Moreover, the separation of white houses and indigenous bungalows tends to happen naturally. It is best, in our opinion, to encourage it.[22]

Certain legislative acts concretized and formalized distinctions between types of neighborhoods. These existed previously, hidden between the lines of discourse and sometimes practiced in reality. Thus administrative and commercial zones, where Europeans lived due to the proximity between place of work and residence, were juxtaposed to the streets inhabited by Africans. This trend remained implicit; it was not instituted by official doctrine, even though it came through in official vocabulary at an early date. In 1889 we find the expression, "European center,"[23] while in 1899 we find "European town" and "indigenous town," both of which were used quite naturally.[24] The lots surrounding the government seat were logically consecrated to administrative functions (the secretary-general's office, the court, the public works office, the post office, the printing press) or religious activities (the two Catholic missions), the two domains being directly linked before the separation of church and state. The lots located near the port were devoted to commerce and customs; both were joined to the administrative center by a boulevard speckled with the most prestigious businesses. This functional division of space was institutionalized by the official partition of the city (1901–1905) into zones according to financial criteria.

With the expansion of the city, this practice also involved the progressive displacement to the city outskirts of activities thought to be noxious or too space-intensive. Thus the prison was reconstructed in the early twentieth century at the other end of the peninsula. The prison was relocated far from the centers of power to a third "indigenous" zone beyond the eighth boulevard (lot 86) (see Map 6.1). This zone was still thinly populated. However, it attracted many migrants who were strangers to urban life and could benefit from the lax property rights practiced in this area.[25]

Following the same logic, a camp for the *tirailleurs* was constructed from 1899 to 1902. Its location was moved from lot 3 (next to the government) to the end of sixth Avenue, on the waterfront (lots 101–102),[26] as was the new lazaret, which was erected at the end of a promontory, beyond the cemeteries. These buildings remained close to the European zone, but they were very isolated. This new policy of transferring so-called baneful activities to the urban periphery is not specific to the colonial situation. It was also practiced in metropolitan France, being the result of late nineteenth-century values that called for the relocation of cemeteries, prisons, and hospitals away from city centers.

In Conakry, the land once occupied by the prison became the main office for a precinct station (transferred, after World War I, to lot 45, to the heart of the African town). Transfers of police forces were also inscribed in space: The *tirailleurs* gave over their locale to the circumscription's guards in the 1920s, and then to the gendarmes (lots 9 and 20bis).[27] Repressive and surveillance activities remained, then, on the same spot even though they took on new, modernized, forms.

In Conakry, the construction of new sites of repression far from the center of town took place according to precise plans and budgetary considerations. This was the case for the barracks in 1901–1902 and, after 1903, the prison.[28] The site across from the prison (lot 87) was devoted to public executions presided over by a Mende (Sierra Leone) henchman named Samawa until the 1920s. Such executions were outlawed—rather belatedly with respect to the metropole—due to the emotions that they provoked. The prison remained in operation for the entire colonial period and still functions today. In 1905, the construction of the penitentiary (at Fotoba on the Los islands off of Conakry, ceded to France by Britain in 1904) represented a more radical eviction, since its jurisdiction was so extensive. Indeed, it consolidated all prisoners of French West Africa serving sentences of more than five years.[29]

The expulsion of the prison beyond the confines of the urban center was standard practice in the French empire during times of rapid development. The city's size was the fundamental parameter for this practice, often determining whether or not the prison was to remain downtown, near centers of power. Thus, in small towns and administrative centers, the prison generally remained close to the district officer's residence, since he presided over justice and utilized prisoners for tasks such as hauling water, emptying latrines, and agricultural work in government fields. On the other hand, relocation was imminent for all towns that reached a certain demographic level. Initially set under the administrative gaze, the prison was then relocated to the confines of the allotted zone, as in the case of Grand Bassam, the capital of the Ivory Coast from 1893 to 1899.[30] After several years however, this process could lead to the placement of the prison in a densely populated area that, often being recently inhabited, was a popular and not an administrative neighborhood. However, this latter scenario was less frequent since few colonies made heavy investments in real estate beyond the initial period of intense construction activity.[31] In certain large cities, the extension of the agglomeration and prison overpopulation led to the doubling of penal infrastructures after the Second World War.

This general logic of displacement and construction was easily contravened for insufficient financing, lack of urgency, or practical reasons. Thus the new prison in Lomé was erected in 1904 in the heart of the city so as to preserve its proximity to the residence of the district officer, who rendered justice. The French maintained this placement due to the proximity of the tribunal. The prison, surrounded by a large wall, still functions today.[32]

In Freetown, which presents a different social and political context, the prison was also transferred toward the edge of the city after a century of spatial continuity. During this time, the city had grown to more than 30,000 inhabitants. It was only in 1914—rather late, relatively speaking—that a new building, still in operation today, was erected at the end of Pademba Road on the outskirts of the municipality, far from the city center. Since a new European residential quarter (Hill Station, the construction of which began in 1904) had been built within six miles from the city, the old city center was less attractive to the colonists. Moreover, public real estate investments remained very low in Freetown after the founding phase of construction at the beginning of the nineteenth century. At this time, the old prison was demolished and the cleared land was used to enlarge the hospital. Here, the use of space followed the same logic as in Conakry, being driven by the dilapidated state of the first prison and demographic growth.

NEW EDIFICES, NEW PENITENTIARY PRACTICES

The construction of new buildings for incarceration resulting from the relocation policies put into practice at the turn of the twentieth century took place at the height of the colonial period. Their designs testify to the will to omnipotent surveillance that was true to Enlightenment formulae and internal logic of organization that reflected the hierarchy of colonial society.

The transfer of the Conakry prison was justified by combined arguments about limited space and the disadvantages of its placement in the middle of the "European neighborhood."

> The construction, built in summary manner from 1892 to 1896 to serve as the Conakry prison, [has] become, during these last years, absolutely insufficient for the prisoners, who number about one hundred. Also, since the building is now situated in the heart of the European neighborhood, the administration has decided to construct a new prison in a more removed neighborhood and following a well-defined comprehensive plan.[33]

This program was part of a plan for the reorganization of the police forces: "Given the close relationships between the police services, the militia, and the prison, we decided to add barracks for the militiamen to the prison, as well as a home for the commissioner *(commissaire régisseur)*." These buildings were constructed with the utmost care, the militia's barracks being graced with a central pavilion.

> The pavilion has three rooms on the first floor, a warehouse, an office for the prison manager, and a room for the guards. On the second floor, four rooms served as lodgings. Two galleries running three meters wide dominate the large façades on both the ground floor and the second story. This building is done entirely in masonry: the second-story floor is done with iron and concrete, with tiling set in cement; the roof is corrugated iron on a timber framework; ventilation is obtained through bull's-eye holes in the side walls and skylights.[34]

This main building was adorned with two ground-level wings that were used for lodging, or twelve rooms for families and two large rooms for bachelors. This was far from the improvisations of the first installations; here, the aims were permanence and efficiency. Nonetheless, if the prisons are given pride of place on all maps of colonial cities, the buildings themselves seem to have been lacking in architectural originality (in contrast to most colonial structures). Questions of function, security, and practicality continued to override in the case of the prison. Thus, for the new prison in Conakry: "The whole project involves a prison in the form of a cross with four branches which each form a separate pavilion running 17 meters wide by 37 meters long. At the intersection of these four buildings, there are plans for a hall running 16 meters sideways, topped with a roof that dominates the other pavilions to facilitate surveillance."[35]

The builders were inspired by the nineteenth-century idea of the central eye of the panopticon elaborated by Bentham in 1787–1791.[36] This same plan existed in other colonies. In the Ivory Coast, for instance, a prison plan for the circumscriptions dated 1931 reiterates the idea of a central tower, which was a sort of kiosk from which one could view all points.[37] The prison in Abidjan included a spiral staircase situated between two buildings organized around two courtyards; its upper landing was to serve as a watchtower.

While this plan was not specific to the colonial world, it was nonetheless minimally adapted to the tropics. For instance, much care went into providing for ventilation, which had to accommodate small size for reasons of security: "Ventilation of the prison pavilions will be assured by large openings in the side walls and barred transoms placed high enough to prevent the sun and rain from entering; porch roofs will be used on every large façade."

This newfound concern for construction coincided with serious deliberations over the internal organization of buildings at a time when the slowly evolving judicial system had matured. Prisoners were separated by sex and sentencing, as in metropolitan France, as well as by function of their penal status, a practice specific to colonial prisons. This illustrates the transposition of a segregationist mentality to all levels of colonial policy. Indeed, this reflects the existence of diverse, parallel codes of justice. Thus, in the French colonial system, distinctions were made between those "condemned by European justice" and those "condemned by indigenous justice." The condemned of the latter category were divided according to their status in the colonial system and the nature of their crime. In Abidjan, the first courtyard, located just behind the entryway and the prison director's lodgings, was designated for Europeans and assimilated persons, as well as women and political detainees. The second set of buildings consisted of simple cells, differentiated for those condemned by the war counsel and those condemned by indigenous chiefs. Those condemned by the war counsel had access to a toilet and individual showers, while prisoners with the "indigenous" status had to use the communal bathrooms situated in the middle of the courtyard. Likewise, the indigenous kitchen was separated from the European kitchen. The prison faithfully reproduced the status hierarchy of colonial society. What happened, however, to the distinction between the condemned and the accused? Did the expeditious manner of colonial justice lead to confusion between the two in one site of detention? Unfortunately, the documents we consulted do not specifically address this question.

The analysis of penal practice in Conakry reveals the concomitant development of rules for the construction of buildings and codes regulating prisons at the turn of the twentieth century. Beyond the imperatives of security, principles of order, hygiene, and the separation of types of people determined the new organization of colonial spaces of incarceration. As we have noted, these principles were hardly different from those found in metropolitan France.

An examination of secular penitentiary practice in Freetown highlights the passage from a typically pre-industrial approach to incarceration to the application of new norms inspired from the metropole. We can thus juxtapose the stability of structures to accommodating methods for incarceration over time. Initially, the internal organization of the prison was as follows: The first floor was consecrated to the mass of prisoners, the second floor to debtors (offenders having a separate status inherited from the justice system of the old regime) and guards' living quarters, and the third floor to the court of justice. As in Europe at the beginning of the nineteenth century, this space also sheltered the mentally ill whose social and medical statuses were still fairly undetermined. Generally speaking, the prisoners could circulate freely in the interior of the edifice and in the courtyard, which was closed off by walls. For economic reasons and in order to occupy the prisoners in a constructive manner, the prisoners were chained and employed in public works projects along roads or in the government quarry.[38]

In keeping with the reform process unfolding in Europe, modifications in the prison system evolved little by little. In 1836, people considered mentally insane were transferred to the colonial hospital; in 1862, the tribunal was transferred outside of the detention center. This relieved the congested and overpopulated building somewhat, but it was insufficient for the application of the principle of separation of detainees. The very concept of imprisonment was transformed by the policies of Governor Arthur Edward Kennedy during his second term from 1868 to 1872. Being the former administrator of the penal colony of Australia, Kennedy was particularly interested in penitentiary practice. Encouraged by a succession of secretaries of state who wanted to spread new metropolitan ideas to the colonies, he attempted to modify lax behavior by instituting a disciplinary regimen for the prison and imposing forced labor. In brief, Kennedy did not want to make the prison an adequate place of stay, to which detainees returned for refuge. Instead, he wished to make the prison a place that marked prisoners with the seal of social disgrace. His reform plan called for the pejoration of the dietary regime and the elimination of corporal punishment, such as the whip and shackles, in favor of physical exercises.[39] The treadmill was reestablished: "Close by, over a high wall, a huge fan-like windmill is grinding its useless way with well-greased throbs. This is the treadmill of the prison, and eight men, stripped to their loins, and perspiring from the result of such labor, are doing their ten minutes on, to cause that revolving shutter to spin round."[40]

Otherwise, the progressive separation of prisoners by sex and types of sentence was enabled by the acquisition of another building, in 1869, situated on the King Tom Peninsula outside the city center. Seen as a house of correction, the authorities imprisoned women, juveniles, and those serving a first sentence in this new location. They brought an experienced prison guard over from Europe, but he died soon after arriving and his successor sank into alcoholism. In the end, Kennedy named a captain from the first West India Regiment to head the prison.[41] But these efforts waned during the following years, as the description of the late 1880s shows. The small size of the prison, which held about 300 people, did not allow for strict application of the separation of detainees by category; and yet other, previous practices continued:

> The prison is one difficult to manage, the building being so small that no solitary system can be carried out; and what is still more disadvantageous, through want of accommodation, batches of prisoners have to occupy the same cell, while the prison yard is so littered with benches, tables, and kitchen buildings that it is impossible to maintain anything beyond the merest show of discipline.
>
> The youth incarcerated for his first offence, probably a minor one, is drafted into the same gang as the hardened convict. The murderer, and the repeatedly-convicted thief, mix not only with those doing penance for less serious offences, but with untried men who are compelled to occupy the same yard until the sessions come which decide their fate.[42]

Only political prisoners had their own quarters in the guardians' area. Therefore, while preserving an obsolete building, penal practice was slowly brought into line with the new expectations of the second half of the nineteenth century. The example of Freetown confirms the direct relationships that existed between the location of the prison, its design, and the evolution of judicial practice.

CONCLUSION

In the penal domain, as in many others, the colonizers grafted European practices onto African societies. Although this assertion must be nuanced with regard to judicial codes that distinguished offenders according to status, it is clear that prison sentences, designs for spaces of incarceration, and principles regulating the installation of prisons in space were all transferred without much adaptation. The colonizers introduced the European repressive arsenal in a seemingly unconscious manner. The prison was thus the preeminent site of punishment alongside more expeditious techniques such as corporal punishment, which was the basis of laws applied to indigenous peoples in the French system *(indigénat)*. Reserved, in fact, for the most serious crimes or for those who escaped the "indigenous" label, the prison was a pre-eminent structure in all important cities and administrative centers. In very large agglomerations, prisons were eventually detached from the head offices of circumscriptions. Deemed indiscreet and potentially dangerous in city centers,[43] they were relegated to the outer limits of political space, even though they were simultaneously improved through new techniques of construction. Far from the improvisations of the early years, the prison building came to symbolize solidity, permanence, and the authority of colonial powers. Likewise, the internal hierarchy of detainees according to status and sentencing was refined as well.

The evolution of places of incarceration in terms of architecture, placement in urban space, and internal organization was largely transferred from European metropolitan centers during the nineteenth century. The colonial dimension was only a secondary influence on these developments.

NOTES

1. A. Hyland, *"Le Ghana,"* in J. Soulillou, ed., *Rives coloniales. Architectures, de Saint-Louis à Douala* (Paris: Parenthèses/ORSTOM, 1993), 135–70.

2. M. Foucault, *Surveiller et punir. Naissance de la prison* (Paris: Gallimard, 1975); M. Ignatieff, "State, Civil Society and Total Institutions: A Critique of Recent Social Histories of Punishment" in S. Cohen and A. Scull, eds., *Social Control and the State* (New York: St. Martin's Press, 1983), 75–105; M. Perrot, ed., *L'impossible prison. Recherches sur le système pénitentiaire au XIXe siècle* (Paris: Seuil, 1980).

3. O. Goerg, "Sierra Leonais, Créoles, Krio: La dialectique de l'identité," *Africa* 65, no. 1 (1995), 114–32.

4. A. Sinou, "Les moments fondateurs de quelques villes coloniales," *Cahiers d'études africaines* 21, nos. 81–83 (1981), 373–88.

5. Heir to the Verminck family enterprise, this public company was created in 1881, acquiring its final status in 1887. First titled *Compagnie du Sénégal et de la Côte Occidentale d'Afrique*, the enterprise was eventually renamed *Compagnie française de l'Afrique occidentale*.

6. As of February 1, 1885, Bayol, the lieutenant-governor of the *Rivières du Sud* obtained the chief of Dubreka's signature to an additional clause to the 1880 treaty, ceding coastal territories.

7. *Archives nationales de Guinée (ANG)*, 2 B 2, Péreton, district officer of Dubréka district, to the governor of the *Rivières du Sud* district, July 15, 1885.

8. ANG, 2 B 1, Governor Ballot, July 31, 1885.

9. ANG 2 B 2, Letter of the district officer Ly, Dubréka district, to the governor of *Rivières du Sud*, November 7, 1886.

10. *Archives nationales du Sénégal* (ANS), 7 G 3, Péreton to Governor, September 10, 1889.

11. Ibid.

12. ANS, 2 G 2/9, Annual report 1902, 67, "*construction de la route circulaire.*"

13. ANS, 2 G 9/2, Annual report 1909. This is not specific to Guinea; prisoners were also used for similar tasks in Lomé. Chained during the time of German Togo, they were liberated from their shackles by the English (I am thankful to Yves Marguerat for this reference).

14. *Archives nationales, section outre-mer (Aix-en-Provence)* (ANSOM), Guinée XII, d. 3, correspondance of lieutenant-governor Cerisier, to the secretary of state for the colonies, June 7, 1890.

15. Maps: ANSOM, Guinée XIX D. 1b 1894 inspection Hoarau-Desruisseaux; ANSOM AF 1378: "*Konakry. Ville et port;*" Famechon LMF, "La ville de Conakry en 1900" in *Notice sur la Guinée française* (Paris: Alcan-Lévy, 1900).

16. *Comptes définitifs de la Guinée française* for 1892: expenditure of 5,327 francs, or 2.8% of the post for "new construction, maintenance, repairs." The report for the year of 1899 refers to the enlargement of the prison for a total of 2,500 francs.

17. ANS, 2 G 2/9, Annual report 1902, 74.

18. A. Sinou, *Comptoirs et villes coloniales du Sénégal* (Paris: Karthala/ORSTOM, 1993), 140.

19. ANS 2 G 1/40, Annual report 1899, 42–43.

20. Ibid., 100 cases of which 53 were prison sentences (39 for theft and complicity to theft, 1 for cutting down a tree).

21. ANS, 2 G 2/9, Annual report 1902. The verdicts included 77 prison sentences for 1 day to 3 months, 73 sentences for 3 months to 1 year, 25 sentences for 1 to 3 years, and 3 sentences for 3 to 5 years. There were also 58 fines and 14 acquittals.

22. ANSOM, Public Works, c. 147, d. 4, report signed by Fontaneilles, October 30, 1901, 35.

23. ANSOM, Guinée XII, d. 1, letter signed by the governor of Senegal, September 1, 1889, asking to prepare "an adjustment project, for the proposed European center on the site which has become the seat of the government of the *Rivières du Sud.*"

24. ANS 2 G 1/40, Annual report, 111.

25. O. Goerg, "Conakry: un modèle de ville coloniale française? Règlements fonciers et urbanisme, 1885—années 1920," *Cahiers d'études africaines* 25, no. 3, (1987), 309–35; O. Goerg, *Pouvoir colonial, municipalités et espaces urbains. Conakry-Freetown des années 1880 à 1914*, vol. 2 (Paris: L'Harmattan, 1997), 107–13 and 147–56.

26. It is interesting to note that this same process was not applied to Dakar, where the hospital was maintained on its original site, the Plateau, not far from the governor general's residence. It is true that the hospital in Dakar had been established on a well-ventilated site at the end of a promontory. Begun in 1880, after the yellow fever epidemic of 1878 that had overburdened the medical facilities at Gorée, the hospital opened in 1890 and enlarged several times. Le Dantec hospital, originally established for the *tirailleurs*, was erected on the same site in 1914.

27. G. Ternaux, *La Guinée française; ses origines, son administration actuelle, ses gouverneurs, son commerce, ses cercles* (Conakry: G. Ternaux, 1910); includes a map.

28. Final accounts for 1901: 750 francs [FF] for the police barracks. Final accounts for 1902: 99,918 FF for the militia's barracks. Final accounts for 1903: 64,559 FF for the prison. Final accounts for 1906: 61,938 FF for the prison enclosure and annexes. Final accounts for 1911: improvements on the prison. Between the two world wars, a wall was built by Jacquemin-Berguet, the mayor-administrator in 1935 (interview with E. Tompapa, February 1, 1989, Conakry).

29. Chérif Mamadou Dian Diallo, "Histoire de la répression pénitentiaire en Guinée française (1900–1958)," (*Thèse de l'université, Université de Paris-7*, 1998).

30. F. Doutreuwe, *Architecture coloniale en Côte d'Ivoire* (Abidjan: Ministère des Affaires culturelles/DEDA, 1985), 156. This is also the case for Grand Lahou, cf. ibid., 106–8.

31. This point should be analyzed city by city, according to the possibilities and financial choices made during the FIDES, for example.

32. Communication by Yves Marguerat.

33. ANS 2 G 2/9, Annual report 1902, 49–50, includes a photo of the barracks and the precinct as well as a map; ANSOM, T.P., box 147, d. 4, Report of October 30, 1901, by Fontaneilles.

34. General report for *Guinée française*, 1902, 49–50.

35. Ibid. Materials were also selected for their solidity: "This prison is to be built with masonry using local stone, concrete and cement floors, reinforced concrete ceilings like those of the Ballay hospital, corrugated iron roof, room height of 4.50 meters on a 0.50 meter foundation." The same was true in Abidjan, where the solidity of structure was insisted upon: "The foundations were made of laterite rubble stone, the walls of cement bricks, the coating of cement. Iron bars on the windows, doors made of two layers of perpendicular wood planks reinforced with bars and sashes were designed to prevent escapes. The heavy outside door, made entirely of iron and thick metal sheets also gave the impression of unshakeable solidity. The framework was made of wood and the roof of machine-made tiles." Doutreuwe, *Architecture coloniale*, 231.

36. Foucault, *Surveiller et punir*, 228 ff. J. Bender, *Imagining the Penitentiary: Fiction and the Architecture of Mind in Eighteenth-Century England* (Chicago: University of Chicago Press, 1987).

37. Doutreuwe, *Architecture coloniale*, 230.

38. R.F. Burton, *Wanderings in West Africa*, vol. 1 (London: Tinsley Brothers, 1863), 204, who refers to detainees who appeared unfriendly, identifiable as such by the marking "convict" on their backs. See also, C. Fyfe, *A History of Sierra Leone* (Oxford: Oxford University Press, 1962), 302 and 361.

39. The latter were both difficult and pointless. For example, Kennedy introduced the "shot drill," which involved moving balls from one pile to another as in a form of military exercise.

40. G.A. Lethbridge Banbury, *Sierra Leone, or the White Man's Grave* (London: Swan Sonnenschein & Co., 1889), 155. The author, who was a colonial administrator in Sierra Leone during the 1880s, gives a very detailed description of the prison and penal practices while others, like T.J. Alldridge—an otherwise verbose man—writing *A Transformed Colony. Sierra Leone, its Progress, Native Customs and Undeveloped Wealth* (London: Seeley & Co., 1910) does not even mention the building.

41. These facts are taken from Fyfe, *A History of Sierra Leone*, 134, 229, 302, 360 and 608.

42. Lethbridge Banbury, *Sierra Leone*, 156.

43. See H. Diabaté, *La marche des femmes sur Grand Bassam* (Dakar: NEA, 1975). The prison, which held political detainees in the Ivory Coast, was attacked in 1949 by prisoners' wives, who eventually forced the government to back down.

7

BETWEEN CONSERVATISM AND TRANSGRESSION

Everyday Life in the Prisons of Upper Volta, 1920–1960

Laurent Fourchard

At first glance, the prisons of the Upper Volta seem to follow the tormented history of the colony itself. For forty years, colonial powers constantly modified penitentiary legislation. French rulers signed the first decree on penitentiary establishments at the founding of the colony in 1920.[1] But the decree was only applied after 1932 when Upper Volta was partitioned between the colonies of French Sudan (Mali), Ivory Coast, and Niger. From this point on, three different regulatory regimes directed prisons in the former Upper Volta.[2] Despite the reorganization of the colony of the Upper Volta in 1947, the three different regimes endured until 1950,[3] when a general decree standardized prison regulations for all prisons of the colony. A closer look at the social history of incarceration demonstrates, however, that these legal shifts remained formal; they did not affect daily life in the Upper Volta penitentiaries. (See Map 7.1.)

In this chapter, I will not attempt to retrace the entire history of incarceration in the Upper Volta. Instead, I will examine the disjuncture between official regulation and everyday uses of the prison. By focusing on the lived experiences of those involved in the colonial penitentiaries, I hope to document whether or not transformations in official regulations led to grass-roots modifications in penitentiary practice, and in the daily lives of African prisoners. The archives consulted are sparse and incomplete, but they allow for a comparative approach through time since they are particularly well preserved for the 1920s and the 1950s.

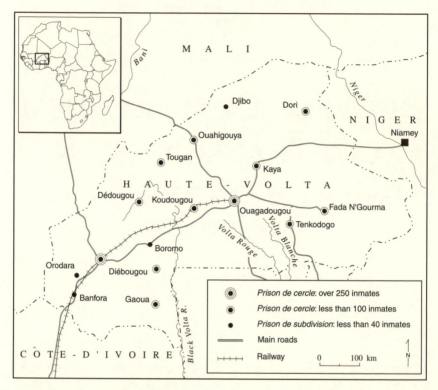

Map 7.1. Prisons in Upper Volta.

To begin with, penitentiary authorities did not systematically apply official regulations. For example, after the colonial government tried to implement a prison reform during the 1950s,[4] the actual conditions of detention changed little on the ground. While penitentiary authorities were inclined to maintain existing practices in the colonial prisons, African guards and detainees invented everyday practices and a specific culture that both largely escaped colonial authority. As a result, the prison became a symbol of the inertia of colonial power, as well as a site of African disobedience, corruption, and transgression.

THE INERTIA OF COLONIAL INCARCERATION

From 1920 to 1960, a series of legal reforms seemed to have dramatically altered the regulatory regime of the Upper Volta prisons. In 1920, the first decree regulating the prison system of Upper Volta contained only 11 articles, while the 1950 decree comprised 107 articles. Modeled after a Senegalese decree of 1947 that reserved numerous rights for prisoners, the 1950 decree appeared quite liberal, and sought to regulate prison life in its finer detail.[5] In fact, the reform proved to be mostly formal in nature. The 1950 decree guaranteed more rights for prisoners (the right to visits from lawyers and parents, the right to correspondence), but the pentientiary administration seldom abided by the law. Moreover, the governor of the Upper Volta was particularly inspired by the disciplinary measures set forth in the Title IV of the Senegalese 1947 decree, titled "discipline and internal police," which provided for strict control of the most liberal measures.[6] The 1950 decree hardly improved the living conditions of the detained; on the contrary, it combined the most severe practices set forth in 1920 and 1947, and codified longstanding practices such as racial segregation and forced labor. The administration could open all correspondence (art. 46), send suspect mail to a higher authority (art. 47), require inmates to wear prison uniforms (art. 70), and fix rewards for the capture of escapees (art. 54).

Theories and Practices of Racial Segregation

Even if the first mention of separate living quarters for Europeans only dates from 1928,[7] the separation of European and African prisoners was as old as colonial prisons. Problems associated with segregation in prisons surfaced when large numbers of Europeans came to the colony after the Second World War.[8] The 1950 ruling sought to prevent any promiscuity between European and African prisoners, without violating the principles of equality laid down in 1946 by the Lamine Gueye law.[9] Therefore, differential treatment of European and African prisoners was justified by differences in living standards. In order to explain why European prison uniforms were less rudimentary than African ones,[10] the authorities argued that "the majority of African prisoners of local law[11] have never worn a hat, a pair of shoes, or a shirt."[12] A 1950 decision instituted stricter residential and alimentary segregation. Europeans who were imprisoned as defendants were housed in separate quarters (art. 20) and their food came from the noncommissioned officers' mess hall, as opposed to the prison kitchen (art. 62). The penitentiary administration enforced this culinary form of segregation until the very end of the colonial period: "Separate living quarters prevent the most evolved of the European prisoners from becoming the ring-leaders of the most frustrated amongst their companions in captivity."[13]

Official justifications argued that the distinctions between prisoners were social in nature, although in practice, they were racial. Only a year after the signing of the 1950 decree, the governor reiterated that prisoners originating from the *Quatre Communes* in Senegal—who had been French citizens since 1916—could not benefit from the European food service[14] in the prison at Bobo-Dioulasso. Indeed, racial segregation was most visible in the prison at Bobo-Dioulasso, where most European and Senegalese prisoners lived under the same roof.[15] Detainees coming from Senegal—who, since the 1920s, had enjoyed a privileged social position in Bobo-Dioulasso that differed little from that of the French—were forced to live alongside African delinquents in the prison.[16] In 1958, Mamadou N'Diaye, a Senegalese detainee, expressed his consternation to the prison director, arguing that his incarceration denied his rights as a French citizen, acquired since 1916.[17]

In part, financial considerations explain the endurance of racial discrimination in the prisons of Upper Volta. In 1958, food for an African prisoner cost 8,500 francs a year while that of a European prisoner cost about 55,000 francs—6.5 times more expensive.[18] Therefore, "this [latter] diet must be reserved for Europeans since it would entail too high costs."[19] The will to segregate was readily apparent. In 1959, the director of the Bobo-Dioulasso prison supported an increase in 50 francs per day for each European prisoner so as to diversify their dietary regime.[20] The following year, the African prisoners of Ouagadougou received only 45 francs' worth of food per day, a drop from the 50 francs earmarked for the previous year.[21]

Therefore, the prison maintained a segregationist structure, which was increasingly out of phase with the Upper Volta colonial society of the 1950s, when the administration was in the process of "africanizing" some of its positions.[22] The modern prison's principle of "egalitarian punishment"[23] could not function in the colonial context. Subjecting Europeans to the same conditions as prisoners of common law meant assimilating them—lowering them—to the precarious position of the Africans, and invalidating their civil rights. This was one reason why European prisoners did not labor outdoors. As the governor of the colony of Ivory Coast explained: "It would be immoral insofar as it would damage French prestige to send [European detainees] out to public work sites."[24] In Upper Volta, racial segregation was enforced during the 1950s beyond the walls of the prison itself. While African prisoners endured forced labor and had to wear prison uniforms in public, European detainees were always exempt from both.

The Proper Use of Prison Labor

Before the First World War, colonial powers routinely employed prison labor to construct colonial buildings.[25] Thereafter, criminal detainees along with prisoners held under the disciplinary regime of the *Code de l'indigénat*[26] were used for road maintenance, the upkeep of gardens and plantations, and tasks related to water provisioning and hygiene.[27] These daily chores were sometimes coupled with urgent municipal works that necessitated large numbers of workers for which administrative detainees served as surplus labor. In 1924, the governor recognized that, "disciplinary punishment in the prison varies over the course of the year. The highpoint is the month of March, when the administration works hardest; in June, the native is liberated from administrative obligations and returns to his fields."[28] The governor thus officially confirmed that the prison served as a reservoir of cheap labor. But the analysis of a seasonal distinction, which did not take into account the economic cycles of the peasants, was wrong. According to Figure 7.1, the only period in which disciplinary punishments truly decreased was during the months of October, November, December, and February, when the peasants had already finished agricultural work. Contrary to the governor's pronouncement, the peasants of Upper Volta experienced increased administrative constraint at the time of most intensive farming duties.

If this form of administrative labor disappeared with the abrogation of the *indigénat* regime after World War II, forced labor continued to be imposed in the prisons despite the Houphouêt-Boigny law of April 5, 1946, outlawing all forms of mandatory labor. Not only all African prisoners should labor (art. 91) but, in the Upper Volta, the ban on work during Sundays and holidays prescribed by the Senegalese decree did not apply to "forced labor in the municipality of public utility" (art. 90). This disposition is reminiscent of the 1920 decree stating that "the prisoners can be forced to work on Sundays through justified directives from the commander of the circumscription" (art. 8).

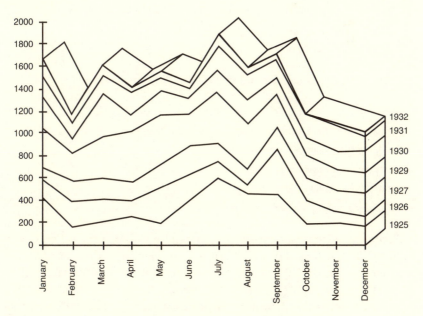

Figure 7.1. Monthly Variation of Disciplinary Sanctions (1925–1932).

Penal labor remained gratis until the end of the 1950s. During the 1920s, the governors of Upper Volta and the Ivory Coast opposed the establishment of compensation, which would have allowed prisoners to earn some savings.[29] While not very surprising during the time of the *indigénat*, this logic persisted during the postwar period in the Upper Volta; the 1950 decree carefully erad-icated all articles of the 1947 Senegalese decree that referred to compensation for penal labor.[30] In 1957, 135 years after the establishment of salaries for detainees in French jails, Upper Volta's Minister of the Interior, Michel Dor-ange, requested its institutionalization in the country's prisons—without success.[31]

From the end of the nineteenth century to 1960, prisonners did not earn wages for laboring inside or outside of the prison, a situation justified by unchanging colonial rhetoric about budgetary needs. In 1914, in order to cut costs, the administration used penal labor to erect the new prison at Bobo-Dioulasso.[32] In 1954, the governor proposed that detainees would serve their sentence in the prisons of their native circumscriptions.[33] This was done to satisfy local commanders lacking in sufficient labor for the maintenance of their posts.[34] The economy of forced penal labor remained unchanged during this entire period and the supply of labor hardly varied. In the prison at Bobo-Dioulasso in 1927, of 220–230 detainees:

20 sick people are exempt from service

45 do not go out due to the risk of escape

36 are in the gardens, 34 are doing public works, 9 of which are for the circumscription

38 are doing water and W.C. tasks

40 work in the area of hygiene[35]

In the prison at Ouagadougou in 1954, of 220 prisoners:

33 are doing forced labor for the government

29 are unavailable (sick persons, minors, dangerous)

31 are doing forced labor for the prison

13 are at the disposition of the circumscription commander

30 are doing forced labor in town

84 accused persons are not obligated to work[36]

According to this data, prison officials did not force accused persons to work in 1954 as they did in 1927 (when this category of detainee was not even mentioned). But the distinction was probably purely formal. In 1954, the director of the Ouagadougou prison was sincerely astonished that accused persons did not labor alongside convicted detainees.[37] The colonial prison remained therefore a considerable reservoir of cheap labor during the entire colonial period. After 1946, prison labor was all the more attractive since forced labor for free African citizens was prohibited by law. This explains why district commanders remained eager to maintain a local jail and to use local detainees for public works in their posts, even though the existence of numerous small prisons throughout the Upper Volta proved costly for the administration. This conservative policy and budgetary logic was pursued to the detriment of the prisoners, leading to derelict living conditions in most local prisons.

The state of decay in the prisons of Upper Volta in 1958–1960 is indicative of the public authorities' financial abdication. All prisons were built in banco[38]—with the exception of the prison at Bobo-Dioulasso—and required regular and onerous repairs.[39] Administrative reports *(procès-verbal)* regarding prison inspections document the unsanitary conditions and dilapidated state of the prisons at the time of independence. At Fada-N'Gourma (an eastern town of the Upper Volta), "Conditions of hygiene are extremely bad, the building is totally decrepit. The cells are very poorly ventilated; prisoners sleep on the bare floor at about three per cell on rotting mats. There is no separate area for toilets in the prison; there are just latrines under the open sky in the middle of the tiny courtyard. During the rainy season, the gutters inundate the cells; the timberwork is on the verge of collapsing. A new building of sturdy materials is necessary in order to assure a minimum of hygiene and a decent shelter for the prisoners."[40] In 1960, this description was not the exception; it was the rule.[41] Even the administrative centers *(chef-lieux)* prisons were not much better off. "There is no sanitary installation in the infirmary. On a daily basis, medical care is assured by a detainee. The kitchens have no equipment and the WCs leave much to be desired; there is a single water tap for the entire prison (265 prisoners) and there are no showers. . . . This collectivity is totally unsanitary."[42] In 1960, the prisons of the Upper Volta bring forth images of Howard's descriptions of European jails in the eighteenth century.[43]

The prisoners' hygiene and health did not improve during the colonial period. Unfortunately, statistics are lacking, but the causes of mortality during the 1920s and the 1950s, respectively, seem fairly similar. In Dédougou, in 1925, "A dysentery epidemic struck a certain number of elderly detainees."[44] In 1929, 66 percent of the prison population at Ouagadougou died from dysentery while the African population of the circumscription fared much better (less than 10 percent).[45] In 1959, an inspector visited the Ouagadougou prison after the suspect deaths of five accused persons. He concluded that the causes of death were clearly linked to the chronic lack of hygiene, and warned that "morbidity and mortality will be very high in the case of an epidemic and, in particular, an illness spread from feces."[46]

Therefore, despite the establishment of commissions for the surveillance of the prisons in 1950, and in spite of regular visits and constant requests for repairs, the colonial administration never promoted the reconstruction of the prisons and improvements of living conditions as priorities. The new investments for economic and social development in the colonies, as put forth at the Brazzaville conference (1944) and partially enacted by the *Fonds d'investissement pour le développement économique et social* (FIDES), never reached the penitentiary system. FIDES funds helped hospitals and dispensaries multiply in town, giving local people better access to medical care; and supported public hygiene services to organize vast campaigns for urban sanitation against malaria. While not very effective,[47] these projects widened the gap between the penal community and a part of urban society.

Colonial authorities resisted change in the colonial penal institutions. The postwar reinforcement of racial segregation, the various forms of forced and unpaid labor, the refusal to improve living conditions for African prisoners all speak to the ways in which the prison was the conservative space of a colonial regime that refused to recognize African emancipation within the walls of its penitentiary. Prisons remained the bastion for colonial rule's control over Africans, in spite—or maybe because—of the French administration's loss of power outside the prison. Yet, within the walls of the colonial prisons, African detainees' everyday lives also largely escaped colonial control.

COLONIAL PRISON: A SITE OF TRANSGRESSION

The colonial state had to rely on inadequate means for controlling prison guards and detainees. Prison management was never ensured by professional penitentiary personnel, who could have devoted themselves entirely to this task.[48] Most often, European *gendarmes*[49] served as prison managers, and in some cases African guards took charge of the smaller prisons in rural circumscriptions.[50] During the 1950s, in the central prison of Ouagadougou, the capital of the colony, the prison director was a *gendarme* without specific remuneration or time off for this additional task.[51] Europeans only fulfilled this role if they had sufficient time, often acting in bad faith. Without effective authority, a well-defined program, and clear regulations about the penitentiary regime,[52] the prison was often abandoned to the prisoners and the guards.

Guard-Prisoner Relations: Complicity among the Colonized?

Many African novelists described colonial prisons as places where brutal and corrupt guards mistreat prisoners.[53] This was probably true, but reliable data is hard to find. The few indications of assaults on prisoners appear in the context of more serious affairs.[54] The silence in the sources can be explained by the lack of outside witnesses to this self-contained world. Nonetheless, the penitentiary cannot be reduced to a Manichean confrontation between prisoners, who are hostile to colonial discipline, and guards, who guarantee colonial order. To the contrary, the relative absence of European authorities in the penitentiary world created opportunities for Africans living and working in the prison. To what extent did complicity between guards and prisoners encourage escapes, minor rule-breaking, and the granting of small privileges?

"The only positive aspect of the penitentiary regime in the Upper Volta is that it is not inhuman . . . the personnel are indulgent. The prisons of the Upper Volta are unable to keep the prisoners. Escapes occur almost every day . . . the African prisoners are compliant since those living behind bars are those who wish to be."[55] Even incomplete statistical sources confirm and nuance this point. During the second half of the 1920s, there were approximately 50 to 100 escapes per year for 650–1,000 detainees, which amounts to about 10 percent.[56] The Ouagadougou prison registered more than one escape per month between 1928 and 1931,[57] and one every two months between 1947 and 1950.[58] Despite this slight decrease, escapes were extremely frequent during the entire colonial period.

The dilapidated state of the prisons and the lack of personnel were among the main reasons for escapes.[59] Most took place while prisoners completed forced labor outdoors, when the lack of guards increased opportunities for escape.[60] Numerous examples can illustrate this point: One guard refused to pursue prisoners who fled from the prison courtyard; another let prisoners leave unaccompanied; unescorted prisoners were caught stealing in Ouagadougou; and one prisoner was found dead drunk in a neighborhood near the Bobo-Dioulasso prison.[61] These accounts illustrate how guards wittingly neglected the surveillance of forced labor and the comings-and-goings of prisoners. Colonial authorities in the 1930s deplored the situation: "Recommendations were made to prevent guards from being excessively severe with prisoners or, to the contrary, becoming so familiar with them that surveillance is neglected."[62] Again, in the 1950s, administrative reports complain that "Forced labor is too insignificant, too dispersed, and poorly guarded by the personnel, whose complacency sometimes borders on complicity."[63]

Active complicity was not systematic. Escape could occur due to negligence that arose out of lack of interest in a poorly paid job; guards fell asleep while supervising prisoners' forced labor, they often left their posts in order to attend to their own business.[64] But complicity could easily arise out of the fact that the prisoners and guards shared similar living standards. The guards living quarters were only slightly better maintained then the prison itself. And during the 1930s, circumscription guards' salaries in the Upper Volta were the lowest in all of French West Africa.[65] As for the lack of equipment,[66] the guards were dressed in almost as rudimentary fashion as the detainees: shorts and a shirt made of raw canvas. The guards often turned a blind eye to prisoners who wanted to improve their daily existence: "The prisoners are used to making fires in the courtyard for their personal cooking. If the rules were observed and if the personnel demonstrated a bit of authority, we might manage to have a clean locale."[67] Furthermore, the line between prisoners and guards was blurred. In the 1950s, any guard whose negligence was noted during an escape received punishment of eight to fifteen days in prison. In Ouagadougou, about every two months, one or two guards found themselves imprisoned.[68] These sanctions brought wardens and prisoners so close together that they proved to be an ineffective means of dealing with the supposed negligence of guards.

A considerable underground life, which gained ground over the prison courtyard, emerged from this situation. Guards and detainees subverted prescribed discipline and created a whole array of strategies, from ignorance of regulations to deliberate violations thereof. This parallel life, which is impossible to glean from the administration's annual reports, surfaced only on particular occasions, such as when the most glaring instances of fraud were discovered. In 1941, the Ouagadougou prison director unveiled close relations between former prisoners, who were working in the kitchen, and circumscription guards: "While surveying the grounds surrounding the prison, it was discovered that a prisoner brought loads of wood to the sergeant and the sergeant major two times a week."[69] A few years later at Bobo-Dioulasso, the prison accounting clerk *(greffier économique),* who was a former African detainee, embezzled large sums of money. In 1953, this amounted to 1 million francs, 126,500 of which involved false receipts.[70] Fraud clearly resulted from the colonial administration's failure to control the prison system. The directors' absenteeism and disinterest explain how corruption, which was fairly easy to detect, remained undisclosed for several years. And the existence of extortion demonstrated the possibility of complicit relations between African prisoners and European managers.[71] On the other hand, the prisoners did not always present a united front against colonial authority: For example, an African detainee who was promoted as a prison clerk at Bobo-Dioulasso granted himself a European dietary regime, which he partook of in hiding."[72] This privilege incited jealousy among the other prisoners, and the clerk was severely bullied when he was relieved of his duties.[73]

Ultimately, it seems that every actor in the prison tried, above all, to survive by obtaining small profits. Prior relations between prisoners and guards were surely strengthened in prison in the interests of the general good: "There are instances of familiar relations that were established prior to the prisoners' detention, from which arise a certain receptiveness between them and us and, from that, verbal requests to third parties in town for assistance, which do not compromise us."[74] Such relationships with the outside world, which were formally forbidden by the regulations,[75] improved the ordinary lives of the prisoners[76] and allowed the guards to earn commissions.

Survival in prison depended on these negotiations. The guards were always in a position of power and thus able to acquire privileges for themselves quite easily. For instance, individual persons were strictly forbidden to assign penal labor. Colonial correspondence from the 1930s denounces the European administrators' use of prisoners as unpaid domestic personnel.[77] But this practice probably endured after the 1950s to the profit of prison guards: "We have no profit and no advantages linked to our work, except appropriating prisoners as house boys for diverse chores in our homes."[78]

What is interesting here is not the fact that regulations were transgressed, but rather the guards' certainty that these practices were common and supposedly licit. This demonstrates how wide the gap had become between prison regulations and the habits of the prison, or how far removed the daily lives of prisoners and guards were from the texts in force. The administration seemed to disregard the regulation of daily life inside the prison and, in turn, seemed to authorize all sorts of illegal practices among prisoners and guards.

The Prison as a Site of Corruption

In Europe, nineteenth- and twentieth-century reformers put forth numerous programs that sought to transform the prison into a site of correction and re-education.[79] These theories never appear in colonial correspondence, and even comments on the social or moral functions of the prison are few and far between. In the 1950s, the small administrative steps taken to reform the prisons in the Upper Volta did not trigger any larger debate. The first oversight committees were created in 1950 and only operated regularly at the end of the decade, leading to very rare transformations in the prisons.[80] The interventions of Catholic priests in the penitentiary system during the 1950s and, after 1956,[81] the placement of some children (seven to sixteen years old) in the Orodara center near Bobo-Dioulasso did not modify conditions of detention for minors in the prisons.

However, in 1957, the blatant dysfunctionality of prisons in the Upper Volta led the Minister of the Interior, Michel Dorange, to write a report and to propose general reforms.

> The prisons [of the Upper Volta] do not fulfill any of the objectives assigned by all modern societies to the penitentiary system: to guard, to punish, and to reform.
>
> a. The prisons of the Upper Volta are unable to guard prisoners. Escapes occur almost every day. . . .
>
> b. The present regime does not inspire terror such that the liberated person does everything possible to avoid being incarcerated again. . . .
>
> c. The results of the reform process are disastrous. The Upper Volta prison does not amend, it corrupts. Due to the lack of prison earnings, the discharged prisoner who has neither friends nor family is almost forced to

commit new crimes. The magistrates have noted that repeat offenses occur during the first few days of liberty.[82]

Following this statement about the failure of the colonial penal program, the minister elaborated a reform project that was not applied before independence. The proposed solutions involved policing more than reforming. They sought to reinforce surveillance (create a distinct administration for the penitentiary service) and limit escapes by concentrating prisoners together (abolishing secondary prisons, constructing a central prison for long sentences and recalcitrant prisoners). The idea of prison earnings suggested by Dorange was not retained. The European community felt that African prisoners led an idyllic life, being better fed, better housed, and working less than free men.[83] Preaching in part from ignorance of the penitentiary world, they invoked a cliché that is as old as the prison itself: that is, the idea that prisoners are better off than the poorest people in society.[84] In refusing all improvements in the conditions of incarceration for Africans, this colonial good conscience set the stage for the development of promiscuity and corruption in the heart of the prison.

Astonishing Promiscuity

"The astonishing promiscuity that reigns in the prison is a factor of corruption. The separation of men and women, minors and adults, and accused and condemned is poorly enforced. There is no discrimination between repeat offenders and petty delinquents, those condemned to long sentences and those locked up for a few days, authors of money crimes and authors of blood crimes."[85] This description of the central prison in Ouagadougou is true for all establishments in the Upper Volta—although Bobo-Dioulasso did have two prisons, one for the accused and the other for the condemned.

Colonial sources insist on the consequences of this promiscuity for minors in Ouagadougou. During the 1950s, numerous reports express concern about the rise in urban delinquency. In 1956, in response to a request made by the service for social affairs, the police force in Ouagadougou and Bobo-Dioulasso increased "their surveillance of vagabond minors and attempted to arrest delinquents even for the smallest infractions."[86] From March to December 1956, in a concerted effort to rid the capital of adolescents who were more or less abandoned, fifty-four cases involving minors were tried by the court in Ouagadougou alone. After trial, most of these adolescents were placed in the Orodara center, which had just opened its doors. During the phase of inquiry, however, which lasted about a month, the children were detained in the Ouagadougou prison, where they were not separated from other prisoners or offered specific activities.[87]

Three main consequences arose from this poorly devised program for delinquency. First, children who lived on minor theft became conscious of their status as delinquents upon entering prison.[88] Through contact with the adult prisoners, they learned better techniques for thievery: "In the old Ouagadougou prison, we sometimes attended practical courses on how to cut pockets with razorblades, which were presented by a twenty-year-old to thirty minors, some of whom were not even twelve years old. Standing nearby, the guard observed the scene with amusement: during this time, they don't bother me."[89] But the consequences of mixing minors and adult prisoners were well understood in the French prison system; since the Restoration, "the magistrates loathed sending children to these houses of corruption."[90]

The second consequence was no less logical. The Ouagadougou prison became the cradle of organized gangs of petty street thieves. The birth of these gangs in Ouagadougou coincides with pursuit of repressive policy against minors. "These gangs exist since the mid-1950s, and seem to originate in relations that are established in prison between adults and minors. Each minor is 'protected' by an adult prisoner and the resulting friendship endures even after exit from prison. The letters received by minors at the Orodara mission leave no doubt about the solidarity that has formed between adults and minors."[91]

The third consequence was a bit more unexpected. The Ouagadougou prison became a site for homosexual initiation. All detainees discovered this practice in prison. "They say that they did not even know that this was possible before coming to prison and that it is always a prisoner, generally an adult, the minor's "protector," who initiates them, mostly by force. Once initiated, the minors conclude that this is part of the necessities of life in prison and do it willingly amongst themselves."[92] This phenomenon was hardly marginal. Indeed, it was massive: in 1960, of 60 young boys in rehabilitation at the *Maison de l'Enfance*, about 50—all ex-detainees—continued homosexual practices.

CONCLUSION

In the French colony of Upper Volta, penitentiary policies rested on concerted inertia, both at the level of legal reforms and at the level of practices on the ground. One can read, through the paralysis of the conservative regulations, the imported flaws of the old European prison system: from the morgue-prisons of the eighteenth-century jails to the repressive houses that "punish, eliminate, and hardly correct" of the nineteenth century.[93] But the specific traits of the colonial situation reveal themselves in the colonial penitentiary. Racial segregation remained stronger in prison than elsewhere in the colony. The use of penal labor—which was forced, unpaid, and applied to all categories of prisoners, with no rest days—*de facto* protected the endurance of the *indigénat* regime in the colonial prisons after it was abolished in all French colonies in 1945.

In order to survive, guards and prisoners reinvented a life of their own on the margins of colonial regulations. Informal contacts with the outside world, unaccompanied outings, and frequent escapes all served to sustain hope for the prisoners. In the prison itself, the transgression of rules improved everyday life. During the 1950s, the prison became the site for learning delinquency. The colonial administration was aware of these facts, but chose to ignore them. Instead, officials enforced separation between European and African prisoners. By enforcing racial segregation, which was officially prohibited and extremely costly, rather than the separation of minors and adults, which was mandatory, the colonial authorities demonstrated that the penal function of prisons in the Upper Volta was not to reform, correct, or improve African prisoners, but to save European prisoners from African promiscuity.

This colonial "model" of the prison was transferred, practically untouched, to the African elite during the 1950s. Colonial penitentiary practices endured through the use of unpaid penal labor.[94] The government of the Upper Volta (after independence, Burkina Faso) also continuously refused to consider any improvement in penitentiary life. In 1959, the restoration of three prisons that were on the verge of collapsing were listed in the 1959 national budget well after funds allocated by the deputies for the construction of a villa for Bernard Ilboudo, a prominent politician in Ouagadougou.[95] Today, however, rhetorical platitudes about prisoners' idyllic living conditions continue to provide mundane conversation topics for all Burkina Faso's social classes.

NOTES

1. *Journal officièl de la Haute-Volta (JOHV), Arrêté du 4 avril 1920 réglementant le régime des prisons en Haute-Volta*, 1920.

2. In the circumscription attached to the Ivory Coast, the administrators were to apply a decree dating from 1916. The circumscriptions attached to the French Sudan and Niger followed, respectively, the 1927 and 1932 decrees.

3. *Archives du Ministère de l'Administration territoriale à Ouagadougou* (MATS) 2F1c, *Correspondance du haut-commissaire de la République au gouverneur de la Haute-Volta*, February 23, 1952.

4. JOHV, *Arrêté du 4 décembre 1950 réglementant le régime des prisons en Haute-Volta*.

5. *Journal officiel du Sénégal* (JOS), *Arrêté no. 3653 du 22 octobre 1947 réglementant le régime des prisons au Sénégal*.

6. Of these thirty articles, only five related to prisoners' rights while twenty-one others treated questions of order, surveillance, prohibitions, and punishment.

7. "A la prison de Ouagadougou, les Européen possèdent deux chambres qui leur sont réservées," *Archives nationales de Côte d'Ivoire* (ANCI), FF 5646, *Correspondance du régisseur de la prison de Ouagadougou au commandant de cercle de Ouagadougou*, June 8, 1928.

8. The European population went from 1,800 inhabitants in 1948 to more than 3,300 in 1949. *Archives nationales françaises*, Paris (ANP) 200 MI 1905, *Inspection du travail de Haute-Volta*, Annual Report 1949.

9. The Lamine Gueye Law (May 7, 1946) granted French citizenship to all those living in French overseas territories. It was one of the most popular decisions made by the Constituent Assembly.

10. Article 71 accorded "a pair of shoes, a shirt, and a hat" to European prisoners, thus overriding the mandatory use of prison uniforms.

11. A differential status of "local law" *(statut personnel)* continued to discriminate among Africans and Europeans even after the 1946 Lamine Gueye law.

12. *Archives personnelles de l'administration pénitentiaire à Ouagadougou* (AAP), *Correspondance du secrétaire général du Territoire au haut-commissaire de la République*, July 18, 1957.

13. Ibid.

14. MATS 2F1b, *Correspondance du gouverneur de la Haute-Volta au commandant de cercle de Bobo-Dioulasso*, August 24, 1951.

15. This is due to the fact that the largest number of European and Senegalese residents in the colony of the Upper Volta was located at Bobo-Dioulasso.

16. L. Fourchard, "Un modèle de ségrégation spatiale presque parfait. Bobo-Dioulasso à la fin des années 1920," *Cahiers du groupe Afrique noire* (Paris: L'Harmattan, forthcoming).

17. *Archives non-classées du cercle de Bobo-Dioulasso (ACB), Lettre du citoyen français Mamadou N'Diaye, détenu à la prison civile de Bobo-Dioulasso au directeur de la prison*, November 19, 1951.

18. ACB, *Dépenses matérielles du budget 1958-de la prison de Bobo-Dioulasso*.

19. ACB, *Correspondance de l'administrateur de Bobo-Dioulasso*, March 12, 1959.

20. ACB, *Correspondance du régisseur de la prison de Bobo à l'administrateur de Bobo-Dioulasso*, February 5 1959.

21. MATS 2F2c, *Procès-verbal de visite du médecin Ladji Traoré à la prison civile de Ouagadougou*, April 21, 1960.

22. C. Sissao, "Les enjeux du pouvoir communal pendant la colonisation: le cas de Ouagadougou. 1927–1960," in *La Haute-Volta coloniale* (Paris: Karthala, 1995), 117–28.

23. Michel Foucault, *Surveiller et punir* (Paris: Gallimard, 1975), 268.

24. ANCI FF 6835, *Correspondance du lieutenant-gouverneur de la Côte-d'Ivoire au gouverneur général*, August 28, 1929.

25. This included European houses and the new prison at Bobo-Dioulasso in 1914. ACB, *Rapports du cercle de Bobo-Dioulasso 1913–1918, Rapports sur les travaux, 1913–1915*.

26. A specific administrative and penal code that applied to the African populations of the French colonies before 1945. [NDT]

27. ANP 200 MI 1705, *Service des prisons, Rapport politique de la Haute-Volta*, 1924.

28. ANCI 5EE 58, *Rapport du gouverneur sur l'indigénat et son fonctionnement en Haute-Volta*, October 18 1924.

29. ANCI FF 6835, *Correspondance du lieutenant-gouverneur de la Côte-d'Ivoire au gouverneur général de l'AOF*, August 28, 1929.

30. Articles 51, 74, and 108–18.

31. MATS 2F1c, *Rapport du ministre de l'Intérieur, Michel Dorange au chef du territoire de la Haute-Volta, 30 août 1957*. "Compensation was instituted in 1823 in France. Applied to the jail in Toulon, it then spread to the jails of Brest and Rochefort." J.-G. Petit, ed., *Histoire des galères. Bagnes et prisons. XIIIe–XXe siècles* (Paris: Privat, 1991), 209.

32. ACB, *Rapport du cercle de Bobo-Dioulasso 1913–1918, Rapports sur les travaux*, May 1914.

33. MATS 2F1b, *Circulaire du gouverneur de Haute-Volta aux commandants de cercle*, April 16, 1954.

34. The circumscription commanders at Yako, Boromo, Kaya Diébougou, and Tenkodogo only had from ten to twenty prisoners in 1952, while the prison in Ouagadougou held 400 and that of Bobo-Dioulasso held 300. MATS 2F1b, *Liste des prisons civiles de Haute-Volta en 1952*.

35. ANCI DD 1398, *Correspondance du commandant de cercle de Bobo-Dioulasso au gouverneur de Haute-Volta*, September 12, 1927.

36. MATS 2F2c, *Correspondance du commandant de cercle de Ouagadougou au gouverneur de Haute-Volta*, May 7, 1954.

37. *Archives non-classées du cercle de Ouagadougou (ACO), Correspondance du régisseur de la prison de Ouagadougou au procureur de la République*, April 12, 1954.

38. During the 1950s, the Upper Volta comprised eleven circumscription prisons, five subdivision prisons, and two annexes for the prisons at Ouagadougou and Gaoua, at Ziniare and Kampit respectively. MATS 2F1b, *Liste des prisons civiles*.

39. AAP, *Correspondance du gouverneur de Haute-Volta au gouverneur général de l'AOF*, January 11, 1955.

40. MATS 2F4b, *Procès verbaux de visite de prison de Fada-N'Gourma*, October 10, 1959.

41. See, for example, MATS 2F4b, *Procès-verbaux de visite de prison de Dédougou du 1er mars 1960, de Gaoua du 15 mars 1960, de Banfora du 31 mars 1960, correspondance du 7 juillet 1960 du commandant de cercle de Boromo au ministre de l'Intérieur*.

42. MATS 2F4b, *Rapport d'inspection de la prison civile de Ouagadougou fait à la demande du ministre de la Santé par le Docteur Roux*, August 26, 1959.

43. "Several prisons have no water . . . no latrines, or are poorly maintained . . . straw beds become completely infected." J. Howard, *L'état des prisons, des hôpitaux et des maisons de force en Europe au XVIIIe siècle*, new translation by C. Carlier and J.-G. Petit (Paris: Éditions de l'Atelier, 1994), 75–77.

44. ANP 200 MI 1708, *Service des prisons, Rapport politique annuel, 1925*.

45. AAP 120, Mairie de Ouagadougou, "*Certificats d'indigents du cercle de Ouagadougou de 1929*."

46. MATS 2F4b, *Rapport d'inspection de la prison civile de Ouagadougou*, August 26, 1959.

47. C. Sissao, "Urbanisation et rythme d'évolution des équipements. Ouagadougou et l'ensemble du Burkina-Faso (1947–1985)" (*Thèse de l'université, Université de Paris 7*, 1992), 328–87.

48. In 1957 the Minister of the Interior only asked for budgetary provisions to recruit two prison directors. MATS 2F1d, *Correspondance du ministre de l'Intérieur au ministre de la Fonction publique*, November 20, 1957.

49. *Gendarmes* were policemen whose command was attached to the army headquarters.

50. "It is not normal that certain circumscriptions were authorized to designate native agents as prison directors. This is a sufficiently important service that it should not be handed over to indigenous people." ANP 200 MI 2198, *Rapport de l'inspecteur des Colonies, Bernard Sol, concernant la situation administrative de la Haute-Volta, 1932*.

51. "I am only a temporary director. I did not seek out this job; I was appointed to it. The management of the prison is only supplementary work, which I ensure along with my

functions as the sergeant of the gendarmerie. In most administrative centers that have large numbers of prisoners, a civilian has been appointed as director of the prison, which is not the case for me." ACO, *Correspondance du régisseur de la prison civile de Ouagadougou au procureur de la République*, July 12, 1954.

52. In 1954, Ouagadougou's prison—and probably all the prisons of the territory—possessed no documentation on prison regulations in French West Africa. Ibid.

53. R. Chemain, *La ville dans le roman africain* (Paris: L'Harmattan, 1981).

54. For example, in 1941, the complaint of a prisoner in Ouagadougou against one of the guards for mistreatment is set against the backdrop of the trafficking in merchandise. ACO, *Correspondance du régisseur de la prison de Ouagadougou au commandant de cercle*, November 17, 1941.

55. MATS 2F1c, *Rapport du ministre de l'Intérieur, Michel Dorange au chef du territoire de la Haute-Volta*, August 30, 1957.

56. Prisoners escaping from prisons in Upper Volta amounted to 103 in 1924; 48 in 1925; 56 in 1926; 91 in 1927; and 66 in 1929. ANP, *Rapports politiques annuels de Haute-Volta*.

57. ANCI FF 5646, *Procès-verbaux d'évasions de la prison de Ouagadougou, 1928–1931*.

58. AAP 71 Mairie de Ouagadougou, *Décisions cercle de Ouagadougou: 1947–1950*.

59. The disrepair of the buildings allowed bars to be unhinged from windows, which incited mass escapes from the Bobo-Dioulasso prison in December 1958, and from the Fada-N'Gourma prison in February 1959. MATS 2F4b2, 2F4B2, *Correspondance du commandant de cercle de Fada-N'Gourma au ministre de l'Intérieur, 13 février 1959*. "The Bobo-Dioulasso prison (112 prisoners) is guarded by three wardens at night and one during the day." ACB, *Correspondance du régisseur de la prison de Bobo-Dioulasso à l'administrateur-maire de Bobo-Dioulasso*, November 25, 1954.

60. Of forty-seven escapes from the Ouagadougou prison between March 1928 and September 1931, six prisoners escaped from the prison courtyard, four from the hospital, and the others during forced labor in town. ANCI FF 5646, *Procès-verbaux d'évasions de la prison de Ouagadougou*. Between 1947 and 1950, of twenty-one escapees, four escaped from the prison courtyard, eleven during outdoor forced labor, and six for unknown reasons. AAP 71, Mairie de Ouagadougou.

61. ANCI FF 5646, *Procès-verbaux d'évasions de la prison de Ouagadougou*. MATS 2F4b2, *Correspondance du procureur de la République au régisseur de la prison civile de Ouagadougou, "Construction de prison,"* May 19, 1958. In the last case, the prisoner was not punished for having left the prison unaccompanied, but rather for troubling public order. ACB, *Punition de détenu, Régisseur de la prison civile de Bobo-Dioulasso*, August 13, 1951.

62. ANP 200 MI 1729, *Service des prisons, Rapport politique de la Haute-Volta, 1930*.

63. MATS 2F1c, *Rapport de Michel Dorange au chef du territoire de la Haute-Volta, Projet de réforme*, August 30, 1957.

64. AP 71, Mairie de Ouagadougou, Decision no. 78, November 2, 1950. At the Ouagadougou prison, there are three instances of the abandonment of a guard post so as to return to agricultural fields, or to return home. AAP 71, Mairie de Ouagadougou, *Procès-verbaux d'évasion*.

65. "The wages and benefits of the subaltern personnel of the administration are lower than those of neighboring colonies for reasons of budgetary equilibrium." ANP 200 MI 2198, *Rapport de l'inspecteur des Colonies, Bernard Sol, concernant la situation administrative de la Haute-Volta, 1932*.

66. "Not enough arms for the sentinel, no raincoats, no flashlights." Interview with Rabi Pascal Ouedraogo, retired prison guard, Ouagadougou, 1996.

67. MATS 2F4b2, *Rapport du médecin chef du service d'hygiène à la prison de Ouagadougou, Construction de prison*, June 4, 1959.

68. AP 71, Mairie de Ouagadougou, *Procès-verbaux d'évasion*.

69. ACO, *Correspondance du régisseur de la prison de Ouagadougou au commandant de cercle*, November 17, 1941.

70. ACB, *Correspondance de l'administrateur-maire de Bobo-Dioulasso au gouverneur de la Haute-Volta*, May 3, 1954.

71. Embezzlement could only take place with the tacit agreement of the prison director. The circumscription commander admitted this implicitly when he averred that fraud was discovered at the time of a change in directors: "Gendarme Cutulic has excuses, but he delegated too much." Ibid.

72. "The secret must remain guarded so that the other prisoners do not ask for the same thing." ACB, *Lettre d'Etienne d'Almeida adressée au régisseur de la prison civile de Bobo-Dioulasso, 1954*.

73. MTS 2F4b2, *Lettre du détenu Etienne d'Almeida au gouverneur de la Haute-Volta*, November 9, 1954.

74. Interview with Rabi Pascal Ouedraogo, retired prison guard, Ouagadougou, 1996.

75. Article 10, *Arrêté du 4 décembre 1950*.

76. Alcohol and tobacco were forbidden to the detained. Art. 65 and 66, *Arrêté du 4 décembre 1950*.

77. ANCI FF 6835, *Correspondance du lieutenant-gouverneur de la Côte-d'Ivoire à tous les cercles concernant la cession et l'emploi de la main-d'œuvre pénale dans les chantiers publics*, October 12, 1933.

78. Interview with Rabi Pascal Ouedraogo, Ouagadougou, 1996. In France during the interwar period, prison guards used detainees as gardeners for derisory fees. C. Carlier, *L'administration pénitentiaire et son personnel dans la France de l'entre-deux-guerres* (Paris: Ministère de la Justice, 1989), 162.

79. Examples include the late nineteenth-century "social defense" school, or the theoretician Paul Amor after the Second World War. Petit, ed., *Histoire des galères*, 290–97.

80. In Bobo-Dioulasso, the committee consisted of the circumscription commander, the attorney general, a representative from the Chamber of Commerce, a doctor, a police commissioner, and an African notable. The commission was charged with the inspection of prisons in the presence of detainees. *Arrêté du 7 juillet 1950 créant une commission de surveillance près de la prison de Bobo-Dioulasso*. (ACB). All memos of the oversight committee are dated prior to 1959. (MATS 2F2b).

81. *Projet d'arrêté du 6 janvier 1956 créant une maison d'éducation et de l'Enfance à Orodara. Archives des Députés du Peuple à Ouagadougou* (ADP), 1107.

82. MATS 2F1c, *Rapport de Michel Dorange au chef du territoire de la Haute-Volta*, August 30, 1957.

83. Ibid.

84. "When the economic conditions of the laboring classes tend to improve in the country (France), one can then begin to think about the fate of prisoners: it would be indecent to do so too early on." J. Léonard, "Les médecins des prisons en France au XIXe siècle," in J.-G. Petit, ed., *La prison, le bagne et l'histoire* (Geneva: Librairie des Méridiens, 1984), 141–49.

85. MATS 2F1c, *Rapport du 30 août 1957*.

86. ANP 200 MI 2756, *Affaires sociales de Haute-Volta, Rapport annuel 1956.*

87. "A small credit allowed for the creation of two rooms and a courtyard, which were set up for the minors, who do not have their own living quarters. A prisoner who is literate agreed to look after them, give them reading and writing classes, watch them play, and assure their cleanliness until small manual tasks can be found for them. A small amount of school materiel and a ball were purchased." ANP 200 MI 2756, *Affaires sociales de Haute-Volta, Rapport annuel 1956.*

88. J. Hochet, *Inadaptation sociale et délinquance juvénile en Haute-Volta, Recherches Voltaïques*, no. 9 (Paris and Ouagadougou: CNRST, 1967, 1967), 90.

89. The narrator was an eyewitness to the scene in 1962. Ibid., p. 92.

90. C. Carlier, *La prison aux champs. Les colonies d'enfants délinquants du nords de la France au XIXe siècle* (Paris: Éditions de l'Atelier, 1994), 8.

91. Hochet, *Inadaptation sociale*, 86.

92. Ibid.

93. Petit, ed., *La prison*, 4.

94. The new political administration refused to give up free and vital labor. In 1959, a circumscription commander was able to reopen the prison that had been closed since 1955 so as to house about twenty prisoners who undertook forced labor in order to alleviate the circumscription's expenses. The Minister of the Interior, Kargougou Moussa, made no objection. MATS 2F4b2, *Correspondance du commandant de cercle de Djibo au ministre de l'Intérieur*, October 16, 1959.

95. The construction of the three prisons would have cost three times less than Ilboudo's building. MATS F4b, *Plan de campagne des travaux pour l'exercice du budget de 1959.*

8

ULTIMATE EXCLUSION

Imprisoned Women in Senegal

Dior Konaté

African women experienced a major aggravation of their status as punished criminals in the prisons of colonial Senegal. Carceral policies neglected women as a leftover category. Whereas they bore the same hardships as men—dilapidated jails, lack of clothing and basic needs—their triple otherness as women, prisoners, and Africans led to further discriminations.

In the coastal towns of Senegal, urban security started to preoccupy French authorities as early as the mid-nineteenth century. In St-Louis, the French first promoted public order by expelling bums, alcoholics, and vagabonds.[1] Later, they opened a police precinct and a prison (1840), and organized a battalion of *gendarmes* (police troops under army control) (1848). At that time, the French measured the success of colonization by their ability to control dangerous classes through an efficient penal apparatus. According to this ideology, colonial tribunals would sentence, and prisons neutralize, African delinquents.

The colonial project, however, met with resounding failure as the lack of material and financial means rapidly undermined the burgeoning carceral system. Confronted with an increasing number of arrested delinquents, the police faced an acute shortage of penal housing. In this context, women experienced the harshest conditions of detention. I will examine first the profile of female detainees within the general context of penal detention in Senegal. Second, I will explore the evolution of women's carceral conditions, focusing on housing, surveillance, penal labor, and abuses.[2]

THE COLONIAL PENITENTIARY

In precolonial Senegambia, repressive systems were characterized by the absence of penal confinement.[3] Sentences ranged from public blame or notification, to whipping, fines, exile, and death. A number of ordeals, some-times in the form of ingesting a concoction of plants, helped to convict the guilty party. In Senegambia, the famous "red hot iron" ordeal required the accused person to lick a red-hot blade. If the victim's tongue did not heal, he or she was convicted.[4] Such sanctions receded after colonial powers and tra-ditional rulers signed treaties to "abolish corporal punishments, and replace them with imprisonment," for example in the Serer province (in Jegem, Jo-baas, and Mbayaar).[5] From then on, French authorities progressively forced the prison upon colonized societies.

Before 1791, the penitentiaries of the *ancien régime* colonies of France had served primarily for convicts sentenced to deportation and hard labor.[6] Until the mid-nineteenth century, however, the French government had de-ported criminals to French Guyana instead of Senegal, "where dysentery was prevalent."[7] Therefore, penitentiaries diffused in Senegal later, during the co-lonial conquest, as tools for French repression over Africans. First tested in the urban areas of St-Louis and Gorée, prisons invaded the colony at the end of the nineteenth century, as the imperial power erected a network of correc-tion houses, penal camps and farms, and carceral facilities.[8] Prisons became a tool for banishing Africans who tried to resist French hegemony. The early colonial state relied on violence, and authorized private colonizers to inflict punishments on Africans,[9] and administrators to sentence reluctant individ-uals to arbitrary imprisonment under the *Code de l'indigénat*.

The importance of penal labor has often been underestimated by compar-ison with the forced *prestations* and *corvées* imposed on ordinary subjects.[10] Yet, the colonial prison fully participated in the forced labor economy. Po-litical circumstances also shaped the prison in Senegal. For example, the Vichy regime in French West Africa arrested many partisans of Général Charles de Gaulle after 1940. The total number of prisoners in Senegal in-creased by 39.8 percent between 1941 and 1942. French West Africa had four detention centers for Europeans at the beginning of the war: More than fifteen existed at the end of 1942 and imprisoned American, British, Gaullist, and African activists.[11] Simultaneously, criminal imprisonment increased, then de-clined at the end of the war: from 3,724 in 1941, imprisonment rates in Sen-egal declined to 2,015 in 1945.[12]

Africans resisted the prison vigorously, as they equated incarceration with social degradation, and slavery. In the Fouta-Toro, "Whatever the crime, a free man shall never be enslaved."[13] Local memories of captivity and enslave-ment fueled terror of the prison among the colonized: To some extent, these representations helped the French to enforce colonial repression. Yet, among Africans, no social category managed to escape the prison entirely: Adults, minors, men, and women were forced to live together in the new penitentiaries.

MIXED DETENTION

Penal infrastructures remained poor in colonial Senegal, since the administration neglected the maintenance of prisons even when the number of detainees increased. In theory, penal law separated the accused and the convicted, military and civilians, and, most importantly, African and European detainees. In reality, with the exception of racial segregation, administrators seldom observed classifications established by law. In addition, penal codes did not separate prisoners according to their sex, and did not pay attention to female detainees.[14] Whereas in metropolitan France the law had enforced specific facilities for females since 1850, colonizers never built prisons for women in Senegal.[15]

Colonial regulations, however, provided for separate wards for women inside the prison. In 1929, a decree specified that "women should be detained in separate wards, so as no contact could be made with other prisoners."[16] In reality, the penitentiary administration never enforced physical separation between sexes. Such neglect derived from patriarchal ideologies shared by Europeans and Africans, and from colonial perceptions of female delinquents.

WOMEN IN PRISON

Colonization played a crucial role in eroding the status of women in Senegal. The increased monetarization of local economies combined with the French legal system, undermined matrilineal traditions. In addition, the colonial ideology, "imbued with moral values inherited from Christian and Roman law,"[17] tended to reinforce patriarchal authority. Some authors argue that African women remained outside the colonial system, partly because colonial rulers failed to implement specific policies for them.[18] Women were hardly visible in colonial state structures: even the educational system enforced gender segregation by opening "sub-schools" for female students.[19] Another reading of the period locates African women within the larger context of power relationships between colonizers and colonized. To defeat African societies, colonizers needed to weaken the status of women. Fragilized by constant attacks, African women became more easily prone to social marginalization, and, as a consequence, they often committed crimes in order to survive. Many ended up in prison.

Inside the walls of the colonial penitentiary, African women suffered a threefold exclusion. First, colonial and African patriarchal ideology considered female detainees as inferior beings because of their gender. Second, as Africans, women belonged to the subaltern category of colonized subjects: Colonial racial coercion backed gender discrimination. Finally, female prisoners were suspected of resisting colonial rule, since they were imprisoned alongside African convicts who had defied colonizers.

FEMALE LODGINGS

In theory, the law required penitentiary authorities to provide female prisoners with separate lodgings, but the legislation was almost never enforced. In most prisons no separate cells, nor female wards existed. Colonial memos described female quarters using general terms such as "room," "kitchen," "veranda," or "pantry."[20] The lack of special wards partly derived from the general lack of local funding. A colonial inspector wondered in 1938 about "local administrators' greediness when it came to the management of penal facilities."[21] In the context of colonies' financial autonomy, the colonial administration in Senegal, not the French government, was in charge of providing for the prisons and for the prisoners.

On the ground, female prisoners suffered extreme neglect. In 1929, in the prison at Kaolack, "[women] slept under a shack that served as the prison's kitchen."[22] Up to 1943, although the law required specific buildings or wards for women, in many prisons, "nothing was prepared for female detainees."[23] In 1930, research on women in French West Africa reported how "oftentimes, female prisoners did not have a reserved ward. They slept under a veranda, or in more or less dilapidated storage rooms."[24] In 1933, members of the surveillance committee for the prison at Ziguinchor asked the penitentiary administration "to build a reserved room and some cells for female prisoners who currently sleep in the prison kitchen."[25] Seven years later, in 1940, the Ziguinchor prison still had no specific lodgings for women, as all detainees lived in the same collective cells, without any distinction based on their legal status.[26]

In other facilities, emergency decisions betrayed a enduring shortage of material means. To move female prisoners from the kitchen, administrators envisioned the possibility of converting adjacent rooms as female wards. Many prison directors adopted this solution.[27] An inspector further advised that "when rooms did not exist near the kitchen, one could use storage rooms for recycled equipment, or firewood dumps."[28] The penal administration did not address female housing in a systematic way; rather, it came up with emergency solutions that left women in dire living conditions. In the prison of Tambacounda, the director hastily organized makeshift arrangements every time a woman was incarcerated, housing the detainee in a separate room "so she could avoid undesirable contacts with other inmates."[29] In other prisons, such as St-Louis, several detainees shared a single room, "initially reserved for a single inmate."[30] In the Thiès penitentiary, "only one cell out of the existing eight was destined to women."[31]

The situation prompted in 1937 the central administration to send a *circulaire* to all prison directors in Senegal: "A number of unfortunate habits have been identified in the management of prisons. Too small rooms where, contrary to the most elementary hygienic principles, a mixed population of female and male detainees were packed without discriminating their penal status. Please remedy to this situation immediately."[32] Sent one year after the inspection of Mr. Monguillot, the *circulaire* failed to change the fate of female prisoners. In Ziguinchor, in 1938, women lived "in the same courtyard with men."[33] In 1943, Puyot, an inspector for administrative affairs, explained how "Accused persons, convicted criminals and administrative detainees[34] are imprisoned together, in spite of official legislation. I did not find any separate quarters for women anywhere."[35]

These shortcomings encouraged colonial authorities to propose a penal reform in August 1944, in order to improve the quality of penal facilities. A section of the law provided that newly built prisons "should have a special ward for female detainees, with larger cells (2 meters of ground width per detainee) since many female inmates were incarcerated with their young children."[36] Unfortunately, the project did not receive financial backing, and was never implemented.

As a result, women's living conditions in prison remained extremely poor. They experienced the hardship of exiguous lodgings and insufficient equipment, the poor quality of makeshift wards made of poor materials such as banco, hay, clay, or barbed wire, oftentimes lacking adequate ventilation; an unsanitary environment by virtue of its lack of hygiene and strong odors; and finally, promiscuity with other inmates. Only European detainees escaped this fate, and benefited from private lodgings outside the prison.[37] For all other female inmates, life in prison promoted psychological and physical morbidity, and the risk of sexual abuse.

SEX

The deterioration of the physical environment in the prison, combined with insecurity and promiscuity, encouraged deviant sexual behaviors. Female detainees had to face constant harassment from both male inmates and guards. In 1944, a report denounced the situation in the prison in St-Louis: "At night, some guards such as Alimansa Konaté used to open the door to the female ward, and to choose several women to make them sleep with Malick Sy, Malick Faye and Madiaw."[38] The letter further described how "the detainee Tacko Ly slept every night with Malick Sy. They were caught a number of times. The detainee Fatou Tine, sentenced to six years in prison, became pregnant and gave birth to a child. Some detainees put pressure on her to denounce the ex-brigadier Demba Ndiaye, who is now deceased. This is the reason why she finally accused him."[39] The author of the letter, an ex-guard laid off by the administration, accused the director of encouraging the lack of discipline and order in the prison, as "he appointed some ex-convicts as heads of the prison, who just did as they pleased." In other places, similar affairs occurred routinely. In the prison at Diourbel, "female detainees lived with guards, and a child was born from the relationship between Amy Sène and Cheikhou Bigué Sy, two famous recidivists."[40]

These case studies shed light on the violence experienced by women. Female detainees, deprived of social support and visibility, could neither end such excesses nor call for justice. In this regard, sexual violence in prisons resembled that which prevailed between colonial masters and servants.[41] Assessing the role of women in this situation proves difficult. Did the guards blackmail female prisoners? Did women agree to provide sexual services in order to survive, or get better treatment? Or did they long for a sexual life after being imprisoned? These questions cannot be fully answered without the help of oral testimonies from ex-female detainees. However, the enduring existence of sexual harassment in the post-colonial prisons of Senegal confirms that much sexual activity probably derived from violent abuse.

SURVEILLING FEMALE PRISONERS

Prison regulations imposed a strict hierarchy of guards and surveillance personnel in the colonial penitentiaries. In each important prison, the governor was supposed to appoint a director, a chief-guard who could replace the director in exceptional circumstances and oversee a team of several guards or police officers, a clerk in charge of secretarial duties, and, finally, a female warden for women. In case of absence, the female warden could be replaced by a guard's spouse, or by any other person approved by the administration. In the smaller prisons in rural circumscriptions, the presence of a female warden depended on the number of female detainees.[42] In fact, female wardens existed only in major prisons next to French tribunals, in Dakar and St-Louis. Even there, female, wardens did not receive any training. No specific criteria guided their recruitment, a pattern common to both male and female wardens, as penal legislation only defined clear criteria for the position of prison director. Subaltern guards had only a status of "auxiliaries," and could not be promoted, or appeal in case of unfair treatment.

The guards' vulnerability, combined with the deterioration of material settings, account for the small number of female detainees' attempting to escape from jail. Women escaped less frequently then men, and they often failed, as the case of Ndioba Tine demonstrates. Accused of murder, and detained in the prison of Thiès, her native town, Ndioba Tine tried to escape, but the guards captured her four days later in the rural village of Mékhé.[43] Escape proved easier for men, since they labored outside the prison. Women, by contrast, were exempted from outdoor labor: they typically worked inside the prison.

FEMALE PENAL LABOR

Colonial authorities did not care about the social rehabilitation, or re-adaptation of prisoners. The French administration was preoccupied with "repressing deviance, and putting the natives to work."[44] In this context, female detainees experienced the worst exploitation.

Colonial authorities implemented a gendered division of labor in the prison. Men were forced to labor outside the prison, and earned wages, however low; but women were confined in unpaid domestic duties inside the prison. During their transfer to the prison, therefore, female convicts did not experience significant changes in their daily chores. They cooked for the prisoners, pounded food, cleaned and swept the wards. The law provided neither guidance nor personnel for feeding the prisoners, and left the preparation of meals to the director's initiative. Oftentimes, the prisoners, and particularly women were forced to prepare the food. Female prisoners in the largest prisons of Dakar and St-Louis experienced the worst exploitation. In her report, Mrs. Savigneau denounced how, in the prison of Sédhiou, six female detainees were in charge of pounding 60 kilograms of rice and 60 kilograms of millet daily in order to feed a total population of 190 to 200 prisoners."[45]

Women condemned to long sentences became easy victims. In the prison of St-Louis, the liberation of several women, combined with the necessity of feeding an increasing number of prisoners, encouraged the director to require his colleague in the prison of Dakar in 1925 to send him "four women condemned to long sentences who knew how to pound and cook millet."[46] Directors routinely organized such transfers, and the overall necessity of women's chores encouraged tribunals to pronounce longer sentences over female convicts.

Female work in the colonial prisons sheds light on gender discrimination in the larger colonial society. Women were deprived of wages, under the pretext that their work related to the "domestic" sphere. As a consequence, they could not accumulate any capital during their time in prison. In fact, women's unpaid chores subsidized the reproduction of male penal labor. While female prisoners had to confront daily arbitrariness and oppression, their fate and well-being remained entirely neglected by the penal administration.

CONCLUSION

Gender discrimination reigned inside the colonial prison. As colonizers opened educational reformatories for minor male convicts, they imprisoned underage female detainees in regular jails with adult convicts. Deprived of special wards, subject to promiscuity and sexual abuses, and forced to labor without wages, female detainees—both adults and minors—experienced a harsher exclusion than male convicts. As a result, women's health and psychological security deteriorated dramatically in prison. Morbidity and mortality reigned among female prisoners, and did not spare the young children incarcerated with their mothers.

Post-colonial regimes in Senegal have inherited this situation. Today, female quarters do not differ significantly from colonial ones. Yet, in 1972, a project of penal reform was undertaken to solve the enduring discrimination of female prisoners. The Senegalese government opened a new prison for women in the city of Rufisque, and organized projects for the education of female detainees and the hiring of professional female guards. However, many additional efforts remain necessary to ensure the improvement of female prisoners' living conditions and their ultimate reintegration into society. Only then will Senegal break away from the dramatic legacy of gender discrimination in the colonial prison.

NOTES

1. P.M. Diop, *"L'éducation de la jeune fille indigène en AOF, 1903–1958,"* in C. Becker, S. Mbaye, and I. Thioub, eds., *AOF: réalités et héritages. Sociétés ouest-africaines et ordre colonial, 1895–1960* (Dakar: Archives nationales du Sénégal, 1997), 1142.

2. This chapter is based on extensive archival and field research in Senegal.

3. E. O'Kubasu, "Les prisons en Afrique," in *Les conditions de détention en Afrique* (Paris: International Penal Reform Pub., 1997). M. Guèye, "Justice indigène et assimilation," in Becker, Mbaye, and Thioub, *AOF*, 153–69. P. Lagier, *La criminalité des adultes au Sénégal* (Montréal: University of Montréal, 1971).

4. Lagier, *La criminalité*, 38.

5. A. Sène, *"L'impact économique de la fiscalité dans le cercle de Thiès de 1895 à 1945"* (*Mémoire de DEA, Université Cheikh Anta Diop,* 1993), 12.

6. J.-G. Petit, ed., *Histoire des galères, bagnes et prisons, XIIIe–XXe siècles* (Paris: Éditions Privat, 1991). I. Voulet, *Les prisons* (Paris: PUF, 1951).

7. Petit, ed., *Histoire des galères*, 235.

8. I. Thioub, *"Sénégal: La prison à l'époque coloniale,"* in F. Bernault, ed., *Enfermement, prison et châtiments en Afrique du 19e siècle à nos jours* (Paris: Karthala, 1999), 285.

9. E. Le Roy and T. Von Trotha, *La violence et l'Etat. Formes et évolution d'un monopole* (Paris: L'Harmattan, 1993). J. Suret-Canale, *Afrique noire. L'ère coloniale, 1900–1945* (Paris: Editions sociales, 1977), 418.

10. Thioub, "Sénégal: la prison," in Bernault, ed., *Enfermement*, 287.

11. C. Akpo-Vaché, *L'AOF et la Seconde Guerre mondiale* (Paris: Karthala, 1993), 65.

12. Ibid., 68.

13. *Coutumier juridique de l'AOF*, vol. 1: Sénégal (Paris: Larose, 1939), 5.

14. Although the colonial state had created a few educational facilities for minors and asylums for the insane, see Thioub in this book, and R. Collignon, "Le traitement de la folie au Sénégal à l'époque coloniale," in Bernault, *Enfermement*, 227–57.

15. M. Foucault, *Surveiller et punir. Naissance de la prison* (Paris: Gallimard, 1975), 247.

16. *Arrêté 478, article 2,* February 29, 1929, on the regulation of prisons in Senegal.

17. C. Coquery-Vidrovitch, *Les Africaines* (Paris: Éditions Desjonquères, 1994).

18. A. Mama, *Etudes sur les femmes et par les femmes en Afrique durant les années 1990* (Dakar: CODESRIA, 1997), 71.

19. Diop, "L'éducation de la jeune fille".

20. ANS, 17G/381/126, Mme Savigneau, "La condition de la femme en AOF durant les années 1930," 1937, 40. ANS, 3F/00100, Report on the renovation and building of new penal facilities in Ziguinchor and Kaolack, signed by the inspector for administrative affairs at Diourbel, February 1938.

21. ANS, 3F/00100. Report 29B on prisons (St-Louis, Louga, Thiès, Kaolack), by Inspector Monguillot, 1938.

22. ANS, 3F/00159. Letter from the prison director at Kaolack to the commander of Sine Saloum, May 8, 1929.

23. ANS, 3F/00105. Report on the Bambey prison, September 1943.

24. ANS 17G/381/126. Savigneau, "La condition de la femme en AOF," 40.

25. ANS, 3F/00092. *Procès-verbal du comité de surveillance pour la prison de Zinguinchor*, January 5, 1933.

26. ANS, 3F/00112, Letter from the prison director to the commandant of Ziguinchor, January 5, 1940.

27. ANS, 3F/00103, Report on the prison at Diourbel, 1938.

28. ANS, 3F/00100, Report 29B on prisons (St-Louis, Louga, Thiès, Kaolack), by Inspector Monguillot, 1938, 7.

29. ANS, 3F/00122. *Prisons des cercles. Correspondance générale 1940*. Letter from commander of Tambacounda to the Governor of Senegal, April 14, 1940.

30. Idem.

31. ANS, 3F/00130. *Prisons des cercles 1942–43*. Letter from the commandant of Thiès to the Governor of Senegal.

32. ANS, 3F/00101. *Prisons des cercles. Fonctionnement et effectifs. Circulaire adressée à tous les régisseurs des prisons des cercles*, 1937.

33. ANS, 3F/00112. Letter from the director of the prison at Ziguinchor to the commandant of Ziguinchor, January 5, 1940.

34. The expression "administrative detainees" referred to Africans imprisoned after they had refused to comply with administrative demands, such as taxes, forced labor, etc. The *Code de l'indigénat* allowed white administrators to sentence Africans, without trial, to a maximum of fifteen days in prison.

35. ANS, 3F/00105. *Note de l'inspecteur des Affaires administratives aux commandants de cercle du Sénégal*, September 6, 1943.

36. ANS, 3F/00135. *Prisons des cercles*. Reform of the penitentiary regime, August 18, 1944.

37. ANS, 3F/00034. *Prison civile de Dakar*. Letter from Prosecutor Teulet to the Governor general of FWA, August 18, 1924.

38. ANS, 3F/00123. *Prison de St-Louis*. Letter send to the Inspector of colonies, May 11, 1944.

39. Idem.

40. D.C. Bâ, "La criminalité à Diourbel de 1925 à 1960" (*Mémoire de maîtrise, Université Cheikh Anta Diop*, 1993), 51.

41. O. Faye, "Un aspect négligé de l'histoire sociale de la colonisation: les domestiques dans la vie de relations à Dakar de 1885 à 1940. Etude d'un salariat urbain à la périphérie du monde du travail," *Annales de la Faculté des Lettres et Sciences humaines de l'Université Cheikh Anta Diop* (Dakar), 23 (1993), 77–95.

42. *Arrêté no. 487*, article 11, on the legislation of prisons in Senegal. February 22, 1929.

43. ANS, 3F/00114. *Prisons des cercles. Evasions de détenus. Télégramme officiel du commandant de cercle de Thiès*, December 13, 1935.

44. I. Thioub, "Sénégal: la prison," in Bernault, ed., *Enfermement.*

45. ANS, 3F/17G/381/126, Savigneau, "La condition des femmes."

46. ANS, 3F/00027. Letter from the director of the prison at St-Louis, October 1925.

9

L'ENFERMEMENT DE L'ESPACE

Territoriality and Colonial Enclosure in Southern Gabon

Christopher Gray

The notion of *l'enfermement* refers not only to individual incarceration but also to larger political processes where the colonial administrative unit came to exercise its power, power associated with the concept of "territoriality" as distinct from "space." Colonial authority based on territoriality served as the substructure for the legal pretensions to "incarceration." This chapter deals with the establishment of that essential administrative substructure.[1]

THE THEORY OF HUMAN TERRITORIALITY

Geographers have long practiced spatial analysis and French social scientists and historians of Africa have been particularly keen to make use of space as a conceptual key to change and the past.[2] Yet "space" is a vast and bewildering concept that can be manipulated to fit or to function in a wide variety of research agendas.[3] A more precisely defined instrument needs to be employed. The work of the geographer Robert David Sack brings the necessary precision to this concept of social space. Sack develops a theory of human territoriality that can be usefully applied to the "enclosure" that occurred in Southern Gabon during the period of French colonial rule.

For Sack, "territoriality" is "a particular kind of behavior in space" and "forms the backcloth to human spatial relations and conceptions of space";[4] it is defined "as the attempt by an individual or group to affect, influence, or control people, phenomena and relationships by delimiting and asserting control over a geographic area. This area will be called "territory."[5] Territoriality points out that human spatial relationships are not constructed in a power vacuum. Indeed, the practice of territoriality "is the primary spatial form power takes."[6]

How a particular group of people uses the land, how they organize themselves in space, and how they give meaning to place are all components of territoriality. These will vary according to historical and geographical context. Sack argues that territorial uses of space have a history in which there has occurred an evolution from less sophisticated forms of territoriality in what he terms "classless-primitive" societies to the more developed practices of "pre-modern civilizations" and finally to the full exploitation of territorial techniques found in "modern capitalist" society. He further posits that the exploration of how and why modern capitalist society employs the complete range of territorial effects can help "to unravel the meanings and implications of modernity."[7]

In Equatorial Africa, historical transformation occurred as more and different instruments of territoriality were introduced by Europeans during the colonial period. This transformation was characterized by a radical discontinuity between precolonial and colonial practices as well as a major shift in social category of those who exercised territorial power. The order of precolonial society was grounded in a territorial kinship ideology of clans and lineages; power over people and things was primarily expressed through the manipulation of this kinship ideology.[8] This contrasted dramatically with the modern territoriality that developed with the rise of capitalism in Europe. Here it was the capacity to create territory—not the manipulation of kinship ideology—that allowed for control over people and things. French colonial rule attempted to impose its authority by means of modern territoriality and thus altered the economic and social structures of the Equatorial forest. In this way, the peoples of Southern Gabon became more intimately linked to the needs and rhythms of capitalism. The identities of those exercising territoriality shifted as African clan elders were replaced by European administrators and African colonial auxiliaries.

FROM APPROPRIATING GAZE TO NAMING SPACE

The particular form and sequence of modern territoriality and its potential for the "enclosure" of space in Gabon stemmed from a fundamental mutation in Europe's "gaze" out upon the world that occurred in the eighteenth century. The geographer David Harvey describes an "Enlightenment project" in which a European "totalizing vision of the globe" sought to order knowledge according to universal categories.[9] For the critic Mary Louise Pratt, these categories are the expression of a "planetary consciousness" that emerged in the first half of the eighteenth century; this new consciousness was "marked by an orientation toward interior [geographical] exploration and the construction of global-scale meaning through the descriptive apparatuses of natural history."[10] Both Harvey and Pratt owe a debt to Michel Foucault and his reflections on the mutations of power in Western society since the Renaissance.[11] The upshot of this "Enlightenment project," or European "planetary consciousness," was that by the end of the nineteenth century, the world's spaces were deterritorialized, stripped of their preceding significations, and then reterritorialized according to the convenience of colonial and imperial administration.[12]

The first stage of this process was the enclosure of physical space within the "appropriating gaze" of the European observer. By the middle of the nineteenth century, sight had long since become the dominant sense in European bourgeois modes of perception and when explorers such as Paul Du Chaillu or Pierre Savorgnan de Brazza ventured into uncharted areas like Southern Gabon they did so with "imperial eyes" capable of incorporating the specificity of all they surveyed into the universalizing categories of the Enlightenment.[13] Indeed, a recent book on the creation of colonial space in German South West Africa suggests "there is a certain sense in which vision amounts to colonization";[14] or indeed, in which vision amounts to enclosure.

Du Chaillu's account of his 1858 visit to the Apindji-speaking clans of the Koï district on the Ngounié reveals several key elements of the European appropriating gaze. First, he viewed their labor in terms of capitalist notions of productivity and remarked that the "Apindji are, for Africans, a very industrious people" as "the men do some work here" making a fine quality raphia cloth.[15] Second, he interprets clan-controlled access to fruit trees as evidence of private property, this showing "that the Apindji have made a very important step in advance of the Bakalai and Shekiani, and all the other tribes I have met." Finally, he presages the colonial concern of controlling population movement and fixing the peoples of Southern Gabon in colonial territory by noting these Apindji-speaking clans "are a settled people, and need only flocks and cattle to make them a prospering nation." Du Chaillu contrasts this to the mobility of villages found in districts closer to the commercial nodal points on the coast.[16]

The mysteries of the forest had long disturbed European vision.[17] However, the Equatorial forest of Gabon presented an acute challenge to the appropriating gaze of the explorers, missionaries, and colonial administrators who sought to bring order to its perceived chaos. The perspective required for the "landscape discourse" of the "seeing-man" was simply unobtainable from within such closed quarters.[18] The dense Equatorial forest served as a formidable obstacle to the visual dominance of space and effectively disoriented the European gaze. Mary Kingsley noted that spending a night in the Gabonese forest was "like being shut up in a library whose books you cannot read all the while tormented, terrified and bored."[19] The French administrator

George Bruel equated the impossibility of grasping the fullness of the forest landscape to the condition of a myopic "[who, without his glasses, can only see the details]."[20]

Thus it took a man of extraordinary vision and energy to see beyond the details and conjure up the images required to carve a colony out of this daunting environment. Pierre Savorgnan de Brazza, the Italian-born aristocrat who became a French citizen due to his service as an officer in the French Navy, was this man. The three voyages he undertook to the interior of Gabon between 1875 and 1885 culminated in the formation of the colony of French Congo in 1886. Brazza's dreams have been rightly labeled "visionary" but his was a passionate gaze, bordering on obsession, as he often wildly exaggerated the impact of his missions and the commercial potential of the regions he explored. The explorer Henry Morton Stanley thought he was crazy when they met at Malebo Pool in 1882. Yet it was from Brazza's vision that the physical form of Gabon the colony took shape. Thus he has been referred to as "a prodigious 'invertor of space'".[21]

Writing served to mediate the impact of the gaze. Brazza's vision was expressed through his travel accounts, maps, and bureaucratic reports; these existed in a textual space that prefigured the changes in physical space that occurred under colonialism. The act of Europeans writing about the nonliterate peoples and the hitherto "unseen" environment of Southern Gabon in the mid-nineteenth century had two important consequences. First, it initiated an ongoing dialogue between texts and physical space through which the territorial units of colonial and independent Gabon were forged. It was the power afforded by writing that ultimately allowed the French to impose their modern practice of territoriality in Southern Gabon.

Second, writing provided the European gaze with the ability to negate the spaces and practices of the nonliterate peoples of Southern Gabon and to create an "emptiable space" that was to be filled with the activities of capitalist commercial enterprise. The ability to write allowed European explorers, missionaries and colonial administrators "to classify and supplant existing *unwritten* meaning,"[22] thus enabling the exercise of "real" power in the physical space of the colony.

One of the objectives of Brazza's West African Mission of 1883 to 1885 was to break up the complex network of trade relations that controlled commerce on the Ogooué River so as to clear space for the unhindered long-distance trade of the recently established European factories. Although Brazza was only partly successful in his project, the passage below from his report nicely reveals this capitalist conception of "emptiable" and "fillable" space:[23] "We need to clean the ground and entirely transform trade in this region." This "clearing the ground" was first accomplished in the travel account and accompanying maps before it became a reality in the physical space of Southern Gabon. Indeed, it would not be until the 1920s that the commerce of the region was effectively organized on a capitalist basis.[24] However, the power of the written text and other literate tools (such as mapping) to empty space of its local, unwritten significance has been described as "a real inability of the European eye to look at the world and see anything other than European space—a space which is by definition empty where it is not inhabited by Europeans."[25]

The appropriating gaze and the ability to write that which was previously unwritten allowed European colonial agents to impose their practice of "naming space," in this way advancing the process of enclosure.[26] At its most pompous level, explorers named natural wonders like lakes and falls after European royalty; Du Chaillu, for example, named the series of rapids on the middle Ngounié "Eugénie Falls" in honor of the French Empress.[27] The production of a name in the textual space of a travel account or on a map was the first step to its entering into local parlance. Some geographical terms, such as Eugénie Falls, never made it beyond a textual reality but others, such as the "Du Chaillu" massif and the "Ngounié" River, came to be widely used as the practices of modern territoriality became effective.

The naming practices of the peoples of Southern Gabon during the precolonial period reflected a different perception of space. The "birds-eye-view" perspective provided by mapmaking was not available to the local inhabitants who gave names to rivers, streams, lakes, savannahs, and mountains but who did not have names for vast expanses of space. Thus, though there existed a rich local toponymy in precolonial Southern Gabon and such features as individual mountain peaks and peak clusters were given names, there existed no local term for the larger geographical expanse of forested mountains that came to be known as the "Du Chaillu Massif." Indeed, it would have been virtually impossible to identify this type of geographical feature without the perspective gained from mapping.[28]

The naming of the key waterway in Southern Gabon further illustrates this confrontation between fundamentally different conceptions of space and the power of writing. What has come to be known as the "Ngounié" River on the maps of the colony and independent nation of Gabon is known to Gisir- and Punu-speakers as *Durèmbu-du-Manga*, to Apindji-, Eviya-, and Tsogo-speakers as *Otèmbo-a-Manga* and to Kele-speakers as *Mèlèmbyè-a-Manga*. The first part of each of these names is a generic term for "body of water" while *manga* refers to a species of dwarf palm abundant along the river's banks. "Ngounié" is the French deformation of *Ngugni* a term used by Vili-speaking clans settled around Samba—a key nineteenth century commercial center (see Map 9.1)—to refer to the northern frontier of their district[29] (*Nsina-Ngugni*). This term *Ngugni* was then employed to refer to the river by the Galwa-, Enenga-, Ajumba-, Orungu-, Nkomi-, and Mpongwe-speaking traders who came to trade at Samba in the first half of the nineteenth century. The first Europeans to reach the river, Paul Du Chaillu in 1858 and the British

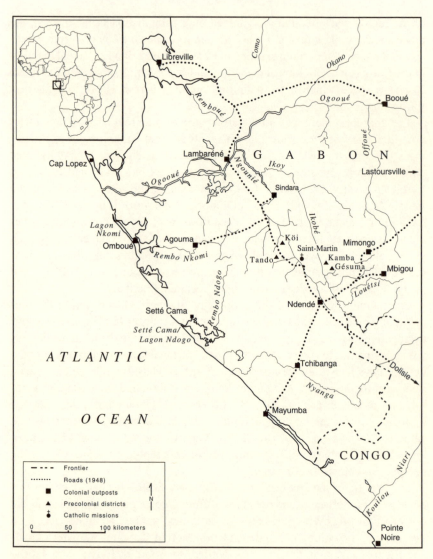

Map 9.1. Gabon (1948).

trader Robert Bruce Walker in 1866, did so with guides speaking the above languages and thus initiated the name-appropriation process by writing down "Ngouyai" or "Ngunyé" on their maps and in their text.[30]

MAPS AND MAPPING

On the map of Du Chaillu's initial travels of 1856 to 1858, the Ngounié is inaccurately depicted, since the explorer believed he had penetrated 200 kilometers farther into the interior than he had actually gone. In addition, the middle and upper segments of the river are labeled "Rembo Apingi" (Apindji) and "Rembo Apono" (Punu), this reflecting local conceptions of space where naming was limited to segments of large rivers and determined by the linguistic identity of those inhabiting its banks. The more precise conception of a single, all-inclusive name for a European geographical feature called "river" was not part of local knowledge. Du Chaillu's map, then, effectively symbolizes a historical moment when European and African conceptions of space confront and mutually contaminate each other. The map's "errors" can be seen as reflecting the competing notions of territoriality that would come to define the colonial encounter.

Du Chaillu, having received a good deal of criticism for the many inaccuracies found in his first map, sought to develop a more refined appropriating gaze. On his return to Europe, he learned how to specify positions through astronomical observation and compass bearing. He returned to Southern Gabon in 1864. His efforts resulted in a more accurate map for European purposes and one in which the term "Ngouyai" effectively replaced local river terms in textual space. In this way he advanced the process of emptying the space of Southern Gabon of its specificity and clearing the ground for the imposition of modern territoriality.[31]

Maps were particularly effective instruments in this regard. Recent studies in the history of cartography seeking to insert the map and process of its creation into social and cultural history have shed light on this process. From this new vantage point, "maps constitute a specialized graphic language, an instrument of communication that has influenced behavioral characteristics and the social life of humanity."[32] Firmly ensconced in the tide of historical events, maps and mapmaking lose their innocence and are no longer viewed as neutral, objective representations of physical space. They embody instead a form of knowledge subject to the manipulation and control of those who exercise, or seek to exercise, territoriality. European explorers, missionaries, and colonial administrators were part of a culture where "mapmaking was one of the specialized intellectual weapons by which power could be gained, administered, given legitimacy and codified."[33] The geographer J.B. Harley plainly states that "as much as guns and warships, maps have been the weapons of imperialism."[34] The ability to map, as with the ability to write, allowed for the creation of a textual space where the physical space of the real world was abstracted, reified, and emptied of its autochthonous unwritten meaning. Thus, "while the map is never the reality, in such ways it helps to create a different reality."[35]

The Portuguese had begun the naming and mapping of the coastal space of Gabon in the fifteenth and sixteenth centuries but virtually nothing was known about the interior until the latter half of the nineteenth century.[36] The mapping of the Ogooué was begun in 1862 and grew in sophistication as explorers traveled further upstream toward its source. Yet its complex delta system was not accurately drawn until a colonial hydrographic mission was undertaken in 1911.[37] Du Chaillu's maps remained the principal sources of information for the peoples and geography of the Ngounié until the creation of the French Congo colony in 1886. There was, however, a rough map published by Père Bichet in 1882 of the lower Ngounié, indicating villages and factories between the Ikoy and Samba as well as affixing ethnic designations.[38]

At about the same time, Aloysius Smith, in service to the trading firm of Hatton and Cookson, tells of making a "navigation chart" of the Ngounié and of a map he "drew of the big slave roads" to the coast servicing Samba and the middle portion of the river. These maps were privileged information, as maps so often were throughout history, and as "trade secrets" specific to the concerns of Alfred Aloysius "Trader" Horn's firm they were not meant for publication. These different mapping projects represented multiple and sometimes competing European interests, thus demonstrating that colonial territoriality was hardly a monolithic enterprise.[39]

Brazza's West Africa Mission had as one of its tasks the correction of cartographic errors and the filling in of blank spaces. A good deal was accomplished along the Ogooué but it would be the task of the new French Congo colony to map the Ngounié River basin.[40] Missions cutting across the Du Chaillu Massif from the colonial post of Lastoursville (created in 1885) on the Ogooué to Samba on the Ngounié were organized in 1890 and 1893. Jules Berton, the head of the 1890 mission, claimed that one of his main accomplishments was the creation of a more accurate list and map of Gabonese "tribus" than those provided by Du Chaillu.[41] In affixing ethnic names to the abstracted space of a map, Europeans fixed Gabonese identity and attachment to place in ways that did not reflect precolonial conceptions. Thus from Du Chaillu through the end of the colonial period, the map assumes a central role in the invention and crystallization of modern Gabonese ethnic identity.[42]

It is significant that during the 1893 mission the colonial administrator Godel was accompanied by Monseigneur Le Roy and Père Bichet of the French Holy Ghost Fathers Catholic mission.[43] The enclosure of the Gabonese forest was effected from a network of colonial nodal points that were actually outposts of European constructed space. The Catholic and Protestant missions were the first to establish such networks; they differed from the European commercial factories in that their stated objective was to transform the cultural practice of the peoples of Southern Gabon.[44] Nineteenth-century European traders did not seek transformation but were rather more concerned with inserting themselves into the networks of local commerce. The missionary vision for the radical transformation of the cultural practices of Southern Gabon paralleled that of Brazza's for the landscape and employed the same literate instruments to chart its trajectory in textual space. Yet in comparison with the colonial administration, the Catholic missions had very few resources and thus no real power to impose their vision. Truly effective colonial nodal points capable of imposing modern territoriality only began to form with the advent of concession companies in the closing years of the nineteenth century.

Brazza, as Commissioner General of the French Congo colony from 1886 to 1898, squandered the resources made available to him by the French government in trying to conquer Chad and was singularly ineffective in promoting any kind of economic benefit for France. In spite of his efforts to attract French capital, commercial activity in Gabon continued to be dominated by British and German firms, a severe affront to the intensely patriotic colonial servant. By 1898, the French government was frustrated as well and Brazza was recalled to France.[45] Before his departure, Brazza set in motion the project of creating concession companies on the model of those operating in King Leopold's Congo Free State. After a couple of false starts, *the Société du Haut-Ogooué* (SHO) began its operations on both banks of the middle and upper Ogooué in 1897; by 1900 more than 70 percent of the French Congo colony had been divided up into some forty-two different concessions. These concession companies operated from a radically different approach than trading firms like Hatton and Cookson, as they claimed both monopoly control over commerce and ownership rights to land within their concession. Simply put, "all rights of possession and exploitation" accrued to the concession company, this based on a legal argument positing that:

Land can only be owned through individual or collective property, or as public domain. Only temporary use of land exists in black Africa, not individual property. No charge is asked for the temporary or permanent use of collective property, and land cannot be sold either within or outside the community. Natives cannot sell land legally, therefore the selling of any land is fictive.[46]

In concluding that all the land of the French Congo was public domain with the local populations having only usage rights, not only were precolonial territorial practices emptied of their significance but so were the accommodations negotiated by the existing European factories.

The most potent symbol of this crucial shift in the European *cognitive* map is the 1900 *cartographic* map published in *La Dépêche Coloniale* illustrating the holdings of the various concession companies (see Map 9.2).[47] This is a very different product from the tentative mapping efforts of Du Chaillu forty years earlier. The appropriating gaze that first looked out on the physical space of Southern Gabon through the eyes of individual explorers now precisely rendered the perceived chaos of the Equatorial forest through the ordered textual space of the cartographic grid. The bold and sharply geometrical lines

Map 9.2. Concessionary Companies in the French Congo (Map published in the *Dépêche coloniale,* 1900).

delimiting the concessions are expressions of an enhanced imperial confidence poised to impose a modern capitalist territoriality over its domain.

Yet these bold lines drawn up in Paris betrayed an ignorance of the actual terrain and a number of geographic expeditions were required to effectively apply the "textual reality" to real physical space. Several brigades were organized in 1899 to provide the "geodesic canvas" on which the concessions could work out the precise boundaries of their holdings and the colonial government could determine the contours of its administrative units.[48] Further data was obtained by the administrator Georges Bruel during his 1907–1908 assignment to determine the boundaries between the SHO, the *Société des factories de Ndjolé* (SFN), and the *Société de la Haute-Ngounié* (SHN) concessions. All of this information was put together to produce the kind of detailed and accurate map required for modern administration.[49] The combined obsessions of the colonial administration's pursuit of tax revenue and the efforts of the concession companies to profit from their monopoly claims resulted in the creation of truly effective colonial nodal points that began to enclose and irreversibly transform the physical landscape of Southern Gabon. Colonial posts existed on the Atlantic coast at Cap Lopez from 1885 and at Setté Cama and Mayumba from 1887. By 1905 and the arrival of the Brazza Commission to investigate concession company abuses, administration and concession actions had not only served to stifle what had been a lively commerce with British firms in these areas but had also disrupted networks in the interior, notably at Agouma on the Rembo Nkomi. The surrounding population at each of the above posts balked at trading with the French concessions and simply moved their villages in search of other trade opportunities. Increasingly brutal administrative efforts to collect tax revenue were further motivation to abandon villages that had been commercially active in the early 1890s. Violent resistance was also a strategy. The military post of Mouila, established in 1904, was created in response to the rebellion of the Tsogo-speaking clans in the Kamba and Gésuma districts—a rebellion that was partly stimulated by concession and administrative action to shut down the local salt trade out of Mayumba.[50]

Attempts begun in 1894 to organize a per capita tax obliged the French colonial administration to conduct information-gathering activities like census-taking so as to determine the rolls eligible for taxation. Census-taking is a very powerful instrument of modern territoriality and its use is always a significant historical development.[51] In all modern states, the main objective in delimiting and asserting control over geographic area is to collect revenue. In the colonial state of Gabon, tax collection became the gauge of colonial hegemony for the French and the symbol of submission for the Gabonese. So powerful was this symbol that it was integrated into the origin myths of the Mitsogo people to explain the relations between the races of humanity: *Min-ombe* (the Blacks), *Ebamba* (the Whites), and *Babongo* (the Pygmies). In these myths, the pygmy *Babongo* are seen as the older brothers of the white *Ebamba* because the colonial administration did not force them to work or pay taxes.[52]

In the first decade of the twentieth century, French attempts to enclose the physical space of Southern Gabon only functioned to disrupt local commerce and stimulate revolt. The most notable rebellion was that of the Tsogo-speaking clans of the Gésuma and Kamba districts, lasting from 1903 to 1913. The end of 1906 marked an intensification of French efforts to bring an end to this revolt. Conrad, the captain of a company of *tirailleurs* dispatched from Dakar, started to make alliances with the leaders of Punu-, Gisir-, Apindji-, or Tsogo-speaking clans whose villages had either been attacked or intimidated by forces loyal to Mbombé, the key leader of the Mitsogo resistance. In February 1907, Conrad initiated a strategy that would ultimately bring about the enclosure of space in Southern Gabon: he organized the building of a "road." Actually, the task was simply to widen the trail between Mouila and Kembélé, but the project shared with later road-building efforts the goal of delimiting and asserting control over a geographic area in order to influence the people inhabiting that area. The consequence of this particular effort was the flight of all the villages along this trade route further into the forest and the fractioning of the Kamba district. A temporary post was established at the village of Mabaga on the Onoy and dubbed "Fort Sampic" after a French sergeant killed in a 1904 skirmish. This was about 20 kilometers from Mouila and one-third of the way to Kembélé. It took three months to clear the remaining distance as there were almost daily ambushes on the locally recruited labor gangs and the *tirailleur* protection forces. By mid-April, the colonial force was in Kembélé, attempting to build a military post in the face of continuous attacks from hostile Tsogo-speaking clans.[53] The post was effectively established and manned by a French officer but: "However, the country was still escaping our control. The road between Kembélé and Mouila was still relatively unsafe. The natives did not wish to establish relations with us; they avoided the immediate surroundings of the administrative outposts, and sought refuge in the forest."[54]

Patterns of village settlement and land use were severely disrupted as the populations began to spend more time in seasonal *mpindi* (temporary camps) so as to avoid contact with agents of the colonial administration. This kind of disruption of fragile agricultural and hunting practices could not go on for very long without producing serious food shortages. This process accelerated in the decade between 1910 and 1920. Precolonial districts virtually disappeared from the landscape as the unprecedented volume and different kinds of population movement—due to labor recruitment for the timber industry and the need for porters in the Cameroon campaign of World War I—swept away their loose and fragile structures. Clusters of good-sized villages participating in patterns of exchange over generations were broken up by trade competition, military campaigns, disease, famine, and flight deep into the forest away from the well-worn commercial routes. The "salt route," which had supported the large, neat villages of the Tsogo-speaking Kamba district encountered by Du Chaillu fifty years earlier, was abandoned by 1916; all that remained of the villages were the bands of banana and palm trees that had encircled the dwellings. Their former inhabitants had fled into the forest.[55]

The colonial military post at the recalcitrant village of Kembélé had been shut down once again in 1914 due to a lack of personnel but the incessant disruption had left its mark; four years later Kembélé's inhabitants "disbanded in their forest dwellings and did not plant their fields; they feed on palm nuts and fruits from the forest."[56] Kele-speaking clans who had established villages on the Ikoy River at the end of the nineteenth century abandoned these sites following numerous deaths from famine. Once relatively prosperous, this stretch of the river was an uninhabited dead zone in the 1930s, as the former inhabitants believed the land cursed.[57]

The experience of disease, forced labor, and famine in Southern Gabon during the second decade of the twentieth century has been correctly viewed as a crucial watershed in the imposition of colonial enclosure. Precolonial territoriality as the predominant practice in the organization of social space effectively ended. When Le Testu, perhaps the most-gifted observer to have served in the colonial administration in Southern Gabon, began work on a census in the Ofooué-Ngounié circumscription at the end of 1916, he remarked: "The diverse groups in the subdivision of Mouila, Apindji, Bapounou, and Mitsogo entirely lack organization and structure. After we complete the census, we need to group them by administrative territories."[58] By this time pre-colonial district structure was in such a state of disarray that it escaped Le Testu's usually keen powers of observation. The chaos and turmoil of the period had effectively erased the district from the physical space of Southern Gabon, thus implementing the textual act of erasure accomplished by colonial cartography some decades earlier.

THE TRIUMPH OF MODERN TERRITORIALITY: ROADS AND ENCLOSURE

> Roads, railroads, schools, markets, military service, and the circulation of money, goods, and printed matter . . . swept away old commitments, instilled a national of view of things in regional minds, and confirmed the power of that view by offering advancement to those who adopted it.[59]
>
> —Eugen Weber, *Peasants into Frenchmen*

The imposition of modern territoriality in rural France in the final decades of the nineteenth century was accomplished by the same instruments of change that rearranged the physical space of Southern Gabon from about 1920. Though it is striking to note that these developments occurred within a generation of each other, the contexts were, of course, very different.[60] The disorder that resulted from the ordeal of famine and disease left the peoples of Southern Gabon severely shaken and extremely vulnerable. The *tabula rasa* that Europeans had thought they had been seeing all along had, to a certain degree, become reality as the Equatorial tradition, which for centuries had ordered the physical space in this region of Africa, was no longer the dominant territorial influence.[61] The forests and savannahs of Southern Gabon were now fully primed for the imposition of modern territoriality and enclosure.

The hegemony of the French colonial state was dependent upon its ability to create modern communications and transportation infrastructures. The peoples and forest terrain of Southern Gabon presented particular challenges to this project. The penchant for decentralization and the aversion to the consolidation of authority that defined the complex networks of clan and lineage relations ran counter to the requirements of the colonial state. There were no centralized state structures or figures of authority upon which the French could build; power and authority were diffused across interwoven networks of male clan elders; their function and operations were poorly understood by Europeans. Nor were there nodal regions containing a metropolitan center serving a well-defined hinterland over a well-developed system of roads. All of this had to be created.[62]

Many observers note just how little was accomplished in terms of modern infrastructure during the colonial period when Gabon was justifiably considered the classic example of a neglected backwater.[63] Yet from the perspective of the peoples who lived through this period the colonial presence was not so slight; radical transformation occurred and, though the colonial towns and road networks that grew in the decades following First World War pale in comparison to physical changes in other colonies, their impact was just as drastic and perhaps even greater given the fundamental differences between precolonial and modern territorial practices.

Permanent roads are the key, indicator that modern territoriality has been established, that physical space is undergoing enclosure. The geographer Roland Pourtier notes that "Only the buildings of roads can achieve the real appropriation of the national territory. The material as well as the mental construction of the territory is based on the road network."[64] The first "road" project in Southern Gabon sought to connect the colonial post at Sindara to the cluster of villages that eventually became the post of Fougamou. This would have created a more efficient bypassing of the rapids on the Ngounié and thus have improved communications and transport between Mouila and Lambaréné. The organization of a labor force to undertake this task between 1910 and 1912 represented a public works project on a scale hitherto unknown and served to heighten ethnic awareness, as workers were grouped together by Europeans according to European colonial ethnic categories.

The goal at this time was to create an enlarged trail for the transport by porter of palm kernels, the main source of tax revenue in the Middle and Upper Ngounié, to the post and factories at Sindara. The trail fell into a state of disrepair during the period of chaos and food shortages. In 1920, the colonial administration proposed constructing a dirt road capable of handling automobile and truck traffic and duly began organizing work teams. These teams were euphemistically labeled *main d'œuvre prestataire* and their creation required coercive tactics from the Regional Guards. The general shortage of labor that existed throughout the colony forced the administration to recruit among Apindji-speaking clans, still reeling from famine and disease, located on the Middle Ngounié some 80 kilometers away from the road site.[65]

These efforts failed because two years later the road had yet to be built. The colonial administration recognized that road-building at this level was beyond the competence of the circumscription administrator and that the presence of a specialized public works technician was required. A study was duly commissioned at the end of 1924 but the technician was slow in completing his work. In the meantime, porterage traffic along the tortuous 30-kilometer trail (there were ninety-two bridges between Sindara and Fougamou) continued to increase. In 1923, it was estimated that 60,000 loads were carried up and down the path annually; the local Eviya-and Vili-speaking clans, now decimated, as well as the Gisir- and Fang-speaking clans, who preferred employment in the booming timber industry at Lambaréné and the Lakes Region, abhorred this work. Thus, the colonial administration and the SHO were obliged to recruit porters from the Punu- and Nzabi-speaking clans on the Upper Ngounié, 500 of whom were under the charge of the SHO at Sindara in 1923; a total of 720 porters toiled along this route in 1924. The work was grueling—six trips to be made within twenty-five days—and took its toll on the health of those engaged in it. A road suitable for motor vehicles was viewed as an absolute necessity.[66]

This had been a goal of the colonial administration for five years before serious work was finally undertaken in 1925.[67] The earlier failed efforts to forcibly recruit labor had only served to frustrate the surrounding population by involving them in a seemingly pointless endeavor. The 1925 administrative reorganization, which moved the Sindara subdivision from the Bas-Ogooué to the Ngounié circumscription, facilitated the more intense recruitment needed to finally complete the road project; the shifting of colonial boundaries in Gabon was usually undertaken for purposes of labor recruitment. By March of that year, 900 workers were stationed at Fougamou, a number deemed excessive by the priests at the Saint-Martin Catholic mission who feared food shortages.[68]

By the end of 1927, the road was completed and motor vehicles were able to make the trip between Sindara and Fougamou; the colonial administration was optimistic that the Ngounié circumscription would prosper now that the burden of porterage was lifted and the local populations could focus on exploiting produce from the groves of palm trees found in the area. However, the forced recruitment of labor for the Sindara-Fougamou road—which coincided with recruitment for the less arduous but longer route along the savannah from Mouila to Ndendé[69]—led to food shortages in several parts of the Ngounié circumscription in 1929, poor harvests resulting from the disruption to the planting season two years earlier. Further tempering the optimism from the completion of the Sindara-Fougamou road was the necessity for almost continual maintenance and the considerable drain this made on revenue. The growth anticipated from the exploitation of palm products never materialized because by the mid-1930s low prices paid by the SHO and the high tariffs the concession charged to transport produce from Fougamou to Sindara totally discouraged village producers.[70]

There is a good deal of irony in this example of the imposition of modern territoriality. If permanent roads are an expression of territorial power, then the French infrastructure projects described above might be seen as rather feeble and fragile. Clearly they are not indications of a mastery over the space of the Equatorial forest; yet it was precisely the feebleness and fragility of these efforts that resulted in excessive demands on Gabonese labor and rendered the local populations vulnerable to abuse and food shortages.[71]

The completion of the Fougamou-Sindara road signaled the decline of Samba as a colonial nodal point. This move also heralded, however tentatively, the coming triumph of the road over the river as the dominant means of long-distance transportation in Southern Gabon. Although this would not be fully accomplished until after the Second World War, the flurry of road construction in the 1930s signaled an end to precolonial commerce based on water transport; by 1948 a road linking Dolisie in the Congo to Libreville and passing through Mouila, Fougamou and Lambaréné had replaced the Ngounié River as the main transport axis in Southern Gabon.[72]

The contrast between the situation at the beginning of the 1930s and that at the decade's close is revealing not so much in what was completed in terms of suitable roads but rather in how it was accomplished. In 1929 forced recruitment for the Sindara-Fougamou (30 kilometers) and Mouila-Ndendé (75 kilometers) routes had led to serious food shortages in much of Southern Gabon. These remained the only roads in the region until the mid-1930s when work was begun on routes connecting Mouila to Fougamou (100 kilometers) and linking Ndendé to Tchibanga and Mayumba (200 kilometers). The administration was hesitant to forcibly recruit workers, fearing yet another food shortage; furthermore, the powerful European timber interests in Gabon frowned upon diverting scarce labor from their camps on the Lower Ogooué.

By 1937, when the administration organized workers for the Mouila-Fougamou route, colonial bureaucratic practice had become more efficient and work registers were employed to control labor: "A book for registering compulsory labor should keep the name of each worker, and the work he is supposed to do, so that the calling of workers is facilitated. Recruitments and administrative reports should be sent to the canton chiefs in charge of the workers in each location . . . 13,600 labor days have been necessary to the building of the road between the towns of Fougamou and Mouila."[73] The use of such bureaucratic instruments, now implemented by *canton* chiefs in addition to the Regional Guard, allowed officials considerably more control over the people and activities within the physical space of colonial administrative units. For the stretch of the road between the Douya and Doubou rivers, workers were fed and paid 40 francs per month, though on sites further north they only received food.[74]

The administration thus claimed that only "voluntary" labor had been employed in this project; officials further asserted that some elements of the local population saw the benefits of road-building: "Large numbers of natives worked to build the road between Fougamou and Mouila. If the 'Mitsogos' did not grasp the importance of the new means of communication, the 'Eshiras' by contrast are pleased about the road, even though they had to provide considerable labor for building it."[75] Indeed, an informant in the village of Mussondji who worked on the road as a young boy recalled receiving brutal treatment at the hands of the Regional Guard.[76]

The Mouila-Fougamou route was completed in 1938; the justification for its construction was to ensure year-round transport as steamer traffic on the Middle Ngounié was not possible in the low waters of the long dry season. The same problem existed on the Lower Ngounié; thus the Mouila-Fougamou route was useless unless another road were cut over difficult terrain connecting it to the important commercial center at Lambaréné. A 50-kilometer stretch was built from the village of Fouramwanga between 1940 and 1943; this time there were no food shortages, as laborers from Chad were brought in to do much of the work. The administration also profited from the availability of timber workers idled by the industry's shutdown during World War II. In this way, the Ndendé-Tchibanga-Mayumba route was also finally completed.[77] Neither of these efforts required the degree of coercion seen at the beginning of the 1930s nor did they result in severe food shortages. In just over a decade, the French colonial administration and the timber industry had succeeded in altering the pattern of labor exploitation in Southern Gabon; by the 1940s there existed a "labor market" in French Equatorial Africa sufficiently integrated into the capitalist wage-earning sector and capable of accomplishing infrastructure projects without disastrous consequences for the local population.[78]

VILLAGE REGROUPMENT

Modern territoriality, as employed by the colonial or nation state, seeks first to "fix" people and their relationships through the bureaucratic textual space of the map and census. This bureaucratic knowledge is then exploited to control and influence people and their relationships in real physical space; the initial goal is to obtain revenue. In Southern Gabon from about 1920, the construction of roads or the improvement of trails provided state-controlled axes along which the local population was forced to move. The bureaucratic term for this was "regroupment"; the goal of regroupment was to "fix" villages in accessible physical space so that the colonial administration and timber industry could recruit labor.

Yet with regard to the timber industry, this "fixing" was only momentary, as once workers were recruited from their villages, they were obliged to move into temporary lumber camps on the Lower Ogooué or in the Lakes Region, the sites for timber concessions. Given the industry's transient exploitation and the fluidity of the labor market, there developed a pattern of mobility when it came to settlement and population movement that differed from the mobility that characterized precolonial society.[79] There also developed a competition between the colonial administration, which desired access to labor available in its own circumscriptions for infrastructure projects, and the timber industry, which recruited throughout the colony with little regard for the needs of areas outside the Lower Ogooué exploitation zone. Yet, on other occasions, the administration's desire for infrastructure development was lukewarm and colonial officials came to assist the timber industry in its attempts to recruit labor.[80]

Attempts to regroup Punu- and Apindji-speaking clans into larger villages in the area of Mouila date from 1910 but concerted regroupment efforts were only undertaken in the 1920s. By the end of 1921, the Apindji-speaking clans of the Mouila subdivision were consolidated in thirty-five villages but only "after numerous difficulties and palavers."[81] The administrator had only been concerned with grouping together what he believed was a sufficient number of inhabitants and paid no attention to clan and lineage relations; within a year these settlements no longer existed.[82] In 1922, Kembélé was once again the site of a colonial post and efforts were made to regroup the clans of the former Kamba district along the abandoned path heading out of Mouila; two villages were established near the Onoy river. Given that labor recruitment possibilities had been exhausted in the Nyanga, Bongo, and Bas-Ogooué circumscriptions during World War I, the administration and timber industry started to focus recruitment efforts on the Tsogo-, Sango-, and Nzabi-speaking clans in the relatively populous area around Mbigou; to this end villages were to be grouped along the path connecting Mbigou to Kembélé. However, Tsogo- and Nzabi-speaking clans frustrated administration plans as a colonial official noted at the end of 1922 that they would rather live in forest camps and in filthy conditions"[83] the same complaint was made two years later, though the administration now expressed an awareness of the importance of lineage relationships.[84]

In 1918, Le Testu had stressed to colonial officials the importance of obtaining information about clan and lineage relationships; yet his advice was little heeded. As a consequence, village regroupments were pell-mell affairs and had to be maintained by force. In a 1924 report, Le Testu cited the attempt to group a number of villages along the trail connecting Mouila to Ndendé as particularly wrong-headed. Not only was the location poorly chosen, but the name of the regrouped village, "Keri, (fear)" referred to the dread the different lineages felt now that they were obliged to live next to each other. Le Testu thought village regroupment was a poor policy and believed it was easier to administer four villages of twenty-five inhabitants than one of one hundred. These attitudes earned him the animosity of the new Governor-General of the A.E.F., Raphael Antonetti.[85]

Thus throughout the 1920s and 1930s the Regional Guard was continually sent out into the forest to destroy the temporary *mpindi* settlements in which the clans of Southern Gabon distanced themselves from colonial rule. This "passive resistance" was most effectively practiced by peoples ensconced in hilly, thickly forested areas: the Tsogo-speaking clans of the Gésuma district; the Gisir-speaking clans of the Tando district; and the Vungu- and Varama-speaking clans in the hills to the east of the Setté Cama lagoon. In the latter half of the 1920s, the administration adopted an energetic plan to force re-calcitrant Varama-speaking clans to participate in the life of the colony. When it was implemented the subdivision commander reported in frustration: "Since then, what did the Waramas [Varamas] do? They only dance the bouiti [bwiti]."[86] Another attempt to regroup them was attempted in 1931. In the Gisir-speaking Tando district, a chief named Boukouendzi dismantled his village in 1928, destroyed the coffee trees he had been required to grow, and fled with his followers into the forest; the following year the subdivision commander ordered the Regional Guard to regroup Boukouendzi's dispersed *mpindi* back into villages.[87]

In 1936, the colonial official Maclatchy described the Tsogo-speaking clans of the Mimongo subdivision in the following fashion:

They tolerate our presence more than they accept it, and they take on ad-ministrative requirements as they would carry a necessary evil for the sake of protecting their tranquility. But it is clear that our influence on them is virtually nonexistent, as water sliding on a hard surfaced rock. For example, they build villages for the sake of meeting administrative demands and official activities. Yet the natives' real life occurs in the "*pindi*,' those small and filthy camps built in the bush by every family next to their plantations and hunting grounds. The Mitsogos spend most of their life there, away from official control, thanks to the immensity of the bush. The natives make a clear distinction between "the village for the commandant" and the "pindi: the village for the blacks." Plantations also fall into these two categories.[88]

This double existence represented a creative compromise with modern ter-ritoriality, in effect ceding it the spaces of what were once large villages located on active trade routes. The superficial investment in "show" villages for the colonial administration allowed Tsogo-speaking clans to gather the remnants of precolonial territoriality and practice them on a smaller scale in the relative security of the forest.

Flight into the forest was the most effective form of defense; villages in the Du Chaillu Massif organized surveillance teams that kept watch night and day over the trails running through the area so as to warn inhabitants of the coming of the Regional Guard. When their arrival was imminent, the shouting of a single phrase sufficed to organize the rapid exodus into the forest of all the young men and women of a village, where they would remain for up to several weeks. On occasion, defense became more aggressive, with secret societies organizing revenge attacks against abusive guards. However, by the

1930s when a small portion of the local population acquired literacy skills, written complaints to colonial officials became common. In 1931, for example, young Punu-speakers submitted a petition in the name of Punu clan chiefs regarding systematic patterns of abuse in the Mouila subdivision attributed not only to the Regional Guard but to the post interpreters and French commander.[89]

The local population had good reason to avoid the colonial administration and it was not until the late 1930s that a trickle of villages began to see the advantages of establishing themselves on the growing network of roads in Southern Gabon.[90] The most dramatic developments in terms of village regroupment occurred after World War II, and this farther to the north in the Woleu-Ntem.[91] Village regroupment continued throughout the colonial period and after independence. The 1960s witnessed a major effort to move isolated villages onto roads in the Nyanga and Ngounié provinces.[92] Yet, by 1940, it was quite apparent that modern territoriality had triumphed in Southern Gabon; the physical space of the region had been effectively "enclosed" so that the agents of the colonial presence could influence and control people, phenomena, and relationships in a more or less hegemonic fashion. This transition, occurring within the span of a single generation, was radical. In the conclusion to his masterful study on the spatial development of the Gabonese nation-state, Roland Pourtier describes a historical process where "The fluid and mobile space from earlier times has ossified and has shrunk around a restricted number of places."[93] In Southern Gabon, these "places" were colonial nodal points with names like Lambaréné, Mouila, and Fougamou. Pourtier further proposes that in present-day Gabon "the space crystallizes around such fixed clusters."[94] This "crystallized space" is the outcome of the enclosure process.

NOTES

1. This paper is drawn from my doctoral dissertation; see Christopher Gray, "Territoriality, Ethnicity, and Colonial Rule in Southern Gabon 1850–1960" (Ph.D. Thesis, Indiana University, 1995).

2. A very influential work has been H. Lefebvre, *La Production de l'espace* (Paris: Anthropos, 1974); see also P. Clavel, *Espace et pouvoir* (Paris: *Presses Universitaires de France*, 1978) and F.P.-Lévy and M. Segaud, eds., *Anthropologie de l'espace* (Paris: Centre Georges Pompidou, 1983). For space and African history, see the contributions presented by Marc Augé, Jean-Pierre Chrétien, and Claude-Hélène Perrot under the rubric "L'Afrique: un autre espace historique," in *Annales E.S.C.* 40, no. 6 (1985). Gabon has been given the spatial treatment in Roland Pourtier, *Le Gabon, Tome 1: Espace-Histoire-Société, Tome 2: État et Développment* (Paris: L'Harmattan, 1989); for an interesting theoretical statement, see *Tome 1*, 11. Foucault produced three influential pieces; see Foucault, "Space, Knowledge and Power," in P. Rabinow, ed., *The Foucault Reader* (New York: Pantheon, 1984), 239–56; "Of Other Spaces," *Diacritics*, 16 (1986), 22–27; and "Questions

on Geography," in C. Gordon, ed., *Power/Knowledge: Selected Interviews and Other Writings* (Brighton: Harvester, 1976), 63–77. Pierre Bourdieu has a relevant article, "The Social Space and the Genesis of Groups," *Theory and Society* 14, no. 6 (1985), 723–44. For an excellent summary by a geographer, see D. Harvey, *The Condition of Post-Modernity: An Enquiry into the Origins of Cultural Change* (Oxford: Basil Blackwell, 1989). Yi-Fu Tuan, *Space and Place: The Perspective of Experience* (Minneapolis: University of Minnesota Press, 1977) is a stimulating introduction to key issues.

3. For studies concerned primarily with domestic space and gender, see S. Ardener, ed., *Women and Space: Ground Rules and Social Maps* (London: Croom Helm, 1981); H.L. Moore, *Space, Text and Gender: An Anthropological Study of the Marakwet of Kenya* (Cambridge: Cambridge University Press, 1986); Mamphela Ramphele, *A Bed Called Home: Life in the Migrant Labour Hostels of Capetown* (Athens: Ohio University Press, 1992); and H.J. Nast, "The Impact of British Imperialism on the Landscape of Female Slavery in the Kano Palace, Northern Nigeria," *Africa* 64, no. 1 (1994), 35–73.

4. R.D. Sack, *Human Territoriality: Its Theory and History* (Cambridge: Cambridge University Press, 1986), 23, 26.

5. Ibid., 19.

6. Ibid., 26.

7. Ibid., 6, 53–91, for the full development of this argument; see also Sack, *Conceptions of Space in Social Thought: A Geographic Perspective* (Minneapolis: University of Minnesota Press, 1980), 170–85. Sack insists that the term *primitive* be read in its original meaning—that of "being primary" or "coming first"—and not according to the pejorative connotations it later acquired.

8. For a detailed discussion of territoriality in Southern Gabon just prior to colonial rule, see Gray, "Territoriality," 94–191; also G. Dupré, *Un ordre et sa destruction* (Paris: ORSTOM, 1982).

9. See Harvey, *Condition of Post-Modernity*, 240–59.

10. M.-L. Pratt, *Imperial Eyes: Travel Writing and Transculturation* (London and New York: Routledge, 1992), 15.

11. See in particular Foucault, *The Order of Things: An Archaeology of the Human Sciences* (New York: Vintage, 1973); see discussions in Harvey, *Condition of Post-Modernity*, 213–14, 237–38, 252–53; and Pratt, *Imperial Eyes*, 28–29.

12. Harvey, *Condition of Post-Modernity*, 264.

13. The notion of "imperial eyes" is from the title of Pratt's book. For Pratt, Du Chaillu and Brazza would be examples of the "seeing-man," which she describes as "an admittedly unfriendly label for the European male subject of European landscape discourse—he whose imperial eyes passively look out and possess"; Pratt, *Imperial Eyes*, 7; see 208–16 for interesting interpretations of Du Chaillu's writings as well as those of Mary Kingsley. For a fascinating study of the transformation of European vision, see D.M. Lowe, *History of Bourgeois Perception* (Chicago: University of Chicago Press, 1982).

14. J.K. Noyes, *Colonial Space: Spatiality in the Discourse of German South West Africa 1884–1915* (Philadelphia: Harwood Academic Publishers, 1992), 190–91; see also 163–64.

15. P.B. Du Chaillu, *Explorations and Adventures in Equatorial Africa* (London: T. Werner Laurie, 1861; reprinted London: Live Books Resurrected, 1945), 445–46 (emphasis in original).

16. Idem.

17. See R.P. Harrison, *Forests: The Shadow of Civilization* (Chicago: University of Chicago Press, 1992).

18. The terms are from Pratt, *Imperial Eyes*, 7.

19. M.H. Kingsley, *Travels in West Africa: Congo Français, Corisco and Cameroons* (London: MacMillan, 1897), 102.

20. G. Bruel, "La boucle de l'Ogooué," *Revue Coloniale* 93 (1910), 642; the forest as obstacle to European vision is a theme Pourtier addresses on several occasions; see Pourtier, *Le Gabon, Tome 1*, 35–36, 40–41, 52, 65, 147, 151–52.

21. Pourtier, *Le Gabon, Tome 1*, 83; for discussions of Brazza as visionary, see H. Brunschwig, ed., *Brazza explorateur: les traités Makoko 1880–1882* (Paris: Mouton, 1972), 213–14; E. Rabut, ed., *Brazza Commissaire Général: Le Congo Français 1886–1897* (Paris: Éditions de l'EHESS, 1989), 12; C. Coquery-Vidrovitch, "Les idées économiques de Brazza et les premières tentatives de compagnies de colonisation au Congo Français 1885–1898," *Cahiers d'études africaines* 5, no. 1 (1965), 57, and *Brazza et la prise de possession du Congo: La Mission de l'Ouest Africain 1883–1885* (Paris: Mouton, 1969), 214.

22. Noyes, *Colonial Space*, 136; see Sack, *Human Territoriality*, 48, for a discussion of capitalism and emptiable space.

23. "Rapport de Brazza au ministère de l'Instruction publique, Madiville, 20 mai 1885," in Coquery-Vidrovitch, *Brazza et la prise de possession du Congo*, 281.

24. Coquery-Vidrovitch, *Le Congo au temps des grandes compagnies concessionnaires 1898–1930* (Paris: Mouton, 1972).

25. Noyes, *Colonial Space*, 196.

26. See Pourtier, *Le Gabon, Tome 2*, 62–72 for an interesting discussion.

27. Du Chaillu, *Explorations and Adventures*, 258.

28. For examples of local names for falls and rapids on the Upper and Middle Ogooué, see Raponda-Walker, "Chutes, seuils et rapides de l'Ogowe de Franceville à Alembe," *Réalités Gabonaises* 12 (1961), 39–41.

29. In the precolonial political tradition of Equatorial Africa, the "district" was the largest social organization of space; districts were clusters of villages that grouped together for security and to facilitate matrimonial and economic exchange; see J. Vansina, *Paths in the Rainforests: Toward a History of Political Tradition in Equatorial Africa* (Madison: University of Wisconsin Press, 1990), 81–83.

30. See Du Chaillu, *Explorations and Adventures*, 458, map endpiece; and R.B.N. Walker, "Relation d'une tentative d'exploration en 1866 de la rivière de l'Ogowé et de la recherche d'un grand lac devant se trouver dans l'Afrique centrale," *Annales des voyages de la géographie, de l'histoire et de l'archéologie* 1 (1870), 70; local names are found in Raponda-Walker, *Notes d'histoire du Gabon* (Montpellier: Imprimerie Charité), 105, 147; Raponda-Walker and R. Sillans, *Les plantes utiles du Gabon* (Paris: Éditions Paul le Chevalier, 1961), 16; M. Mbigui, "Recherche sur l'histoire de Sindara 1858–1946" (*Mémoire de maîtrise, Université Omar Bongo, Libreville*, 1984), 18.

31. Du Chaillu, *A Journey to Ashango-Land* (New York: D. Appleton, 1867), x; also vi–ix and map endpiece.

32. J.B. Harley, "The Map and the Development of the History of Cartography," in J.B. Harley and D. Woodward, eds., *The History of Cartography, Volume 1, Cartography in Prehistoric, Ancient and Medieval Europe and the Mediterranean* (Chicago: University of Chicago Press, 1987), 1.

33. J.B. Harley and D. Woodward, "Concluding Remarks," in *The History of Cartography, Volume 1*, 506.

34. Harley, "Maps, Knowledge, and Power," in D. Cosgrove and S. Daniels, eds., *The Iconography of Landscape* (Cambridge: Cambridge University Press, 1988), 282.

35. Harley, "Deconstructing the Map," *Cartographica* 26, no. 2 (1989), 14.

36. For details, see Pourtier, *Le Gabon, Tome 1*, 45–65.

37. Ibid., 60.

38. Du Chaillu, *Explorations*, endpiece; *Ashango-Land*, endpiece; R.P. Bichet, "Quelques jours dans l'Ogowé," *Les Missions Catholiques* (1882), 583.

39. E. Lewis (ed.), *Trader Horn: Being the Life and Works of Alfred Aloysius Horn* (New York: Simon & Schuster, 1927), 124–25, 137, 193; for a discussion of maps and secrecy, see Harley, "Maps, Knowledge and Power," 284; for a more recent example concerning prospecting maps and the Gabonese timber industry, see Pourtier, *Le Gabon, Tome 2*, 151.

40. For the mapping objectives of the West Africa Mission and a list of what was produced, see Coquery-Vidrovitch, *Brazza et la prise de possession du Congo*, 185–87.

41. J. Berton, "De Lastourville sur l'Ogooué à Samba sur la N'Gounié (septembre et octobre 1890)," *Bulletin de la Société de géographie* 7, no. 16 (1895), 211–18.

42. M.-A. de Suremain, "Cartographie coloniale et encadrement des populations in Afrique française dans la première moitié du XXe siècle," *Revue française d'histoire d'outre-mer* 181, nos. 3–4 (1999), 29–64, provides a number of insights into this process as it developed across Francophone colonial Africa. In my own work, I argue that modern territoriality requires that cultural identity be linked to territory and that the categories of modern Gabonese ethnicity are a consequence of its imposition; see Gray, "Territoriality," 248–71.

43. "Relation du voyage de Lastourville aux chutes de Samba (Ngunyé) par Godel (extrait), le 1er décembre 1893," in Rabut, *Brazza Commissaire Général*, 182–83.

44. For a fuller discussion of Christian missions as colonial nodal points, see Gray, "Territoriality," 221–33.

45. For this period, see Rabut, *Brazza Commissaire Général*; M.-A. Menier, "Conceptions politiques et administratives de Brazza 1885–1898," *Cahiers d'études africaines* 5, no. 1 (1965), 83–95; Coquery-Vidrovitch, "Les idées économiques de Brazza," 57–82 and *Le Congo*, 25–48.

46. Quoted in Coquery-Vidrovitch, "Les idées économiques de Brazza," 71, from a 1895 correspondence of A. Le Chatelier, a key colonial figure in the initial efforts to establish concessions.

47. Reproduced in Coquery-Vidrovitch, *Le Congo*, 56–57.

48. See E. Jobit and Ch. Loeffler, "Mission Gendron au Congo français," *La Géographie* 3 (1901), 181–96; and R. Avelot, "Dans la boucle de l'Ogooué: Conférences sur les opérations de la Brigade Topographique de l'Ogooué-Ngounié," *Bulletin de la Société de géographie de Lille* (1901), 225–56.

49. See G. Bruel, "Note sur la construction et la rédaction de la carte du Moyen Ogooué et de la Ngounié," *Revue Coloniale* 85 (1910), 209–24, 297–305; this information was then incorporated into G. Delingette, "Carte générale de l'Afrique Équatoriale Française," *Échelle au 1/1,000,000, en 5 feuilles, publiée par ordre de M. le Gouverneur général Merlin, Paris, A. Challamel, éditeur (Feuille IV, Gabon et Congo, 1911)*; I would like to thank Marie-Claude Dupré for providing me with a photocopy of the relevant portions of Feuille IV.

50. For details, see Gray, "Territoriality," 290–320.

51. I have been very much influenced by the ideas of Benedict Anderson in this regard; see B. Anderson, *Imagined Communities: Reflections on the Origin and Spread of Nationalism* rev. ed. (New York: Verso, 1991) 163–78.

52. See O. Gollnhofer, "Bokudu ethno-histoire Ghetsogo: Essai sur l'histoire générale de la tribu d'après la tradition orale" (*Mémoire de diplôme*, EPHE, 1967), 168–70; for taxes as a symbol of power, Pourtier, *Le Gabon, Tome 2*, 80–81.

53. AOM-AEF (Aix), D 4D 4(1)D3 1905–1908; *Rapport Annuel d'ensemble, Rapport sur la situation politique de la colonie au Gabon en 1908*; 4(1)D4 1909, *Rapport sur les causes de la révolte de Mocabe*; Commandant M. Denis, *Histoire Militaire de l'Afrique Équatoriale Française* (Paris: Imprimerie Nationale, 1931), 88–90.

54. Denis, *Histoire Militaire*,

55. "Le secret de l'Ofoué," *Annales Apostoliques de la Congrégation du Saint-Esprit* (1923), 58–63.

56. AOM-AEF (Aix), D 4D 4(1)D17 1919, *Rapports d'ensemble trimestriels, 1 er trimestre 1919*.

57. A. Maclatchy, "Monographie de la sub-division de Mimongo" (Unpublished document, Layoulé), 3, 23.

58. AOM-AEF (Aix), D 4D 4(1)D14 1916, *Résumés des rapports mensuels, Circonscription de l'Ofooué-Ngounié, décembre 1916*.

59. E. Weber, *Peasants into Frenchmen: The Modernization of Rural France, 1870–1914* (Stanford: Stanford University Press, 1976), 486.

60. I develop this comparison in Gray, *Modernization and Cultural Identity: The Creation of National Space in Rural France and Colonial Space in Rural Gabon*, Occasional Paper No. 21, MacArthur Scholar Series (Bloomington: Indiana Center on Global Change and World Peace, 1994).

61. See Vansina, *Paths*, 239–48.

62. See discussions in Pourtier, *Le Gabon, Tome 2*, 9–14 and G. Sautter, *De l'Atlantique au fleuve Congo: Une géographie du sous-peuplement, Tome 1* (Paris: Mouton, 1966), 194–96; for a discussion of the difficult position of colonial-appointed African chiefs and the new kinds of authority they were supposed to wield, see Gray, "Territoriality," 410–30.

63. The French West Africa federation received considerably more metropolitan attention than its poor relation, the French Equatorial Africa federation, and Gabon was the forgotten colony in the latter. Pourtier cites as evidence the fact that Libreville in 1935, after nearly a century of French colonial rule, remained marginalized from the rest of the colony as there existed no modern roads connecting it to the interior; this at a time when Brazzaville and Yaounde were already centers in considerably more developed transportation networks; Pourtier, *Le Gabon, Tome 2*, 220–21; see also G. Lasserre, *Libreville: la ville et sa région* (Paris: Armand Colin, 1958).

64. Pourtier *Le Gabon*, 217; see also Sautter, *De l'Atlantique*, 1018–20; and P.-P. Rey, *Colonialisme, néo-colonialisme et transition au capitalisme: Exemple de la 'Comilog' au Congo-Brazzaville* (Paris: Maspero, 1971), 380–81.

65. For colonial administration plans, see AOM-AEF (Aix), D 4D 4(1)D18 1920, *Rapports trimestriels d'ensemble, Circonscription de Sindara, 3e trimestre; Exposé de la situation de la colonie du Gabon.*

66. AOM-AEF (Aix), D 4D 4(1)D20 1922, *Rapport annuel 1922*; 4(1)D22 1992, *Rapports mensuels, Circonscription Bas-Ogooué, janvier 1922*; 4(1)D24 1923, *Rapports mensuels, Circonscription Bongo, novembre-décembre 1923*; 4(1)D26 1923, *Rapports mensuels, Circonscription Bas-Ogooué, mars-avril 1923*; 4(1)D29 1924, *Rapports mensuels, Circonscription Ngounié, décembre 1924*; 4(1)D30 1924, *Rapport mensuels, Circonscription Bas-Ogooué, août, novembre 1924*; 4(1)D31 1925, *Rapport trimestriel, Circonscription Bas-Ogooué, le trimestre 1925.*

67. The administrator Le Testu asked in exasperation at the end of 1924, "when will the road between Fougamou and Sindara be finally built?" "*Quand fera-t-on la route Fougamou-Sindara?*"; AOM-AEF (Aix), D 4D 4(1)D29 1924, *Rapports mensuels, Circonscription Ngounié, décembre 1924.*

68. *Archives Congrétion des Pères du Saint Esprit, Boîte 991 IV, Journal de la Communauté de St. Martin des Apindjis, janvier 1923–13 août 1927*, entry March 15, 1925.

69. In 1928, 10,000 locals had been engaged at work sites along this route; see AOM-AEF (Aix), 5D 5D58 1923–1948, *Dossier Confidentiel au sujet de la situation Vivrière de la Circonscription de la Ngounié, 25 mars 1930.*

70. AOM-AEF (Aix), D 4D 4(1)D33 1927, *Rapport du 4e trimestre (Gabon)*; 4(1)D34 1928, *Rapport politique et economique à la fin de l'année 1928*; 4(1)D36 1930, *Lieutenant Gouverneur du Gabon à M. le Gouverneur Général de l'AEF, Rapport de tournée (13 mai au 26 juin 1930); Rapport trimestriel, Circonscription de la Ngounié, 1er trimestre 1930*; 4(1)D38 1932, *Rapport annuel 1932*; 4(1)D43 1936, *Rapport trimestriel, Département de la Ngounié-Nyanga, 1er trimestre 1936*; 5D 5D58 1923–1948, *Dossier confidentiel au sujet de la situation Vivrière de la Circonscription de la Ngounié, 25 mars 1930*; ANG, *Fonds de la Présidence, Carton 99, Rapports Politiques, Département de la Ngounié, 1929–1944, Rapport trimestriel, 4e trimestre, 1929.*

71. Phyllis Martin makes reference to "the rule of the feeble" in characterizing European rule in parts of Central Africa; see P.M. Martin, "The Violence of Empire," in D. Birmingham and P.M. Martin, eds., *History of Central Africa, Volume Two* (London: Longman, 1983), 8–15.

72. See V. Moulengui-Boukossou, "Une population flottante dans un espace non-maîtrisé: La population de la forêt Gabonaise" (*Thèse de doctorat, Université Paul Valéry, Montpellier III*, 1985), 46.

73. AOM-AEF (Aix), D 4D 4(1)D45 1937, *Rapport politique, Département de la Ngounié, 1 er semestre 1937.*

74. Ibid.

75. *Archives Nationales du Gabon (ANG), Fonds de la Présidence, Carton 35, Politique Générale, Subdivision de Sindara, 1937–1944, Rapport politique, Département de la Ngounié, Subdivision de Sindara, 2e semestre 1937.*

76. Mussondji/Moulandoufala, Interview Notes XXII, Mussondji, September 19, 1991.

77. Mbigui, "Histoire de Sindara," 15; Pourtier, *Le Gabon, Tome 2*, 182.

78. In positing an articulation between lineage, and colonial and capitalist modes of production, Rey emphasizes the construction of the Congo-Océan railroad as the key element in bringing about this shift to a capitalist labor market in the Congo colony between the years 1924 and 1934; he makes reference to a telling 1932 quote from Governor-General Antonetti: "The building of the railroad started with forced labor, we will be achieved thanks to voluntary workers" *Colonialisme*, 411–12, see also 342–43. Due to the timber industry's need for workers, Southern Gabon was off limits to labor recruitment for the Congo-Océan. However, the railroad's completion and a road connecting Ndendé to Dolisie drew the region into Congo's economic sphere after the Second World War; see Pourtier, *Le Gabon, Tome 2*, 224–25.

79. For the mobility and settlement patterns of precolonial populations, see Gray, "Territoriality," 15–38.

80. For a related discussion, see Pourtier, *Le Gabon, Tome 2*, 102–9.

81. AOM-AEF (Aix), D 4D 4(1)D19 1921, *Rapports trimestriels, 3e trimestre 1921*; for earlier efforts 4(1)D5 1910, *Résumé des rapports politiques des administrateurs de*

circonscriptions, Circonscription de l'Ofooué-Ngounié, septembre 1910; 4(1)D6 1911, *Résumés des rapports mensuels des chefs de circonscriptions, Circonscription de l'Ofooué-Ngounié, août 1911.*

82. AOM-AEF (Aix), D 4D 4(1)D29 1924, *Rapports mensuels-Ngounié, décembre 1924.*

83. AOM-AEF (Aix), D 4D 4(1)D20 1922, *Rapport annuel 1922.*

84. AOM-AEF (Aix), D 4D 4(1)D29 1924, *Rapports mensuels-Ngounié, mai 1924*; also 4(1)D20 1922, *Rapports mensuels, Circonscription des Bandjabis, août 1922.*

85. Antonetti was very much a proponent of village regroupment; see AOM-AEF (Aix), D 4D 4(1)D31 1925, *Le Gouverneur Général de l'AEF à M. le Lieutenant-Gouverneur du Gabon, Réponse aux rapports (1925).*

86. AOM-AEF (Aix), D 4D 4(1)D37 1931, *Rapport de 2e trimestre 1931, Circonscription des Ouroungous.*

87. ANG, *Fonds de la Présidence, Carton 99, Rapports politiques, Département de la Ngounié, 1929–1944, Rapport trimestriel, 2e trimestre 1929.*

88. Maclatchy, *"Monographie,"* 30; for specific references to the passive resistance of the Gésuma district, see AOM-AEF (Aix), D 4D 4(1)D29 1924, *Rapports mensuels-Ngounié, juin 1924*; 4(1)D40 1934, *Rapport trimestriel, Circonscription de la Ngounié, 3e trimestre 1934.*

89. See AOM-AEF (Aix), D 4D 4(1)D37 1931, *Réclamation de tous les chefs Bapounous demeurant dans la Subdivision de Mouila, Mouila, le 21 novembre 1931*; for leopard men revenge attacks, see J.-H. M'Boukou, *Ethnologie criminelle du Gabon* (Le Vésinet: Ediena, 1984), 17; for surveillance techniques, see Moulengui-Boukossou, "Une population flottante," 39–40.

90. AOM-AEF (Aix), D 4D 4(1)D46 1938, *Rapport politique, Département de la Ngounié, 2e trimestre 1938.*

91. See G. Balandier and J.-C. Pauvert, *Les villages gabonais: aspects démographiques, économiques, sociologiques, projets de modernisation* (Brazzaville: *Institut d'Études Centrafricianes*, 1952), 11–15, 58–79; also J.-H. Aubame, *Renaissance gabonaise: programme de regroupement des villages* (Brazzaville: Imprimerie officielle, 1947); and the discussion in F. Bernault, *Démocraties ambiguës en Afrique centrale, Congo-Brazzaville, Gabon: 1940–1965* (Paris: Karthala, 1995), 111–13

92. See Pourtier, *Le Gabon, Tome 2*, 102–22.

93. Ibid., 308.

94. Idem.

10

SPACE AND CONFLICT IN THE ELISABETHVILLE MINING CAMPS, 1923–1938

Sean Hanretta

You arrive in a new country, in a place of work to which you are unaccustomed, where you feel uprooted [un-countried]. The Congolese watches you at every moment; he judges you. This first contact with your work-team is of great importance. Your reputation and the success of your colonial career may depend on it.
　　　　　　—from a UMHK guide for incoming colonial officials[1]

Such is the story of the city of Lubumbashi as we, the boys, saw it. Also, we heard many things from the people from Europe. There wasn't a thing they could hide from us.
　　　　　　—André Yav, Lubumbashi historian[2]

These two quotes, from two very different perspectives on the experience of European and African relations in the mining camps of the *Union Minière du Haut-Katanga* (UMHK) may seem somewhat startling at first. Rather than referring, as we might expect, to the panoptic sight of the European overseer, the first reflects instead an almost paranoid fear of the gaze of the African worker, a gaze that, turned upon the displaced and off-balance European, has the potential to disrupt the entire moment of contact. The second statement, by André Yav, a historian and resident of Lubumbashi, is a forthright expression of this challenge; the "boys" of Lubumbashi have seen all, more even than they will tell.

This is, indeed, an accurate reading of these statements; but there is another reading as well. Behind the paranoia of the anonymous[3] UMHK author lies an idea that may help explain *why* the mining company considered the African gaze to be so dangerous: Central-African workers were, in the minds of their Belgian employers, extremely impressionable. Africans learned, so the UMHK believed, by an uncritical mimesis; a worker would imitate both his employer's good habits and his bad,[4] or, in the words of L. Mottoulle, director of the UMHK's labor policy throughout the 1920s, '30s, and '40s, "The colonizer must never lose sight that the blacks have the spirits of children, spirits which mold themselves to the methods of the teacher [*éducateur*]; they watch, listen, feel and imitate."[5] While this mimicry made the maintenance of proper behavior crucial for employers, it also gave those employers (so they believed) a powerful tool in altering the behavior of workers. Colonial and mining company officials believed that Africans tended to imitate not only the people who surrounded them but also the material environment in which they were placed. This belief eventually led the UMHK to develop an entire physical institution, the "mining camp"—halfway between city and prison—whose express purpose it was to transform the "detribalized" African—at once unfit for both rural and urban life—into a well-disciplined, loyal, immobile, and skilled "worker," by taking advantage of his or her mimetic behavior. This process, initiated by the UMHK over the period from 1925 to 1933, came to be known as "stabilization."

From this perspective, André Yav's claim, that "there wasn't a thing they could hide from us," seems doubly subversive. In *The Vocabulary of Elisabethville*, a Swahili-language history of Lubumbashi written around 1965, André Yav provides an "insider's" perspective on the colonial period. From Yav's text, it becomes apparent that workers were acutely aware of the acts of colonial employers; they *saw* "what was going on," shattering the passive imitation the UMHK tried to ascribe to them. By becoming visually (and aurally and tactilely) conscious of the power and plans of the UMHK, workers undermined the mine-owners' attempts to mold them by example. In their spatial surroundings, Africans read the instruments of power, and when possible they manipulated these instruments to suit their own uses or they resisted them directly. This study is about the history of these mining camps, the colonial discourses that produced them and gave meaning to the project of their creators, and the ways in which Africans viewed them, lived in them, and tried to change them.

If the carceral technologies of the prison proper often come in response to a particular construction of criminality, in the colonial labor camps of Katanga they were the result of the intersection of a universalist discourse on labor and health with an asymmetrical relation of compulsion based on the pliability—and incapacity for conscious self-fashioning—presumed of the colonial subject. That such an intersection could place the colonial worker in the structural position of a criminal—bringing to bear on him or her such techniques of control as enclosure, the "rationalization" of space and activity, and surveillance—is perhaps not as surprising as how ambiguous workers' positions remained even under such regulated conditions. The need on the part of camp officials to imbue workers with more fully fleshed-out identities than those of "mere criminals" required ever more complex and rich apparatuses of subjectification, multiplying thereby the possible lines of contestation and resistance.

Ultimately, the colonial labor camp, like the colonial prison, was a totalitarian institution only insofar as the universalism of the administrative discourses that produced it were able to fully and convincingly account for the daily life experiences of those whom they sought to explain, mold, and control. More so, perhaps, than some colonial prisons, the labor camps of the UMHK were planned constructs, clearly dependent for their shape on the nuances of domestic theories of psychology, biology, and labor. Yet if we take these discourses too much at face value, we risk missing the obvious ways in which the physical institutions to which such theorizing gave birth were shaped in highly contested debates over the nature of work, family life, and personal and collective autonomy—debates in which the (often invisible) theories of African laborers played an equally determining role.

The development of the UMHK's mining camps has typically been analyzed from one of two main perspectives. Bruce Fetter has outlined what can be considered the materialist history of space in the mining camps.[6] In the early 1920s, in response to rising copper prices, higher copper demand, and new technologies, the UMHK began to need a labor force greater in size and more skilled than was currently available. The company believed that workers would only remain employed long enough to send back a fixed sum of money to their rural homes. Thus it was felt that raising wages to create an incentive for workers to stay would backfire: They would merely leave the camps sooner, their goal all the more quickly achieved. Instead, the UMHK outlined a plan to make the mining camps "more attractive" to workers than either their rural homes or the urban mass of the city of Elisabethville. The vindication of this costly project came, so the story goes, in the late 1920s when the UMHK was able to successfully move from employing workers on six- to twelve-month contracts to three-year contracts, to lower worker mortality and thereby reduce its dependency on outside recruiters; and to transfer many skilled positions from unionizing white Belgian, Rhodesian, and South African workers into the hands of African workers. This was, by all accounts, a tremendous economic savings for the UMHK and a political victory over other companies competing for labor, over the colonial administration and over the British. In fact, stabilization was so successful, Fetter claims, that in 1933 when a drop in copper prices and available capital caused by the Depression forced a drastic cut in production, African workers rioted rather than be forced to return to their former homes; they had become truly fixed, loyal workers.

In his commentary on André Yav's history of Elisabethville, Johannes Fabian presents a history of the mining camps that focuses more upon the power that the UMHK exercised over workers and how this power was expressed in the camps. For Fabian, the camps were ultimately a manifestation of a distant, uncomprehending, colonial project, and the camps' material design was ultimately rejected and disdained by workers. The camps were built around a blueprint imported from Europe and plopped down upon workers, an expression of the height of the UMHK's naïveté and arrogance.[7] Yet what both of these explanations overlook is that the colonial planners who designed the camps and the mine workers who struggled to shape, affect, and appropriate the space in which they lived shared a common framework when they looked at the camps. UMHK officials embedded the policy of stabilization in years of anthropological and medical discourses designed precisely to tailor living space to the "rules of etiquette" of the UMHK's employees.[8] It is perhaps indicative of the success of the UMHK's ethnographers' attempts to identify some crucial elements of its workers' social relations that mine workers interpreted the spatial layout and design of housing in the camps in essentially the same way as did the camps' designers. Both the employers and certain employees, for example, saw in the individualized, "nuclear family"–centered, homogenous brick homes a profound attack on workers' kinship-based social relationships. But, contrary to the expectations of the architects of stabilization, these places did not exert a straightforward, orthopedic force upon the behavior of presumably passive, mimetic miners; rather, workers perceived in these new dwellings an attempt to impose a particular type of identity upon them and many of them responded to this attempt with active disgruntlement.

This difference in evaluation was crucial. African workers saw the camp not as a group of discrete, disciplining places, but as an overarching, planned space of power. Keeping this in mind, we can organize the individual elements of resistance that appear in the historical record—isolated in the accounts of Europeans, since Europeans could only interpret them as isolated, specific reactions to particular places—into a more coherent if still heterogeneous, picture of responses to the colonial project. Once the possibility is accepted that mine-workers shared a spatial frame of analysis with the camp designers, previously underused sources begin to reveal a sophisticated and conscious discourse on the power of the UMHK's camps among the workers themselves. A set of life histories of men interviewed in 1966 for an oral history project organized by Bruce Fetter,[9] Yav's *Vocabulary of Elisabethville* and the life history of Clémentine Kawama, a woman who grew up and lived in the camps of the mining company,[10] all give evidence of the types of conflicts over space that took place within the UMHK's compound at Lumbumbashi. When read alongside the writings of camp designers and other officials, these sources emphasize that, whatever misconceptions either the workers or their employers may have had, each developed complex approaches to space and place that reflected close analysis of conditions in the camps and that served as tools in the struggle to control them.

THE *UNION MINIÈRE DU HAUT KATANGA* AND THE INVENTION OF "STABILIZATION"

The UMHK grew out of the *Comité Special du Katanga*, an organization to which Leopold had given control over the entire southeast corner of the Free State, and the Tanganyika Concessions Limited, a Rhodesia-based mining organization run by British entrepreneur Robert Williams. With the the arrival of the CFK/BCK railroad in 1912–1913, the UMHK began exploiting the copper deposits of southern Katanga (see Map 10.1). Over the next fifty years, the company took a series of steps designed to increase its productivity and to decrease its reliance both on South African capital and expertise and on the Belgian government itself. Investment in the UMHK was partially privatized by bringing it under the control of the *Société Générale*, a Belgian

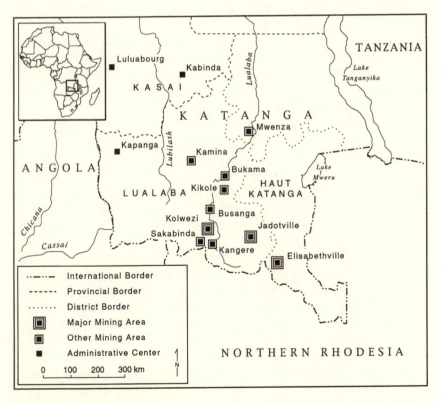

Map 10.1. Katanga Region.

bank. The period from the early 1920s until World War II was something of a "golden age" for the UMHK; except for brief riots in 1933 and a labor strike in 1941, the company greatly increased its productivity, the efficiency of its work force and its position within the global copper economy through "worker stabilization."

Three distinct developments gave shape to the employment principles and aspects of camp design that constituted this policy of stabilization. Beginning around 1923, Belgian colonial officials and the *Société Générale* developed a particular theory about the behavior of the "African" in the contexts of both the "city" and the "forest." Secondly, a series of scandalous medical reports emanating from the UMHK's mining camps in the early 1920s began to force the UMHK to develop new approaches toward living conditions around the mines; these new approaches gave camp planners the opportunity to put into practice the new principles being theorized about African behavior. Finally, a sudden and intense need for a labor force that was large, skilled, and free from entanglements with rural recruiters or British authorities convinced the UMHK that the best solution to all of these problems involved not only re-designing its camps' layout, but retooling its entire employment philosophy. The shape that the mining camps eventually took derived from the intersection of these three historical threads.

From early on, the UMHK relied on what it considered anthropologically sound descriptions of local African customs, behaviors, and mentalities to provide a guide for the implementation of work strategies. In 1923 a group of missionary supervisors assembled in Stanleyville to discuss perceived threats to the civilizing mission of the Church posed by a tendency in the Belgian government toward a policy of "indirect rule." One participant in this meeting, S. De Vos, expressed the group's conclusions: founded on a mis-guided desire to "respect indigenous cultures," government policy had un-wittingly contributed to an escalating violence by local Africans against colonial churches, Church officials, Westerners in general, and African *évo-lués*.[11] The Belgian government was not, the missionaries claimed, taking into account the fact that after twenty-five years of colonialism, African societies had, through their contact with the capitalist West, begun to degenerate: Health in villages had declined, the authority of chiefs had weakened, mo-rality had been relaxed, and societies were, in general, moving toward the dissolution of familial and social order and the reign of anarchy.[12] Drawing on a mix of theology and a belief in the malleability of African minds, the missionaries advocated a strong interventionist policy that would teach by example. Its goal was the re-institution of "authentic" African customs tem-pered with a Christian, humanist individualism that opposed polygamy, ini-tiation rituals, and, especially, the monopolization of wealth by lineage elders.[13]

Although opposed and derided by government officials, this policy gained currency with an important figure in the history of the UMHK, Monseigneur J. de Hemptinne, who was head of the Benedictine missionaries in Elisabethville and in charge of the education of mine workers.[14] Even before the 1920s, the UMHK's copper operations were so vital to the Belgian colonial economy that an almost completely free reign had been granted to the company, so the protestations of colonial officials had little or no effect on what happened in the camps.[15] After successfully driving out more moderate Protestant missionaries, the Benedictines established their first school in the Elisabethville camps in 1925 with de Hemptinne in charge of the curriculum. UMHK officials, influenced by the thinking of men like de Hemptinne, believed that African customs were incompatible with hard work, and went so far as to pay workers to attend classes that focused on "Christian values," loyalty and discipline, reading, and basic arithmetic. In particular, the company thought that group ownership of property was especially bad for Africans' work ethic, and the missionary schools obediently undertook the project of instilling a sense of individual ownership in their pupils.[16]

At approximately the same time, a series of devastating epidemics and social disturbances in the camps prompted several studies by doctors and medical officials on the hygiene and security of the workers' living environments. Two Belgian physicians, A. Boigelot and P. Polidori, examining the camps around Elisabethville after the influenza epidemics of 1912, 1916, and 1918–1919, issued a scathing report critical of the sanitary conditions in the camps, worker safety, and the prevalence of African drunkenness, absenteeism, and workplace negligence.[17] In part to placate the objections of reformers in Belgium, who had used the medical reports to criticize colonial policy in general, and in part to help provide a solution to the very real problems of worker mortality and lack of discipline, the UMHK undertook some preemptory reforms in the areas of housing and sanitation. The UMHK instructed its own company physician, R. Mouchet, to investigate the camps and to suggest a long-term policy.

Previously, the high levels of mortality and desertion in work camps had posed a real problem for the UMHK, but as long as recruitment of new workers from Northern Rhodesia and the areas north and west of Elisabethville was unrestricted, the company could replenish workers as quickly as they died or fled. In fact, in the late 1910s and early 1920s, when employment was based on either the six-month or the twelve-month contract, workers were forcibly repatriated to their rural homes for a period equal to the term for which they had been employed.[18] No worker was allowed to return to the UMHK until s/he had spent this entire period "outside." This policy, sponsored by the colonial government, had its roots in the fear that the countryside was being depopulated by the extent of recruitment. Too heavy a depopulation of an area or even too lengthy an absence of men, officials feared, would cause a serious decline in agricultural productivity. By forcing workers "home," the government could protect the agricultural base of the area while still providing labor for the industrial work at the mines.[19]

Approximately five years after the end of the first World War, the nature of the UMHK's labor needs changed, and the company began to require many more skilled laborers. In the previous years, a move toward "Belgianization" had stripped away most of the British and South-African administrators, while union-busting programs had forced the dismissal of the majority of skilled white labor. As a result, the company needed to begin training its African labor force to staff these new positions without substantial supervision.[20] UMHK executives were understandably hesitant to train workers who were expected to either die or return home after only a half-year on the job. Yet company officials also doubted that black workers, in their current state, could supervise themselves and feared that merely increasing the length of contracts would proletarianize the work force.[21] As a result they determined that a "new type" of worker needed to be formed—one who was highly skilled, self-disciplined, interested in long-term employment and had the physical strength and health to spend an entire career in the mines.

Yet, despite the impression given by the UMHK's official history,[22] not all workers the company employed in the next ten years fit this description. By the late 1920s and 1930s, the company was developing a new image of a type of worker who needed to be kept *out* of the camps as well. Some of the massive, labor intensive, construction projects the UMHK began at this time—including building the new camps—required an even more temporary and unskilled labor force than its earlier mining operations. It was decided that this group of workers should, under no circumstances, mix with the group of workers the company was trying to "stabilize." There is, perhaps, something ironic about the employment of as many as 4,000 workers on intentionally short-term contracts for the purpose of constructing the very buildings used to entice other workers into signing long-term contracts, but the juxtaposing of the two groups was more than coincidental.[23] Fetter has called these targeted exiles "non-productive natives," but it was not a lack of productivity that made the UMHK want to keep them out of the camps.[24] Nor was it merely an absolute increase in the numerical quantity of long-term employees that the UMHK had in mind in its stabilization program. The division of useful laborers into two distinct groups, with two distinct sets of expected behavioral characteristics, makes it clear the long-term employment of a certain *type* of worker was the UMHK's real goal in stabilization. The new camp was the tool intended to create this type of worker and to separate him or her from other laborers.

Similarly, in the mid-1920s the UMHK began taking an active interest in managing the affairs of those Africans living in the larger region around Elisabethville. The project of stabilization would, from the perspective of the Belgian industrialists, integrate the entire region of upper Katanga (Map

10.1); the UMHK would control the labor needed for rural agricultural production and urban industrial production and would manipulate the balance between the two to ensure both an adequate labor supply for the mines and an adequate agricultural yield to feed mine workers.[25] At the same time, stabilization implied that the African mine worker, rather than being a free-moving part of this integrated system, would be tied to a single location and a single productive activity. In a situation characterized by the absorption of space into an economic system, the UMHK wanted to manufacture for its African workers an identity dominated by local place. Just as workers in the camps were to be confined to carefully manipulated places, rural workers were to be positioned with respect to roads and industrial zones around urban centers; their production was to be commanded and regulated, while the prices of their goods were to remain open to market fluctuations.[26] To an extent, then, the emphasis on keeping certain workers out of the camps was predicated on a certain "negative potential" seen in the hinterland; just as an inadequate, or inappropriate, containment of workers could result in degradation of the industrial site by exposing them to bad influences, so too could an overly permeable boundary around the camp contribute to rural degradation.

It was in this context that de Hemptinne's ideas about the degeneration of tropical-African civilization and the health and morality crises of the early camps became fused with Mouchet's observations about health and camp design. Thoughts about the effect of colonization on Africans became a theory of the relationship between Africans and "place." The guiding metaphors for these theories of deculturation were "detribalization"[27] and "disacclimation." According to Mouchet, Africans in rural areas existed in a sort of equilibrium with respect to both their biological environment—its altitude, humidity, and bacterial and viral regimes—and their cultural environment. The tropical African was attuned to his *milieu*, where he was surrounded by familiar types of food, his parents, his family, those who spoke the same language and were of the same "ethnic group." Only the rare individual with "nomadic instincts" would voluntarily leave his village home to work in a mining camp. For the "normal" African, once wrested from this environment, biological and moral deterioration set in.[28] Since African customs were, he believed, so place-dependent, Mouchet advocated sending out expeditions to any new area from which recruits were beginning to be drawn to study local housing layouts, methods of life and work and, especially, women's roles in these societies.[29]

For Mouchet, and especially his superior Mottoulle, women had an important role to play in shaping the relationship between an African worker and his *milieu*; mortality and desertion in the mines were as much a result of the lack of women and the improper behavior of those women who were at the camps, as of the other deculturating effects of displacement. To the company, a worker with a family in the distant countryside was, by definition, only a temporary worker. A worker with his wife and family around "suffers less from isolation, is better fed, happier with his situation and a more efficient worker." Yet, unfortunately, high infant mortality rates and the "breakdown" of the *cellule familiale* had begun to threaten the "future of the race."[30] The death of most of the infants born in the early camps was, in Mottoulle's view, not an effect of poor nutrition or other causes relating to the economic conditions of workers, but of "the dissolution of morals and of venereal diseases." A large part of the project to keep workers for a longer period of time centered around attracting the right kind of women to the mining camps and educating those who came in "their roles as mothers."[31] However, women were considered as both the harbingers of domesticity and particularly susceptible to the "degrading conditions" of the urban environment in terms of both its moral and physical threats.[32] Indeed, part of the reason women had not been brought into the early camps was that they had been considered too fragile and too costly to maintain; so when the UMHK decided it needed women in the camps, an entire program—Mottoulle's *Oeuvre de Protection de l'Enfance Noire* (OPEN)—was established.

The effects of spatial dislocation were what Mouchet fingered as the cause of the scandalously high mortality and desertion rates in the camp. By focusing on the African and his and her relationship to place, Mouchet was able to conclude that the type of work carried out in the mines was not related to levels of mortality.[33] To combat this fragility, and in the words of Mottoulle, to rid the camps of their "reputation for immorality and sterility" that was driving away the most desirable workers, what was needed was a new understanding of the camp as a spatial tool that could change workers' minds and bodies.[34]

Thus, when the UMHK took steps to counter the perceived problems of camp hygiene, training, labor recruitment, and rural depopulation that arose in the mid-1920s, they set themselves the task of reshaping the entire region of upper Katanga as well as the mining camps at Elisabethville. The space within and outside the camp was, in the minds of these officials, a complex tool to reshape the nature of African workers, a vast and complex *milieu* whose formative power was dependent on African workers remaining passive, unreflective, and unknowing imitators. To say, then, that the project of worker stabilization was a set of employment practices manifested in space is not merely to say that the effects of the new approaches being taken by the UMHK were primarily visible in the form of spatial changes. This was certainly the case and spatial changes did occur; but, in addition, the entire project of worker stabilization was one that was formulated, theorized, and executed in the domain of space. For the UMHK, the problem of creating new, industrialized workers was primarily a problem of manipulating workers' *milieu*, and of correctly placing workers at appropriate points within it.

THE WORKERS' VISION: AFRICAN ANALYSES OF THE POWER OF SPACE

It was not, however, only the mine owners who saw power in spatial control. As is likely the case with any concentrated group of workers, the mine-laborers at Lumbumbashi were acutely aware of the power their employers exercised over them. Their often carefully calculated responses to UMHK policies and projects belied de Hemptinne's, Mouchet's, and Mottoulle's assumptions about their passivity and mimesis. Indeed, just as the designers of the labor camps were fixated on the importance of controlling space, and on the assumed behavior of Africans when placed within a certain point in space, workers themselves chose space as the dominant metaphor around which to organize their thoughts about struggles with the mine owners.

André Yav's *Vocabulary of Elisabethville* is preeminently a spatial history, which consistently embeds its narratives in a sense of place. The text is not only fully cognizant of the fact that the colonialists' gaze was one that sought to control people by controlling space, but also creates its own reverse gaze to critique this power.[35] The *Vocabulary* puts what seems a disproportionate amount of emphasis on streets and street corners, often associating them with the European forces that brought them into existence. Illustrative is Yav's formulation: "The father of the streets and the mother of the streets were these: . . . 2. Avenue Sankulu [Sankuru], its force ended at the rails, near the military camp, this is where the force of that road ended."[36] For Yav, roads were not simply neutral places running through the surrounding space, nor merely mnemonic tags for historical events and the names of people; they had a "force," the force of the companies that called them into existence. Physical structures in the city are similarly implicated in the history of colonial power. Yav devotes a fair portion of the *Vocabulary*'s length to lists of buildings, organized by type. His descriptions often begin by pointing out buildings in contemporary Lubumbashi to the reader, giving their history and focusing on the white officials associated with them.[37]

This sensitivity to spatial power was not unique to consciously historical analyses of the relationships of power in Elisabethville; when individual inhabitants of the mining camps and the city reflected on their own lives, they too expressed employer-employee conflicts in the language of space. The life stories collected for Lumbumbashi's *Journée de la lettre*—an oral history project Bruce Fetter coordinated with the Zairian government in 1966—and the life story of Clémentine Kawama reflect many of Yav's themes. For Fetter's interviewees, buildings and streets, in particular, were seen to embody directly the power of white employers. Even though most of the life stories recorded in Lubumbashi contain less than 200 words, eight out of thirty-one spend a significant portion of their time describing the appearance, position, and function of various buildings in the mining camps and the city.[38] Many of the life stories recorded in Elisabethville begin with remarks that, when the individuals first arrived in the city and the camps, there was nothing there but "the forest"; only over the course of human action—action directed by a colonial project labor—had the streets and buildings been formed. The "military camp" mentioned by Yav also appears as a common theme in the recorded life histories, part of a general association of space with official force; descriptions of streets and buildings are often preceded or followed by mentions of the police or the army, both in the *Vocabulary* and the oral histories.[39]

Another life story, that of Clémentine Kawama, gives a rather dramatic version of the association of buildings and other defined spaces with disciplinary force, focusing specifically on the UMHK and its missionary assistants. In her narrative, Kawama constructs the entire first two-thirds of the text—covering the period from her childhood until marriage—as a journey through various buildings and spaces. Each place is, in turn, associated with a particular representative or group of representatives of the UMHK and with a particular disciplinary technique exercised by those representatives. Born in a camp hospital, Kawama outlines her life as a series of spatial journeys: her narrative moves from the camp school room—where an inspection of clothing and personal hygiene was required every morning before a student could enter the building—to the supervised recreation area where children played, to the fields of priests or teachers where students worked when disciplined, to the enclosure of the Church on Sunday, to inside her home where she helped her mother with chores, to the "practice space" of the *foyer social* (social center) and finally to her own home for which she, as the wife of a UMHK worker, was responsible.[40]

The sense one gets upon reading Kawama's story is one of near claustrophobia, a constant, unshakable sense of containment, an overwhelming sense of the constrictions of space. However, some of her reflections countermand such a straightforward reading. Despite the strong connection she makes between life and space and between space and power, Kawama did not simply passively inhabit these spaces. Having mastered the teachings of the nuns in the *foyer*, she herself sought a religious vocation, an ambition that her parents blocked for reasons on which she does not elaborate. Yet, even though Kawama did not become a nun, she still managed to parlay her experience and work into a job teaching at the *foyer* itself, which improved both her material condition and her status vis-à-vis other women in the camp.[41] It is perhaps revealing of how certain aspects of status functioned among the residents of the camps to note that, while most workers moved frequently between the city of Elisabethville and the camps, because of her higher status as a teacher, Kawama was able to reject a suitor who lived in the city as "beneath" her, and held out for a "child of the camps" who was therefore, she implies, well brought up.[42] So while Kawama was clearly aware of the power that saturated the spaces of the camps, she was nonetheless able to live in and make use of those very spaces.

A COMMON FRAMEWORK FOR CONFLICT: THE MINING CAMPS

So if the UMHK conceptualized its project in the mining camps as a spatial one, there is little doubt that the Africans who worked in the mines also saw the company's power expressed in the control and manipulation of space. This mutual recognition of the importance of space not only manifested itself in the discourses of these groups, it also profoundly affected and shaped the conflicts and struggles that took place between mine-owners and mine-workers over how the mining camps would be designed and how they would be lived in. Mouchet's actual designs reflected his ideals of using space to create workers, but these ideals were themselves forced to take into account and to respond to attempts by residents to reshape and redefine these spaces.

For example, the long, straight lines of identical, perfectly symmetrical houses separated by the "zone boisée" (Figure 10.1) and the more complex but just as symmetrical and infinitely repeating inward-facing *quartiers* (which was the layout the UMHK preferred, Figure 10.2) evoke nothing so much as Le Corbusier's *Plan Voisin* for Paris. Such a similarity could lead us to concur with Fabian that the mining camps were indeed just the imposition of European aesthetics upon tropical Africa, anthropological and medical discourses and the counterstruggles of workers notwithstanding. Yet this apparent homology with European cities is deceptive—the straight rows of houses,

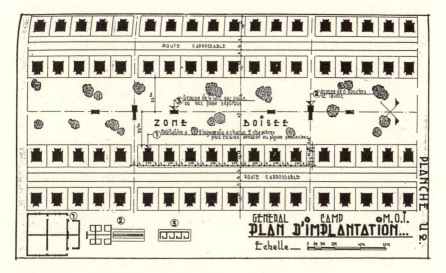

Figure 10.1. UMHK Mining Camp with *Zone Boisée*.

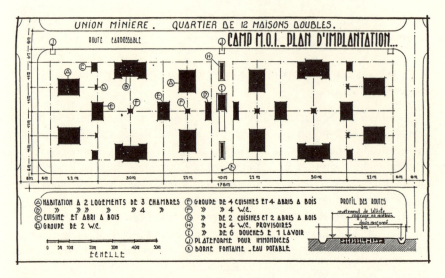

Figure 10.2. UMHK Mining Camp with Block of Houses (*Bulletin CESPI*, 12 (1950), 130).

the open central courtyards and the long, wide boulevards meant very different things to the UMHK's planners than they did to the theorists of Western cities, who were already "conceiving of the city as a place that . . . encourages the concentration of difference" rather than as a fortuitous place to exercise hegemony.[43] And they certainly meant something very different to the workers who lived in them, who, even had they been aware of the intricacies of European urban theories would have been reluctant to admit their relevance to their lives in the camps.

But when we shift from analyzing Mouchet's ideal camps to the history of the actual implementation of the stabilization project, it becomes apparent how deeply often subtle conflicts between the UMHK and its employees shaped the real camp. The physical features of the camp can be loosely organized into two main categories: those that the UMHK intended to use to isolate and distinguish the *milieu* of the mining camp from the carefully managed rural *brousse* (bush) and the potentially dangerous urban area of Elisabethville; and those that, in Mouchet's formulation, were supposed to help refine, direct, and apply the UMHK's worker-creating power within the fence of the camp. In each of these areas the UMHK had to struggle to apply its theoretical ideas about worker *milieu* to practical conditions, as mine-workers identified the power expressed in particular spatial elements and found ways to subvert, overcome, or otherwise reappropriate those spatial elements.

From the outset, the UMHK's organizing concept for the redesign of the camps, the notion of "stabilization" itself, begins to fall apart when examined not as an abstract "project" but as a specific expression of power that workers contested. Luise White has pointed out that "both migrancy and stabilization were employers' categories that when taken up by historians have tended to obscure the various strategies by which workers enhanced the value of their wages."[44] From the perspective of the mine-owners, the mining camps and the seal around them were intended not only to keep workers in, but also to keep others out. Who these others were reflected closely on the changing use of space to stabilize "mine-worker" as an identity. For the UMHK, the greatest fear was that the mining camps would begin to resemble the African section of Elisabethville. The nonwhite quarter of Elisabethville was set up as a *centre extra-coutumier*—an urban area restricted to Africans but not governed by "customary" law—which meant that judicial and partial legislative powers were vested in a group of "traditional" African authorities selected from each major "ethnic" population of the city. This arrangement assumed the distinctness of each separate ethnic community, their different interests and need for separate representation.[45] In sharp contrast, the UMHK operated under the fear that "inter-ethnic collaboration" could weaken the camp boundary. To prevent this, it manipulated recruitment to bring into the camps people from areas inhabited by different ethnic groups than those living in the city.[46] Members of the same group were intentionally placed at different camps to break up any "ethnic blocs" that had become dominant within sectors of the camps. It was this difference in the nature of interethnic relations, more than anything else, that served, from the perspective of the UMHK, to define the mining camp as a space separate from Elisabethville itself.[47]

Space in the *centre extra-coutumier* was more erratic than in either the white sections of the city or in the camps; streets were not laid out along a grid; the surveillance capabilities of the police (who were often drawn from the same "ethnic" group they policed) were severely limited. Movement between the city and the rural areas was far more free than in the camps, and the governmental organization of the city allowed many political, cultural, and social influences from the hinterland to take hold there.[48] While the colonial government saw Elisabethville as a testing ground for eventual self-government, from the perspective of the UMHK it was nothing but a haven for every sort of danger and vice.[49] The UMHK saw the city as the perfect example of what could go wrong if Africans were allowed to "deculturate" without being subjected to a careful discipline.

As a result, every possible effort was made to differentiate and geographically separate the area of the camp from that of both the surrounding rural areas and the *centre extra-coutumier* of Elisabethville. From the early days of the UMHK's operations, the mining camps had often been defined in opposition to the more "open" city sitting beneath them at the bottom of the Lubumbashi River valley. This opposition was formalized in the erection of a high wire fence around the camp. Beginning in the early 1920s, the Euro-

pean mine-workers who had previously been living in the camps were given
the option to leave and settle in the white areas of the city, an option nearly
all took.[50] The movement of Africans through the fence surrounding the camp
was carefully controlled; visitors from the outside were only allowed in with
special permission, a permission that also had to be acquired before camp
residents could leave for even short periods.[51] Increasingly, then, one's presence in the camp became inseparable from either being employed in the mines
or being in the family of a miner.

Yet among the first things one is struck by on reading the life stories of
those who lived and worked in the mining camps is how great the gap was
between the UMHK's ideal of the stable worker and the degree of permanency
workers actually experienced. Almost all of the UMHK's statistics purporting
to prove the success of stabilization were based on the number of three-year
contracts it entered into with workers after 1928.[52] While these were substan-
tially longer than the old six- and twelve-month contracts, a three-year resi-
dency in the camps hardly reflected the kind of multigenerational permanence
the camps' theorists had imagined.

In fact, the life stories available from UMHK employees and their families
suggest that the dominant experience in the lives of workers was a highly
fluid relationship with place. Over one-third of the men interviewed in 1966
by Bruce Fetter recount having had multiple employers over the course of
the years of the stabilization project.[53] Not one of the remaining two-thirds
specifically mentions having been employed by the UMHK for the entire
period. Not only did most workers not spend their entire careers with the
UMHK or any other one company, they tended to circulate not between the
camps and their rural homes, but between different jobs for Europeans.[54] Most
of those interviewed described having been initially employed by the Bas-
Congo Katanga railroad company (BCK) or another local construction enterprise before going to the UMHK, and later alternated between the mines and
various jobs in the city proper. This type of fluidity completely undermined
both the expectations and wishes of their employers who wanted to keep the
city and the camps rigidly separate and who conceived of migrant labor as
alternating between industry and agriculture and of stabilized labor as fixed
in one place.

One of the most troublesome problems that faced the UMHK administrators and the colonial officials in Katanga province was the surveillance and
control of those workers who did leave the mining compounds. During the
stabilization project, the company urged unmarried workers to maintain contact with family members back home, for the sake of ensuring their eventual
marriage. Occasionally the company allowed other workers to visit their rural
homes as well, but the UMHK was uniformly insistent on permitting travel
only to a worker's "village of origin." To control this, all recruited workers
as well as those who had joined "voluntarily" had to have their state-

determined ethnicity and point of origin marked on their work ticket; workers' outside trips could thus be controlled, and violators could be detained and reprimanded. Here, the tactics of resistance employed by mine workers were straightforward. Workers frequently gave false information to recruiters and labor processors, "lost" the portions of their tickets that contained the relevant information, or simply avoided giving the information out in the first place. As a result, tracking the movements of all workers became a logistical nightmare. Similarly, by hiding visitors in their houses, or failing to report the exact day on which a relative had arrived, mine-workers and their families were able to circumvent restrictions on contact with outside family members.[55]

Yet the divisions that the UMHK tried to create between the mining camps and the "outside world," and the strategies workers used to blur these divisions were both overshadowed by efforts to control space within the camps themselves. For the UMHK, the design of the camps was intended to effect the transformation from "deculturated African" into "stabilized worker" through the creation and regulation of residential space. The company sought to define and control the spaces of communal interaction and activity; to create individual domains with an eye toward eliminating the African "taste" for common property and to carefully separate these domains from communal space; and to create gendered spaces that were intended to shape women into wives and mothers who would contribute to the stabilization and reproduction of the work force.

Before stabilization began, neither communal nor individual spaces were clearly demarcated or organized in the mining camps. In contrast, by 1926 Mouchet's camps had begun to reflect everywhere the intent to distinguish the personal from the communal. African workers had largely used food sharing to create communal bonds with other workers; the UMHK sought to replace these ad hoc social groups with gatherings of its own making. As a first step, it moved to break up the communities created by food sharing. Kitchens were located outside, in between houses, because the African custom of communal eating was thought to be too deeply ingrained to be changed. It was considered preferable that families assemble to eat in an open space rather than crowding into one family's dwelling where illicit behaviors would be easier to hide.[56] Types of residential space were themselves fragmented to retard the development of worker solidarity—the company gave members of a new class of African supervisors better housing, located at strategic points throughout the camps, and ordered them to maintain surveillance of their fellow workers.[57] Surveillance was very important in the camps, since the colonial government had set certain restrictions on the use of corporal punishment. Unlike officers in the army, UMHK officials had to rely more on the deterrent effects of their gaze.[58]

The use of kitchens and the small regularized gathering spaces between houses would, it was thought, contribute to stable, controllable group relations; but much of the planning behind the camp was also intended precisely to delimit such relations and to enhance a sense of personal space. The most dramatic change in living environment was the switch from group dormitories to personal family dwellings. The provisional reforms in housing, which the UMHK undertook in the early 1920s, replaced long rows of straw huts with large dormitory-style housing holding up to sixty single men.[59] Rather than serving an elaborate theory about workers' mentalities, these reforms were a stopgap to improve sanitary conditions; they emphasized undifferentiated shared space. The partitions between beds in the dormitories were there to retard the transfer of germs to other men rather than to demarcate the space belonging to an individual worker. Latrines were enclosed and rationalized, but individuals had no privacy. After 1926, the typical family's house (Figure 10.3, although the kitchen and wood shelters were usually detached) gave each worker, his wife, and his children their own domestic space. The UMHK considered it to be a weapon in its longstanding battle against polygamy in the camps, but the creation of family space also had the goal of making each worker responsible for his own family's living conditions, and of making each adult woman in the camp responsible for cleaning and maintaining the house. For the company, good workers were necessarily parts of "nuclear families."

Even the toilets of the new camps reflected this attempt to enforce a Western style of individualism and the types of resistance it engendered. One of the more surreal aspects of the history of these camps involves Mouchet's

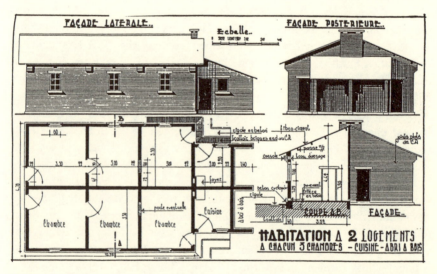

Figure 10.3. Plan of Lodgings for Two Families (*Bulletin CESPI,* 12 [1950], 129).

continually thwarted attempts to get workers to use latrines in what he considered a hygienic manner. Spiral-shaped enclosures contained individual seats with buckets and were designed to create a private space in which workers could relieve themselves (Photo 10.1). Yet such latrines were notoriously unpopular with workers; part of the purpose of the fence around the camp was to keep people from "running into the bush" instead of into the toilets. Bedeviled by the inhabitants' tendency to squat instead of sit on latrine seats, Mouchet contemplated building a set of constraining boards designed to make it physically impossible to squat within a latrine building. At no moment perhaps was, to borrow from Foucault, the orthopedic approach of the camps more clear.[60]

Spaces that lay at the intersection of the personal and the communal were carefully gendered. Public fountains, from which women fetched clean water, and group laundries were areas for the visible modernization of housekeeping. Trash cans were placed between houses and the women of the adjoining residences were responsible for making sure that no refuse fell out of them onto the ground of the courtyard.[61] All these tasks defined spaces where women participated in group activities contributing to the establishment of proper domestic roles. Here women interacted with one another outside of the boundaries of their personal living quarters; yet the types of activities engaged in within these spaces and the people who were expected to occupy them separated them from other communal areas.

Space within the house was also divided to create a restricted sphere within the already delimited domestic zone. The segmentation of dwellings into two or three separate rooms for each family allowed for the creation of hierarchical, gendered spaces within the houses themselves (Figure 10.3). The important role that women played in Mouchet's and Mottoulle's theories about workers' behavior in their home villages meant that each part of the house,

Photo 10.1. Building for Latrines in Mining Camp (Mouchet and Pearson, *L'Hygiène pratique*).

and each activity within it, was saturated with psychological and social meanings. Women were first of all expected to have certain proprietary feelings toward their homes, some of which were to be encouraged while others were rechanneled. Practices like the blocking of ventilation openings with canvas sacks or pungent incense, and seemingly unsound nursing strategies were combated in the *foyers sociaux*. Women with young children had to attend these domestic science classes, run by nuns, in order to receive bottles, food, and medication for their families. Teachers made surprise visits to homes to see how well women were complying with what they learned at the *foyers*.[62] A tightly regulated approach to domestic spaces was often "prompted" by women's general reluctance to abide by UMHK rules. Kawama noted that women had considered the common areas in between houses to be the responsibility of the company, not of the women whose compounds abutted it, and they thus refused to help clean it. Such a flat-out refusal infuriated the company's officers and they responded by using force to compel cooperation.

But as frustrating as such janitorial defiance may have seemed, Mouchet and Mottoulle feared that women's sexuality would pose a far more substantial threat to camp security. They assumed that an unchaste wife would likely not care as much for her house or her children, and the personal conflicts such behavior would ultimately provoke would only spark more serious conflicts among male workers.[63] The UMHK's solution was to create a space in which women's time would be more productively and safely spent: family gardens. While such gardens, of course, helped offset the costs of importing fresh vegetables into the camp, they also kept women "absorbed in gardening while their husbands were at work," in full view of the other women of their quarter, ensuring that they "would not be unfaithful."[64] It also went without question that women's and men's toilet and bathing facilities needed to be segregated in order to promote more "civilized" attitudes toward bodies and bodily functions in general.[65] The careful determination of which activities needed to be done in public, under a normative gaze, which had to be undertaken in an isolation that was equally normative, and which were to be executed in a private space that was nonetheless open to scrutiny was the guiding project in constructing gender in the mining camps.

But in all three of these types of spaces—communal, individual, and gendered—the colonial policy was continually forced to reorient and reorganize itself to account for Africans' unexpected responses to the control of space. In every exasperated story by a medical officer or other camp official about "special problems" faced by the designer of camps lies the historical trace of a resistance to spatial power. Workers often acted in ways directly counter to the type of "individual work ethic" that the UMHK wanted to instill. For example, taking advantage of the food given out by the company, men with work would often take on other men and their families as "clients." A worker could go to the mines most of the time, sometimes sending one of his clients in his place, and then distribute the food and clothing he received to those others who were living in his house as his "family."[66] Kawama gives a brief description of the "inspection" techniques used by the UMHK to try to prevent such behavior, but it appears that it was nonetheless common.[67]

The housing of workers and the ways in which housing integrated women into the camp were in many ways the linchpins of the UMHK's stabilization program. However, rather than having a mollifying effect upon residents, it was precisely this aspect of the mining camps that workers found to be most offensive. Yav's *Vocabulary* provides one of the most startling and challenging depictions of worker resistance to the creation of domestic and gendered spaces. Yav's history of Elisabethville paints a somewhat surprising picture of the overall relations between workers and the mining company. He characterizes the mining operations of the UMHK as a sort of heroic endeavor on the part of the Europeans with which the African miners agreed to help. Yav speaks of the "loyal help" offered to the Belgians by the first workers, discusses the hardship that the workers suffered "with the whites," and paints comradely scenes of mine-owners and -workers sleeping together on the ground and being bitten by snakes together.[68] Yet this was not indicative of a naïveté on the part of the workers about the economic foundation of their employment; the history of workers' financial and employment strategies as a whole gives no doubt but that they understood full well that they were not simply "helping the Belgians with a project."[69] Nor should it be taken to mean that workers felt as if they were true companions of their employers. Rather Yav's depiction focuses on the workers' contributions to the mining enterprise as a whole; since the Africans went out of their way to help with the mining, which was, Yav implies, for the Belgians' benefit, it was only fitting that the workers should seek just compensation.

This becomes clearer after the abrupt transition that follows Yav's pastoral description of the mining project. After discussing how the whites were "real men" who accomplished much, Yav notes, "[a]s far as sleeping goes they failed us by building for us those outhouses which have remained the same up to now."[70] In a fascinating passage he goes on to comment at length that:

They thought to build for the black man just a one-room house. [But] this man had his wife and his children some of them male, some of them female. Now this poor man with his wife and children suffered when he went to sleep and when he awoke. Who is this man? The poor man, the boy, who sleeps in one small room together with his children, female and male. When he goes to work, the poor boy, when he wakes up, he says to all his grown-up children: Mothers and fathers, you must excuse me. Get up and leave, or go first outside. Me, your old man, I want to put on my clothes first. . . . The children would all have to get out until their father had finished dressing. . . . And when his wife came to wake up, it was the same, no difference. This has been our, the boys', suffering [editor's interpolation].[71]

What is startling about this quote is how thoroughly it conflicts with not just the perspective of the UMHK, but with the information available on the layout of the camps themselves. Between the earliest time to which Yav refers, the post–World War I era, until when he wrote his history, in 1966 at the latest, there had been several series of changes in housing in the camps. What then could it mean to claim that the houses had "remained the same up to now"? Similarly, the UMHK was at great pains to provide multiroom houses for workers with families, precisely in order to maintain the types of private and gendered spaces that Yav complains about not having.

One possible explanation rests on what the house signifies in Yav's recounting. Fabian has already noted that the usage of "little latrines" to describe the lodging can be usefully read as referring to the effects of the housing arrangement in a more abstract sense.[72] Cues to this shift in metaphor are given by the language of Yav's text. The passage quoted above and its continuation through the next paragraph are the only time in the entire work in which Yav uses the pronoun "he" to refer to a hypothetical, unnamed, or otherwise identified character. Other times, when he wishes to refer to the experience of workers in general, he employs such expressions as "we boys," or just "we." The switch midway through the description from past to present tense also serves to place the passage in a narrative frame that contrasts sharply with the two other styles of description that dominate the *Vocabulary*: past-tense historical narration and lists of names and places.

Within the "one bedroom" dwelling that serves as the setting for the quote, gender and generational relations are chaotic. Yav mentions the worker's "grown-up children" living with the man in the same house, where such an extended family would not have fit into the UMHK's "nuclear family" definition used for housing assignments. In the space, generational distinctions are confused and inverted; work intersects with and interferes with domestic life. Taken as a metaphor, Yav's critique stands as a description of the mass confusion about proper place and behavior workers experienced. The fact that Yav used the layout of the home to express the disrupted power relationships that resulted from the UMHK's policies is indicative of how centrally space encoded the conflicts in the lives of Africans; and the fact that he presents the home not as a utopian area enclosing a passive worker, but rather as a "failure" on the part of the UMHK that caused a sense of dislocation and violated the "gentlemanly bond" between workers and employers, is indicative of how misguided the image of the passive, mimetic African was.

The example of the *butwa* dance helps clarify the difference in perspective between workers and mine officials and illustrates how this difference often confounded the UMHK's projects. One of the primary causes of "worker immorality" in the old, prestabilization camps, was thought to be the large number of dances that took place in the evenings and on days off.[73] The *butwa* dance, in particular, was thought to be obscene, and curfews were even imposed to try to eradicate its performance. The new camps tried to avoid this problem by eliminating any central open space where workers and their families could gather. Both the grid scheme (Figure 10.1) and the quarter design (Figure 10.2) eliminated the large central assembly lawns of earlier layouts, the first by creating long narrow rows not large enough in which to congregate and by filling any large spaces with trees, the latter by displacing a single center into several smaller, dispersed courtyards. Social events calling for large open spaces, like dances and football matches, required special permission from the camp's "director of leisure"—a new post created by Mottoulle.[74]

The UMHK saw the *butwa* dance as evidence of the persistence of immoral, "tribal" behavior among workers who had not yet been fully assimilated into camp life; this necessitated the careful control of public space. As communal, public ceremonies taking place in the open, these dances were a direct challenge to the UMHK's attempts to regulate social behavior. But miners also used these dances to develop networks of social connections—to provide assistance to workers who had become ill or injured and to coordinate the preparation of food for groups larger than the UMHK had intended.[75] Such organizations, often based on religious associations present in the hinterland areas, gave employees the ability to regulate their own internal social life and counterbalanced white officials' and African supervisors' authority.

Yet these social organizations often ran directly counter to the plans of the company. The UMHK, believing that Africans needed strong political organizations to control them, had favored the promotion of African supervisors whom they believed to have been elites in rural societies. By giving this rural aristocracy supervisory jobs, they hoped to reproduce the methods of political control that existed outside the camps' confines. What the UMHK misunderstood was that political authority in rural societies was often offset by broader, trans-village associations, and mine-workers quickly imported these organizations into the compounds to serve the same purpose. Furthermore, according to Fetter, the *butwa* dances were the major public ceremonies through which these associations coordinated food distribution and maintained contacts with groups outside the camps. Thus the social links created by the *butwa* were direct counters to the power of UMHK-backed elites. As ways of reappropriating the fragmented spaces that remained in the mining camps for group interaction, they were an active subversion of the mining company's control over collective space. Rather than being places where Western ideas of gender, property, and family were disseminated, they became the sites of political exercises that completely escaped the understanding of the UMHK, and gave workers the ability to mediate the types of interaction they would have with the rural hinterland and to modify and adapt rural forms of social organization to the new conditions of the camps.

Contrary to the beliefs of Mouchet and Mottoulle, then, African workers were quite vigilant of the relationship between elements of their physical surroundings and the meanings given to them by the systems of power in which they were embedded. As a result, the UMHK's evaluation of African motives in deciding whether or not to stay in the camps—that it was the high quality of material conditions in the camps that made workers want to stay even when there were no jobs to be had—proves inadequate. A picture of mining camps as "totalitarian" institutions elides the very real accomplishments of miners in resisting camp authority and fashioning new forms of social organization. It also overlooks the highly conscious and insurgent knowledge of employees and fails to penetrate beneath the surface of the UMHK's motives in camp design. After all, in the words of Mouchet and Mottoulle, these elaborate designs were intended not so much to provide a more "attractive" living environment that would root Africans in the camps, but rather to take a group of "Blacks, coming from the forest, new to work, impregnated by centuries of the practice of sorcery and of a superstitious fear of medicine and accustomed from childhood to filthy and negligent habits" and transform them into "workers" who would "quickly subscribe to the new form" of labor and who would be trustworthy in their "attachment and submission to the discipline of the *Société* [the UMHK's parent company]."[76] And while there can be no doubt that the Africans impregnated by superstition were colonial fictions, a reduction of the colonial project to a vast *méconnaisance* misses the very complex forms of knowledge that were wrapped up in the theories generated by the UMHK.

What is at issue in the history of the mining camps in Elisabethville is not whether Mouchet, Mottoulle, and de Hemptinne were wrong about what spatial relationships were like in certain Central-African villages or about how these spatial relationships affected sanitary conditions or work efficiency on the camps. Nor should the historiographic project be to determine what parts of African experience were accurately reflected in European models and what parts of European models were derived from western biases. The UMHK and its theorists had a stake in making sure that their discourses on Africans and space overlapped with those of Africans themselves. But the existence of a common spatial framework also served to sharpen workers' analyses of the company's power and helped them more accurately direct their resistance. What has animated my examination of space in the mining camps is a sense of the power that the UMHK officials believed their knowledge gave them, and of the fundamental assumptions about Africans on which that feeling of power depended. It is not by an analysis of which Africans resisted which strategies of power and which Africans colluded with them—an analysis of whether, for example, Kawama's work in the *foyer social*, whose disciplinary functions she knew only too well, constituted a naive or an insurgent understanding of power—but rather by an examination of how these workers positioned themselves within a field of power, how they generated their own knowledge about the techniques of discipline being exercised upon them, that the spirit of resistance in the mining camps is foregrounded.

NOTES

1. Union Minière du Haut-Katanga [hereafter UMHK], *Européens et congolais au travail* (Bruxelles: UMHK, 1954), 5.

2. J. Fabian, *History From Below: The Vocabulary of Elisabethville by André Yav: Texts, Translation and Interpretive Essay*. Translation and commentary by Johannes Fabian with Kalundi Mango. Linguistic notes by W. Schicho (Philadelphia: J. Benjamins Pub., 1990), 99. Unfortunately, almost nothing is known about the author of this text.

3. Most probably L. Mottoulle, director of the UMHK's "indigenous labor" division and writer of many such handbooks. In all likelihood, this particular version was edited down by a later official from an earlier Mottoulle manual.

4. UMHK, *Européens et congolais*, 5. An older guidebook (1932?) put it in these words: "The White . . . must focus on his role as educator as much from a moral point of view as from a professional, and . . . in his acts and words must maintain his own prestige towards the *indigènes* . . . [whom] he must regard as does a good father [original text in English]." Anonymous, *Main d'œuvre indigène* [sic], 26–27, 30; in Belgian Congo Colonial Documents: Kasai and Katanga Provinces (Louvain: 1978), University of Wisconsin-Madison, Microfiche 2612 [hereafter JLVC].

5. L. Mottoulle, "Politique sociale de l'Union Minière du Haut-Katanga pour sa main-d'œuvre indigène et ses résultats au cours de vingt années d'application," *Institut Royal Colonial Belge, Bulletin des Séances de Sciences Morales et Politiques, Mémoires in–8°* vol. 14, fasc. 3 (1946), 5.

6. He first expressed this argument in his article, B. Fetter, "L'Union Minière du Haut-Katanga, 1920–1940: La naissance d'une sous-culture totalitaire," *Cahiers du CEDAF* 6 (1973), which he later worked into his monograph *The Creation of Elisabethville: 1910–1940* (Stanford: Hoover Institution Press, Stanford University, 1976). My treatment of Fetter's argument here is, at best, highly compressed; yet it captures, I believe, the salient aspects of his position. Fetter's account of the stabilization project is largely based on the UMHK's own official history. See UMHK, *1906–1956* (Bruxelles: L. Cuypers, 1956), 163–65. There is, in addition, a long tradition of Marxisant works, most notably by J. Higginson, which, despite their great usefulness, all but ignore issues of space. J. Higginson, "The Making of an African Working Class: The *Union Minière du Haut Katanga* and the African Mine Workers, 1907–1945" (Ph.D. Dissertation, University of Michigan: 1979); Banjikila Bakajika, "Capitalisme, rapport salarial et régulation de la main-d'œuvre: La classe ouvrière noire dans les camps de l'Union Minière du Haut-Katanga, 1925–1967" (Ph.D. Dissertation, Université Laval: 1993).

7. See, for example, Fabian, *Vocabulary*, 137. For an analysis that stresses the origins of the camps' features in Belgian urban planning, see B. de Meulder, "Camp and Plant: The Belgian Colonial Housing Policy as an Eugenic Experiment: The Case of the *Union Minière du Haut-Katanga*, 1910–1930," in G. Vanderhulst, ed., *Industry, Man and Landscape* (Brussels: n. p., 1992), 187–91, and "At Home and Abroad: Belgian Planning and

Urban Design Policies in the Congo, 1925–1960" (unpublished paper, International Conference on Africa's Urban Past, London, School of Oriental and African Studies, June 19–21, (1996). Unfortunately, as of the time of publication I have not been able obtain copies of de Meulder's articles.

8. Until after the Second World War, these discourses circulated exclusively among colonial officials like Mottoulle; Monseigneur J. de Hemptinne, a missionary and head of camp education; and R. Mouchet, the UMHK's company physician. See Mottoulle, "Politique Sociale"; "Un imposant bilan social: Les résultats de la politique sociale de l'Union Minière du Haut-Katanga pour ses travailleurs indigène," *Revue Coloniale Belge* 25, no. 10 (1946), 230–35; and "Historique, organisation et résultats obtenus d'une œuvre de protection de l'enfance noire dans la population indigène industrielle de l'Union Minière du Haut-Katanga," *Institut Royal Colonial Belge, Bulletin des Séances* 2 (1931), 531–44; J. de Hemptinne, "La politique indigène du gouvernement belge," *Congo* 9, no. 2 (1928), 359–74; and *"Précisions sur le problème de la politique indigène,"* *Congo* 10, no. 2 (1929), 187–207; R. Mouchet and A. Pearson, *L'hygiène pratique des camps de travailleurs noirs en Afrique tropicale* (Bruxelles: Goemaere, 1922); and *The Practical Hygiene of Native Compounds in Tropical Africa* (London: Baillière, Tindall and Cox, 1923); and R. Mouchet and R. Van Nitsen, *La main d'œuvre indigène au Congo belge: Les problèmes qu'elle évoque* (Bruxelles: Impr. des Travaux publics, 1940).

9. Katanga Documents and Field Notes, Bruce Fetter, comp., 1966. University of Wisconsin–Madison Microfilm 4500 [hereafter KDFN].

10. C. Kawama, "Récit de vie de Clémentine Kawama: Recueilli par Dibwe dia Mwembu et Claude Milambwe," in B. Jewsiewicki, ed., *Naître et mourir au Zaïre* (Paris: Karthala, 1993), 229–38.

11. For the conclusions of this group, see S. De Vos, "La politique indigène et les missions catholiques," *Congo* 4, no. 2 (1923), 635–57, esp. 635–36.

12. Ibid., 639–40. De Vos's words were echoed almost verbatim by the anonymous author of the report of 1927, JLVC, F618, according to whom, the lack of stabilization *"fatigu[e] la population, amèn[e] l'anarchie et épuis[e] la force de reproduction de la race."*

13. Ibid., 647–53.

14. De Hemptinne's views, which increase De Vos's emphasis on the degeneracy of contemporary African culture and the receptivity of Africans to Western models, were expressed in 1928 by "Gouvernement belge," esp. 365, 368–69; and in 1929 by "Précisions sur le problème," esp. 196–97, 203.

15. For an overview of the economic importance and corresponding power of the UMHK, see J.-L. Vellut, "Mining in the Belgian Congo," in D. Birmingham and P. M. Martin, eds., *History of Central Africa*, vol. 2 (New York: Longman 1983), 130. As late as 1936, the colonial government was still issuing condemnations of the UMHK's labor practices, seemingly to no avail. See, for example, the report of Georges Brouxlon, *Substitut du Procureur du Roi*, JLVC, F1436.

16. Fetter, "Sous-culture totalitaire," 25–28.

17. Quoted in Higginson, "Working Class," pp. 121–29, 159.

18. C. Perrings, *Black Mineworkers in Central Africa: Industrial Strategies and the Evolution of an African Proletariat in the Copperbelt 1911–41* (London: Heinemann, 1979), 64–65.

19. The lengthy debate over the balance between agricultural subsistence and industrial production was fought out at the level of the provincial government. See *Comptes rendus*

des Conseils des provinces du Congo Belge and Examens des prévisions budgétaires: Comité Régional de la Province du Katanga. 1921–1948. University of Wisconsin–Madison, Microfilm 5003 (reels 14 and 15), hereafter CRPK.

20. For an overview of the UMHK's changing technologies and labor needs, see Bakajika, "Rapport salarial," 92–94. For the history of the UMHK's destruction of local white labor unions, see Fetter, "Sous-culture totalitaire," 10, and B. Jewsiewicki, "Contestation sociale au Zaïre (ex. Congo Belge). Grève administrative de 1920," *Africa-Tervuren* 22 (1976), 57–67.

21. Fetter, "Sous-culture totalitaire," 18–21.

22. UMHK, *1906–1956*, 163–65.

23. Perrings, *Black Mineworkers*, 76.

24. Fetter, *Creation of Elisabethville*, 59.

25. J.-L. Vellut, "Rural Poverty in Western Shaba, c. 1890–1930," in R. Palmer and N. Parsons, eds., *The Roots of Rural Poverty in Central and Southern Africa* (Berkeley: University of California Press, 1977), 309–10. For an in-depth description of the UMHK's plans for the rural areas of Katanga, see the report of 1927, JLVC, F618.

26. B. Jewsiewicki, "Unequal Development: Capitalism and the Katanga Economy, 1919–1940," in Palmer and Parsons, *Rural Poverty*, 323–35.

27. Mouchet and Van Nitsen, *Main d'œuvre indigène*, 1.

28. Ibid., ii, 20–22. "*Une plante transplantée porte rarement des fruits la première année.*" Mottoulle, "L'enfance noire," 531, 533.

29. Mouchet and Pearson, *Camps de travailleurs*, 104–5. Mouchet believed that agricultural peoples made the most disciplined workers, followed by pastoralists, and finally by riverain groups, who made the worst.

30. Mouchet and Van Nitsen, *Main d'œuvre indigène*, 9.

31. Mottoulle, "L'enfance noire," 531, 533.

32. Mouchet and Pearson, *Camps de travailleurs*, 9.

33. Ibid., 20.

34. Mottoulle, "L'enfance noire," 532. In one of his more literal moments, Mouchet even suggested creating "practice villages" in which workers could be partially trained in the ways of the camps without having to work. They would then be moved into the mining camps where they could be expected to behave quite appropriately and could begin working without disruption. Mouchet and Pearson, *Camps de travailleurs*, 16–17.

35. I owe this formulation to Angel Adams, "Narratives-in-Place: Critical Reflections on Place in the Vocabulary of Elizabethville," Unpublished Seminar Paper, University of Wisconsin–Madison, Fall 1996.

36. Fabian, *Vocabulary of Elisabethville*, 83.

37. Ibid., 73–75, 85, 93, 99.

38. Those of Jean Fataki, Laurent Mumba, Prosper Kandango, Bembeleza Tshikwasi, Ambroise Mateta, Henriette Balenge, Pilipill Sihumbile, and Léon Mutombo, KDFN.

39. Jean Fataki, KDFN. For the same theme, see Fabian, *Vocabulary of Elisabethville*, 83, 93.

40. Kawama, "Récit de vie," 230–33. The *foyers sociaux*, administered here under the UMHK's OPEN program, were a common feature of Belgian colonial projects. Analogous in many ways to Mouchet's practice camps for male workers, *foyers* were practice homes where European and, later, African women instructed young wives on the arts of homemaking and family raising. See N.R. Hunt, "Domesticity and Colonialism in Belgian Africa: Usumbura's *Foyer Social*, 1946–1960," *Signs: Journal of Women in Culture and*

Society 15 (1990), 447–74. Hunt has discussed the ways in which the *foyers* served to "solidify the class structure" of urban African societies. In cities like Usumbura, those who attended the *foyers* were in daily juxtaposition to the "lower class" women who did not. In Elisabethville, by contrast, the opposition was less one of class than of mine-worker versus city-dweller. The UMHK's employees were in an ambiguous position vis-à-vis other Africans; more highly trained, and considered more "assimilated" than others, they nonetheless were marked by the UMHK for a life of manual labor and not self-governance. Kawama's expressed feelings of superiority over the residents of Elisabethville emphasizes the cultural and social distinctions between the groups, not their political or economic position.

41. Kawama, "Récit de vie," 235.

42. Ibid., 237.

43. R. Sennett, *The Conscience of the Eye: The Design and Social Life of Cities* (New York: Knopf, 1990), 126–27.

44. L. White, "Class Struggle and Cannibalism: Storytelling and History Writing on the Copperbelts of Colonial Northern Rhodesia and the Belgian Congo," in *Speaking with Vampires: Rumor and History in Colonial Africa* (Berkeley: University of California Press, 2000), 288.

45. J. Dresch, "Villes Congolaises: Etude de Géographie urbaine et sociale," *Revue de géographie humaine et d'ethnologie* 1 (1947), 21–23.

46. B. Fetter, "Immigrants to Elisabethville: Their Origins and Aims," *African Urban Notes* 3, no. 2 (1968), 28.

47. B. Fetter, "African Associations in Elisabethville, 1910–1935: Their Origins and Development," *Etudes d'Histoire africaine* 6 (1974), 215.

48. Idem.

49. Fetter, "Sous-culture," 36.

50. Fetter, *Creation of Elisabethville*, 73–75.

51. Kawama, "Récit de vie," 233–34.

52. Mottoulle, "Bilan social," 231.

53. KDFN, *passim*. See also Kawama's descriptions of both her father's and husband's employment history; "Récit de vie," 229.

54. Kasimoto Mbuyi, for example, reported: "Once I arrived in Elisabethville in 1929, I never again returned to the village of my birth," KDFN.

55. See *Compte rendu*, 1935, CRPK.

56. Mouchet and Pearson, *Camps de travailleurs*, 28.

57. Ibid. 33–34.

58. Mouchet and Pearson, *Native Compounds*, 19.

59. Fetter, "Sous-culture totalitaire," 12.

60. Ibid., 32.

61. Kawama, "Récit de vie," 233.

62. Mouchet and Pearson, *Native Compounds*, 22; Mottoulle, "L'enfance noire," 534–35; neither discusses directly the surprise visits or the giving of food and medicines on condition of attendance, but these are attested to by Kawama, "Récit de vie," 232–33, 235.

63. The seemingly ineradicable nature of polygamy, for example, baffled the UMHK and the government long past the end of the period under discussion here. See the report of 1938, JLVC, F2407-8.

64. Fetter, "Sous-culture totalitaire," 37.

65. Mouchet, *Camps de travailleurs*, 45.

66. Fabian, *Vocabulary of Elisabethville*, 107.

67. Kawama, "Récit de vie," 233–34.

68. Fabian, *Vocabulary of Elisabethville*, 69–71.

69. Higginson, *passim.*

70. Ibid., 71.

71. Ibid., 75–77.

72. Ibid., 137.

73. Fetter, *Creation of Elisabethville*, 38.

74. Fetter, "Sous-culture totalitaire," 11, 21–22.

75. Fetter, "African Associations," 208–9.

76. Mouchet, *Camps de travailleurs*, 7; L. Mottoulle, "Bilan social," 231.

11

ADMINISTRATIVE CONFINEMENTS AND CONFINEMENTS OF EXILE

The Reclusion of Nomads in the Sahara

Pierre Boilley

During the colonial period, the Tuareg nomads of Adagh (Map 11.1) progressively became sedentary herders and in doing so, they experienced significant social transformations.[1] In order to better control this supposedly turbulent population, French authorities had recourse to two methods: first, they froze existing social dynamics among the Tuareg; second, they tried to limit pastoral migrations, deemed as anarchic. In this chapter, I will be refer to colonial strategies under the generic term of "administrative confinement."

After independence, administrative confinement endured in the Adagh. But the Tuareg had to confront other forms of enclosure, both as refugees and as military recruits. The repression of the Tuareg revolt in 1963 and subsequent massacres committed by the Malian army, followed by the severe droughts of the 1970s and 1980s, drove most Tuareg onto the road of exile. Confined in refugee camps in Mali, Algeria, Niger, and Mauritania, the Tuareg had to adapt to novel and often unwelcome situations. In order to escape from the social misery they encountered in the refugee camps, young Tuareg often looked for jobs in the Libyan army. In Libya, military commanders barracked Tuareg troops in training and housing camps, and kept them under close surveillance. Halfway between the refugee camp and the military camp, these enclosed spaces provided the Tuareg with new sites for social innovation. I will refer to the series of post-colonial experiences as "confinement through exile."

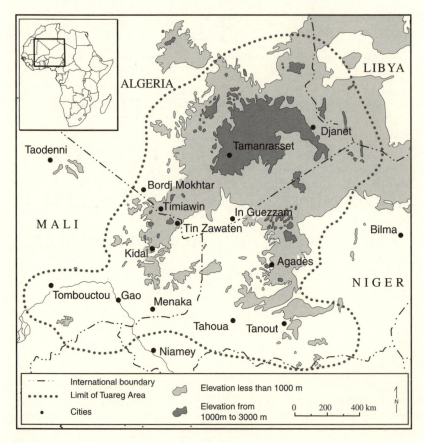

Map 11.1. Tuareg Living Space in the Sahara.

These different types of incarceration are linked to one another. Colonial administrative confinement engendered considerable social changes that often led to economic and social disasters among the Tuareg. Far from being mere epiphenomena in the region's modern history, or the painful but logical outcomes of exceptional catastrophes, these disruptions proved structurally determinant for the future of the Tuareg community, exposing the nomad societies of the Adagh to long-term mutations.[2]

ADMINISTRATIVE CONFINEMENT

The Tuareg had dominated the vast space of the central Sahara up to the border of the Sahel for several centuries, when, at the beginning of the twentieth century, the colonial conquest brought them into a situation of absolute dependence. Despite their determined opposition to the French invasion,[3] colonial rule finally integrated the Kel Adagh into the territory of French West Africa. The military defeat, followed by five decades of foreign occupation, initiated a series of considerable political and spatial traumas among the Tuareg. French administrators perceived nomads as unstable and untrustworthy. They sought, therefore, to impose French sovereignty by suppressing nomadic movements, enforcing colonial borders, and altering the Tuareg chiefs' powers.

Social Confinement: The Colonial Rationalization of the *Tiwsaten*

Before the colonial conquest, relations between nomad groups and the *tiwsaten*[4] were protean, constantly reconfiguring according to climatic variations, migrations, and the changing context of power relations. For instance, the *tawset* of Ahaggar had reached the Adagh for the first time during a drought. The group then carried out a series of temporary migrations before settling down definitively in the region. Tributary groups could free themselves from the tutelage of a noble *tawset* by migrating to new pastures and forming allegiances with those who controlled the area. Such examples are typical of the ways in which Tuareg communities adapted to their milieu and frequently restructured political relationships, either through progressive changes or through abrupt and violent ruptures. By contrast, the French colonial administrators belonged to a sedentary civilization where people and geographical spaces had been linked in a quasi-permanent manner for centuries; hence, they could not easily understand Tuareg realities. Moreover, the forms of political control that the colonial administration sought to enforce proved hardly compatible with the forms of spatial and political mobility prevalent in the region.

Furthermore, upon first contact, the French attempted to understand the organization of Tuareg groups, in order to transform it into a tangible and lasting reality, one that they could describe on paper and codify for administrative control. These principles of organization were quite explicit: "We will easily establish order in Adrar once we clearly divide families into groups and tribes. Classification is indispensable."[5] This phase of study lasted up until the effective occupation of Adagh in 1909. The first description of Kel Adagh society dates from 1904.[6] At that time, the names and distribution of the groups comprising the *tiwsaten* were still uncertain. However, a general framework was established by French colonizers. In 1907, lieutenants undertook the first reconnaissance mission in the region by traveling from north to south, and refining earlier descriptions.[7] In 1908, the battalion officer Bétrix, who was in charge of preparing the military occupation of Adagh, definitely imposed Arnaud and Cortier's classification.[8] From then on, up until decolonization, the normative representation of the Kel Adagh rigidified the political evolution of the *tiwsaten*, as Adagh groups were ordered to conform to the administration model. In fifty years, the administration modified its diagram only in minor details so as to weaken certain groups or better control them (as in the case of the Kel Telabit, who were separated from the Taghat Mellet around 1914).[9]

Moreover, the French administration created a hierarchical pyramid structure in which heads of families were subordinated to the *tawset* chiefs, who were themselves under the control of the *Amenokal*.[10] The chief of the French subdivision required *Imenokalen* to provide regular reports about their group's political and economic activities. Modeled after a colonial chiefdom, this system locked Tuareg groups into rigid, hierarchical divisions. French authorities interfered in the designation of chiefs, imposing an official authorization. Of course, they deposed *Imenokalen* who refused to comply with French policy. Subdivision officers registered all Tuareg chiefs, and they graded and commented on their actions in files later sent all the way up to the governor of the colony. In addition, the French endowed the chiefs with new prerogatives (tax collection, transmission of administrative messages, political information), thus transforming the nature of *Imenokalens'* authority. In pre-colonial Tuareg society, where spatial but also political mobility was prevalent, the chief's people expected him to guarantee the cohesion of the community. By imposing a rigid political hierarchy of *Imenokalen*, French colonial rule thoroughly transformed the chiefs' exercise of power and sources of legitimacy.

Colonial Rule and Spatial Confinement

Spatial confinement reinforced the process of social fossilization among the Tuareg. Under colonial rule, each *tawset* could only move through a precise territory, defined by known water sources and wells in each subdivision. This territorial space provided the basis for a census and fiscal revenues. Since colonial sovereignty in nomadic regions was essentially expressed through the head tax, each French subdivision chief imposed a close surveillance over Tuareg communities. Members of each *tawset* had to report the exact composition of their group, and their itineraries. Resistance to this program was very strong. Since the *tawset* chief was responsible for the collection of taxes, anyone who wished to avoid the head tax had to escape the official census. Paradoxically, therefore, administrative control provoked a greater dispersion of smaller encampments trying to avoid colonial observation. In turn, this encouraged the administration to create an arsenal of measures that aimed to keep the *tiwsaten* under the authority of designated chiefs, and within designated territory.

When patrols discovered nomads outside the official zones, colonial administrators forcefully resorted to military raids called "driving-back" operations *(refoulement)* that "pushed back" *(rabattre)* delinquent and scattered encampments towards a regrouping site.[11] Then, the subdivision *goumiers*[12] escorted the Tuareg back to their designated lands and fined them. These "police operations,"[13] with their "seizures of recalcitrant elements," often took on the allure of military campaigns, mobilizing large numbers of troops.[14] Once captured, the disobedient Tuareg groups experienced various sanctions according to the nature of the transgression. First, households (tents)[15] that had abandoned their tribe without reason were brutally reincorporated. Second, groups whose complex networks of alliances served as pretexts for claiming that they "belonged to no one" could be tried on the spot, without appeal, by a marabout from Attaher.[16] Finally, if the flight appeared to be a violation of colonial discipline, the delinquent group was submitted to genuine forms of punitive confinement:

> The Taïtoqs group was taken back to Adrar. These people are dependents of the Idnanes, chief Dauchy. Some of them returned to the Idnanes. The others, with Akoukou, refused to obey the chief of the Idnanes and were thus taken to Kidal where they are in forced residence. This disobedience stems from the chief of the Taïtoqs, Akoukou, who moves farther away from Adrar with the arrival of each new subdivision chief.[17]

In order to identify lawful and illegal residents, colonial authorities distributed official documents to the nomads. Hence, in cases of insufficient rain and mediocre grazing land, the nomads of Adagh could move to better territories outside the subdivision, provided that they acquired a permit from the administrator at Kidal, a copy of which was sent to Gao, the circumscription headquarters.[18] This permit for collective nomadism was valid for an entire group, family, or *tawset*. This helped the subdivision chiefs to identify persons who settled in their circumscription, and those who had just returned from neighboring subdivisions. In addition, French administrators issued detailed family identity cards, thus improving the means for identity checks.

These methods of spatial control did not always prove effective. They curbed the dispersion of families and groups in unauthorized territories but did not eliminate it. This led to odd administrative situations. Since French administrators refused to admit that their policy was inappropriate, they switched from adapting people to borders to adapting borders to people's movements. Colonial authorities frequently modified subdivision frontiers so that they encompassed "illegitimate" groups that had successfully escaped colonial control.

For example, Tuareg frequently crossed the border between the subdivision of Kidal and Menaka, on the one hand, and the circumscription of Tahoua, on the other, since it was located in a poorly supervised territory. The central administration could not decide on a strategy for revising the subdivision limits, and handed the problem over to the subdivision chiefs. Each chief should fix the conditions for authorizing nomads to cross a circumscription to which they did not belong. At the end of the 1930s, the subdivisions of Menaka and Kidal gave nomads from Kidal (Kel Adagh) the right to cross a zone in the north of Menaka. In return, the Kel Adagh agreed to have their permits for nomadism inspected annually. But this agreement did not endure. During the first years, the people of Adagh headed toward the south, beyond the zone in which they had just been accorded right-of-passage. The situation become intolerable and the administration summoned the subdivision chiefs to renegotiate the accord. The new convention fixed the right-of-passage within specific limits, and was signed between Kidal and Menaka on September 18, 1948.[19] Many similar agreements were established between Kidal and neighboring subdivisions, including that of November 6, 1944 with the subdivision of Bourem *(Convention d'Anefis),* February 1945 with the annex of Tamanrasset *(Convention de Tamanrasset),* and December 31, 1948, with the circumscription of Tahoua *(Convention de Mentes).*

Thus, every time colonial regulations proved plainly obsolete, the administration adapted to the circumstances. In many cases, the conventions on nomadism did not enforce existing situations; rather, they merely registered them. Therefore, Tuareg herders' constant and necessary adaptations to climatic conditions and grazing land endured, as many nomads maintained a relative freedom of movement. However, Tuareg experienced considerable constraint under the accumulation of bans, rules, permits, forced returns *(refoulements),* and official pressures that hindered the nomadic capacity of the Kel Adagh and their neighbors. Administrative pressure significantly diminished the fluidity of pastoral life: The Kel Adagh, like most nomadic populations in the French empire, could not entirely escape from spatial restraint and administrative confinement.

Malian Incarceration: A Colonial Legacy

After Mali's independence in 1960, administrative confinement did not disappear in the nomadic regions. The Tuareg had only a vague understanding of the transformation in the relations between France and its former colonies. They remained almost entirely outside the process of decolonization, abstaining massively from colonial elections. Therefore, Tuareg ended up without high-profile political representatives who could defend their specific demands and needs in the new state. Some Tuareg organized a few petition campaigns to claim autonomy in the newly independent country.[20] But these projects failed, and the post-independence authorities, mostly Southerners, inherited the state apparatus and the administrative framework left by the French. Ill informed about the particularities of the nomadic population in the northern regions, Malian political elites generally slipped into previous practices and administrative principles.

The quick departure of the French took the Tuareg by surprise. They did not understand why the sedentary people of southern Mali were taking over administrative posts in the north: From their perspective, a new form of colonization had simply been substituted for the old one. Reciprocal misunderstandings followed, particularly when new laws failed to account for local mentalities, thus exacerbating the Northerners' feelings of being left behind in the process of African emancipation. In 1963, a marginal dispute between two *goumiers* and two young Tuareg threw oil on the fire: Revolt spread through the north of Mali. Facing a modern army, stuck between the troops of southern Mali and its ally, Algeria, the poorly armed rebels and their camels did not resist long. The rebellion was crushed in 1964 and violent repression, interspersed with massacres of men and cattle, followed.

Following this episode, the Malian state and its administration held the Kel Adagh in high suspicion, along with other Tuareg and nomads. Politicians perceived the nomads as potential rebels, and put the Adagh region, deemed a "zone of insecurity," under military control, forbidding foreigners to enter it up until the 1980s. Thus, the Malian state not only inherited French administrative confinement in Adagh, but reinforced it during the early post-independence period. The transformation of colonial administrative borders into frontiers of new independent states (Algeria, Mali, Niger) encouraged this process. As a result, in the 1960s and 1970s, the Tuareg faced increasing political isolation and spatial confinement.

EXILE AND CAMPS

A few years after the 1963–1964 revolt, the Tuareg faced further crises. In the early 1970s, a series of droughts put increasing pressure on pastoral life. The crisis peaked in 1972–1973: During this period, animals died by the thousands and the nomads, deprived of resources, experienced what journalists described as a "mass famine."[21] From then on, having lost everything and incapable of surviving on their usual pastures, the Tuareg fled north or south in hopes of finding some form of assistance. Pushing along their surviving animals, they began by moving toward regions that normally received more rain. This movement was so massive that the year became known as *awatat wa n Tebdhay*—the year of "the flow"—when nomads who left for Algeria and the river regions of Menaka or Niger were so numerous that they formed a human river that flowed slowly away from Adagh. Most fled toward the southeast, the region of Azawakh and the land of the Iwlliminden, and toward Menaka and Niamey (Niger).

Many herders lost all their livestock and continued on foot, abandoning belongings that they could no longer carry. Those who had lost most of their animals at the outset could not take on such a long voyage. In order to find help, they headed for small urban centers on the Algerian border such as Boughessa, Bordj, Mokhtar, Timiawin, or Tin Zawaten. Tuareg who were not able to reach these towns found refuge in the sedentary villages of the Adagh region itself, such as Kidal, Tessalit, and Aguelhoc. The few nomads who had retained a few goats—which are the most resistant animals, though incapable of long migrations—were able to survive for some time in the Adagh. But the large majority of the region's inhabitants (up to 90 percent by some estimates) deserted the region.

Having lost their herds, the majority of Tuareg refugees reached their destinations in a state of exhaustion. Before seeking out assistance, they sold their few belongings (arms, jewelry, bags, saddles, tents) for food. When these goods were gone, there was no longer any choice. Many emigrants who had traveled south sought refuge in camps. In Mali, a report by the Service for Planning and Statistics *(Service du Plan et de la Statistique)* counted 49,000 refugees in the camps in 1973 and 88,000 in 1974 (90 percent of whom were nomads).[22] In Niamey (Niger), 13,000 nomads lived in the camp of Lazaret alone.[23] Those who had headed north ended up in the camps in Algeria. There, the camps of In Edaq (Bordj Mokhtar) and Timiawin sheltered a total of 12,000 Tuareg from Mali.[24] Tuareg who could not leave Adagh went to the makeshift camps set up in the towns of the region, where they also numbered in the thousands. At any point in time, the Kidal camp alone harbored no less than 2,000 refugees, according to figures available for the period from mid-December 1973 to mid-April 1974.

The 1969–1974 drought did not put an end to the series of climatic disasters that befell the Kel Adagh. After a succession of normal years, 1984–1986 suffered again from rain deficits. Pastures dried up, water holes disappeared, wells ran dry, and herds were decimated. Again, hundreds of nomads sought refuge outside Adagh, and outside of Mali. The refugee camps filled once again. People died of famine, disease, or exhaustion upon arrival in the camps or along the way. In 1986, the Algerian Red Crescent accounted for 40,478 refugees on the Algerian territory, in Adrar and Tamanrasset, the two southern *wilayas*.[25] In all, 12,672 refugees (essentially Kel Adagh) lived in the camp of Bordj Bedji Mokhtar, and 27,330 in those of Tin Zawaten and In Guezzam, where Tuareg from Mali and Niger gathered.

Refugee camps represented a new form of spatial confinement for the nomads of the region. Tuareg were often stationed for several years in these sites, which they could not escape for lack of resources. Uprooted from their pastures, forced to deal with unfamiliar modes of social organization, the Tuareg and their companions in misfortune lived in unprecedented conditions of promiscuity, and in a state of complete dependence for daily subsistence and food.

Climatic Catastrophes as Consequences of Spatial Confinement

Before analyzing the social changes that took place in the refugee camps, we must first clarify how drought conditions had worsened through colonial and post-colonial spatial and political confinements of the Tuareg. The 1973–1974 drought represented an unprecedented catastrophe for the Sahel and for the Adagh in particular, deserted by several thousand inhabitants and the majority of the cattle. A disaster of such proportions would have been hard to imagine during the pre-colonial era. When local people recall difficult years, they tend to describe them as less catastrophic than the 1973–1974 crisis. I would like to argue that the political constraints imposed upon the Kel Adagh exacerbated the consequences of climatic variations.

Drought was far from being exceptional in the region. The Kel Adagh still remember the 1913 drought, for example, under the name *awatay wa n Tin Ahamma*, the year of Tin Ahamma, from the name of the well at Tin Ahamma in the region of Menaka, where the Tuareg took their herds to graze because of drought. Cycles of dry periods were typical of this region and the Tuareg developed strategies in response to these situations. First, mobility allowed the Tuareg to utilize a large spectrum of regional resources. Second, if mobility proved insufficient, groups sought out wetter lands, since all regions known to the nomads are rarely struck by the same degree of drought at the same time. The Tuareg also split up their herds so as to distribute them in space; they constituted food reserves in the form of live animals; and, in case of urgent need, they sold surplus animals or precious goods accumulated during better periods. Finally, the system of reciprocal lending of cattle between families allowed those who had suffered from drought to reconstitute their livestock. Drought thus rarely led to general catastrophe, or to famine and mass starvation. However, the 1972–1973 drought and, to a lesser extent, the drought of the 1980s proved cataclysmic for the nomads, especially the Kel Adagh. There are several possible explanations for this. First, the 1972–1973 drought was exceptionally long and spread throughout a large part of the pastoral and agricultural zones of the Sahel. Second, when the drought hit, the 1964 rebellion had already diminished the Kel Adagh's livestock. Finally, new political conditions prevented the Tuareg from using normal strategies against the crisis.

French colonial rule and the Malian administration had made mobility—that is, the basic flexibility needed to confront drought—more difficult. Doubtless, the panic-stricken nomads rushed out of the Adagh as soon as they realized that their survival was at risk. The Malian state could not—and apparently did not—seek to stem this "flow." In any case, it did not have the means to do so. Therefore, legal restrictions against mobility did not prevent Tuareg mobility at the time of panic in 1973. But they had already undermined the Tuareg's capacity to confront the crisis. For instance, rigorous customs barriers had already disturbed economic equilibrium. The Tuareg, of course, could circumvent tax controls in many ways. But the customs service hindered nomadic movements by forcing them to occur clandestinely. Custom officials, when they seized fraudulent caravans, confiscated goods and animals, thus contributing to the restriction of commercial networks and the impoverishment of the region. Nomads commercialized surpluses with more difficulty. In addition, they were forced to obtain supplies from state cooperatives, which did not always carry the goods they desired and charged higher prices than Algerian outlets. As the Tuareg could no longer move freely through the open space of the desert, and were increasingly confined to a controlled, rigid national territory, their strategies for economic accumulation during productive periods lacked efficiency.

Refugee Camps: Loss and Transformation of Social Values

In 1973–1974, and in 1984–1986, the refugee camps both symbolized and accentuated the transformation of the Tuareg's social structures. Life in the camps destabilized Tuareg social and political organization, as well as their particular world view.

Social hierarchies declined. The nobility, impoverished and famished, lost significant authority. Completely dispossessed, Tuareg nobles could no longer support dependents, a duty that had been the aristocracy's primary basis of legitimacy. This loss of prestige meant a decline of social standing in the eyes of the community. However, Tuareg nobles' own sense of humiliation was equally important. Worse, in order to survive, the nobility was forced to adopt what they considered ignominious behavior. In particular, they had to accept food relief, and compete with others for rations. This was a true moral defeat, since the Tuareg cultural code represented the mere show of interest in food as humiliating. Moreover, the nobility viewed most available labor or small chores as dishonorable. As a consequence, nobles had more difficulties overcoming poverty than other refugees. By contrast, those Tuareg who were tributary to the nobility, and were used to manual labor and artisanal work, could partially overcome social decline by taking on jobs such as gardening, construction work, unskilled labor, and herding surviving animals. This situation helped close the gap between different classes, leading to a number of marriages between women of noble origins and once-dependent folk. In 1974, "Slaves asked for the hand of their masters' daughters. In many instances, they succeeded. Economic need, and misery brought this drop in social standing. . . . The fall of the 'nobles' . . . was never so catastrophic as during the difficult hours of the camps."[26] Relations of dependence and domination that linked the nobility to their tributaries (or slaves) largely receded, while all social categories engaged in a mental reconstruction of social relationships.

At the same time, and often as a consequence, life in the camps profoundly modified rituals codifying social relations. Proper behavior based on reserve, the basic marker of Tuareg modesty and dignity, was challenged. In normal circumstances, Tuareg avoided eating in public, expressing one's hunger or suffering, begging, eating dead animals, and looking an old person in the face. But these acts, perceived as inappropriate according to the Tuareg moral code, proved unavoidable in the camps. If Tuareg did not accept them, they had to tolerate them. The respect due to elders and especially to the now discredited nobles dwindled. It became less unusual to see women working. This tendency could be observed even in the details of the dress code. Men wore the veil and the *taguelmoust*—symbols of Tuareg identity—usually covering the face entirely with the exception of the eyes, less strictly. Young people especially no longer respected the injunction to veil the face; they often left the mouth and chin bare even when facing old persons or parents, a behavior previously deemed the pinnacle of impoliteness. Some women cast off their petrol-blue Guinea cloths and started wearing colored fabrics or sometimes even European dresses, following the example of the city dwellers with whom they now lived. The symbolic codes of dress and behavior in the camps dramatically expressed the slackening of social relations and the general confusion that reigned during those years.

CONSENTED CONFINEMENT: MILITARY AND MILITANT CAMPS

The Tuareg who managed to sustain nomadic pastoral activity in spite of rebellions and droughts were unable to provide for many dependents due to the scarcity of cattle. Economic scarcity pushed the youth to seek sources of revenue elsewhere, and especially through migrant salaried work in faraway places. These youth became known as *Ishumar* (sing., *Ashamur*), a Tuareg neologism based on the French word *chômeur*, or unemployed person. The paths of exile led them first to Algeria and then to Libya, the economic Eldorado of northern Africa. Coming up against national frontiers and suspicious states, they undertook a long and perilous journey:

People started leaving by foot for Libya. Every border posed a problem. Thus, for example, the Algerians initially did not want people to go beyond the first habitations on the Algerian border, Timiawin, Tin Zawaten, or Bordj. But they continued on and came to Tamanrasset. There, they were told that this was the final limit, they were not supposed to leave the town. But they went on to Djanet. At Djanet, the Algerians went so far as to create meharist units to prevent an exodus, but the people went on to Ghat, in Libya. The Libyans then said that this town was the final authorized limit, and they even started sending people back to Algeria. But the Algerians refused them because they were not citizens. They continued like this, on foot, until they reached the Mediterranean. It was this way from 1972 to 1978; people reached the Mediterranean, alone or in small groups of five or ten people, very young, twelve or eight years old. And they were hundreds and hundreds, thousands of them.[27]

The precarious conditions of living among labor migrants helped create new solidarities among young *Ishumar* that transcended the typical divisions of Tuareg society. The Kel Adagh were not the only people who participated in this movement. The *Ishumar* came from all regions of the Tuareg world. They could see that other groups had lived through similar experiences, and shared similar problems. The *Ishumar* generally blamed their declining status on the colonial legacy, and on the actions of the now-independent states.

Progressively, a political rationale emerged from the economic constraints experienced by the *Ishumar*. The youth came to perceive wandering and exile as active forms of resistance to adversity, as well as a way of being Tuareg toward and against all—in the face of the bearded statesmen and their rules, responsible for the misfortune of the moment. "People started to think politically about their fate and even the destiny of society. They undertook reflection on the mode of organization that was needed to save our community."[28]

This was the context in which the political structures of the Tuareg rebellion took form. Libya promoted this movement because it served its own strategic interests, using Tuareg demands as a means pressuring Mali and Niger into supporting its foreign policy. In addition, Lybia enrolled the *Ishumar* as hardy and determined infantry to serve in its own conflicts (against Lebanon and Chad). In 1980, Libya inaugurated the first military training camp for Tuareg at Beni Walid on the outskirts of Tripoli, allowing at the same time for the formation of a Tuareg political party, the *Front Populaire de Libération du Sahara Central* (FPLSAC). When the president of Libya sought out the presidency of the Organization for African Unity (OUA), the camp was closed out. In March 1986, Libyans opened a new training camp *(Camp du 2 mars)* for the Tuareg in preparation for a future offensive in Chad (the conflict over the Aouzou strip). During the war, which began a few months later in July, the nomad fighters proved particularly efficient in Saharan conditions. Libyan camps trained Tuareg youth from Mali and Niger until the end of the 1980s. However, they were not the only camps that punctuated the paths of the Tuareg youth's exile. In southern Algeria, a penitentiary camp opened to assemble Tuareg suspects who had been picked up by the police or the army.

These various sites—ephemeral or lasting places for repressive or voluntary incarceration—represented the last vicissitude of the successive waves of confinement that marked Tuareg history during the twentieth century.

Political Camps: Reconstructing Tuareg Identity

The camps allowed a whole generation of *Ishumar*, the future combatants of the Tuareg rebellion, to articulate new social and political ideas, and to build new identities. For example, affiliation with a clan (either as a noble or as a dependent) lost its significance and was even considered negatively insofar as it blocked the *Ishumar*'s solidarity and homogeneity in the face of their adversaries. *Ishumar* saw such affiliations as characteristic of the old order, which was to disappear.

They also looked down upon "traditional" economic and social organization because it had failed to produce appropriate responses to the many crises experienced by the nomads since the beginning of the century. From this perspective, the very existence of former social classes, or the hierarchy dominated by the nobles, was entirely negative. A radical critique emerged:

> The youth experienced a break with the heads of factions and tribes. . . .
> The role that traditional rulers had played during colonization and independence was to avoid the worst for their community. This is why they served as intermediaries between the administration and the populations. . . . They told the administration that they would be responsible for taxes and duties.
> . . . On the surface, this tactic worked, but underneath, it promoted a complete rupture with the new generation. Confusion arose between the administration and the chiefs, the very organization of society in factions and tribes. The youth assimilated the chiefs and their very mode of organization with the administration. So, on the whole, there was conflict in society.[29]

Young Tuareg denounced the state as primarily responsible for the degradation of Tuareg society. Expressions of resentment and bitterness linked the youth and the larger Tuareg society, which had only experienced the coercive, repressive, arbitrary, and unjust side of the various states they had encountered. From their point of view, the state had never assisted the Tuareg in times of need. On the contrary, it had taken advantage of economic disaster to dominate them. The state became the young Tuareg's main adversary. It was embodied by bureaucrats, the army, its representatives, and even those Tuareg who served as *Amenokal*, or administrative chiefs. "The movement also spread the idea, the notion, that we could not leave our destiny in the heads of a central power that was unconscious of our misfortune, did not take care of us, and did not worry about our afflictions."[30]

The youth, full of these ideas, also adopted new forms of behavior that proclaimed their differences and the radical nature of their thoughts. They imported new commodities into this emergent culture, diverting them from their usual usage. For instance, the young *Ashamur* no longer sported a sword at his side, like his father, but rather dreamt of brandishing a "kalash," the kalashnikov machine gun that is now used in many resistance movements, rebellions, and revolts in Africa. Young Tuareg have also abandoned the camel for Toyotas, and they have replaced the *guerba* (goatskin) with plastic canteens wrapped in rags. The *shakmara*, or mariner's sack for transporting belongings, has replaced the tent, as it follows young *Ishumar* everywhere, and provides their only shelter. A new form of poetry exalts the suffering and wandering, no longer sung by women to the sound of the *imzad*, the Tuareg violin, but rather by the *Ashamur* himself, accompanied by a guitar. New repertoires have spread throughout Tuareg communities in West and North Africa via audiocassettes of passionate songs and subversive lyrics. While this new culture has split away from older customs and makes unabashed use of the arms and tools of the Tuareg's adversaries, it does not renounce Tuareg identity. To the contrary, *Ishumar* identity valorizes and defends Tuareg culture in its most intimate manifestations: the Tuareg language, *Tamashaq*, and Tuareg writing, *Tifinagh*.

The *Ishumar* offer a contrasted image to their own society. On the one hand, they appear to be the ones who denounced the old order, including dress codes, which they contested in unprecedented ways by wearing European clothing and neglecting or abandoning the veil. "Some of them came back to their tents from time to time. For the Tuareg, they were an object of curiosity, squatting over their iron-wire brazier, surrounded by bizarre gadgets: oil lamps, canteens, ballpoint pens, teapots, jackets, shirts, closed shoes."[31]

Acting on new codes and personal references almost incomprehensible to some Tuareg, the *Ishumar* became positive heroes when they proved to be able to assist their families, in particular, with the revenues they earned in other countries. Today, many Tuareg invest their hopes for change and improvements in the *Ishumar*, who embody resistance and have become models for young boys. "All of us, especially the youth, we dream about the roads traveled by the *Ishumar* singing the poetry of paths, the *Ishumar* carrying "kalashes" and mariner's bags filled with explosives. We also dream of Toyotas filled with *Ishumar* connecting the lands."[32]

According to this view, the *Ishumar* represent those who did not submit to others; those who stood up to the Tuareg' adversaries, and have become the new "warriors" of Tuareg society. In this sense, they have built a new aristocracy based on combativeness, energy, and experience of the outside world. This differs greatly from the old nobility, based on birth and the force of arms. The new *Ishumar* nobility has its own networks of solidarity, which have given rise to clandestine forms of fraternity, with their own values and specific culture.

The *Ishumar* have transformed their culture into a critique of the future of Tuareg society. In the 1970s and 1980s, the exiled youth rejected the old hierarchical order of status and power; they negated inequalities between the extant classes and refused to be defined by the *tawset*, or the various groups to which they belonged. Through this, they explicitly sought to restore the autonomy and power to rule that had been usurped by the state, and to recover control over their own fate. However, the *Ishumar* have failed to undertake long-term political action. Carried away by their youth and their impetuosity, and also marked by a Tuareg culture that valorized warriors, the *Ishumar* privileged armed struggle as a mode of political action. To bring Tuareg society out of economic and political marginalization, they decided to become combat soldiers and train for modern warfare in order to conquer the adversary by using its own arms. This process gave rise to the 1990 Tuareg rebellion in Mali and Niger.

CONCLUSION

For the Tuareg of Adagh, administrative, spatial, and political confinement sparked a series of crises, which ran their course throughout the twentieth century. Yet, modern confinement, particularly in military and refugee camps, also gave rise to a response to the Tuareg's misfortunes. Destabilized by the administrative confinements imposed by French colonization, later exacerbated by the Malian administration, Tuareg nomads have been unable to ensure the flexibility needed for pastoral life in the Sahara. The catastrophes that accompanied the successive droughts of the 1970s and 1980s were largely due to this restriction of mobility. Driven into a new type of reclusion, the exile in refugee camps, Tuareg society witnessed the demise of its most intimate values. However, in other camps, such as in Libya, the youth found new resources and developed political ideas that gave rise to the 1990 rebellions. The balance sheet of these uprisings is, no doubt, quite mixed. But despite many difficulties, revolt has transformed the Tuareg's political situation. Their economic and political marginalization is less absolute than it was in the past. As a rare case of a nomadic population subjected to a series of spatial and political confinements, the Tuareg illustrate the dramatic effects of multiform and non-penitentiary confinement. The Tuareg youth's active re-appropriation of the constraints of modern states, and of the multiple reclusions they have had to endure, provides an example of their continuing spatial and social creativity, and the possibility of a better future.

NOTES

1. A Saharan and Sahelian region now situated in northern Mali (former French Sudan), and populated mostly by nomads.

2. Tuareg from the Adagh region call themselves "Kel Adagh."

3. Tuareg resistance lasted well beyond the installation of colonial authority. The last large-scale revolts occurred in Fihrun in 1916 and Kaocen in 1917.

4. *Tawset* (pl., *tiwsaten*): a lineage group in Tamashaq (the language of the Tuareg of Adagh). The term is used herein instead of "tribe," which is a inadequate indicator of the political organization of these populations.

5. *Rapport politique*, September 1908. *Cercle de Gao*. Mali National Archives (ANM) 1ᴱ 36–37, *fonds anciens, Rapports politiques Gao, 1899–1920.*

6. The officer-interpreter Durand wrote the report on the basis of information that was sent from envoys at Illi during their initial contact with the annex of In Salah on November 3, 1903. Durand, "Notes sur les Touareg et sur les populations agrégées, alliées ou voisines, d'après des légendes et des renseignements recueillies dans le Tidikelt," *Bulletin de la Société de Géographie d'Alger et d'Afrique du Nord,* fourth trimester (1904). See also the report by Captain Métois, the chief of the In Salah annex and commander of the company of the Saharan oases at Tidikelt, on the submission of the Ifoghas of Idrar: *Archives nationales d'outre mer, Aix-en-Provence (ANSOM), série géographique,* AOF IV, 4, Salah, November 9, 1903.

7. M. Cortier, *D'une rive à l'autre du Sahara* (Paris: Larose, 1908).

8. *ANM 1N114, fonds anciens, Rapport du chef de bataillon Bétrix, commandant de la région de Gao,* January 22, 1909.

9. P. Boilley, *Les Touaregs Kel Adagh. Dépendances et révoltes : du Soudan français au Mali contemporain* (Paris: Karthala, 1999).

10. *Amenokal* (pl., *imenokalen*): head of a Tuareg political group.

11. *ANM 1ᴱ24, fonds récents. Cercle de Gao, Subdivision de Kidal.* Lieutenant Lagarde, *commandant de la subdivision de Kidal, Rapport de tournée No 6-Ki du 22 septembre au 16 octobre 1943.*

12. Nomadic auxiliaries of the French army.

13. "Aims of police operations: a) capture individuals resisting the census; b) reintegrate individuals who have fled to live independently into their tribes; c) pronounce judgment over the numerous tents claiming to be without tribe on the pretense of personal reasons or complicated family alliances; d) drive back approximately 350 tents living permanently on the territories of Tahoua, Agadès and Menaka; e) reinforce indigenous chiefs' authority; f) start applying the program for the repression of the traffic in arms and the slave trade." *ANM 1ᴱ24, fonds récents, Cercle de Gao, Subdivision de Kidal.* Lieutenant Lagarde, *commandant de la subdivision de Kidal. Rapports de tournée 1944–49,* September 1944.

14. "Troops: 11 *goumiers* from Goum in Kidal, 14 armed partisans, the *Amenokal* of the Ifoghas, Attaher ag Illi, the chief of the Iforgomoussen, the chief of the Kel Telabit, the chief of the Tarat Mellet." *ANM 1ᴱ24*, ibid.

15. *Tente,* in French, designated a Tuareg household.

16. Attaher was the *Amenokal* of Adagh.

17. *ANM 1ᴱ24, fonds récents. Cercle de Kidal, Rapports politiques et de tournées,* 1928–1960. Lieutenant of Kidal subdivision to *Cercle de Tombouktou,* October 10, 1930.

18. *ANM 1ᴱ24, fonds récents. Capitaine de Saint-Maur, cercle de Tombouctou-subdivision Kidal, Rapport politique,* third trimester 1933.

19. *ANM 1ᴱ24, fonds récents. Rapports de tournée,* 1944–1949, "*Convention de Tedjerirt,*" September 18, 1948.

20. French officers often supported these claims, and even provoked some. Cf. especially "*Lettre ouverte par les chefs coutumiers, les notables et les commerçants de la Boucle du Niger (Tombouctou, Gao et Goundam), à sa Majesté monsieur le Président de la République Française,*" May 30, 1958.

21. J. Copans, ed., *Dossiers africains. Sécheresse et famines au Sahel* (Paris: Maspero, 1975).

22. DRPS Gao, *Enquête socio-économique réalisée dans la région de Gao en 1975*, October 1977, 15–17.

23. *Courrier de l'UNESCO*, April 1975, 11.

24. Estimates by the Algerian Red Crescent. Figures for 1974 taken from the archives of the *wilaya* of Tamanrasset by I. Ag Litny, *Systèmes éducatifs et société touarègue. Les Kel Adagh du nord du Mali* (Paris: Mémoire de l'EHESS, 1992), 162.

25. The Algerian Red Crescent figures for 1986 are cited in F. Fritscher, "Quelques dix mille Touaregs en situation irrégulière ont été refoulés vers le Niger et le Mali," *Le Monde* (May 14, 1986), 4.

26. E. Ag Foni, *L'impact socio-économique de la sécheresse dans le cercle de Kidal* (Bremen: Borda, 1979), 114.

27. Interview with informant, Bamako, February 10, 1994.

28. Ibid.

29. Ibid.

30. Ibid.

31. Hawad, "La Teshumara, antidote de l'État," *Revue du monde musulman et de la Méditerranée* 3, no. 57 (1990), 127.

32. E. Ag Ahar, "L'initiation d'un ashamur," *Revue du Monde musulman et de la Méditerranée* 3, no. 57 (1990), 142.

12

THE WAR OF THE *CACHOTS*

A History of Conflict and Containment in Rwanda

Michele D. Wagner

The Rwandan flag snapped breezily on the pole in front of the local communal building where dozens of residents, tattered and barefoot, shifted about silently in line. Waiting to enroll for food aid, they presented one example among many of Rwanda's dynamism in the effort to rehabilitate its war-weary population at the end of 1994.[1] Inside the communal building, other more fortunate people who had gained permission for an official audience milled around in the corridor, eyes fixed on a door at the far end. This was the door to the office of the *bourgmestre*, the head of the commune, who with his team of assistants provided the link between Rwanda's central government and its citizens—whom government agents conventionally designated as "the population" and "the peasants"[2]—the men and women who worked the soil of the "land of a thousand hills" (Map 12.1).

Filled with people and the signs of rural life—women enveloped in cloth that bore the smoky aroma of the morning's cooking-fire, young muscular men to whose bare feet the rich red soil of Rwanda stubbornly clung, diminutive elders in long dark coats whose threadbare pockets revealed the outline of the pipe and pouch of tobacco nestled deep inside—the corridor was absolutely silent, quite still. Yet wafting in, unacknowledged by all, was the distinct murmur of human voices—many voices.

Inside the *bourgmestre's* office, as in the corridor, supplicants for official audience stood rigid and silent, speaking only when addressed. Such silence, in the face of so many people, was somehow awkward. Yet again, through

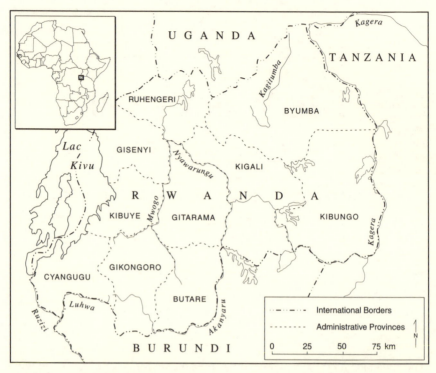

Map 12.1. Rwanda Provinces (1996).

the open window, the murmur of many voices was unmistakably audible. Beyond the window, an adjacent building, in front of which lounged a trio of soldiers, seemed to be the source. What was this building? It had once been a cooperative, although it had been sacked and damaged during the months of the genocide. Was it currently in use? As the *bourgmestre* processed the question, a shadow flickered across his face. Yes, it was now a makeshift *cachot*—a communal jail—temporarily in use because the commune's normal *cachot*, a small cell in the back of this office building, was too small to accommodate the large number of prisoners. The *bourgmestre* shrugged. Who could have guessed that such a large number of genocidal killers would have sprung from the bosom of the local population? Pay no attention to the *cachot*, the *bourgmestre* advised, nor to the soldiers at its door. The killers were being dealt with. The victims were being aided, albeit on an insufficient scale. Rehabilitation would proceed.

Three years after this scene, rehabilitation had proceeded, but only at a snail's pace. Frustrated Rwandan government officials bitterly denounced Western donors for having aided Hutu genocidal killers housed in Zairian and Tanzanian refugee camps, but not having come forth with open arms to aid the "legitimate" Tutsi victims of genocide and war.[3] True enough, foreign donors had balked at aiding Rwanda. The rebuilding assistance that had been so forthcomingly pledged had slowed down or stalled as visiting donor assessment teams brought home reports of widespread killing during "cordon and search" operations, particularly in the north of the country, and "scores of deaths" through violence or neglect of prisoners, particularly those housed in communal detention centers, the *cachots*.[4]

By December 1997, as attacks on sites of detention—and particularly on cachots—multiplied, it was increasingly felt that *cachots* had become a de facto front line of a simmering war between Rwanda's Tutsi-dominated military government and its Hutu-majority population.[5] The strategic objectives for situating this war at detention centers, and the political meanings that each side imputed to it, had not yet become clear. What was clear was that such a "war" would further jeopardize the lives of more than 120,000 untried men, women, and children confined in the approximately 213 prisons and *cachots* throughout Rwanda. These people, both the perpetrators and the survivors of Rwanda's 1994 massacres and genocide crushed together in overcrowded holding cells, had already survived horrendous detention conditions to which countless others of their counterparts—beaten, gangrenous, feverous, asphyxiated—had succumbed. But now these sites of slow, covert death by neglect had become targets of open armed clashes between alleged anti-government rebels and Rwandan government troops. During the course of three weeks in later November–early December 1997, three such attacks took place on *cachots* in Bulinga commune located in Gitarama, central Rwanda, and in Rwerere and Giciye communes located in the northwestern region of Gisenyi, directly involving an estimated 914 detainees, but devolving out to the hillsides where hundreds of villagers died in a hunt for escapees.[6]

What was the nature of the "war of the *cachots*"? Interpretations, like Rwandans themselves, were sharply polarized. The perpetrators, the government asserted, were members of the former genocidal regime and its extremist militia who sought to liberate their Hutu collaborators and propagate widespread public disorder. Their ultimate goal: to complete their 1994 genocide. The true perpetrators, critics countercharged, were government soldiers, who made use of *cachots* to avenge the Tutsi deaths of 1994 by slowly, secretly killing Hutu. The soldiers made use of the attacks, and possibly staged some of them, in order to ravage hillside communities, killing at will.

Between these two extremes, ordinary civilians who had become accustomed to heavy military presence in their daily lives—at crossroads, bridges, and public offices—wondered when they would ever be secure. They recalled the first weeks of 1991 when the Rwandan Patriotic Front (RPF), then a group of rebels led by Major-General Paul Kagame, had launched an assault on Ruhengeri Prison, the largest in Rwanda, with more than 1,000 inmates and a special section, a *cachot* within a prison, for political detainees.[7] The RPF had liberated the prisoners. Some, including the notorious secret police major, Théoneste Lizinde, had joined up with the rebels and become prominent RPF leaders. Was this new campaign against detention centers an "echo" of that 1991 attack? Rwandans also recalled the ethnically focused reprisals, most recently of 1991–1992, conducted by soldiers of the former Hutu regimes against ordinary Tutsi families following incursions, real or rumored, by Tutsi infiltrators.[8] Were these recent attacks a payback? History, they speculated, has a way of repeating itself in Rwanda. The choice of particular sites, dates, details of behavior convey a message in the present and link intimately to the tragedies and hatreds of the past.

The war of the *cachots* was the most recent chapter of Rwanda's twentieth-century history of struggle for ethnically based political power and ethnically defined justice. *Cachots*—crowded, dispersed, teeming with detainees, often situated in remote locales—had become its latest setting. This new twist evoked numerous political and historical associations, from the RPF's own attack on the political *cachot* in Ruhengeri prison, to the notion of "human shields." For Hutu, it was easy to see the detainees as hostages, the means by which the Tutsi-dominated government held the Hutu ethnic group at bay. With the lives of 120,000 people in the balance, the government exacted local cooperation and demonstrated a clear threat to those who would dare to venture to attack it. For Tutsi, the detainees embodied the government's pledge to end impunity. They stood as the guarantee of the RPF promise to genocide victims that justice would be achieved. As targets for rebel attack, these detention centers evoked other meanings. For Hutu, they were sites of RPF government power and symbols of its primary relationship with the Hutu population. For Tutsi, *cachots* signified security, continuous vigilance against the return of the terror of 1994. For Hutu, *cachots* signified Tutsi oppression. The sight of prison work gangs digging the soil—long-term government captives, accused but untried—evoked historical images of the Tutsi-dominated colonial nightmare. For Tutsi, *cachots* signified justice. The punishment of killers promised to bring an end to *their* nightmare.

It had become clear by early 1998 that attacks on *cachots* had become a dominant feature of Rwanda's tragic, ongoing struggle. But what exactly did this mean? If elements of the modern political struggle resonate with meaning for Rwandans because of their historical references, what was the history of *cachots*? What role had communal detention centers played in Rwanda prior to these most recent crises?

Cachots, as understood by Rwandans, have several different references. The primary one is the official communal *cachot* (communal detention center, usually a room in the back of the communal office building), which is part of the communal apparatus. In the current context, because those rooms are overcrowded, other buildings are used as *cachots*, including former schools, cooperatives, offices, etc. The second reference that comes into the minds of

Rwandans is the *cachot* within the prison, a separate holding cell meant to isolate certain prisoners from other prisoners—a jail within a prison. Another reference for *cachot* is a holding cell used by civilian or military security personnel, such as a cell used by the DMI (military intelligence). And then, in the current situation, there is a broad range of "informal" *cachots* (in private houses, abandoned buildings) used by individuals or civilian and military units to hold "suspicious" individuals (a préfet holding his own prisoners at his private home, a military officer detaining suspects at his house, a group of soldiers holding prisoners in a shipping container, etc.) (Map 12.2).

Communal detention centers—*cachots communaux*—have had an ironic double legacy in Rwanda. As part of the apparatus of local-level government, they have been taken as evidence of decentralized regional development. For many onlookers, particularly for international donors during the 1970s–1980s, communal development, including the construction of facilities meant to provide preventive detention in a local setting for alleged perpetrators of minor crimes, appeared to be a very positive sign.[9] The development was interpreted as a milestone on the road toward less centralized—and hence less authoritarian—administration and politics, possibly in the long run even toward de-

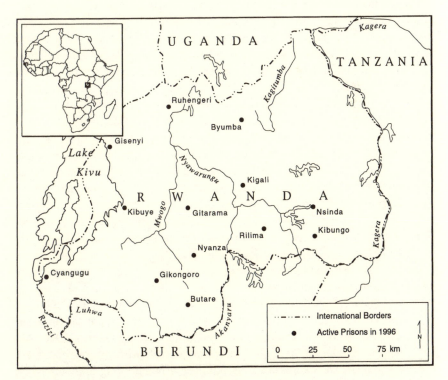

Map 12.2. Active Prisons in Rwanda (1996).

mocracy. Rwandans, too, while not necessarily greeting them as signs of Western-style democracy, welcomed the construction of *cachots* in the 1970s–1980s as a sign of government commitment to local security. *Cachots* had signified protection.

But as the national sense of security in the 1980s gave way to insecurity in the political strife of the 1990s, *cachots communaux* also came to signify intimidation and torture. Although they had represented state decentralization, *cachots* came to evoke a terrifying sense of state power—the unchallenged ability to disrupt families, to make its citizens disappear, and to take its citizens' lives. Initially meant to serve on the front line of justice as part of the infrastructure for granting ordinary citizens more direct access to judicial processes,[10] by the late 1990s *cachots* served on the front line of state terror as well. They became crucial "battlefields" in a simmering war between the RPF government and the civilian population—a war that, as of this writing, has yet to define explicitly its course.

COLONIAL CONTEXT FOR THE INTRODUCTION OF COMMUNES

Communes—the infrastructural units that housed *cachots*—were introduced into Rwanda in 1960 following a wave of violent protest against colonial overrule and against chiefs and subchiefs, its local-level agents. This startlingly bloody and ethnically divisive political struggle forced Belgium, Rwanda's internationally mandated steward[11] since the end of the First World War, to re-evaluate its strategy for administering the tiny multi-ethnic country.

This strategy had relied on the governance of a small, highly advantaged clique of Belgian-appointed Rwandan chiefs and subchiefs over previously politically, economically, and culturally diverse peoples. Violent military expeditions had forcibly consolidated these peoples into a single, overarching colonial structure. Colonial mechanisms of compulsion and constraint had reduced them within the system to the status of *indigènes* or "natives."[12] Reflecting to some degree this precolonial diversity, but also reflecting its collapse and transformation under the Belgian colonizing effort, were the three primary Rwandan identity categories that survived colonialism—albeit profoundly transformed—Tutsi, Hutu, and Twa.[13]

Chiefs, and the majority of Rwanda's aristocratic upper stratum, who tended to invest their resources in cattle, a traditional form of wealth, identified as "Tutsi." This precolonial identity category had a range of context-driven meanings as diverse as pastoralist, privileged, chiefly, patron, member of a particular family, or inhabitant of a particular region. In contrast, a broad spectrum of the population—including farmers, craftsmen, fishermen, small traders, ritualists, and even governing families of neighboring kingdoms that had been forced into Rwanda's orbit by European colonizers—became identified as "Hutu." This identity category signified many different meanings according to context, including commoner, ordinary person, farmer, client or subordinate, member of a particular family, or inhabitant of a particular region. A third and frequently overlooked identity category was the Twa, an identity ascribed to the dwellers of forested and riverain environments, hunters-gatherers, and certain artisan communities.

These categories, first understood by Europeans as "races" and later as "ethnic groups," became operative in the administration of indirect rule during the Belgian overrule of the 1920s–1950s.[14] They were touted as essential divisions in Rwandan society by means of which Rwandan chiefs—the "traditional" rulers—naturally separated themselves from the mass of the population. In this context, political power—and the "natural" right to rule— became ethnically identified as Tutsi.[15]

Actualizing this notion of "natural" and "traditional" Tutsi rule in a new colonial context, tiny Rwanda was divided into administrative units called *chefferies* (chiefdoms)—represented as "traditional," hence authentic and legitimate—which were essentially the products of Belgian administrative expedience. Within these structures chiefs and subchiefs, backed by Belgian-authorized force, placed increasingly excessive obligations on their subjects.[16] This had the effect of creating smouldering animosity—defined by Rwandans in class, family, and ethnic terms—which when it finally exploded in 1959– 1960, revealed such lethal intensity that Belgium moved to scrap the *chefferie* system and replace it with communes, modeled on the administrative structure of Belgium itself.

In introducing communes, Belgium gave Rwanda a new structure and vocabulary for expressing political/administrative relations that were uniform, decentralized—and rooted in European post-Enlightenment philosophy. Historically, communes had developed out of European (particularly French) popular reaction against the extremely centralized and exploitative royal absolutism of their seventeenth- and eighteenth-century monarchs. Hence, embedded in the new commune-based administrative structure introduced into Rwanda in 1960 was an underlying historical agenda promoting such Enlightenment notions as popular self-determination, local-level empowerment, the rule of law, and human rights. From this perspective it was possible to interpret the development of the system of communal *cachots* as a positive step toward bringing the mechanism of justice closer to the people. And *cachots* were received in just such a way when they were established in the early years of Rwanda's independence. While they inspired a certain nervousness among community members—as any punitive apparatus would be likely to do—*cachots* also inspired confidence that security had increased and justice was nearer at hand.[17]

The new communal system which was superimposed on Rwanda in 1960— following large-scale political violence that quickly found rhetorical comparison to the French Revolution[18]—sank its post-Enlightenment roots into a political foundation that was very different from the terrain of western Europe in the age of Absolutism. Rwanda's own system of regional governance, prior to colonialism, had been relatively decentralized. Although the system centered on the *Mwami*, or king, at a regional level Rwanda's human and economic resources had been managed by means of a tripartite system of land *(ubutaka)*, pasture *(umukenke)*, and military *(umuheto)* leaders who maintained separate, and frequently counterbalancing, networks of patronage.[19] In addition, Rwanda's two colonial experiences—administration by Germany until 1916 and by Belgium until 1961—had shaped its political history in uniquely modern and colonial ways. The scale of violence to which the colonial state had taken recourse (due to the existence of automatic weapons) and the insidious manipulation of pre-existing identity categories as a political tool for indirect rule, find no parallel in the history of early modern Europe.[20] Accordingly, communes in Rwanda developed along lines that reflected Rwanda's prior political history and not the post-Enlightenment ideals of the European nations whose patterns they were meant to imitate.

In fact, the political and historical foundation into which Rwandan communes sank their roots was characterized by more than three generations of European overrule in a region that, prior to European occupation, had comprised a number of separate and diverse politico-cultural entities. These pre-colonial entities included kingdoms such as Gisaka in the east, Bugesera in the southeast, and Nduga in the central-south, as well as autonomous "kinglets," "principalities," or locally governed zones such as Kinyaga (in the southwest), Rukiga (in the northwest), and Buyaga, Bwishaza, Ndorwa, and Bugoyi (in the north).[21] These entities, as well as their predecessors, had shared a long and complex regional history. Marriage bonds, magical competition, armed conflicts, and trade marked their intertwined existence.[22] Thus, the initial challenge to govern Rwanda for the Germans and subsequently for the Belgians hinged precisely on the struggle to arrest the separate development of these subregions and amalgamate them into a unified and centralized colonial state. Such centralization would enable a relatively small European cadre to govern in a rational, efficient, and especially, cost-effective manner.

The endeavor entailed two processes. First, formerly autonomous political and cultural regions were incorporated into an expanding colonial "Ruanda."[23] This entity had at its core the ancient kingdom of Nduga, governed by the Abanyiginya dynasty, whose impressive, politically agile royal court seemed to promise cooperation with Europeans. Nduga, bolstered by European alliances, leveled claims against the territories of its neighbors. These claims were realized first with German and then with Belgian support. Thus, a transforming Nduga became, in the context of colonial rule, the "unified" kingdom of Ruanda: a "traditional" African kingdom.

The second step of centralization required that the variety of claims to political and economic resources within Ruanda had to be coalesced or streamlined into one "rational" (and more easily controllable) system. To this end, the early years of the colonial endeavor—particularly the first decades of the Belgian period—focused on suppressing regional autonomy, eliminating "redundant" local leaders, and coalescing the multiple domains of resource control into a uniform system. Within this system, power and authority would no longer emanate from local-level resources, but rather from European support, and it would be consolidated in the hands of the *Mwami* and a small clique of cooperative Tutsi chiefs.

HISTORICAL APPROACHES TO CONFLICT AND JUSTICE

Detention, whether intended to be provisional as in a communal *cachot* or of longer duration as in a prison, was an approach to managing conflict that seemed highly alien to the peoples who suddenly found themselves subject to it when a handful of Germans arrived in their land at the end of the nineteenth century. The German's impulse to contain conflict by shackling and isolating in their military posts those whom they presumed responsible found no equivalent in the practices of the precolonial societies of "the land of a thousand hills." These societies had developed their own practices for handling conflict, many of which differed in detail from one society to another but found a similar basis in a shared vision of the appropriate relationship between human conflicts and the larger community.[24]

What they envisioned was conflict—collectively acknowledged and externalized—existing out in a society that could sustain it, protected by the strength of social institutions. Rather than withdrawing from daily social life, individually "contained" in order to prevent the conflict's spread, disputing parties plunged themselves into community life, mobilizing resources to strengthen and protect their positions. They activated alliances, rekindled relationships, and stimulated a process of broader community alignment in the situation. Drawn in as participants, community members engaged themselves in resolving the quarrel, mindful that should the dispute intensify, they would be called upon to give more active—and potentially more costly—assistance. This "external" approach to managing conflict, rather than whisking the disputants *out* of society, centered on the question of *who* they were *within* society. Taking the question "Who?" as the point of departure, a protocol for handling the conflict developed according to the capacity of each of the parties to garner support.

The stature of each of the parties engaged in a conflict—and particularly their capacity to move others to act in their behalf—had a direct bearing on whether a conflict would exist as a relatively restrained affair, or if it had the potential to challenge the community's sense of well-being. Accordingly, the approach to handling it was congruous with who was involved, and what its potential impact might be.

In most cases in the precolonial societies of greater Rwanda, a conflict that developed out of day-to-day misunderstandings among ordinary people— from the trampling of fields by the neighbor's livestock to accusations of theft—was likely to be addressed in a mediatory forum. In Nduga, this forum was *gacaca*, which literally signified the grassy public space where local elders and parties to the conflict met. *Gacaca* was a limited public meeting called for the purpose of talking through a local dispute. The goal was to find a mutually acceptable (hence, just) solution to the matter, assess restitution if necessary, and ultimately to "dissolve" the conflict in order to ensure collective well-being. The presence of respected neighbors, and especially elders, as witnesses to the mediation lent credibility not only to the quality of the "input," such as testimony, but also to the effectiveness of the outcome. If a satisfactory outcome were not achieved, the aggrieved party had several choices for recourse, all of which could be seen as potential challenges to the community's well-being. He could press his case further at the court of a notable person for whom he served as a client, hoping that the pressure from this more powerful person could elicit results more favorable to his side. He could also seek to satisfy himself through revenge.

Revenge was a very common course of action in the precolonial societies of greater Rwanda, particularly in the case of the murder of a family member. In such a case, *gacaca* was not an option: the damage to the victim family was so great that the words and material restitution possible in *gacaca* could never "repair" it. The action of murder, so profoundly disturbing to the collective sense of well-being, required counteraction. The clearest counteraction was blood vengeance. It was particularly in the resort to vengeance that the protective network of relationships came into play. For a client, it was time to seek recourse with the patron—a consequence that the aggressor family should have anticipated before ever committing the initial murderous act.

If the aggrieved family had no members with a network solid enough to support open, armed revenge—or if it saw itself as mismatched, far weaker than its opponent—it could appeal to the *Mwami* for justice. The family's hope would be that the *Mwami* would "protect" it by punishing the opponent. In other words, the *Mwami* would commit on behalf of the aggrieved family the revenge that it was not strong enough to carry out itself. In this formulation, punishment and the king's justice could be seen as an alternative form of revenge.

In bringing a case before the *Mwami*, the accuser normally bore the responsibility of arresting and maintaining the accused in "preventive detention": bound and confined in proximity to the royal court.[25] For this task, the accuser called on his network of friends to organize the guard and lodging of the accused. According to Belgian administrator-ethnographer René Bourgeois, it was not unusual for the accuser to keep the accused not only physically constrained but also deprived of food and drink until the *Mwami's* judgment was carried out, a period that could last a week or longer.[26] Bourgeois points out that such detention was regarded as provisional and preventive in nature: The detention was not considered punishment in and of itself.[27] In meting out punishment, the *Mwami* decided if the wrongdoer would make a material payment, endure corporal suffering, or be put to death. Punishments such as fatal beatings, tying the arms of the accused behind his back,[28] mutilation, torture and blinding with hot irons, and crucifixion by nailing the accused to the ground have been noted in several ethnographic sources.[29] Painful punishments clearly equated revenge with justice from the perspective of the accuser.

Whereas those of modest social and political stature tended to settle their conflicts in limited ways, more powerful community members, including the heads of large or aristocratic families, had additional means at their disposal. In fact, those who had recourse to extensive networks of relationships commanded considerable power to involve others, even to disrupt society, with their conflicts. This very potential for disruption frequently served to mitigate against pursuing conflicts with powerful opponents. But when both opponents were powerful and decided to pursue the matter, their allies and clients could find themselves embroiled in a situation in which they had little control and much to lose. Conflict among persons of the very highest stature, such as the princes and queen-mothers of the royal court of Nduga, had such capacity for widespread disruption and bore such serious consequences for the individuals and the families involved that these most powerful Rwandans tended to seek recourse in intrigue, deceit, trickery, magic, and poisoning.

CONFLICT AND CONTAINMENT IN THE ERA OF GERMAN COLONIALISM

Members of Nduga's royal dynasty were engaged in unleashing just such tactics in 1896—the year when a German lieutenant and his African troops *(askaris)* arrived to initiate Germany's conquest, or "pacification" of the region. As the small troupe of soldiers patrolled the eastern shores of the lake, asserting their authority over the lake-plain, up in the hills rival factions of Nduga aristocrats, driven by fratricide, fought to assert their authority over their equivalent of the throne—the royal drum.[30] The passing of a strong and long-ruling *Mwami* and the murder of his newly installed successor by an ambitious half-brother had split the royal court into factions. The usurping half-brother, Musinga, was only shakily installed, his leadership threatened by a war that had broken out between two powerful royal lineages.[31]

The unstable, young Musinga, anxious to do whatever it took to secure his kingship, provided just the inroad that the Germans needed to make good on their claim to the region—a claim that the Belgian Congo contested until 1899.[32] Thus, as Germans pushed to establish effective occupation of this newly opened district of their larger East African colony, at minimal cost, they saw in Musinga the opportunity to govern through a local potentate who would offer little, if any, resistance. Promising to bolster Musinga's authority in exchange for his acknowledgment of German supremacy, German officers and their *askaris* launched campaigns against the *Mwami's* challengers. This set the pattern and tone for conflict management for the rest of the period of German overrule in Ruanda—violent punitive expeditions.[33]

The pattern repeated itself throughout the twenty-odd years of German presence in Ruanda. When reports of regional disturbances or threats to the *Mwami's* power arrived at the German headquarters, a fortified post called a *boma*, the commanding officer sent out a patrol consisting of a German soldier and a group of African *askaris* to contain the threat. The conflict management techniques that the German officer applied in the field had developed in the experience of putting down resistance elsewhere in German East Africa. The commanding officer would "hold a *schauri*,"[34] that is, conduct a public inquiry into the problem, and then "make an impression" on the local people.[35]

"Holding a *schauri*" engaged the German officer in seeking to find a solution to an African conflict. The process commenced with the sorting of the "cooperative" from the "troublesome" local leaders. Having identified whom he wanted to privilege—since the larger governing strategy relied on reinforcing the authority of "good" leaders—the officer proceeded to gather facts about the conflict and to formulate his strategy for handling it. In many cases, the plan relied on the rounding up of the alleged troublemakers as well as local leaders deemed responsible for inciting them. If those accused had taken off, a manhunt ensued; "collateral" casualties, including entire villages if they were rumored to harbor the "criminals," were not unusual. The successful capture of the culprits—who had become full-fledged criminals by the very act of attempting evasion—led to the second German technique for conflict management, "making an impression."

"Making an impression" entailed the punishing of the alleged troublemakers, the chiefs who had supported them, as well as the followers of the recalcitrant chiefs, while publicly reinforcing the authority of the "reliable" leaders. Punishments ranged from fines paid in cattle, to imprisonment (generally of influential figures), to the burning of homes and fields, to summary execution by rifle fire or hanging (generally of less controversial figures). In their reports of these expeditions, German officers expressed the belief that, left with the enduring impression of smoldering fields and of their leaders taken away in chains, local residents would be unlikely to cause another disturbance. In this context, imprisonment at the *boma* under the guard of the *askaris* was a virtual privilege, given to those of such stature that it was deemed that their summary execution might provoke further unrest.

In 1906 German military occupation of Ruanda ended, but the punitive expeditions continued under civilian rule. The establishment of a German Resident in 1907 at Kigali, not far from the *Mwami's* court, led to closer contact between the Germans and the Nduga aristocrats, and the German discovery that the *Mwami's* authority was actually quite fragile. The reaction to this discovery led to a split between the civilian Resident and his military counterparts, who asserted that expeditions against the *Mwami's* challengers must be a vital element of colonial administrative strategy.[36] Ultimately, the military prevailed and the precedent for highly violent conflict management, and "protection" of the *Mwami* against his opponents, became established. Rivals, particularly those in the north, saw their regions burned and themselves locked in chains and led away to detention in the *boma*.

It was during the German period that physical restraint and imprisonment were introduced as more than just preventive strategies. The German approach to containment of political resistance by physically restraining local leaders had the effect of making imprisonment a political tool directed by political elites at the center against their elite challengers on the periphery. The effectiveness of the strategy of imprisoning rivals at headquarters made a considerable impression on the young *Mwami* who in 1902 tried it himself.[37] He sent out an urgent appeal to Chief Mpumbika of Gisaka, a rival, to come to his capital where, upon Mpumbika's arrival, he imprisoned the chief and put his traveling companions/escorts to death. It may have been in this era that regional chiefs began experimenting with physical constraint and imprisonment at their courts, the "traditional" character of which was later debated.[38]

In terms of punishment and justice, Germans introduced new concepts and practices into Ruanda during their brief overrule. In addition to the practice of publicly capturing, chaining and dragging away accused criminals, and imprisonment within the confines of the *boma*, Germans also introduced the notion of standardized sets of measured floggings.[39] One offense could be punishable by up to two sets of floggings. One set of floggings was restricted to twenty-five lashes and a two-week waiting period was imposed between the administration of the first set of lashes and the next.[40] Assuming that the recipient of these floggings would have little incentive to wait out the two weeks for the next set, "preventive" detention would have been likely in this case.

In the final years of their overrule, the Germans began to organize a local police force. The domain of these officials was the hillsides and pathways where they were to maintain peace and facilitate the passage of trade caravans. Within their domain, the officers, each identifiable by a brass badge in the shape of a half-moon, had the power to arrest offenders and bring them to the *boma*.[41] As the system developed, the authority of the officer expanded to include problems connected to arms and narcotics smuggling, the unlicensed sale of alcohol, and settling disputes among residents.[42] In 1912, they were mobilized to put down a rebellion in the north. But further development of this system was interrupted by World War I.

MAISONS DE DETENTION DURING BELGIAN RULE

The impulse to incarcerate as a means of managing conflict created the need for detention centers from the early days of Belgian rule following World War I.[43] A detention center was one of the first pieces of Belgian colonial apparatus to appear in Ruanda. One was established at headquarters in 1918.[44] Within three years, *maisons de détention* (literally, houses of detention) had multiplied and existed at each administrative and police post.[45] The logic of having so many sites, explained the Annual Report of 1921–1922, was that it reduced the risk of mortality during prisoner transfers.[46] Prisoner mortality soon proved to be a problem regardless of the growth of detention sites. Outbreaks of contagious diseases in the central lock-ups at Kigali and at Kitega in neighboring Urundi in 1923–1924 resulted in the deaths of numerous prisoners.[47]

Although the proliferation of regional *maisons de détention* reflected an increase in decentralization over the previous German system, from the perspective of a local chief the system could still seem centralized and distant. At times, chiefs acting on the basis of this sense of distance, sidestepped the matter of lack of authority and detained their subjects in a variety of ways. For example, in 1939, when subchief Mihana had a dispute with his chief, Semugeshi, he found himself under de facto house arrest:

> Then I stayed at my house several months and it was really as it [sic] I were under arrest. Semugishi's [sic] police kept away people who wanted to visit me and my servitors were maltreated, and so on. After two months had gone by without an answer from the Resident I wrote him a letter and one of my brothers took it to him. I told him that I was being held prisoner . . .[48]

Confined to his home, Mihana had been preventively detained.

Preventive detention, like detention itself, had existed from the early days of Belgian rule, necessitated in part by the itinerant nature of the judicial system. In the early 1930s, territorial agents like René Bourgeois and his mentor Phillipart (*"Bwana Morisi"*)[49] regularly spent fifteen days each month circulating through their territories. In this way, they conducted inspections, gave orders to chiefs and subchiefs, conducted police and judicial inquiries, and presided at native tribunals.[50] This heavily charged schedule, and the requirement that a Belgian be present at indigenous judicial proceedings, imposed delays and created the need for preventive detention. References to early cases of preventive detention appear throughout the rich and detailed memoirs of R. Bourgeois, who began his career as a colonial agent in 1931. One example appears in connection with the case of murder suspect Rwamigabo, whom Bourgeois placed in preventive detention during the first week of August 1932, after finding the man in possession of a suspicious knife.[51] Implicated by the knife, but requiring fuller investigation, Rwamigabo remained in preventive detention until early September, when Bourgeois returned to the man's hill to conduct a formal inquiry. This time a suspicious spear turned up. One day later, Rwamigabo and another man, Shakubundi, now formally accused (hence having the status of *prévenus*), were forwarded to Kigali for further processing. In late October 1932, their case was presented before the Territorial Tribunal, seated at Ruhengeri. Bourgeois, having already handled the case and the suspects in several different capacities, participated in the Ruhengeri proceedings in his capacity as Officer of the Public Ministry (OMP).[52]

Another, more controversial, case of preventive detention occurred in July 1943 in connection with the Astrida Territory Chief Semugeshi, evidently the same man who had detained subchief Mihana four years before. Bourgeois, suspecting that this highly influential and well-connected chief had embezzled a large sum of tax money, decided to handle the situation by locking him up in a secret location for the duration of a preliminary inquiry. For this location, he settled on the kitchen of the government guest house in the neighboring territory of Gikongoro. The chief managed to escape and went straight to Bourgeois's superiors to charge him with illegal detention.[53] To the chief's great surprise, he was sent back to Bourgeois and locked up in yet another "secret" place: this time in a special cell inside Astrida central prison. Two weeks later, Semugeshi was still detained in this secret cell when his case was forwarded to the Territorial Tribunal. Finally, in early September, he was placed on trial and sentenced to ten years of prison labor. Semugeshi served out a year and a half of his sentence in the central prison of Usumbura (Urundi), where he died suddenly in mid-March 1945.[54]

The itinerant nature of the Rwandan judicial system, and the need to respond flexibly to "on the spot" situations led to a growing body of informal and formal practice that, when legally formalized in October 1943, envisioned two kinds of preventive incarceration. The first was detention under a warrant of summons *(mandat d'amener)* which allowed for incarceration for a period of up to three days, renewable for a maximum of five additional days. The second, preventive detention *(détention préventive)*, was subject to the same limits and extensions as detention by summons.[55] Both forms were possible without an actual arrest warrant *(mandat d'arrêt)*.

Despite the formalization of preventive detention, and the establishment of clearly defined time restrictions, lengthy and ongoing pretrial detention was still possible. This occurred in the 1948 case of S——. S—— was a former subchief who, having been dismissed for alleged irregularities, had subsequently taken a position with a European businessman as the foreman of a woodcutting team. S——'s activities came to the attention of Bourgeois in October 1948, when the businessman for whom he worked was charged by fellow Europeans with encroaching on their land and harvesting their trees. Bourgeois arrived to make inquiries into the matter, and, on the basis of the spotty backgrounds of both the foreman and his employer, who had been similarly charged before, became convinced that illegal activity had probably taken place. This, the administrator decided, merited preventive detention of S——.[56] His employer was not similarly detained because he had left on vacation in Europe and could not be reached.

S—— waited in preventive detention inside the prison of Shangugu,[57] pending investigation upon the return of his employer, while the European took an extensive vacation and then returned to Africa—to the Belgian Congo, but not Ruanda. Month by month, a judge renewed the preventive detention order for S——, on the basis that he might violate the secrecy of the affair or possibly flee, while his former employer, now living in Congo, ignored a series of summons. Inside Shangugu prison, S—— remained in confinement, separated from the rest of the prison population. He was prohibited from contact with all others. He was not even required to work, as the other prisoners were.[58] Six months later, in March 1949, S—— was released from prison on bail. He immediately charged Bourgeois with arbitrary arrest and detention. Bourgeois defended himself, claiming that it was only through his humanitarian interest and intervention that the man had been released. Preparing his memoirs decades later, Bourgeois wrote defensively, "I acted in a humanitarian way because in that epoch it was not the custom to accord such favor to an accused native."[59] Humanitarian or not, Bourgeois clearly stretched the rules of preventive detention and guarded S—— in a special *cachot* because of the "political" nature of his alleged activities: they implicated a European.

Despite recourse to a kitchen in the case of Semugeshi, preventive detention in the Belgian system ordinarily took place at a site designated for this purpose, the *cachot*. A *cachot* could be a specific place formally established for detention, such as a small hut, or it could be a place informally designated for this purpose, such as the guest house kitchen. A *cachot* could also be a separate holding cell within a prison, such as the place where S—— was placed in solitary confinement. This latter arrangement seems to have been quite common. Evidence for the existence of a separate *cachot* within Astrida Central Prison also appears in the Bourgeois memoirs. On November 11, 1943, he notes that Monsieur Houben, guardian of the Prison of Astrida, was injured from blows he received while fighting with a *cachot* detainee whom he encountered in the prison latrines: a place strictly off-limits to those assigned to the *cachot*.[60]

Cachots confined soldiers as well as civilians. On October 6, 1932, Bourgeois notes that he ordered the detention of disorderly soldiers in the *cachot* for eight days and in the *salle de police* (police room) for four days.[61] In this latter case, the use of the *cachot* seems to have been punitive rather than preventive.

In the later years of Belgian rule, *cachots* out in the *chefferies* away from the Belgian post and central prison took the form of detention huts. One Rwandan remembered:

> When I was growing up in the 1950s, under the chefferie system, what I saw was there were central prisons but no regular [system of] jails. Prison was more centralized then—people were taken away to prison, sent there. But if you were caught red-handed, you might be detained in a hut, or in a certain house set apart.[62]

Another Rwandan recalled from his mid-1950s childhood: "There was no jail [locally] but there were huts for prisoners."[63]

CONTAINMENT AND DETENTION AFTER INDEPENDENCE

With structures, and especially with precedent established by their departing European *tuteurs*—such as the model of the innovative, improvising "man on the spot"—the first generation of independent Rwandan authorities moved into uncharted political territory in 1960. It was a territory that they had opened up for themselves through violence and that they were prepared to maintain with violence as well. The disturbances of 1959 had led to a flurry of elections in mid-1960 that brought 229 new *bourgmestres* into power.[64] These men, nearly all of them unversed in public administration and law, set about improvising modern communal administration.[65]

Conflict containment ranked high on their agendas, as it had for new German and Belgian authorities before them. Replicating a pattern established in past eras, the new *bourgmestres* circulated through their communes, addressing conflicts, identifying threats, using their policemen to escort recalcitrants back to improvised tribunals and jails.[66] With a shaky sense of legitimacy, newfound power, little sense of legal procedure, and the Rwandan view that justice was linked to revenge, *bourgmestres* set curfews and went roving at night to arrest people.[67] At Remera, the new Hutu *bourgmestre* "Ijeri and his gang patrolled the hill at night to see to it that his orders were obeyed. He bragged that he was out to get the Tutsi. . . . He arrested more and more Tutsi."[68]

It was in this context of new Hutu empowerment and anti-Tutsi revenge that Rwanda moved from a monarchy to a republic in the January 1961.[69] But although the central government was undergoing tumultuous change, out in the rural locales communal administration followed a certain order—based on the patterns that had been visible and accessible to Rwandans during German *schauris* and the actions of peripatetic Belgians. These familiar patterns provided a certain continuity during this period of massive political change. In local settings throughout Rwanda the birth of the republic was ushered in on a wave of abuses, as the newly empowered moved to contain and detain their opponents.[70] This next generation's *maisons de détention* soon materialized, for example, at Sake in southeastern Rwanda, in a house where the makeshift government had its headquarters. Extremists reportedly established a *cachot* where they detained and tortured suspected adversaries.[71] Additional *maisons* developed: makeshift jails in makeshift situations. In one commune of Gitarama Prefecture, a depot used for the storage of the hazardous agricultural chemical DDT became a makeshift *cachot*. Local residents jokingly called it *la maison de DDT*.[72]

In these early years of independence, abuses against challengers spawned more challengers—or at least those suspected as such—and generated a continuing cycle of arrests and abuses. In settings throughout Rwanda, from Kibungo to Cyangugu, local-level officials—*bourgmestres* and *préfets*—arbitrarily threatened, detained, and abused their competitors.[73] The March 1962 arrest and subsequent disappearance of L. Bunagu and the September 1962 arrest and physical abuse of V. Kalima were only two of many examples of arrests of political opponents by new officials. Abuses increased with the communal elections in 1963, which unleashed yet another wave of arbitrary arrests, torture, imprisonment, and summary executions.[74] In this context, the general concept of preventive detention—the immediate detention of an alleged or potential troublemaker in order to constrain him physically, "contain" the threat he posed to society, and prevent his escape—found application as a political tool. Authorities reveled in the effectiveness of preventive detention of competitors before an election as a means of containing political challenge. The legalities of preventive detention, and the tedious problem of justifying renewals, were non-issues in this era, since magistrates had little training and were beholden to political authorities.[75]

If, in the opening years of the 1960s, preventive detention had been transformed from a judicial into a political tool for winning elections, it was transformed again in late December 1963 when it was applied in a new context: the armed invasion of Tutsi refugees into Bugesera.

Preventive detention, implemented on massive scale, proved an effective means of silencing potential critics—those Hutu and Tutsi who would be inclined to challenge the government's harsh repression in response to the invasion. It was also a means of separating and containing Tutsi, whom the Hutu-dominated government saw as potential internal enemies. The lack of outcry at the enormous number of civilian, mostly Tutsi, deaths following the invasion—estimated from 5,000 to 14,000[76]—underscored the efficacy of dealing with potential critics as well as potential enemies by "containing" them in government custody.

Both Grégoire Kayibanda and his successor, Juvénal Habyarimana, took this lesson to heart. Throughout the 1960s, Kayibanda continued his strategy of arbitrary arrests against potential challengers.[77] Habyarimana, who wrested power from him in a 1973 coup, carried the strategy into the next two decades, expanding and entrenching it through extensive use of *cachots* and mass arrests.

It was Habyarimana who propagated the use of *cachots*, both special *cachots* for political prisoners and communal *cachots* for local detainees. Early in his presidency, Habyarimana made extensive use of a section of Ruhengeri Central Prison as political *cachot* in which he is believed to have detained ex-President Kayibanda and key ministers of the former government. Cloistered away in a separate cell in Ruhengeri Prison, these men were not seen, and were rumored to be dead, until a trial was conducted in mid-June 1974 during which the still-unseen ex-president was sentenced to death.[78] Some of the former ministers also went to trial in 1974–1975, and received sentences of twenty years. Others, however were neither tried nor accounted for until years later, when they were finally declared dead.[79] Even as these former officials were placed on trial—though they were not necessarily physically present—the Habyarimana government unleashed new waves of politically motivated arrests. The pattern of these newer arrests—particularly the inclusion of key military officers among those detained—suggested power struggles within a small group of military strongmen who controlled the country and called themselves the Committee for Peace and National Unity.

By the late 1970s, these struggles at the center seemed to abate, with Habyarimana emerging victorious. Immediately, he angled to consolidate his personal position by reaching outward to "the population." Launching a new political party, the MRND *(Mouvement révolutionaire national pour le développement)*,[80] by means of which he linked himself directly to political action cells[81] throughout the country, Habyarimana remade himself into a "man of the people." He reinforced this new image by calling for a new campaign of rural development that included the construction of communal buildings and *cachots*. This apparent move toward democracy was received enthusiastically by international partners. The fact that much of the new infrastructure, including the *cachots*, was constructed by forced peasant labor *(umuganda)* was overlooked. In 1979, the fledgling regime received a firm vote of support from the U.S. government, which asserted in its human rights report:

> Since coming to power in 1973, President Juvénal Habyarimana has made continued progress on human rights a key objective of official policy. The Rwandan Government emphasizes development of rural areas to improve the lot of its poorest citizens and has undertaken efforts to make local justice more consistent. . . . Rwanda has been in the forefront of the African human rights movement.[82]

Despite this expression of confidence by a new partner courting closer relations, President Habyarimana found himself under fire in the same year from a rather different quarter—human rights organizations and journalists. The new president of a small country whose previous regime had shunned international contact, now found that opening oneself to international aid opened one to international scrutiny as well. The foreign press published allegations of a broad array of human rights violations, including arbitrary arrests, abuses of preventive detention, and ill-treatment of political prisoners. Throughout the 1970s, the reports of abuses continued. In 1978 and 1979, human rights reports cited incidents of detained persons waiting for up to two years without being tried, physical violence committed by police officers against detainees, arbitrary arrests of young people subsequently sent to forced-labor "re-education" camps, and political prisoners of the former regime living in dismal *cachots*, denied visitation rights and even dying in detention.[83]

Inside Rwanda, the procedure for preventive detention was so extensively violated that the president himself was forced to address it in 1979. In a public pitch for human rights, he acknowledged the prevalence and arbitrary nature of preventive detention and called for bringing it to an end. By this time, it was clear that although he tried to place himself at the forefront of Africa's human rights movement through his oratory, Habyarimana continued to make extensive use of preventive detention and *cachots* as political tools. The most serious abuses were reportedly taking place in security *cachots*, popularly called *amigo*.[84]

Despite the president's rhetoric, abuses of preventive detention, and of detainees generally, continued unabated into the 1980s. Even the U.S. government noted that Rwanda's practice of preventive detention was problematic. In a 1981 human rights report explaining the legal procedures for preventive detention, the State Department noted that it was quite legal in Rwanda for a detainee to be held without charges under certain kinds of warrants, and that under the provisions of preventive detention, persons could be held indefinitely for renewable periods of thirty days. The report added that, in theory, individuals thus preventively detained had a right to appeal their detention, but, in practice, appeal was so rarely successful that it was rarely invoked.[85] It noted that the International Red Cross had been refused the right to visit political detainees, a standard Red Cross procedure, and that "beatings of prisoners and suspects may be common," according to a credible human rights organization.[86]

Abuses of preventive detention, in conjunction with mass arrests or "sweeps" of opponents or public "examples," increased in the 1980s, a decade ushered in by the detention of more than thirty persons without charge and without trial in the *cachot* of Ruhengeri for more than a year.[87] Held incommunicado, some in cells of total darkness *(cachots noirs)* for nearly a year, the untried detainees could neither be visited, nor rendered medical assistance, despite reports that some of them had been tortured by beatings and electric shock in order to elicit confessions and after preliminary inquiries had found that some of the defendants had no accusations filed against them.[88]

In addition to these political prisoners, ordinary Rwandans were massively arrested in a 1983 campaign against "vagabonds" and "delinquents." They were illegally detained and physically abused, even raped, while in detention.[89] Mass arrests of persons belonging to minority religious groups, including Jehovah's Witnesses and other groups advocating nonviolence, generated hundreds of detainees in the mid-and late 1980s. During this decade, pretrial detention lengthened: by 1984, for certain political detainees it exceeded two years—even for detainees who, when they finally went before a judge, were acquitted and released.[90] This lengthy pretrial detention, and the increasing number of detainees, led to prison overcrowding and an overload of the judicial system by the end of the decade.

Attempting to get a handle on the situation in October 1989, the minister of justice ordered the Kigali prosecutor either to charge or to release the 1,900 prisoners held in Kigali Central Prison without charge or trial. These prisoners, most of whom had been arrested without warrants, had already been held for periods ranging from a few months to several years. Mounting reports of torture of uncharged or pretrial detainees in many sites, from *cachots* inside prisons to rooms inside the headquarters of the national intelligence service *(Service Central de Renseignements)* led to increased pressure for change from international human rights groups, and ultimately to the 1986 government revelation that some fifty-six political prisoners had been extrajudicially killed.[91] This revelation, while it may have generated some political capital for the government, which claimed to have "come clean" on human rights, did not lead to a diminution of abuses against detainees.

Indeed, the situation grew exponentially worse in 1990, following an October attack on the north of the country by RPF guerrillas. The government responded by arresting thousands of Rwandans in mass sweeps, and holding more than 4,000 until April 1991. In *cachots* throughout the country, suspected RPF sympathizers were subject to a variety of abuses. In some *cachots,* groups of Tutsi were picked up and held without charge, beaten, and then released.[92] Suspects held by the national intelligence service were reportedly beaten with electric wire and hoe handles, given electric shocks, tied at the elbows with their arms behind their backs, and made to drink urine and eat vomit.[93] Thousands of others never made it to detention; they were simply executed.

Mass arrests continued to play a significant role in the political struggles of 1991–1994, which pitted political moderates, who challenged the Habyarimana regime's abuses of power and called for a negotiated settlement with the RPF, against hard-liners, who vehemently opposed power-sharing or concessions of any kind and sought to galvanize support by appeals to Hutu ethnic solidarity. In addition to new waves of mass arrests, beatings, grenade attacks, and assassinations became increasingly commonplace.

The steadily mounting violence of the early 1990s leaped to a new level in April 1994, following the assassination of President Habyarimana. The political void that his death created opened up a lethal struggle for power between political moderates and hard-liners. The hard-liners seized the opportunity of confusion and void at the political center, and called their network of supporters into action. Swiftly, these hard-liners transformed mass shock and uncertainty into a deadly motivating force as they called upon their countrymen to contain "the enemy within." In the two waves of reaction to the crisis, hard-liners targeted, first, political "enemies," and then, ethnic "enemies," this time not by detention but by massacre. In the events of 1994, *cachots* played little role. Containment of opponents—or "enemies"—now relied on mass execution.

THE WAR OF THE *CACHOTS* SINCE 1994

Several months after the July 1994 takeover of Kigali by the armed forces of the RPF, killing began to give way to mass arrest as the dominant means of conflict containment. Particularly in September 1994, as international relief workers poured in to assist with Rwanda's reconstruction, the unchecked summary executions and disappearances perpetrated to avenge the genocide began to subside and detentions were on the rise. The 800 genocide suspects whom the RPF government held in mid-August 1994, a month and a half into its administration, climbed to 10,000 three months later, and to 15,000 by the end of the year. The arrest rate at year's end was 1,500 persons per week.[94]

This wave of arrests took place in a context of collapse: Rwanda had neither the physical infrastructure nor the judicial personnel to cope with the detentions. With almost no trained judicial authorities to investigate, issue arrest warrants, process inmates, or establish the circumstances of their cases, suspected or accused criminals were apprehended and detained in all manner of arbitrary ways. And although Rwandan law laid out the procedures for preventive detention and judicial inquiry, followed by transfer or release, most communes had no means to either investigate and shelter large numbers of detainees or to transport them on to the central prisons.

The system stalled at the local level: The pressure on local *cachots* became enormous. By late 1994, *cachots*, meant to be provisional, were holding detainees for lengthy periods of time. More alarmingly, rumors indicating the existence of a wide variety of irregular *cachots* were increasingly substantiated. Detainees were being amassed and often tortured in private houses, in abandoned buildings, in sheds and outhouses, in military barracks, in shipping crates, and even in holes in the ground.[95] Although the system for monitoring the arrest and transfer of detainees was barely developed, it quickly became clear that detainees were disappearing. Human rights monitors, attempting to track the whereabouts of persons who had been seen leaving their homes in the custody of authorities, began to find cases where the arrestees were neither recorded nor present in the *cachot*, and their whereabouts could not be explained by authorities.[96]

By early 1995, with prisons at five times their maximum capacity,[97] Rwandan authorities and international observers debated whether it was better to keep detainees in the *cachots* or to transfer them to the central prisons. Many considered *cachot* facilities superior to prisons, where burgeoning inmate populations, some packed at a density of six inmates per square meter, risked epidemic. Butare prison, designed for 1,500 but with an inmate population of over 4,000, recorded a death toll of 166 persons in the last six weeks of 1994. The well-monitored Kigali Central Prison, designed for 1,500 but holding over 5,000 inmates in early 1995, recorded an average of 7 deaths per day.[98] Others argued that *cachots*, more difficult to monitor, were centers of abuse and torture.

The debate shifted decisively toward the latter view after March 1995 when the forced closure of camps for internally displaced persons (IDPs) spilled tens of thousands of persons out on Rwanda's hillsides. Almost immediately, mass arrests began, adding new detainees, many exhausted, sick from a widespread viral infection, or wounded from gunfire or beatings, into the *cachots*. Although not all *cachots*, not even all official communal facilities, were open to monitoring, those that were proved highly overcrowded. An aide worker described a *cachot* of six square meters (390 square feet) holding 150 detainees, who were so tightly packed that no one could lie down at night.[99] In the days that followed, suffocations began to occur. In the lock-up of Muhima at the Kigali *gendarmerie*, 74 persons squeezed into a cell designed to hold no more than 5 to 10, caused the suffocation deaths of 24 people.[100] In the southern commune of Rusatira in Butare prefecture, the cramming of 300 detainees in the small *cachot* killed 28 people by suffocation.[101]

In addition to the overcrowding, physical evidence indicated that detainees were being tortured. Detainees reported being beaten with sticks and wooden clubs, particularly on the genitals. Women detainees reported being raped by security officials. Detainees also reported witnessing the fatal beatings of fellow inmates,[102] testimony supported by sudden decreases in inmate counts that authorities were unable to explain. Throughout this period, prison over-crowding had slowed or stalled prison transfers, even though the United Nations had stepped in to facilitate the transport. Detainees were thus being held for longer periods in *cachots* and other decentralized sites, which monitors believed, increased their chances of being tortured or killed.[103] Therefore, despite reports of abysmal conditions in the central prisons—of high death rates, of amputations of gangrenous limbs caused by endlessly standing in mud and filth—international human rights organizations pushed for *cachot* inmates to be transferred to the central prisons for their own safety.

As 1996 and the second anniversary of the genocide approached, clandestine abuses of *cachot* inmates, including severe overcrowding causing suffocations, continued; in addition, new developments indicated a growing pattern of inmate killings through open, armed attack. In April 1996, with *cachots* filled anew due to mass arrests resulting from an identity card campaign, and recorded detainees nationwide numbering 67,000,[104] on-and-off bouts of violence along Rwanda's western border, which had become commonplace in the previous year, now began to center on *cachots*. On April 10, 1996 at the Muramba Detention Center in Gisenyi Prefecture, at least nine detainees were killed following the shooting death of an RPA soldier, allegedly by an "infiltrator."[105] A similar but more extensive attack took place one month later in Cyangugu Prefecture where at least forty-six detainees died of grenade and gunshot wounds in an attack on the *cachot* at Bugarama Commune.[106] Authorities attributed the killings to infiltrators, who had attacked RPA soldiers and killed the detainees in a bungled attempt to free them. Forensic evidence, however, established that the gunfire and explosions had come from inside the *cachot*.

The year continued with suffocation deaths and shootings of alleged escapees. By early June 1996, forty-three people had died from suffocation in *cachots*, including twenty-two detainees at the Kivumu communal *cachot* in Kibuye Prefecture on May 11, 1996.[107] In an October incident, sixteen detainees suffocated in the *cachot* of Gitesi Commune, Kibuye Prefecture. Amnesty International reported: "The authorities claimed that the deaths were caused by fighting among the detainees, but the detainees apparently died as a result of lack of air and extreme heat in the grossly overcrowded cells. Prison guards had refused to open the cell doors, although they heard detainees screaming for air and water."[108] Numerous cases of individuals being shot dead at close range, allegedly while trying to escape, were also reported in 1996, particularly in Kibuye and Gitarama prefectures. Others detainees died of malnutrition.[109]

The shootings of detainees, justified by authorities as legitimate means to thwart escape, continued into 1997, claiming at least 100 lives between January and early August. In addition to this, violence broadened and escalated in the north of the country, evolving into large-scale attacks on civilian communities.[110] The context of this shift was the violent, forced return of refugees from camps in former Zaire in November–December 1996. Within days of the return of the first wave of refugees, monitors noted a pronounced rise in arrests, disappearances, and killings, particularly in the northern regions of Gisenyi and Ruhengeri. By 1997, having pushed out most of the international aide workers in the North, the Rwandan military engaged in open attacks on the civilian population. It characterized the large number of civilian deaths as collateral damage in the defense of the country against rebel- and infiltrator-initiated offensives. Prominent among the massacres reported—and suggesting an enlargement in scale of the previously established pattern of killing inmates during real or alleged escapes—were those situated in or near *cachots*. For example, in early August 1997, ninety-five detainees at the *cachot* in Gisenyi Prefecture's Rubavu Commune, and an unknown number of detainees at neighboring Kanama, were killed during clashes between government forces and "infiltrators" whom authorities claimed had attempted to liberate them. During the military operations that ensued, several hundred residents of the region were killed. Reports of similar skirmishes continued to filter out of northern Rwanda in mid- and late 1997, culminating in massive military operations conducted against civilians in November and December, following alleged attacks on the *cachots* of Giciye, Rwerere, and Bulinga Communes.

CONCLUSION

The decentralization of Rwanda's state apparatus into communes, of which *cachots* are a vital element, was hailed as a hopeful sign in the 1960s–1980s. Onlookers celebrated this move as evidence of Rwanda's development toward Westernized democracy. Rwandans too welcomed communes, including *cachots*, as a step away from colonial authoritarianism, and a step toward bringing the mechanisms of government and justice closer to the people. In the 1990s, however, with Rwanda's hope for democracy having gone terribly astray, decentralization has provided a cover for abuse. In 1994, government-ordered killing teams combed the remotest corners of the country hunting for victims. In 1997, widespread manhunts and killings in remote northern corners threatened security once again.

Rwanda is presently a country of graves and *cachots*, in which the dialogue on justice is encoded in body counts. Crucial among the figures associated with "justice by numbers" is 120,000. This figure refers to the detainees whose lives, as of this writing, remain extremely precarious, as evidenced by regular weekly death tolls as well as by the casualties generated in incidents of attacks on *cachots*. As the period of their detainment in degrading conditions has stretched into years, the detainees have teetered on the edge between life and death on a continuous and ongoing basis. In 1990s Rwanda, preventive detention was transformed into provisional existence for guilty and innocent alike.

NOTES

1. This article is based in part on personal experience and research conducted in Rwanda from October 1994 to October 1995. I would like to thank the *gacaca* scholars from the *Université Nationale du Rwanda*, the *Institut de Recherche Scientifique et Technologique*, and the *Grand Séminaire*, as well as current members and exiled former members of the Rwandan human rights organization *(Association rwandaise des Droits de l'homme— ARDHO)*, whose input into the research for this article is greatly appreciated.

2. Called *abaturage* in Kinyarwanda and *les paysans* or *la population* in French, ordinary people are conventionally referred to by educated Rwandans as a collective mass who think (or respond) and behave in a collective manner. Imputing to them a herd-like, easily manipulated nature, many educated Rwandans, both Tutsi and Hutu, compare their less educated counterparts to sheep. This comparison is especially invoked in explaining popular participation in the 1994 genocide.

3. For a discussion of the Rwandan government's ethnicized definition of "legitimate" survivors, and how this definition plays into its "politics of victimization," see Michele D. Wagner "Whose Justice?" *Tribunal* 6, no. 1 (December 1996), 6. Michele D. Wagner "All the Bourgmestre's Men," *Africa Today* 45, no. 1 (1998), 25–36.

4. For examples of incidents reported during the year 1996, see: Amnesty International, *Amnesty International Report 1997* (New York: 1996), 271–73. Despite numerous reports of violent incidents, which circulate within the small community of humanitarian aid and development organizations existing in Rwanda, few international organizations operating in Rwanda have publicly reported or denounced these incidents. Organizations that have made public statements about these incidents, such as the French group *Médecins Sans Frontières (Doctors Without Borders)*, have been placed on lists of "suspicious" organizations, denied visas, and/or expelled.

5. Didier Lauras boldly characterizes rebel attacks on detention centers as a "war" in his article "Les rebelles intensifient la 'guerre des cachots' " *(Agence France-Presse*, December 4, 1997). Prior to this, other observers such as Amnesty International remarked upon a developing pattern of violence at detention centers: "A pattern of killings of detainees by the security forces emerged during the year. Most occurred while detainees were held in communal detention centres before being transferred to central prisons." Amnesty International, *Report 1997*, 273.

6. Attack on Giciye Commune, Gisenyi Prefecture, November 1997. "88 Prisoners die at Giciye" *(Agence France-Presse*, November 16, 1997); "300 personnes tuées dans un raid contre une prison rwandaise" *(Reuters*, November 20, 1997). Attack on Rwerere Commune, Gisenyi Prefecture, December 1997. "Hutu Attack Frees Inmates" *(Associated Press*, December 3, 1997). Attack on Bulinga Commune, Gitarama Prefecture, December 1997. Didier Lauras, "Les rebelles intensifient la 'guerre des cachots.' " (Agence France-Presse, December 4, 1997).

7. G. Prunier, *The Rwanda Crisis* (New York: Columbia University Press 1995), 119–20.

8. Idem., 56, 136–39.

9. C. Legun, ed., *Africa Contemporary Record 1976–1977* (London and New York: Africana Publishing Co., 1977), B308–B309 (hereafter referred to as ACR) records that decentralized rural development based on the commune was the focal point of government policy in 1976–1977. U.S. Government, Department of State, *Country Reports on Human Rights Practices for 1979*, Report Submitted to the Committee on Foreign Relations, U.S. Senate, and the Committee on Foreign Relations, U.S. House of Representatives (Washington: 1980), 155. "Since coming to power in 1973, President Juvénal Habyarimana has made continued progress on human rights a key objective of official policy. The Rwandan Government emphasizes development of the rural areas to improve the lot of its poorest citizens and has undertaken efforts to make local justice more consistent. Lack of resources rather than appropriate policies impedes faster human rights progress."

10. The intended function of *cachots communaux* was the preventive detention of local residents accused of minor crimes. According to the Rwandan penal code, in effect prior to November 1994, a local police officer (either the *Inspecteur de la Police Judiciaire*, IPJ, or an *Officier de la Police Judiciaire*, OPJ) had the right to detain a resident on a preventive basis for up to forty-eight hours. A national police officer (*Officier du Ministère Public*, OMP) had the right to detain a person for up to five days. The OMP could, if necessary, prolong the detention for up to thirty days, renewable, with authorization from a judge. In addition, within the commune, the *bourgmestre* acting in the capacity of an OPJ had the right to detain a resident for a maximum of seven days.

11. Germany, Rwanda's first colonial overruler, was forced to surrender its colonies at the end of the First World War. At that point, Rwanda became League of Nations–mandated territory under the stewardship of Belgium. Later, the United Nations continued that mandate.

12. *Indigène*, the nomenclature used during most of Rwanda's colonial experience, later became *paysan*, a nomenclature that endures into the present. It is used by educated Rwandans to refer to less educated, subsistence-sector farmers and artisans.

13. In Kinyarwanda these identities are expressed as *Batutsi, Bahutu*, and *Batwa*.

14. For an example of the interpretation of these identity categories as "race," see A. Arnoux, *Les Pères Blancs aux Sources du Nil* (Namur: Grands Lacs, 1948), 20–7. For an official view that also relies on "races" to explain Rwandan identity categories, see Belgium, Ministère des Colonies, *Rapport présenté par le Gouvernement Belge au Conseil de la Société des Nations au sujet de l'administration du Ruanda-Urundi pendant l'année 1926* (Brussels: 1927), 50. (Hereafter referred to as *Rapport Annuel* [year]).

15. By 1959, at the end of the period of colonial rule, 43 of the 45 chiefs and 549 of the 559 subchiefs were Tutsi. J.-P. Chrétien, "Hutu et Tutsi au Rwanda et au Burundi" in J.L. Amselle and E. M'Bokolo, eds., *Au Coeur de l'ethnie* (Paris: La Découverte, 1985), 145.

16. See, for example C. Newbury, "Ubureetwa and Thangata: Comparative Colonial Perspectives," in *La Civilisation Ancienne des Peuples des Grands Lacs* (Paris and Bujumbura: Centre de civilisation burundaise, 1981), 138–47.

17. Personal communication with BNU, December 1997. Also inspiring confidence in the accessibility of justice was the new system of tribunals introduced into Rwanda in the early years of its independence, the most local of which was the *tribunal de Canton*.

18. Belgians and others saw the violence of 1959–1960, which quickly became termed the "Hutu Revolution," as a Rwandan version of the French Revolution. This interpretation

sprang quite naturally from the characterization of Rwanda in the anthropological and historical literature of the era, which focused on Rwanda as a "feudal kingdom" imposed by Tutsi "feudal lords" on Hutu "serfs." The important difference between the image of the "Hutu Revolution" and the actual ideals that informed the French Revolution was that, in the French case, the dynamics of conflict was rooted in social class. In the Rwandan case, the dynamics of conflict were embedded in ethnicity as well as class, and could never seem to escape ethnicism. "Revolutionary" ideology and terms were overlaid on top of ethnicity, which remained as the ideological bedrock. For an example of an analysis of the events of 1959–1961, which draws upon comparison with the French revolution, see R. Lemarchand, *Rwanda and Burundi* (London and New York: Praeger Publishers, 1970), 187.

19. J. Vansina, *L'évolution du royaume rwanda des origines à 1900* (Brussels: Académie royale des sciences doutre-mer, 1962), 57. C. Newbury, *The Cohesion of Oppression* (New York: Columbia University Press, 1988).

20. For "divide and rule" in the Belgian era, see P. Ryckmans, *Dominer pour Servir* (Brussels: Universelle Editions, 1948).

21. These precolonial entities *(abahinza)* have been described as "Hutu kinglets" *(roitelets)* as in M.C. Atterbury "Revolution in Rwanda," 10. An alternative expression is "Hutu principalities" *(principautés hutu).* F. Nahimana, *"Les Principautés Hutu du Rwanda Septentrional"* in *La Civilisation Ancienne*, 115–37.

22. For a history of the complex and varied interactions among these regions, see Vansina, *L'évolution du royaume rwanda.*

23. *Ruanda*, the colonial name for the region, became *Rwanda* at independence.

24. This ideal vision of society's ability to sustain conflict focused primarily on men's conflicts, and disputes between relatively equal opponents. Conflicts among women, who had more limited means to express themselves openly and to avail themselves of support networks, or conflicts between those of unequal social stature, often relied on other means—poisoning or magical attack. It is important to note that these societies were highly stratified and that their approach to conflict explicitly incorporated this stratification. Higher status afforded one "protection" in a conflict's resolution. Very low status translated into limited ability to protect oneself.

25. R. Bourgeois, *Banyarwanda et Barundi, Tome 2, La Coutume* (Brussels: Académie royale des sciences coloniales, 1954), 399, 400, 438.

26. Idem., 400.

27. Ibid.

28. The practice that the ethnographic sources mention may be the one currently in widespread use of tying the person's arms together behind his back at his elbows, which effectively breaks his rib cage open, while administering severe beatings.

29. Bourgeois, *Banyarwanda et Barundi*, 398. A. Lestrade, *Notes d'Ethnographie du Rwanda* (Tervuren: Musée royal Afrique centrale, 1972), 111.

30. Anonymous, *Historique et Chronologie du Ruanda* (Kabgayi, 1956), 13–14. Kigeri IV Rwabugiri (whose rule lasted approximately from 1853 to 1895) died in 1895. His son Mibambwe IV Rutarindwa succeeded him in 1895 but was murdered in 1896 and replaced with his half-brother Yuhi V Musinga (1896–1931), whose enthronement was met by much resistance at court. For a history of the early colonial era, see W. Roger Louis, *Ruanda- Urundi, 1884–1919* (Oxford: Clarendon Press, 1963), 104–5, 121, 145–46.

31. These two rival factions were the Bega and the Banyiginya royal clans. Louis, *Ruanda-Urundi*, 126, 153–54.

32. Anonymous, *Historique*, 13, on the Bethe-Hecq Agreement.

33. Louis, *Ruanda-Urundi*, 153: "The most prominent features of the administration in Ruanda were not the day to day judicial problems, but the punitive expeditions."

34. *Schauri* was adopted into German colonial terminology from the Swahili language, from which originates most of the German colonial terminology for practices they developed to govern East Africa. In Swahili, *shauri* has a variety of meanings, including "advice" and "opinion."

35. M.D. Wagner, "Whose History is 'History'? A History of the Baragane People of Southern Burundi, 1850–1932" (Ph.D. dissertation, University of Wisconsin–Madison, 1991), 361–428. Louis, *Ruanda-Urundi*, 129.

36. The conflict between the civilian Resident, R. Kandt, and the military establishment is discussed in Anonymous, *Historique*, 21–22.

37. Ibid., 14.

38. Bourgeois, *Banyarwanda et Barundi*, 400, asserts that detention as a punishment was unknown "traditionally," but Lestrade, *Notes*, 111 suggests that it may have existed.

39. For a list of German-era crimes and punishments, see Louis, *Ruanda-Urundi*, 150, footnote 3.

40. Idem.

41. Ibid., 152.

42. Idem.

43. The Orts-Milner Agreement of May 30, 1919, legalized Belgian administration of Ruanda, which was established as a League of Nations trusteeship.

44. Detention centers were established at each of the headquarters, or "Résidences," of Ruanda and Urundi by *Réglement du Résident de l'Urundi*, No. 8 of October 5, 1918.

45. In 1919, *Réglement du Résident de l'Urundi* No. 2 of June 7, 1919, created more *maisons de détention*: at the headquarters of each police prison in Ruanda and at all headquarters other than Kigali. By 1921, they had proliferated further.

46. *Rapport Annuel 1921–1922*, 41.

47. Ibid., 1923–1924, 11. In Kitega, a 1923 outbreak of bronchio-pulmonary disease was labeled an "epidemic" in the annual report. Several inmates of Kigali prison died of "recurrent fever and malaria." Government statistics for that year indicate that thirteen died while incarcerated.

48. H. Codere, *The Biography of an African Society, Rwanda, 1900–1960* (Tervuren: Musée royal de l'Afrique centrale, 1973), 69. Spelling of the name has been modified to reflect the conventions of Kinyarwanda.

49. Bwana Morisi described in R. Bourgeois, *Témoignages, Tome I, Vol. 1* (Tervuren: Musée royal de l'Afrique centrale, 1987), 12. Identification of Morisi as Phillipart: Anonymous, *Historique*, 134–35.

50. Ibid., Tome 1, Vol. 1, 12–18.

51. Ibid., Tome 1, Vol. 1, 42.

52. With few Belgian administrators on the ground, each one performed multiple duties. One man would serve as local administrator, police investigator, judge of various kinds of tribunals, and guardian of the prison. With a single authority serving in multiple capacities, it is clear that the sense of due process that Belgians claimed to want to inculcate in Rwandans would be rather strongly countered by the picture of capriciousness and personal power that Rwandans would see in the example of their administrators. For example of multiple duties, see F. Reyntjens, *Pouvoir et Droit au Rwanda* (Tervuren: Musée royal de l'Afrique centrale, 1985), 164–65, and Bourgeois, *Témoignages*, Tome 1, Vol. 1, Chapter 2.

53. Bourgeois, *Témoignages*, Tome 1, Vol. 2, 75–76.

54. Ibid., 77.

55. G. Mineur, *Juridictions Indigènes du Ruanda-Urundi* (Astrida: 1944), 77. Articles 29 and 35.

56. Bourgeois, *Témoignages*, Tome 1, Vol. 2, 149.

57. The contemporary region of Cyangugu.

58. Bourgeois attributed S——'s exemption from group labor to the necessity of protecting the dignity of a former subchief.

59. Bourgeois, *Témoignages*, Tome 1, Vol. 2, 166.

60. Ibid., 80.

61. Bourgeois, *Témoignages*, Tome 1, Vol. 1, 50.

62. Interview with BCD, March 1997.

63. Interview with HM, February 1997.

64. After the violence of November 1959, an interim decree was issued in December 1959, establishing communes and calling for communal elections. The elections for communal officials—*bourgmestres* and counselors—were held in June through September 1960. Lemarchand, *Rwanda and Burundi*, 178, 184.

65. Ibid., 178, 182–83, 187.

66. Ibid., 185, 187.

67. The system had changed so quickly that a framework of laws had not been been developed to structure it. Hence, the 229 new *bourgmestres* worked a "kind of legal blank check," dispensing "a rough and ready kind of natural justice." Lemarchand, *Rwanda and Burundi*, 178, 182–83. Further, with the eviction of Tutsi judges between 1959 and 1961, no Rwandan had a law degree. Magistrates named in that period, having little or no training, were given thirty-year appointments. Lemarchand, *Rwanda and Burundi*, 437–38.

68. P. Gravel, *Remera: A Community in Eastern Rwanda* (Paris and The Hague: Mouton, 1968), 193.

69. Lemarchand, *Rwanda and Burundi*, 192–93.

70. Ibid., 195–96, and footnote 49. "These politicised functionaries . . . used their prerogatives to arrest, torture and incarerate their political adversaries." Quoted from a letter to Max Dorinsville, Chairman of the United Nations Commission for Ruanda-Urundi.

71. Ibid., 211.

72. Interview with BHM, February 1997.

73. Reyntjens, *Pouvoir et Droit*, 382, 451. Lemarchand, *Rwanda and Burundi*, 219.

74. Reyntjens, *Pouvoir et Droit*, 382, 451, 453–54.

75. Lemarchand, *Rwanda and Burundi*, 437–38. This situation from the early 1960s closely parallels the judicial situation in late 1990s Rwanda.

76. Ibid., 219–23, gives an estimate of 10,000–14,000 deaths. *African Contemporary Record*, 1986, 193, places the number of deaths at 5,000.

77. Reyntjens, *Pouvoir et Droit*, 391.

78. During the trial of June 13–29, 1974, Kayibanda was sentenced to death. However, "There was no indication that Kayibanda was himself present at the trial; some diplomats in Kigali believe that he was actually shot dead on the night of the coup." In July 1974, Habyarimana commuted the sentence, an act undoubtedly meant to garner political points. ACR, 1974–1975, B254–B255. Other sources state that Kayibanda died in late 1976. Amnesty International, *Report 1977*, 94.

79. *Country Reports, 1981*, 198. Amnesty International, *Report 1982*, 69 noted that these prisoners were still missing in 1982 and that about thirty were rumored to be dead. Am-

nesty International, *Report 1986*, 78, reported that these "disappeared" political prisoners, who numbered more than fifty, had all been secretly killed in prison.

80. In July 1975, Habyarimana called for the ending of the military-controlled Committee for Peace and National Unity and launched the civilian political party the MRND (*Mouvement révolutionaire national pour le développement*, or the National Revolutionary Movement for Development). By 1976, during a national political congress, the MRND was lauded as the instrument for the new national goal of decentralized rural development.

81. *ACR*, 1976–1977, B308–B309.

82. *Country Reports, 1979*, 155.

83. Ibid., 156. *ACR*, 1979–1980, B283.

84. Ibid, B284.

85. *Country Reports, 1981*, 198.

86. Ibid, 198, 201.

87. Amnesty International, *Report 1981*, 73–74, reports the plight of persons arrested in April–May 1980, suspected of conspiring against the government and held without official charge for more than a year, although the president gave public assurances that they would be charged and tried. Amnesty International, *Report 1982*, 67, reports that they were brought to trial in September 1981, but had no legal representation.

88. Amnesty International, *Report 1983*, 71.

89. *ACR*, 1983–1984, B231. *Country Reports*, 1983, 278–80.

90. Amnesty International, *Report 1984*, 84.

91. Amnesty International, *Report 1986*, 78–80.

92. Human Rights Watch, *World Report 1992* (New York: 1991), 101.

93. Amnesty International, *Report 1992*, 223–24.

94. Amnesty International, "Rwanda: Crying Out for Justice," AFR 47/03/95 (April 1995), 1. Human Rights Watch/Africa and *Fédération Internationale des Ligues des Droits de l'Homme* (FIDH), "Rwanda: The Crisis Continues" (April 1995), 4.

95. Interviews with United Nations human rights monitors, 1994–1995. Eve-Ann Prentice and Sam Kiley, "Thousands 'Detained at Torture Centers' in Rwanda," *The Times of London* (April 6, 1995), 10.

96. Experience as United Nations human rights monitor, Kibungo Prefecture, 1994–1995.

97. Prisons built to accommodate 4,000 held 20,000 inmates by early 1995.

98. Amnesty International, "Rwanda: Crying Out for Justice," AFR 47/03/95 (April 1995), 2.

99. J. Bedford, "Mass arrests making Rwanda's jails lethal" (*Reuters*, March 4, 1995).

100. "Twenty-two suffocate in tiny Rwandan jail cell" (*Reuters World Service*, March 19, 1995, also reported by *BBC World Service*, March 21, 1995). Twenty-two persons died at the scene and two more died in the hospital later.

101. Annie Thomas, "Rwandan President Announces Independent Enquiry into Massacre" (*Agence France-Presse*, April 27, 1995, also reported by *BBC World Service*, May 1, 1995).

102. Gilmore Inigo, "Prime Minister Forced to Step Down in Lawless Rwanda," *The Times* (August 29, 1995). Amnesty International, "Rwanda: Two Years After the Genocide—Human Rights in the Balance. An Open Letter to President Pasteur Bizimungu," AFR 47/02/96 (April 4, 1996).

103. Amnesty International, "Rwanda: Two Years After."

104. Ibid.

105. Amnesty International, "Alarming resurgence of killings," AFR 47/13/96 (August 12, 1996).

106. Ibid. Amnesty International, *Report 1997*, 273. Forensic details verified in personal communication with human rights monitors who investigated attacks at Karengera, Nyakabuye, and Bugarama, in Cyangugu Prefecture, May 1996.

107. *BBC*, June 4, 1996. Amnesty International, "Alarming resurgence"

108. Amnesty International, *Report 1997*, 272.

109. Amnesty International, "Alarming resurgence." Ian Guest, "After Genocide in Rwanda, a Predictable Crisis of Impunity," *International Herald Tribune* (November 12, 1996).

110. Amnesty International, "Rwanda: Ending the Silence," AFR 47/32/97 (September 25, 1997).

SELECTED BIBLIOGRAPHY

This bibliography privileges general references on the theory of space and on the history of prisons, architectures of confinement, and punishment in Africa. For regional case-studies, see the appropriate chapters.

"L'Afrique: un autre espace historique." *Annales ESC,* 40, 6 (1985).

Anderson, D., and D. Killingray, eds. *Policing the Empire. Governments, Authority and Control, 1830–1940* (Manchester: Manchester University Press, 1991).

Policing and Decolonisation. Nationalism, Politics and the Police, 1917–65 (Manchester: Manchester University Press, 1992).

Arnold, D. "The Colonial Prison: Power, Knowledge and Penology in Nineteenth Century India," in D. Arnold and D. Hardiman, eds., *Subaltern Studies VII. Essays in Honour of Ranajit Guha* (Oxford: Oxford University Press, 1994).

Bayart, J.-F. *La greffe de l'état* (Paris: Karthala, 1996).

Bazin, J., and E. Terray, eds. *Guerres de lignage et guerres d'états en Afrique* (Paris: Archives contemporaines, 1982).

Becker, C., S. Mbaye, and I. Thioub, eds. *AOF: Réalités et héritages. Sociétés ouest-africaines et ordre colonial, 1895–1960* (Dakar: Publication des Archives nationales du Sénégal, 1997).

Bell, L. *Mental and Social Disorder in Sub-Saharan Africa. The Case of Sierra Leone, 1787–1990* (New York: Greenwood Press, 1991).

Bender, J. *Imagining the Penitentiary. Fiction and the Architecture of the Mind in Eighteenth-Century England* (Chicago: University of Chicago Press, 1987).

Berman, B., and J. Lonsdale. "Coping with Contradictions: The Colonial State in Kenya, 1895–1914," *Journal of African History,* 20, 4 (1979).

———. *Unhappy Valley. Conflict in Kenya and Africa,* (London: James Currey, 1992).

Bernault, F. ed. *Enfermement, prison et châtiments en Afrique du 19ᵉ siècle à nos jours* (Paris: Karthala, 1999).

———. "What Absence is Made of: Human Rights in Africa," in L. Hunt, J. Wasserstrom, and M. Young, eds. *Human Rights and Revolution* (New York: Rowman and Littlefield, 2000).

Bickford-Smith, V. *Ethnic Pride and Racial Prejudice in Victorian Cape Town* (New York: Cambridge University Press, 1995).

Bigo, D. "Ngaragba : l'impossible prison," *Revue française de science politique*, 39, 6 (1989).

Bouche, D. *Les villages de liberté en Afrique noire française, 1887–1910* (Paris and La Haye: Mouton, 1968).

Bourdieu, P. "The Social Space and the Genesis of Groups." *Theory and Society*, 14, 6 (1985).

Brauman, R., S. Smith, and C. Vidal, "Rwanda: politique de terreur et privilège d'impunité au Rwanda," *Esprit* (Aug. –Sept. 2000).

Carlier, C. *La prison aux champs. Les colonies d'enfants délinquants du Nord de la France au XIXe* (Paris: Editions de l'Atelier, 1994).

Castel, R. *L'ordre psychiatrique. L'âge d'or de l'aliénisme* (Paris: Les éditions de minuit, 1976).

Cazanove, F. "L'enfance criminelle indigène," *Bulletin de la Société de Pathologie Exotique*, 25, 7 (1932).

Chanock, M. Law, *Custom and Social Order. The Colonial Experience in Malawi and Zambia.* (Cambridge: 1985, and Portsmouth, NJ: Heinemann, 1998).

———. *The Making of South Africa Legal Culture, 1902–1936* (New York: Cambridge University Press, 2001).

Chisholm, L. "The Pedagogy of Porter: The Origins of the Reformatory in the Cape Colony, 1882–1910," *Journal of African History*, 27 (1986).

———. "Crime, Class and Nationalism: The Criminology of Jacob de Villiers Roos, 1869–1913," *Social Dynamics*, 13 (1987).

———. "Education, Punishment and the Contradictions of Penal Reform: Alan Paton and Diepkloof Reformatory, 1934–1948," *Journal of Southern African Studies*, 17, 1 (1991).

Cohen, S. "Bandits, Rebels or Criminals: African History and Western Criminology (Review Article)," *Africa*, 56, 4 (1986).

———, and A. Scull, eds. *Social Control and the State* (Oxford: Basil Blackwell, 1985).

Collignon, R. "Vingt ans de travaux à la clinique psychiatrique de Fann-Dakar," *Psychopathologie africaine*, 14, 2/3 (1978).

———. "Le traitement de la folie au Sénégal à l'époque coloniale," in F. Bernault, ed. *Enfermement, prison et châtiments en Afrique* (Paris: Karthala, 1999).

Cooper, F. "Urban Space, Industrial Time, and Wage Labor in Africa," in F. Cooper, ed. *Struggle for the City: Migrant Labor, Capital, and the State in Urban Africa* (Beverly Hills: Sage, 1983).

Coquery-Vidrovitch, C. *Histoire des villes d'Afrique noire des origines à la colonisation* (Paris: Albin Michel, 1993).

Coutumier juridique de l'AOF (Paris: Larose, 1939).

Crocker, W. *Nigeria. A Critique of British Colonial Administration* (London: Allen & Unwin, 1935).

Crowder, M. *The Flogging of Phineas McIntosh: A Tale of Colonial Folly and Injustice, Bechuanaland 1933* (New Haven: Yale University Press, 1988).

———, and O. Okime, eds. *West African Chiefs. Their Changing Status under Colonial Rule and Independence* (New York: Africana Pub. Corp.,1970).

Crummey, D., ed. *Banditry, Rebellion and Social Protest in Africa* (London: Heinemann, 1985).

Curtin, P. "Medical Knowledge and Urban Planning in Colonial Tropical Africa," *American Historical Review*, 90, 3 (1985).

Deacon, H. "Madness, Race and Moral Treatment: Robben Island Lunatic Asylum, Cape Colony, 1846–1890," *History of Psychiatry*, 7 (1996).

———. "Racial Segregation and Medical Discourse in Nineteenth Century Cape Town," *Journal of Southern African Studies*, 22, 2 (1996).

———. *The Island: A History of Robben Island, 1488–1990* (Cape Town: Mayibuye Books, 1996).

Dembour, M.-B. "La peine durant la colonisation belge," *Recueils de la société Jean Bodin*, LVIII, *La Peine/Punishment* (Brussels: De Boeck, 1991).

———. "La chicotte comme symbole du colonialisme belge?," *Canadian Journal of African Studies*, 26, 2 (1992).

Denis, Commandant M. *Histoire militaire de l'Afrique équatoriale française* (Paris: Imprimerie Nationale, 1931).

Deslaurier, C. "Un système carcéral dans un état en crise: prisons, politique et génocide au Rwanda (1990–1996)," in F. Bernault, ed. *Enfermement, prison et châtiments en Afrique* (Paris: Karthala, 1999).

Diefenbacher, A. *Psychiatrie und Kolonialismus. Zur "Irrenfürsorge" in der Kolonie Deutsch-Ostafrika, 1895–1922* (Franfurt: Campus Forschung, 1985).

Diop, M. "L'administration sénégalaise et la gestion des 'fléaux sociaux'. L'héritage colonial," paper presented at the Colloque L'AOF : esquisse d'une intégration africaine, Dakar, 1995.

Doutreuwe, F. *Architecture coloniale en Côte d'Ivoire* (Abidjan: Ministère des Affaires culturelles/DEDA, 1985).

Dresch, J. "Villes congolaises: Etude de géographie urbaine et sociale," *Revue de géographie humaine et d'ethnologie*, 1 (1947).

Driver, C. "The View from Makana Island: Some Recent Prison Books from South Africa," *Journal of Southern African Studies*, 2, 1 (1975).

Duffield, I. "John Eldred Taylor and West African Opposition To Indirect Rule in Nigeria," *African Affairs,* 70 (1971).

Elias, T., ed. *The Prison System of Nigeria* (Lagos: 1965).

Evans, R. *The Fabrication of Virtue. English Prison Architecture, 1750–1840* (New York: Cambridge University Press, 1982).

Fabian, J. *Remembering the Present. Painting and Popular History in Zaire* (Berkeley: University of California Press, 1996).

Falk Moore, S. *Social Facts and Fabrications: Customary Law on Kilimandjaro, 1880–1980* (Cambridge: Cambridge University Press, 1986).

Faye, O. "Un aspect négligé de l'histoire sociale de la colonisation: les domestiques dans la vie de relations à Dakar de 1885 à 1940" *Annales de la Faculté des Lettres et Sciences humaines de l'Université Cheikh Anta Diop* (Dakar), 23 (1993).

Fisiy, C., and M. Rowlands. "Sorcery and Law in Modern Cameroon," *Culture and History* (Copenhagen), 6 (1990).

———, and P. Geschiere. "Judges and Witches, or How Is the State to Deal with Witchcraft? Examples from Southeastern Cameroon," *Cahiers d'études africaines*, 118 (1990).

Foran, W. *The Kenya Police 1887–1960* (London: R. Hale, 1962).

Foucault, M. *The Order of Things: An Archaeology of the Human Sciences* (New York: Vintage, 1973).

———. *Surveiller et punir. Naissance de la prison* (Paris: Gallimard, 1975).

———. "Questions on Geography." in C. Gordon, ed. *Power/Knowledge: Selected Interviews and Other Writings* (Brighton: Harvester, 1976).

————. "Space, Knowledge and Power," in P. Rabinow, *The Foucault Reader* (New York: Pantheon, 1984).

————. "Of Other Spaces." *Diacritics,* 16 (1986).

Fyfe, C. *A History of Sierra Leone* (Oxford: Oxford University Press, 1962).

Gaitskell, D. "Christian Compounds for Girls: Church Hostels for African Women in Johannesburg, 1907–1970," *Journal of Southern African Studies,* 6, 1 (1979).

Garland, D. *Punishment and Modern Society: A Study in Social Theory* (Chicago: University of Chicago Press, 1990)

Gatrell, V. *The Hanging Tree. Execution and the English People, 1770–1868* (Oxford: Oxford University Press, 1994).

Geary, W.. *Nigeria Under British Rule* (1ˢᵗ ed. London: 1927; 2d ed. New York: Barnes and Noble, 1965).

Gérémek, B. *La potence ou la pitié. L'Europe et les pauvres du Moyen Âge à nos jours* (Paris: Gallimard, 1978).

Glaser, C. *Bo-Tsotsi: The Youth Gangs of Soweto, 1935–76* (Portsmouth, NJ: Heinemann, 2000).

Gocking, R. "Ghana's Public Tribunals: An Experiment in Revolutionary Justice," *African Affairs* (1996).

Goerg, O. *Pouvoir colonial, municipalités et espaces urbains : Conakry-Freetown, des années 1880 à 1914* (Paris, L'Harmattan, 1997).

Goffman, E. *Asylums. Essays on the Social Situation of Mental Patients and Other Inmates* (Chicago: Aldine Publishing Company, 1962).

Gondola, D. "Le cercle de craie : L'enfermement dans le roman africain," in F. Bernault, ed. *Enfermement, prison et châtiments en Afrique* (Paris: Karthala,1999).

Graham, I. "A History of the Northern Rhodesia Prison Services," *Northern Rhodesia Journal,* V (1964).

Gray, C. *Colonial Rule and Crisis in Equatorial Africa: Southern Gabon ca. 1850–1940* (Rochester: University of Rochester Press, 2002)

Gready, P. "Autobiography and the 'Power of Writing': Political Prison Writing in the Apartheid Era," *Journal of Southern African Studies,* 19, 3 (1993).

Guèye, M. "La fin de l'esclavage à Saint-Louis et à Gorée en 1848," *Bulletin de l'IFAN* (Dakar), 28, B, 3–4 (1966).

Guyer, J. "Wealth in People as Wealth in Knowledge: Accumulation and Composition in Equatorial Africa," *Journal of African History,* 36 (1995).

Harley, J. "Maps, Knowledge and Power," in D. Cosgrove and S. Daniels, ed. *The Iconography of Landscape* (Cambridge: Cambridge University Press, 1988).

————. "Deconstructing the Map," *Cartographica,* 26, 2 (1989).

Harms, R. *River of Wealth. River of Sorrow. The Central Zaire Basin in the Era of the Slave and Ivory Trade, 1500–1891* (New Haven: Yale University Press, 1981).

Harries, P. *Work, Culture and Identity: Migrant Laborers in Mozambique and South Africa, c. 1860–1910* (Portsmouth, NJ: Heinemann, 1994).

Harwich, C. *Red Dust. Memories of the Uganda Police, 1935–55* (London: V. Stuart, 1961).

Hay, D., et al. *Albion's Fatal Tree. Crime and Society in Eighteenth-Century England* (New York: Pantheon Books, 1975).

Higginson, J. "Steam Without a Piston Box: Strikes and Popular Unrest in Katanga, 1943–1945," *International Journal of African Historical Studies,* 12, 1 (1988).

Hochet, J. "Inadaptation sociale et délinquance juvénile en Haute-Volta," *Recherches Voltaïques,* 9 (1967).

Howard, J. *L'Etat des prisons, des hôpitaux et des maisons de force en Europe au XVIIIème siècle,* translated by C. Carlier et J.-G. Petit (Paris: Editions de l'Atelier, 1994).

Igbafe, P. *Benin Under British Administration. The Impact of Colonial Rule on an African Kingdom, 1897–1938* (Atlantic Highlands, NJ: Humanities Press, 1979).

Ignatieff, M. "State, Civil Society and Total Institutions: A Critique of Recent Social Histories of Punishment," in S. Cohen and A. Scull, eds. *Social Control and the State* (Oxford: Basil Blackwell,1985).

———, *A Just Measure of Pain, The Penitentiary in the Industrial Revolution* (New York: Pantheon Books, 1978).

Jewsiewicki, B. *Naître et mourir au Zaïre. Un demi-siècle d'histoire au quotidien* (Paris: Karthala, 1993).

Kercher, L. *The Kenya Penal System. Past, Present and Prospect* (Washington: The University Press of America, 1981).

Killingray, D. "The Maintenance of Law and Order in British Colonial Africa," *African Affairs,* 85 (1986).

———, and A. Clayton. *Khaki and Blue: Military and Police in British Colonial Africa* (Athens, OH: Ohio University Center for International Studies, 1989).

———. "The 'Rod of Empire': The Debate over Corporal Punishment in the British African Colonial Forces, 1888–1946," *Journal of African History,* 35 (1994).

———, and D. Omissi, eds. *Guardians of Empire: The Armed Forces of the Colonial Powers, c. 1700–1964* (Manchester, New York: Manchester University Press, 1999).

Lagier, P. *La criminalité des adultes au Sénégal* (Montréal: Université de Montréal, 1971).

Lawrence, A. *Trade Castles and Forts in West Africa* (London: J. Cape, 1963).

Lefebvre, H. *La production de l'espace* (Paris: Anthropos, 1974).

Linebaugh, P. *The London Hanged. Crime and Civil Society in the Eighteenth Century* (Cambridge and New York: Cambridge University Press, 1991).

Lopes, F. X. *Três fortalezas de Luanda em 1846* (Luanda: Museu de Angola, 1954).

Lord Hailey. *Native Administration in the British African Territories* (London: H. M. Stationery office, 1950–53).

Lovejoy, P. *Transformations in Slavery: A History of Slavery in Africa* (2nd ed., Cambridge, UK, and New York: Cambridge University Press, 2000).

Lowe, D. *History of Bourgeois Perception* (Chicago: University of Chicago Press, 1982).

Lugard, F. *The Dual Mandate in British Tropical Africa* (London: Franck Cass, 1965).

———. *Political Memoranda. Revision of instructions to political officers on subjects chiefly political and administrative, 1913–18* (1st ed. 1906; 2d. edition 1919; reprinted London: 1970).

Lyons, M. *The Colonial Disease: A Social History of Sleeping Sickness in Northern Zaire, 1900–1940* (Cambridge: Cambridge University Press, 1992).

M'Boukou, J.-H. *Ethnologie criminelle du Gabon* (Le Vesinet: Ediena, 1984).

Malkki, L. *Purity and Exile. Violence, Memory and Cosmology among Hutu Refugees in Tanzania* (Chicago: University of Chicago Press, 1995).

Mamdani, M. *Citizen and Subject. Contemporary Africa and the Legacy of Late Colonialism* (Princeton: Princeton University Press, 1996).

Mapanje, J. *Gathering Seaweed: African Prison Writing* (Westport: Heinemann, 2002).

Mann, K., and R. Roberts, eds. *Law in Colonial Africa* (Portsmouth, NJ: Heinemann, 1991).

Marchal, R. "Surveillance et répression en postcolonie," *Politique africaine,* 42 (1991).

Martin, P. *The External Trade of the Loango Coast, 1576–1870* (Oxford: Clarendon Press, 1972).

———. *Leisure and Society in Colonial Brazzaville* (Cambridge: Cambridge University Press, 1995).

Mbembe, A. "Traditions de l'autoritarisme et problèmes de gouvernement en Afrique sub-saharienne," *Africa Development,* 17, 1 (1992).

Melossi, D., and M. Pavarini. *The Prison and the Factory. Origins of the Penitentiary System* (1st ed., *Carcere et fabbrica,* Bologna, 1977; English translation, London: MacMillan, 1981).

Miller, J. *Way of Death: Merchant Capitalism and the Angolan Slave Trade, 1730–1830* (Madison: University of Wisconsin Press, 1988).

Milner, A. *The Nigerian Penal System* (London: Sweet and Maxwell, 1972).

Mitchell, T. *Colonising Egypt* (Cambridge: Cambridge University Press, 1988).

Mollat, M. *Les pauvres au Moyen-Âge* (Paris: Editions Complexe, 1978).

Morris, H., and J. Read. *Indirect Rule and the Search for Justice. Essays in East African Legal History* (Oxford: Clarendon Press, 1972).

Morris, N., and D. Rothman, eds. *The Oxford History of the Prison. The Practice of Punishment in Western Society* (New York and Oxford: Oxford University Press, 1998).

Mouchet, R., and A. Pearson. *L'hygiène pratique des camps de travailleurs noirs en Afrique tropicale* (Bruxelles, Goemaere, 1922).

Mwase, G. "Outward and Inward of the Prison and Prisoners," *Strike a Blow and Die: A Narrative of Race Relations in Colonial Africa* (Cambridge, Mass.: Harvard University Press, 1967).

Nast, H. "The Impact of British Imperialism on the Landscape of Female Slavery in the Kano Palace, Northern Nigeria," *Africa,* 64, 1 (1994).

Nédélec, S. "Etat et délinquence juvénile au Sénégal contemporain," in F. Bernault, ed. *Enfermement, prison et châtiments en Afrique* (Paris: Karthala, 1999).

Newbury, C. *The Cohesion of Oppression: Clientship and Ethnicity in Rwanda, 1860–1960* (New York: Columbia University Press, 1988).

Nicolson, I. *The Administration of Nigeria, 1900–1960* (Oxford: Clarendon Press, 1969).

Niel Leitch, J., and M. Watson. *Beriberi and the Freetown Prison. A Report of an Investigation* (Freetown: 1930).

Nkrumah, K. *Ghana: The Autobiography of Kwame Nkrumah* (New York: Nelson, 1957).

Noyes, J. *Colonial Space: Spatiality in the Discourse of German South West Africa, 1884–1915* (Philadelphia: Harwood Academic Publishers, 1992).

Nugent, P., and A. Asiwaju, eds. *African Boundaries. Barriers, Conduits and Opportunities* (London: Pinter, 1996).

Nye, R. *Crime, Madness, and Politics in Modern France: The Medical Concept of National Decline* (Princeton: Princeton University Press, 1984).

O'Kubasu, E. "Les prisons en Afrique," in International Penal Reform, *Les conditions de détention en Afrique* (Paris: 1997).

Pélissier, R. *La colonie du Minotaure: Nationalismes et révoltes en Angola, 1926–1961* (Paris: Orgeval, 1978).

Penvenne, J. *African Workers and Colonial Racism. Mozambican Strategies and Struggles in Lourenço Marques, 1877–1962* (Portsmouth, NJ: Heinemann, 1995).

Perham, M. *Native Administration in Nigeria* (London and New York: Oxford University Press, 1937).

————. *West African Passage* (London and Boston: Peter Owen, 1983).

Perrot, M., ed. *L'impossible prison. Recherches sur le système pénitentiaire au XIXe siècle* (Paris: Seuil, 1980).

Peté, S. "Punishment and Race: The Emergence of Racially Defined Punishment in Colonial Natal," *Law and Society Review* (Natal), 1 (1986).

Petit, J.-G. *La prison, le bagne et l'histoire* (Paris: Librairie des Méridiens, 1984).

————. *Ces peines obscures. La prison pénale en France, 1780–1875* (Paris: Fayard, 1990).

————, et al. *Histoire des galères, bagnes et prisons. XIIIème– XXème siècles* (Paris: Privat, 1991).

Pinnock, D. *The Brotherhoods: Street Gangs and State Control in Cape Town* (Cape Town: David Philip, 1984).

Pratt, M.-L. *Imperial Eyes: Travel Writing and Transculturation* (London and New York: Routledge, 1992).

Prunier, G. *The Rwanda Crisis. History of a Genocide* (New York: Columbia University Press, 1995).

Radinowicz, L., and R. Hood . *A History of English Criminal Law and its Administration from 1750*, vol. 5. *The Emergence of Penal Policy* (London: Stevens, 1986).

Ramphele, M. *A Bed Called Home: Life in the Migrant Labour Hostels of Capetown* (Athens, OH: Ohio University Press, 1992).

Read, J. "Minimum Sentences in Tanzania," *Journal of African Law,* 9, 1 (1965).

Report on the Prison System in Northern Rhodesia and Recommendations for Reorganization (Lusaka 1938).

Roberts, C. *Tangled Justice. Some Reasons for a Change of Policy in Africa* (London: Mac Millan,1937).

Rothman, D. *The Discovery of the Asylum: Social Order and Disorder in the New Republic* (Boston: Little Brown and Co., 1971).

Rules and Standing Orders for the Government of Prisons, Sierra Leone (Freetown: 1941).

Salvatore, R., and C. Aguirre, eds. *The Birth of the Penitentiary in Latin America. Essays on Criminology, Prison Reform and Social Control, 1830–1940* (Austin: University of Texas Press, 1996).

Sarat, A., ed. *Pain, Death, and the Law* (Ann Harbor: University of Michigan Press, 2001).

Schakwyck, D. "Writing from Prison," in S. Nuttall and C. A. Michael, eds. *Senses of Culture* (New York: Oxford University Press, 2000).

Schwartz, S. "The Black Insane in the Cape, 1891–1920," *Journal of Southern African Studies,* 21, 3 (1995).

Silla, E. *People Are Not the Same: Leprosy and Identity in Twentieth Century Mali* (Portsmouth, NJ: Heineman, 1998).

Sinou, A. *Comptoirs et villes coloniales du Sénégal* (Paris: Karthala/ORSTOM, 1993).

Smaldone, J.-P. *Warfare in the Sokoto Caliphate. Historical and Sociological Perspectives* (Cambridge: Cambridge University Press, 1977).

Soulillou, J., ed. *Rives coloniales. Architectures, de Saint-Louis à Douala* (Paris: Parenthèses/ORSTOM, 1993).

Spierenburg, P. *The Spectacle of Suffering. Executions and the Evolution of Repression: From a Preindustrial Metropolis to the European Experience* (Cambridge: Cambridge University Press, 1984).

————. *The Prison Experience. Disciplinary Institutions and Their Inmates in Early Modern Europe* (New Brunswick and London: Rutgers University Press, 1991).

Stoler, A. "Sexual Affronts and Racial Frontiers: European Identities and the Cultural Politics of Exclusion in Colonial Southeast Asia," *Comparative Studies in Society and History,* 34, 2 (1992).

Suremain, M.-A. de. "Cartographie coloniale et encadrement des populations en Afrique française dans la première moitié du XXᵉ siècle," *Revue française d'histoire d'outre-mer,* 324–325 (1999).

Tanner, R. "Penal Practices in Africa: Some Restrictions on the Possibility of Reform," *Journal of Modern African Studies,* 10 (1972).

Thiam, I. Der. *Histoire du mouvement syndical africain 1790–1929* (Paris: L'Harmattan, 1993).

Thioub, I. "Sénégal : La prison à l'époque coloniale. Significations, évitement et évasions," in F. Bernault, ed. *Enfermement, prison et châtiments* (Paris: Karthala, 1999).

Thornton, J. *The Kongolese Saint Anthony. Dona Beatriz Kimpa Vita and the Antonian Movement, 1684–1706* (Cambridge and New York: Cambridge University Press, 1998).

Turrell, R. *Capital and Labour on the Kimberley Diamond Fields, 1871–1890* (New York: Cambridge University Press, 1987).

Van Onselen, C. *Chibaro: African Mine Labour in Southern Rhodesia, 1900–1933* (London: Pluto Press, 1976).

———. *Studies in the Social and Economic History of the Witwatersrand, 1886–1914* (New York: Longman, 1982).

———. "Crime and Total Institutions in the Making of Modern South Africa: The Life of Nongoloza Mathebula, 1867–1948," *History Workshop Journal,* 19 (1985).

Van Zyl Smit, D. "Public Policy and the Punishment of Crime in a Divided Society: A Historical Perspective on the South African Penal System," *Crime and Social Justice,* 21–22 (1984).

Vaughan, M. "Idioms of Madness: Zomba Lunatic Asylum, Nyasaland in the Colonial Period," *Journal of Southern African Studies,* 9, 2 (1983).

———. *Curing Their Ills. Colonial Power and African Illness* (Stanford: Stanford University Press, 1991).

Vellut, J.-L. "La violence armée dans l'Etat indépendant du Congo. Ténèbres et clartés dans l'histoire d'un état conquérant," *Cultures et Développement,* 16, 3–4 (1984).

———. "Une exécution publique à Elisabethville (20 septembre 1922). Notes sur la pratique de la peine capitale dans l'histoire coloniale du Congo," unpublished article, Louvain-la-Neuve, April 21, 1989.

Villemont, R. "Le cas du Sahara occidental," in F. Bernault, ed. *Enfermement, prison et châtiments* (Paris: Karthala, 1999).

Vincent, J.-F., D. Dory, and R. Verdier, eds. *La construction religieuse du territoire* (Paris: L'Harmattan, 1995).

Wagner, M. "Whose Justice?," *Tribunal,* 6, 1 (December 1996).

———. "All the Bourgmestre's Men," *Africa Today,* 45, 1 (1998).

Wells, J. *We Have Done with Pleading: The Women's 1913 Anti-Pass Campaign* (Johannesburg: Ravan Press, 1991).

Western, J. *Outcast Cape Town* (Berkeley: University of California Press, 1996).

White, L. "Separating the Men from the Boys: Construction of Gender, Sexuality, and Terrorism in Central Kenya, 1939–1959," *International Journal of African Historical Studies,* 23, 1 (1990).

Williams, D. "The Minimum Sentences Act, 1972, of Tanzania," *Journal of African Law,* 18, 1 (1974).
———. "The Role of Prisons in Tanzania: A Historical Perspective," *Crime and Social Justice* (1980).
Wright, M. *Strategies of Slaves and Women in East Africa. Life Stories from East/Central Africa* (New York: L. Barber Press, 1993).
Zinoman, P. *The Colonial Bastille. A History of Imprisonment in Vietnam 1862–1940* (Berkeley: University of California Press, 2001).

UNPUBLISHED THESES

This list gives a sample of the growing number of unpublished works on the prison conducted in Francophone universities, particularly in Senegal, Gabon, and Cameroon.

Bâ, C. *La criminalité à Diourbel, 1925–1960* (Mémoire de maîtrise d'histoire, Université Cheikh Anta Diop/Dakar, 1994).
Bounda, G. *Morphologie de la répression chez les Ndumu* (Mémoire de maîtrise d'histoire, Université Omar Bongo/Libreville, 1983).
Diallo, C. *Histoire de la répression pénitentiaire en Guinée française (1900–1958)* (Thèse d'histoire de l'Université de Paris 7, 1998).
Diédhiou, N. *L'évolution de la criminalité au Sénégal de 1930 aux années 1960* (Mémoire de maîtrise d'histoire, Université Cheikh Anta Diop/Dakar, 1991).
Diongue, A. *Evolution démographique et sociale de la ville de Thiès (1885–1960)*, (Mémoire de maîtrise d'histoire, Université Cheikh Anta Diop/Dakar, 1991).
Faye, O. *L'urbanisation et les processus sociaux au Sénégal : Typologie descriptive et analytique des déviances à Dakar, d'après les sources d'archives de 1885 à 1940* (Thèse de 3ᵉ cycle en histoire, Université Cheikh Anta Diop/Dakar, 1989).
Kâ, I. *L'évolution sociale à Saint-Louis du Sénégal du XIXᵉ au début du XXᵉ siècle* (Mémoire de maîtrise d'histoire, Université Cheikh Anta Diop/Dakar, 1981).
Kane, N. *L'évolution de la criminalité à Saint-Louis à travers les archives de la police de 1900 à 1930* (Mémoire de maîtrise d'histoire, Université Cheikh Anta Diop/Dakar, 1988).
Kiki, J.-F. *La justice indigène au Gabon, 1910–1945* (Mémoire de maîtrise d'histoire, Université Omar Bongo/Libreville, 1985).
Konaté, D. *Histoire des modes d'incarcération au Sénégal : Les femmes en prison, 1925–1995,* (Mémoire de maîtrise d'histoire, Université Cheikh Anta Diop, 1999).
Nguiabama-Makaya, F. *Le système pénitentiaire au Gabon, 1887–1957* (Mémoire de DEA en histoire, Université d'Aix-Marseille, 2001).
Sissao, C. *Urbanisation et rythme d'évolution des équipements. Ouagadougou et l'ensemble du Burkina-Faso (1947–1985)* (Thèse d'histoire, Université de Paris 7, 1992).
Takam, M. *Une illustration de la détention au Cameroun sous administration française: La prison de Yaoundé 1923–1960* (Mémoire de maîtrise en histoire, Université de Yaoundé, 2001).
Thioune, O. *L'éducation surveillée au Sénégal* (Mémoire de maîtrise de philosophie, Université Cheikh Anta Diop/Dakar, 1980).

NOVELS AND MEMOIRS

Achebe, Chinua, *Things Fall Apart* (New York: Anchor Books, 1994, 1st ed. 1959).

Bâ, Ahmadou Hampaté, *L'étrange destin de Wangrin* (Paris: Union Générale d'Editions, 1973).

Beti, Mongo. *Le pauvre Christ de Bomba* (Paris: R. Laffont, 1956).

———. *Rumember Ruben* (Paris: Union Générale d'Editions, 1974).

———. *Mission terminée* (Paris: Buchet/Chastel, 1957).

Bhêly-Quénum, Olympe. *Un piège sans fin* (Paris: Présence africaine, 1978, 1st ed. 1960).

Dadié, Bernard. *Carnets de prison* (Abidjan: Ceda, 1981).

Dongala, Bounzéki Emmanuel. *Jazz et vin de palme* (Paris: Hatier, 1982).

Fall, Aminata Sow. *Le revenant* (Dakar/Abidjan: Nouvelles Editions Africaines, 1976).

Fantouré, Alioum. *Le cercle des tropiques* (Paris: Présence africaine, 1972).

Kariuki, Josiah M. *Mau Mau Detainee: The Account by a Kenya African of His Experiences in Detention Camps, 1953–1960.* (London: Oxford University Press, 1963).

Karone, Yodi, *Le bal des caïmans* (Paris: Karthala, 1980).

Kourouma, Ahmadou, *Le soleil des indépendances* (Paris: Seuil, 1968).

Labou Tansi, Sony. *La vie et demie* (Paris: Seuil, 1979).

———. *L'Etat honteux* (Paris: Seuil, 1981).

———. *L'Anté-peuple* (Paris: Seuil, 1983).

Laye, Camara. *Dramouss* (Paris: Plon, 1966).

Ly, Ibrahima. *Toiles d'araignées* (Paris: L'Harmattan 1982).

Mandela, Nelson. *Long Walk to Freedom* (Boston: Little Brown, 1994).

Menga, Guy. *La palabre stérile* (Yaoundé: Editions Clé, 1968).

Ngugi wa Thiongh'o. *Weep Not, Child* (London: Heinemann, 1964).

———. *A Grain of Wheat* (London: Heinemann, 1967).

———. *Petals of Blood* (New York: E. P. Dutton, 1977).

———. *Detainee. A Writer's Prison Diary* (Londonand Exeter, NJ: Heinemann, 1981).

Ousmane, Sembène. *Les bouts de bois de Dieu* (Paris: Presses Pocket, 1960).

Oyono, Ferdinand. *Le vieux nègre et la médaille* (Paris: Julliard, 1956).

———. *Une vie de boy* (Paris: Julliard, 1956).

Saro Wiwa, Ken. *A Month and a Day: A Detention Diary* (1995).

Soyinka, Wole. *The Man Died: Prison Notes* (New York: Harper and Row, 1972).

Tati Loutard, Jean-Baptiste. *Chroniques congolaises* (Paris: P. J. Oswald, 1974).

———. *Nouvelles chroniques congolaises* (Paris: Présence africaine, 1980).

INDEX

Algeria, 33, 228, 230, 231

Angola, 55–68

Architecture, 3–6, 8, 10, 16–23, 25, 26, 34–36, 38, 39, 58, 60, 63, 71, 72, 74, 75, 83, 88, 90, 91, 100, 102, 103, 119–32, 137, 138, 141, 142, 162, 192–95, 201–215, 242, 243, 252, 254; lack of, 11, 32, 59, 61, 106, 141, 142, 157–59, 243, 254–56. *See also* Camps; Cells

Asylums, 13, 14, 38, 43n

Borders, 4, 35, 37, 52n, 58, 223, 225, 227, 228, 231, 262; frontier, 15, 169, 225, 231

Cameroon, 14, 69, 73

Camps, 10, 19, 32, 33, 36, 37, 46n, 47n, 233–35; detention, 13, 14, 104, 105; garrisons, 11, 16, 58–60; military, 27, 119, 126, 202, 231–33, 261; reeducation, 259; refugee, 33, 37, 228–31, 235, 240, 263; sanitary, 14; workers', 3, 10, 191–219

Capitalism, 166, 168, 169, 186n, 189n, 196

Captivity, 4–6, 69, 81, 156; recaptives, 6, 27, 121; war prisoners, 61, 63, 69, 71, 74, 75

Cells, 7, 12, 16–18, 20, 23, 39, 74, 89, 91, 101, 103, 111, 129, 131, 141, 158, 159, 240, 241, 243, 253, 254, 257, 259, 261, 262; clandestine jails, 33, 256–57

Central African Republic, 32, 33, 39

Code, 57, 58, 61, 62, 64; British, 109; French, 82, 83, 91; *indigénat*, 11, 13, 15, 20, 132, 138–40, 148, 156

Confinement, 3–10, 14, 26, 33–35, 37–39, 68n, 75, 76, 89, 111, 155, 199, 221–37, 241, 248, 251, 252, 254, 255; ritual, 4, 37, 76

Congo (Belgian), 2, 14, 30, 36, 37, 191–219

Congo (French), 16, 18, 32

Corporal punishment, 9, 10, 15, 16, 25, 30, 33, 57, 59, 61, 63, 64, 72–74, 106–10, 120, 130–31, 156, 207, 249, 251, 259; treadmill, 23, 102, 130, 131; whip, 72, 98–100, 102, 103, 251. *See also* Torture

Courts. *See* Tribunals

Crime, 2, 3, 5, 6, 10, 15, 23–26, 31, 38, 56, 60, 62, 63, 70, 71 73, 75, 77, 81, 84, 97–99, 100, 101, 105, 107, 109–12, 120, 129, 132, 146, 156, 157, 243, 248; criminality, 2, 4, 24, 61, 63, 83, 192; theft, 3, 10, 68n 84, 89, 91, 93n, 99, 106, 109–110, 143,147

Customary law, 15, 76, 98, 99, 102, 106, 107, 111, 205; African criminal law, 61, 62, 247–49, 251; customs, 196, 199, 207, 213, 214; precolonial social control, 4–7. *See also* Tribunals

Dahomey, 16, 71

Death penalty, 15, 31, 56, 60, 61, 72, 99–101, 110–12, 126–27, 156, 249, 250, 257

Deliquency, 21, 26, 28, 31, 36, 113, 147, 259; deviant behavior, 79, 84; economic; 83, 84; juvenile, 79–92, 109, 131, 146, 147, 161

Deportation, 8, 55, 58, 156. *See also* Exile

Discipline, 3, 10, 15, 23, 25, 26, 33, 34, 36, 83, 84, 89, 104, 106, 131, 137–39, 143, 144, 159, 192, 197, 198, 202, 205, 214, 215, 225; disciplinary sentence, 12

Enclosure of space, 4, 14, 34–38, 165–84, 221–35, 192–219

Escapes, 6, 16, 27, 29, 30, 58, 62, 88, 89, 91, 137, 143, 148, 160, 241, 250, 256, 262

Ethnicity, 4, 34, 37, 73–75, 172, 178, 187n, 199, 205, 207, 242, 244, 245, 260, 264n–266n

Exile, 5, 57, 62, 70, 71, 73; exclusion, 5–7; ostracism, 74, 75. *See also* Deportation

Fines, 57, 58, 62, 98, 106, 108, 156, 250; compensation, 7, 28, 101, 106, 248, 249

Foucault, Michel, 3, 5, 33, 40n, 41n, 167, 184n, 185n, 209

Gabon, 28, 36, 37,165–84

Ghana (Gold Coast), 2, 23, 30, 32, 102, 103, 105

Guards, 10, 20, 25, 27, 28, 30, 33, 34, 58, 74, 89, 90, 103, 104, 107, 110, 112, 131, 136, 142–45, 147, 148, 159, 160, 181–84, 248

Guinea–Conakry, 22, 24, 27, 28, 32, 32, 120–30; Camp Boiro, 32, 73

Hospitals, 3, 10, 119, 126, 142, 202; dispensary, 36, 83, 93n, 142; infirmary, 86

Human rights, 69, 258, 259, 261

Islam, 73, 77; *sharia*, 49n

Ivory Coast, 30, 127, 129, 135

Kenya, 12, 13, 99, 101, 108, 109, 112; Mau Mau, 13, 14, 36, 105, 107, 110

Labor, 3, 8–14, 21–23, 26, 30, 31, 36, 47n, 81, 84, 88–90, 92, 104, 108, 122, 127, 130, 156, 160, 161, 242, 254, 257, 258; agricultural, 83, 87; on prison farms, 9, 60, 105, 156; on roads, 85, 176, 178–81; stabilization of, 191–219

Lombroso, Cesare, 24, 84

Lybia, 33, 221, 231, 232

Mali, 33, 36, 221–37

Maps, 34, 37, 59, 122, 129, 170–75, 177, 181

Missions, 6, 14, 24, 28, 36, 57, 58, 82–86, 100, 107, 113, 126, 129, 145, 147, 167, 168, 171–73, 179, 196, 197, 202, 210

Niger, 17, 19, 23, 28, 32, 221, 227, 232, 235

Nigeria, 11, 98, 100–103, 105, 107–9, 111

Nyasaland, 14

Orphanage, 86, 87, 89

Panopticon, 18, 32, 129, 191

Paternalism, 14, 84, 192; patriarchy, 157–58

Penology, 23–26, 39, 120, 145–46

Police, 12, 13, 31, 33, 89, 91, 106, 122–24, 126, 128, 155, 202, 205, 225, 251, 252, 255; *askaris*, 249–51

Power, 3, 5–7, 12, 15, 26, 28, 29, 32–35, 37–39, 70, 71, 74–76, 81, 90, 92, 99, 100, 106, 108–12, 119, 120, 122, 124, 126, 127, 132, 136, 142, 144, 157, 165–69, 171, 173, 177, 179, 192, 194, 200–5, 210, 212–4, 223, 224, 233–35, 242, 244, 245, 247, 250, 251, 255–58, 260

Precolonial punishments. *See* Customary law

Prison. *See* Architecture

Prison budget, 13, 59, 103–5, 126

Prisoners, 6, 8–11, 13, 16, 20, 21, 24, 27–29, 30, 32–35, 37, 38, 56–59, 61, 63, 97, 100–3, 122, 127–31, 136, 240–43, 252, 254, 255, 257, 259; clothing, 18, 86, 89, 91, 120, 137, 138; diet, 8, 9, 18, 24, 59, 90, 94n, 101, 102, 104, 105, 120, 130, 137, 138, 161; European, 18, 30, 137, 138; homosexuality, 147; isolation, 84, 89, 243; maintenance costs, 83, 85, 86, 138; morbidity, 101, 140, 141, 159, 161, 241, 252, 261, 262; numbers, 12, 83, 105, 124, 131, 156, 240, 241, 259, 260–63; political, 131, 258, 259; racial segregation, 8, 9, 16–19, 21, 23, 25, 129, 137, 157; rebellion, 84, 89; rights, 137, 138; salary, 89, 140, 161. *See also* Labor; Women

Penitentiary schools, 13, 14, 79–92, 113, 119, 145, 146; corrective facilities, 3

Punishment, 2–10, 14–16, 24, 25, 28, 30, 33–35, 38, 57, 58, 60–62, 64, 80, 89, 97–100, 104, 106–10, 120, 122, 130, 132, 138, 139, 144, 156, 207, 242, 248–51; collective, 106. *See also* Corporal punishment

Reform, 24, 25, 32, 33, 90, 98, 100, 102–4, 108–10, 112, 113, 130, 135–37, 145–47, 159, 162, 197, 208

Refugee camps. *See* Camps

Resistance, 10, 11, 14, 22, 23, 27, 29, 37, 38, 142–45, 156, 193, 194, 207, 208, 211, 214, 125; riots, 193, 196; subversion, 213

Rhodesia (Northern), 104, 105, 109, 110, 195, 197

Rhodesia (Southern), 98, 103, 112

Rwanda, 1, 29, 239–70

Senegal, 7, 14, 7, 36, 29, 79–81, 89–92, 156; Gorée, 7, 79–81; St–Louis, 7, 80–81, 88, 123, 155, 156

Shackles, 57, 59, 60, 63, 64, 70, 71, 75, 76, 84, 89, 247; chains, 5, 6, 8, 16, 30, 84, 101, 104, 130, 251

Sierra Leone, 120, 121, 124, 125, 127, 130, 131

Slavery, 5–8, 55, 57, 58, 60, 62–64, 69, 71, 79–83, 100, 124, 156, 172, 230, 236n; pawnship, 28

South Africa, 7–11, 13, 14, 26, 32, 103, 112, 195, 198

Space. *See* Enclosure of space

Tanganyika, 12, 104, 107, 109, 113

Torture, 6, 8, 12, 15, 16, 30, 57, 74, 244, 249, 256, 259–62. *See also* Corporal punishment

Tribunals, 11, 12, 28, 30, 62, 72, 88, 125, 127, 160, 161, 252, 253, 255; *gacaca* 248; native administration courts, 98, 99, 106, 108, 109, 111; *schauri,* 250, 256; trial, 60, 253, 255, 257, 259

Uganda, 11, 32, 104–7, 111, 113

Upper Volta (Burkina Faso), 12, 18, 24

Vagabondage, 9, 26, 31, 36, 81, 93n, 259

Wardens. *See* Guards

Women, 14, 20, 22, 28, 63, 70, 91, 102, 107–8, 110–112, 129, 131, 155–62, 199, 200, 202, 208–11, 231, 234, 241, 262; gender, 93n, 210–13; *signares,* 80

ABOUT THE
CONTRIBUTORS

THIERNO BAH is Professor of African History at the University of Yaoundé (Cameroon). His publications include *Architecture militaire traditionnelle et poliorcétique dans le Soudan occcidental du XVIIe à la fin du XIXe siècle* (Yaoundé, 1985), and, as co-author, *Afrique noire. Histoire et civilisations, XIXe–XXe* (Paris, 1992). He recently served as the editor in chief of the journal *Afrika Zamani*.

FLORENCE BERNAULT is Professor of African History at the University of Wisconsin-Madison. She published a book entitled *Démocraties ambiguës en Afrique centrale. Gabon, Congo-Brazzaville, 1940–1965* (Paris, 1996), and edited *Enfermement, prison et châtiments en Afrique du XIXe siècle à nos jours* (Paris, 1999).

PIERRE BOILLEY is Professor of African History at the University of Paris–1-Sorbonne. He co-edited *Nomades et commandants. Administration et sociétés nomades dans l'ancienne AOF* (Paris, 1993) and recently published *Les Touaregs Kel Adagh. Dépendances et révoltes : du Soudan français au Mali contemporain* (Paris, 1999).

LAURENT FOURCHARD is agrégé d'histoire, and completed his Ph.D. in African history at the University of Paris-7-Diderot. He recently published a book entitled *De la ville coloniale à la cour africaine. Espaces, pouvoirs et sociétés à Ouagadougou et Bobo-Dioulasso* (Paris, 2002). He is directing the IFRA (French Institute for African Studies) at the University of Ibadan (Nigeria).

ODILE GOERG is Professor of African History at the University of Paris-7-Diderot. She recently co-edited a volume on *La ville européenne outre-mer : un modèle conquérant?* (Paris, 1996), and on *Fêtes urbaines en Afrique. Espaces, identités et pouvoirs* (Paris, 1999). Her latest book is entitled *Pouvoir colonial, municipalités et espaces urbains : Conakry-Freetown des années 1880 à 1914* (Paris, 1997).

CHRISTOPHER GRAY was Assistant Professor of African History at Florida International University. He published a book entitled *Conceptions of History in the Works of Cheikh Anta Diop and Théophile Obenga* (London, 1989), and a monograph on *Colonial Rule and Crisis in Equatorial Africa* (Rochester, NY, 2002).

SEAN HANRETTA is completing his Ph.D. thesis at the University of Wisconsin-Madison. His article on "Women, Marginality and the Zulu State: Women's Institutions and Power in the Early Nineteenth Century," appeared in the *Journal of African History*.

DAVID KILLINGRAY is Professor of Modern History at Goldsmiths College London. His most recent books, as author and editor, include *The West Indies* (London, 1999), *Guardians of Empire* (Manchester, 2000), *The Spanish Flu Pandemic 1918–19: New Perspectives* (London, 2002), and *African Soldiers in the Second World War* (forthcoming).

DIOR KONATÉ is completing her Ph.D. thesis at the University of Wisconsin-Madison. In 1999, she defended a master thesis on *Histoire des modes d'incarcération au Sénégal : les femmes en prison, 1925–1995* at the University of Cheikh Anta Diop (Dakar).

IBRAHIMA THIOUB is Professor of African History at the University of Cheikh Anta Diop (Dakar), and founder of the research group on Délinquence et marginalité urbaine. He recently co-edited the volume *AOF: réalités et héritages. Sociétés ouest-africaines et ordre colonial, 1895–1960* (Dakar, Paris, 1997).

JAN VANSINA is Professor Emeritus of African History at the University of Wisconsin-Madison. His latest publications include *Paths in the Rainforest: Toward a History of Political Tradition in Equatorial Africa* (Madison, 1995) and *Le Rwanda ancien* (Paris, 2001).

MICHELE D. WAGNER is Assistant Professor at the University of Minnesota-Minneapolis. She co-edited, with Joseph Miller, Robert Harms, and

David Newbury, *Paths Toward the Past* (1994), and published several articles on the crisis in the Great Lakes. In 1994–95, she collaborated to the United Nations Human Rights Field Operation in Rwanda (HRFOR), and worked for Human Rights/Watch Africa and the Fédération internationale des Ligues des Droits de l'Homme.